Michael Hadley

The German Novel in 1790

A descriptive account and critical bibliography

Herbert Lang Bern
Peter Lang Frankfurt/M.
1973

ISBN 3 261 01065 7

Printed by Lang Druck Ltd., Liebefeld/Berne (Switzerland)

For Anita

Pauline, Michèle, David, Norman

„. . . man kann die Berühmten
nicht verstehen, wenn man die
Obskuren nicht durchgefühlt hat."

Franz Grillparzer: Der Arme Spielmann

C O N T E N T S

I wish to acknowledge my indebtedness to the following bibliographers without whose assistance this study could not have been undertaken:

Dr. Heinz Gittig, Direktor des Auskunftsbüros, Deutscher Bibliotheken, Deutsche Staatsbibliothek,
Berlin (DDR);

Dr. Friedrich Rennhofer, Leiter der Katalogabteilung, Österreichische Nationalbibliothek,
Wien;

Dr. Hugo Alker, Direktionssekretär, Universitätsbibliothek,
Wien;

Dr. H. Peters, Niedersächsische Staats- und Universitätsbibliothek, Göttingen;

Dr. Kiessling, Hessischer Zentralkatalog, Stadt- und Universitätsbibliothek,
Frankfurt am Main;

Dr. Lullies, Berliner Gesamtkatalog,
Berlin-Dahlem (BRD);

Dr. Schneiders, Bayrische Staatsbibliothek,
München;

Dr. Zunker, Zentralkatalog,
Baden-Würtemberg, Stuttgart.

A descriptive account of first editions of prose fiction published
in 1790 requires some justification, particularly in view of the fact
that, with the exception of Moritz' well-known Andreas Hartknopf and
Anton Reiser, no novels of the period have been "zu Unrecht vergessen"
with the passage of time.[1] From an aesthetic viewpoint, they all seem to
have deserved that obscurity peculiar to most popular literary fare, and
it is, in fact, surprising that as many as 35 of the 120 first editions
are still available today.[2] Literary history has traditionally examined
changes in matters of style, form, philosophy, and taste on the basis of
generally recognized masterpieces that are deemed representative of an
epoch or movement. Thus despite certain problems of definition, to cite
but one example, one can trace the changing image of man in the German
Bildungsroman as it develops from Grimmelshausen's Simplicissimus through
Goethe's Wilhelm Meister to Thomas Mann's Der Zauberberg.[3] The results of
this approach to examining literary trends have been corrected to a considerable degree in recent years by broader studies, which show that recognized masterpieces were frequently overshadowed in their own day by
sub-literary works that enjoyed great popularity[4] and that really established the literary tone of their period. This fact was recognized as
early as 1796, when the Neue Allgemeine Deutsche Bibliothek commented
that the authors of the 6000 novels which had appeared in the previous
twenty-four years reflected the spirit of the age.[5] Friedrich von
Blanckenburg and A.W. Schlegel also shared such views on the close relationship between social history and the novel. Popular literature was in
fact a response to the demands of public taste; the public, not the
aestheticians, established the criteria.

The broader studies alluded to earlier seem to have prejudged
their case by specifically singling out 'trivial literature' as the object of their research, thereby distinguishing it from literature as an
art form. However, Hermann Bausinger rightly points out that it may be
quite misleading to distinguish between trivial literature and enlightened or romantic literature;[6] and Dietrich Naumann even finds that literary
and sub-literary forms are rooted in the same uniform world.[7] Certainly,

no writer of fiction who published in 1780 recognized any distinction between the popular novel and literature as an art form;[8] nor for that matter did writers who published in 1790.

Eva D. Becker's Der Deutsche Roman um 1780 examined the 36 available novels published in the years 1779-81, a period regarded as a pause between two distinct developments in the novel: that of the modern novel of the 1770's under the influence of the Enlightenment and Empfindsamkeit, and that of the Romantic movement.[9] She found no evidence of preromantic streams and no romantic and pseudo-romantic Ritter- Räuber- und Schauer-romane, which she claims dominated novel production a decade later.[10] Actually, very little evidence of such novels was to be found "ein Jahr-zehnt später"--in 1790--either. Partly in response to Becker's expectations, but more particularly to the obvious need for reference points against which one might eventually test some of the current assumptions about the 18th-century German novel, there seemed a clear challenge to make a comprehensive study of German novels published in 1790. The effectiveness of such a project seemed dependent on a purposefully narrow historical spectrum. The present study thus forms but one component of a grid, and is predicated on such studies as Becker's 1780 and Manfred Heiderich's The German Novel in 1800.[11] For practical reasons, we define a novel published in 1790 as any book-length work of prose fiction, all or part of which appeared for the first time in that year. Shorter fiction published in short-story anthologies (such as those of Christian Sander and Johann Stutz) or collections of vignettes (such as Friedrich Thilo's Lebensscenen and Johann Haken's Die graue Mappe) is discussed only when it is specially revealing.

Becker found that the novels she studied could be classified according to three dominant types or groups:[12] first, Der Hohe Roman: Empfind-sam-didaktischer Prüfungsroman, which concerned itself with affairs of the upper classes and comprised one-third of the novels she investigated--by far the largest group; secondly, Der niedrig-komische Roman: Satirischer Narrenroman, which portrayed the lower classes in humorous situations and comprised one-quarter of her texts; and finally Der mitt-lere Roman, which was associated with the bourgeois or middle-class milieu. The latter consists of a rather loosely defined group of works which, as Becker explains, "sich vom festen Typus des hohen oder des niedrigen Romans gelöst haben und auf irgendeine Weise versuchen, den um 1780 modernen Roman zu realisieren." These include, in Becker's terminology, novels of education and development, the character novel in dialogue form, and a rather heterogeneous group she defines as 'psychological, pedagogical, sentimental-humorous, and others'.[13]

Becker bases her definition of Der mittlere Roman on examples which Jean Paul had singled out in his Vorschule der Aesthetik; namely, Fielding's Tom Jones (1749), Goldsmith's Vicar of Wakefield (1766), Sterne's Tristram Shandy (1760-67), Hippel's Lebensläufe nach aufsteigender Linie (1778/81), and Goethe's Wilhelm Meisters Lehrjahre (1794-96). This type, as Jean Paul pointed out, "[lässt] gemäß Göthens Meister das bürgerliche oder Prose-Leben [sic] am reichsten spielen...,"[14] a characteristic which was to become more apparent in 1790. The concept also implies a particular type of psychological representation of character by turning away from both the extremely elevated and low types, whose principal characters serve as ideals for emulation or deterrence. As Becker found, the term properly defines the salient characteristics of the novel of Enlightenment.

Study of the 35 available novels published in 1790 reveals that Becker's classification is no longer adequate. The elevated and low comic types, for instance, have virtually disappeared or have assumed characteristics that make re-grouping necessary. It is also impracticable to classify the novels of 1790 according to narrative method (epistolary, dialogue) or social orientation ('high' or 'low'). Only two epistolary novels, but no dialogue novels, are extant, and the fiction of 1790 is largely concerned with the middle-class milieu. Der mittlere Roman, which Becker regarded as modern in 1780, predominates. With the exception of the epistolary novel, most works tend to combine a variety of narrative methods and shift at will from one style to another. Indeed Kurt-Ingo Flessau, who surveys the classification provided by Becker, Beaujean, and Greiner, observes correctly that the types distinguished by these authors are abstractions, and that, in fact, all the novels of the period combine several thematic and formal components and contain at least a latent tendency towards social criticism.[15]

The fact that didacticism is common to all prose fiction of the period provides the method by which the various types of novel can be most meaningfully distinguished: namely, the author's viewpoint, his approach towards imparting moral instruction. Hence the novels in this study are arranged in four groups: 1) The novel of Love and Adventure, which preaches virtue by revealing the dangers of erotic love, 2) The Historical Novel, which tries to authenticate its message by feigning historicity, 3) The Satirical Novel, which instructs through ridicule and humour, 4) The Character Novel, which attempts to edify the reader by offering insights into the hero's personality. Although this classification leads to problems of definition, it seems nonetheless useful. Christiane Naubert's <u>Werner, Graf von Bernburg</u>, for instance, might well have been considered a mere romance if one were solely interested in the intricacies of the traditional love plot; but viewed in the light of the author's intentions of authenticating her narrative, it contributes to our understanding of the historical novel. Wilhelm Heller's <u>Sokrates</u> and Ignaz Fessler's <u>Marc-Aurel</u>, both of which could have been examined as historical novels, are treated here as character novels, as they shed light on the manner in which the development of character was used for didactic ends. In every case, narrow classification into fictional types, no matter how significant the tabulation of these types might be for literary statisticians like Germer,[16] remains secondary to demonstrating the contemporary writer's approach to the craft of fiction.

The task of reading what eventually amounted to some 25,000 pages of fiction (sheer quantity was important to writers, publishers, and public alike!) had scarcely begun when two salient and recurring questions emerged: How did writers of the period define the novel and understand its limits? How did they regard their craft and its problems? Other studies have concentrated upon classification into fictional types and codification of narrative techniques, thereby losing the peculiar flavour that tickled the palate of the reading public of almost 200 years ago. It therefore seemed that the history of literary taste might best be served by trying to capture that flavour again, and by marshalling the material around these basic questions. Novelists of 1790, as will be seen, 'join cookery with authorship' by 'serving up' works of 'considerable corpulence' with 'something for every palate,' and even for 'all digestive systems.' It may be of some comfort to the unwary modern reader to recall Lichtenberg's observations on the often debilitating literature of his day, particularly on the easy disposition favourable to its enjoyment which a cup of coffee and a pipe of tobacco provide:

> Es gibt eine gewisse Art von Büchern, und wir haben in Deutschland eine große Menge, die nicht vom Lesen abschrecken, nicht plötzlich einschläfern oder mürrisch machen, aber in einer Stunde den Geist in eine gewisse Mattigkeit versetzen... Legt man das Buch weg, so fühlt man sich zu nichts aufgelegt, fängt man an zu schreiben, so schreibt man ebenso; selbst die guten Schriften scheinen diese laue Geschmacklosigkeit anzunehmen, wenn man sie zu lesen anfängt. Ich weiß aus eigener Erfahrung, daß gegen diesen traurigen Zustand nichts geschwinder hilft als eine Tasse Kaffee mit einer Pfeife Varinas.[17]

Research for this study was supported by:
The Department of German;
Queen's University, Kingston (Canada);
The University of Winnipeg;
Deutscher Akademischer Austauschdienst.

Publication was assisted by a grant from the
University of Victoria, Canada.

CHAPTER I

ASPECTS OF THE NOVEL IN 1790

1. Contemporary attitudes to the novel

When a mysterious manuscript falls from the planet Sirius in
J.F.E. Albrecht's Dreyerley Wirkungen, its fictional translator faces
the intriguing task of transcribing many strange words. One such word
is "Kingstang," the term for a curious literary genre on Sirius which,
like the novels described in Heinrich Werder's Eduard Rosenhain (2),
was creating a veritable "Sündflut" among the reading public. Albrecht's
fictional translator provides footnotes to foreign words which earthmen
could not be expected to know. Thus "Kingstang" is rendered as brochure,
and includes "Schauspiele, Romane, und dergleichen" (III, 151). Such
writings, the Sirian scribe explains, are mere luxuries and have nothing
to do with life. Now, precisely because of its imprecision, this definition is most instructive. Nobody, Albrecht's scribe insists, is really very clear on the matter, "weil überhaupt von einem Kingstang noch
keine festgesetzte Idee existierte..." Neither contents nor titles are
valid criteria, he argues, for often "ein sehr wissenschaftliches Buch
einen Titel führen könnte, der den Kingstang verrieth," while many Kingstangs frequently express "in wenig Worten nützlichere Dinge und mehr
Wahrheit... als dicke Folianten, die Jahre zum durchlesen erfordern..."
Booksellers, he adds, are unconcerned with pursuing definitions because
business is already brisk. But the paying public, long misled by titles,
has been urging the publishers to define their terms. The challenge, of
course, was not taken up in Sirius.

Albrecht's scribe was correct in assuming that no concept of the
novel as a literary genre was current among novelists--for it is of course
the novel he has primarily in mind when writing about "Kingstangs".
But he overstated his case in contending that no concept had yet been
formulated. Johann Joachim Eschenburg's Entwurf einer Theorie und Literatur der schönen Wissenschaften [[1]1783, [2]1789], for instance, written
in the light of Blanckenburg's Versuch über den Roman (1774), and described in 1790 by the Allgemeine Deutsche Bibiliothek (vol. 92, p.126)

6

as a valuable text-book, devotes nine pages to its definition. He explains in part:

> Grössere [erdichtete] Erzählungen, deren Stof mannich-
> faltiger und ergiebiger, und deren Ausführungen umständ-
> licher ist, nennt man Romane. Diese haben sowohl in
> Ansehung ihres Inhaltes als ihrer Bearbeitung mit dem
> Heldengedichte sehr viel Aehnlichkeit; nur dass die
> Handlung eines Romans von kleinerm Umfang in Betracht
> ihres Einflusses und Wichtigkeit zu seyn pflegt, und
> sich gemeiniglich mehr auf den Menschen überhaupt, als
> auf einzelne heroische Personen und Thaten bezieht;
> dass ferner dem Roman das Wunderbare nicht so wesent-
> lich eigen ist, als dem Heldengedichte; und dass endlich
> die Schreibart des erstern minder poetisch, feierlich
> oder geschmückt seyn, und sich in die Gränzen des
> prosaischen und leichtern Vortrages einschränken muss.

Somewhat later Eschenburg concludes that the novel can to some
extent be regarded as a genuine literary genre and consequently fosters
the traditional dual purpose of delight and instruction:

> Man sieht aus dem allen, daß man die Romane gewisser-
> massen auch als eine poetische Gattung ansehen kann.
> Und so ist ihnen auch der zwiefache Zweck, zu gefallen
> und zu unterrichten, auf den Verstand und auf Phantasie
> und Empfindung zu wirken, mit der Poesie gemein. Je
> mehr beide Zwecke mit einander vereinigt, desto voll-
> kommner ist er. Nur muß man nicht das Gefallen bloß
> im Belustigen, und den Unterricht bloß in eigentlichen
> Lehrvorschriften setzen; sondern beides in einer so
> treffenden, wahren Nachahmung der Natur, die unsre
> Phantasie lebhaft unterhält, unser Herz innig beschäftigt,
> und auf unserm Willen vorteilhaft wirkt. Sodann können
> wir durch Lesung des Romans unser Gefühl verfeinern,
> mit der Welt und der menschlichen Natur bekannter werden,
> und zugleich unsern Geist unschuldig und angenehm unter-
> halten. (338)

Although writers who published in 1790 had no ready definition of
the novel, they did have well-defined attitudes towards it. Most novelists wished to dissociate themselves from the 'usual novel,' which to
their mind everybody else was writing, and decried the increasing public
attention given to it. The 'usual' novel, many argued, was actually a
blight on society; it aroused passions, corrupted innocent girls, and destroyed family life. These views, of course, are essentially no different from those argued in Gotthard Heidegger's Mythoscopia Romantica oder

<u>Discours von den so benannten Romans</u> (1698). In this respect, little
change seems to have taken place. Attitudes of 1790 reflect the wide
range of meaning commonly ascribed to the term <u>Roman</u> and its variants in
18th-century usage.[2] J.F.E. Albrecht (<u>Fackland</u>, II, 66) and Müller von
Itzehoe (<u>Herr Thomas</u>, IV, 451), for instance, use Roman as a synonym for
love affair. Christiane Naubert (<u>Die Familie von Wallis</u>, I, 16; I, 68;
II, 50) uses <u>romanhaft</u> to mean fantastic, incredible, and excessive,
and Leonard Meister (<u>Spaziergänge</u>, 188) uses a variant to describe the
medieval period as "jene romanhafte Zeiten der Vorwelt." Naubert em-
bellishes Meister's description by suggesting that her contemporaries
found models in stories written "in der grauen Vorzeit" on which to
pattern 'the most circumstantial, albeit not most probable relations between mysterious things' (<u>Alf von Dülmen</u>, 452, note). Novels, we might
tentatively conclude from these typical remarks, are books containing
love affairs with incredible plots, and, as G.H. Heinse implies in
<u>Heinrich der Eiserne</u> (I,i), abounding in dark and confusing circumstan-
ces. Indeed Joachim Heinrich Campe's <u>Vaeterlicher Rath für meine Tochter</u>
(1791) asserts that novels are designed to confuse the understanding, de-
file the imagination, and over-excite the feelings.[3]

Nonetheless, most novelists of 1790 feel that readers expected a
novel to be a tissue of adventures and involved love plots, though they
sometimes express the wish to write something different. They generally
display contempt for the 'usual novel.' Their attitude is ambivalent,
for the genre seems to have been an embarrassment even to its most ardent
practitioners, who deny that their works are novels while at the same
time employing the customary techniques and the traditional devices and
forms of popular fiction. A few examples will illustrate this position.
Gottlob Heinrich Heinse, who insists that <u>Heinrich der Eiserne</u> is a historical work and therefore cannot entertain his readers in the manner to
which they are accustomed, grows uneasy in anticipation of his readers'
frustration. Intruding personally into his narrative, he warns those
readers who had begun the book expecting "ein Gewebe von Abenteuern und
verwickelten Liebeshändeln" (I, 51) that they might become disillusioned
if they read further. Yet despite this comment--and there is no suggestion that he is playing with his readers--one finds all the adventuresome involvements one might wish. Christiane Naubert reveals a similar

8

attitude when she informs us in <u>Barbara Blomberg</u> (II, 432) that we will find nothing about the unravelling of confused ideas on love. Yet her earnest apology cannot alter all the unravelling and joys of love in which the work abounds. Friedrich von Oertel's <u>Kilbur</u> reflects a similar disdain of the novel and insists that its reader will find "weder Entführungen, noch wunderbar geschürzten und zerhauenen Knoten" (I, 6). Oertel clarifies his position over two-hundred pages later, insisting that his work is not 'a usual novel' with "Situationen, Begebenheiten, Schilderungen, Verwicklungen und Entwicklungen" (I, 238). Whoever has been expecting a 'usual novel', he asserts, will certainly regard much of his narrative "überflüssig, plauderhaft und langweilig" (I, 238).

Heinrich Werder exploits this attitude toward contemporary fiction in his satirical novel <u>Eduard Rosenhain</u> by frequently refusing to cater to public taste. At one such point--his hero is making a short and uneventful journey to Leipzig--Werder lists the many things which might be done to make his story appeal to the 'fine ladies and gentlemen' who enjoy the customary literary fare. He could interrupt his hero's journey by inserting 'episodes and many adventures ashore and afloat, and by vaguaries, complications in love affairs, illnesses, new acquaintanceships and more such products of a fiery imagination' (147). His suggestion of inserting "manche Fährlichkeit zu Wasser und zu Lande" parodies many titles of the period that the contemporary reader would readily have recognized. Werder's satire lies in declining to do here what he practises elsewhere. His own work too is as much a product of a 'fiery imagination' as the 'usual' kind of novel which he claims not to have written. It finds a ready market among "empfindsame Leser und Leserinnen", a group which to his mind constitutes the greater part of the reading public:

> Du [der Leser] wirst mit jedem klugen Leser leicht einsehen, dass. . . der Held meines Buches durchaus nicht wie ein gewöhnlicher. . . Romanheld handeln kann. Es sind daher keine freygeisterische Grundsätze, keine Spöttereyen über die christliche Religion, kein Ausfall auf die Landesregierung, keine Anweisung Gold zu machen, kein Unterricht, wie man unschuldige Mädchen verführen soll, noch sonst etwas darinn zu finden, woran sich heut zu Tage die feine und aufgeklärte Welt zu belustigen pflegt. (49).

9

With the exception of Werder, these authors are defending themselves against accusations of having contrived incredible tales. In so doing, however, they have described the main features of contemporary fiction and their apparent distaste for it. They have characterized their colleagues and, often unwittingly, themselves as well. Friedrich Rambach's anthology Kraft- und Kniffgenies reveals a somewhat more eclectic rejection of techniques found in the 'usual novel' described by Oertel and Werder. Rambach is particularly averse to the use of miracles. At one point, for instance, one of his heroes falls into the sea during a storm, only to find himself back aboard the boat 'within two minutes.' We never learn just how he managed to get back aboard, but are explicitly told that the feat was achieved without the novelist's stock-in-trade:

> . . . und zwar ohne die Dazwischenkunft eines Delphins, oder Seepferdes, die immer bei der Hand sind, wenn ein Poet oder Geschichtsschreiber sie zu Hülfe ruft, um seine Helden durch die See zu führen. . . (145).[4]

In summary, then, these negative or defensive descriptions portray the 'usual novel' as a fictional narrative with fantastic, contrived, and complicated plots of love and adventure. This attitude contributed to the problem of distinguishing between fact and fiction in narrative prose, since writers felt that the public enjoyed the aura of truth, and seemed convinced that the moral content of their narrative was more effective if based on the lives of ostensibly real people. Certainly the public would have had to be extremely gullible to believe that the average novel of the day was based on facts, and Rambach correctly maintains that the public enjoyed the illusions which fiction provided (Kniffgenies, I, 209 f.). Johann Friedrich Bahrdt exploits the popular view of the novel--decried by the novelists themselves--in the Preface to his autobiography, Geschichte seines Lebens, seiner Meinungen und Schicksale. Von ihm selbst geschrieben. Although his work is a 'history,' he reassures the readers that it has all the attractions of a novel and will therefore satisfy their every need:

> . . . ich kan mir selbst schon von dem Inhalte dieser Geschichte versprechen, dass ich für den Leser, durch die Mannigfaltigkeit der Auftritte, durch die Sonderbarkeit meiner Schicksale, und durch das Neue und

Unerwartete der vielen Aufschlüsse, welche sie über
manche Scenen meines Lebens erhalten werden, so wie
selbst durch Freimüthigkeit und Offenherzigkeit der
Erzählung,--anziehend genug seyn werde (Preface).

Authors who claim to narrate facts, but exploit numerous occasions in their narratives to attack, parody, or objectively criticize a
literary phenomenon with which they are out of sympathy, lend further
support to the defensive writers we have seen. In Das Zauberschloss,
for instance, Adolf von Knigge describes the novel as a complex of 'love
adventures, students scenes and witches tales and such like, which one
can find in the Neue-Original-Romane der Teutschen and other clever collections that every bookfair so richly provides us with' (204). The
reviewer of Heinrich Rehkopf's Franz Wall in the Allgemeine Deutsche
Bibliothek for 1791 (vol. 104, p. 417) supports Knigge's view: "Studen-
ten-Scenen und Liebschaften; das sind die gewöhnlichen Gegenstände, welche unsre neuern Romanschreiber uns darstellen." In Herr Thomas, Müller
von Itzehoe parodies the genre as a "Liebes-auch Ehe- und Wehestandsgeschichte" (I, 244). Müller regards novels as "Plunder und Kram" (III,
115), while in Dreyerlei Wirkungen J.F.E. Albrecht regards the 'host of
fables, histories, novels and whatever else you call the stuff' as utter
rubbish (IV, 197). Fabrication and the writing of novels are all of a
piece, writes Friedrich Hegrad in Felix mit der Liebesgeige (18), and
as Knigge's fictional narrator in Das Zauberschloss insists "Füllen doch
unsre Romanschreiber ganze Bände mit unbedeutenden Scenen an!" (90).

But where some writers malign the novel because of its shapeless
profusion of adventures, events, and reflections, Ernst Göchhausen defends it. His Meines Vaters Hauschronika is supposed to be a hodge-
podge, "dass [es] ein allerley ist, und seyn soll" (xxxix). Here we
might recall J.C. Wezel's assertion in Tobias Knaut (1773) that a novel
should become all things to all men. One might well ask at this point
just who did write novels; every writer seems to decry the genre and to
dissociate himself from a type of fiction to which he himself is clearly
contributing. In fact, they are all novelists who were unable to define
their form. Oertel makes this explicit: "Ich hoffe, man wird die Haupt-
sache in diesem Roman nicht lange als Roman ansehen" (II, 27). He does
not wish to be accused of having contrived an incredible tale while

pretending to relate facts, nor does he wish his reader to judge the work
a flight of fancy. Being called a novelist was an indictment most writers wished to avoid. Heinrich Werder even regarded it as an unenviable
office: "Romanschreiber seyn. . . ein Ehrenamt, welches er Niemanden
beneidet!" (Eduard Rosenhain, 150 f.).

Some writers held the view that the flood of prose fiction in no
way reflected national character. However, Müller von Itzehoe suggested
in Herr Thomas that contemporary fiction was an aberration that might yet
be construed as reflecting the spirit of Germany:

> Die Sitten und den Charakter mancher andern Nation kann
> ein Deutscher aus ihren Romanen kennen lernen. Wer aber
> im Auslande in eben dieser Absicht deutsche Romane lesen
> wollte, der könnte leicht in Gefahr kommen zu glauben,
> ganz Deutschland sey ein einziges Irrenhaus. Das Roman-
> schreiben ist bey uns zu selten das ernstliche Geschäfte
> des reifen, erfahrnen, unter Menschen grau gewordenen Mannes,
> sondern das Handwerk oft sehr junge Jünglinge, die eben
> deswegen nie Männer werden können. (IV, 378)

Müller's assertion that German novelists are 'very young youths' who can
never grow up is not entirely correct. The average age of the authors
who published novels in 1790 is 33 years. The oldest writers were Friedrich Bahrdt (49) and Friedrich Moser (67). The youngest by far was
Johann Bornschein, who was only 16 on publishing his four-volume Der
französische Abenteurer oder Denkwürdigkeiten Greg Merveils. The significance of Müller's charge lies in its emotional response to the novel,
an attitude which characterizes most critics of the genre.

Sheer length is a dominant characteristic of the novel of the period. Müller von Itzehoe parodies this phenomenon in Herr Thomas when
his aspiring hero plans "ein Werklein von einiger Korpulenz" (IV, 394)
simply because 'the bookdealers are not inclined toward the pocket-sized
edition.' J.F.E. Albrecht commends his Dreyerlei Wirkungen as a particularly apt contribution to the genre in view of what he ironically calls
the presently popular small format (I, 30): his novel appeared in eight
parts from 1789-1792 and ran to approximately 2000 pages. Only very few
writers kept their works short, and Christian Sander recommends his collection of short stories, Salz, Laune und Mannichfaltigkeit, as an antidote to the 'usual novel' of which Oertel and Werder spoke. The story

will amuse, Sander writes, as it contains events and occurrences that
will keep all good people breathless, and also because it only rarely
follows 'our ever popular novels' which have 'neither plan nor unity.'
Its 'incomparable advantage,' he points out, is that it will take only
a quarter of an hour to read. But whereas the writer of novels, as we
will see later, always struggles against the anticipated boredom of his
readers, Sander is unique in whimsically regarding his work as a very
useful aid to sleep:

> Nutzen wird sie [die Erzählung]. . . dadurch, dass sie
> manchen braven Leser in den süssen Schlummer einwiegt,
> den er nachmittags im Grossvaterstuhl oder Abends im
> Bette oft allein durch Lesen zu erhalten sucht (135 f.).

2. The purpose of the novel

Few writers of the period, not even writers of love stories, com-
mend fiction for its own sake. If it does not promote specific ends and
values it is rejected as frivolous. Yet most writers seemed to have felt
that the popular novel was not equal to the task of moral persuasion.
Thus a reviewer in the Allgemeine Deutsche Bibliothek for 1790 (vol. 96,
p. 141) gives us to understand that the "Roman von gemeinem Schlag" is
churned out of a "Romanfabrik in Dachstuben" and has miserable heroes
who earn their wretched bread by journeying from place to place. It is
for this reason that Müller von Itzehoe describes most novels as 'junk
and trash' in Herr Thomas, but extols 'Nicolai's Sebaldus, Lessing's
Emilie, Wieland's Oberon' as models for aspiring novelists because of
their disciplined craftmanship:

> Es ist ein hässlicher Irrthum, wenn mancher glaubt, ein
> vortreffliches Buch ströme nur so auf das Papier hin, weil
> eigne kunstleere und marklose Prosa oder Poetery, was es
> nun eben ist, die Er freylich vortrefflich findet, ihm
> selber so gewaltig hinströmet, wie der Regen aus einer
> Dachrinne. . . Die glücklichen Wendungen kommen nicht im
> Fluge, und der natürliche Ausdruck, obwohl man ihn ungesucht
> nennet, läuft dem grossen Schriftsteller nicht so von selbst
> in die Feder, als dem Jüngling das Wasser: es kostet Mühe
> ihn zu suchen, und Anstrengung ihn zu finden, ja, nicht
> selten entschlüpft er Dir in dem Momente wieder, wo Du
> eben glaubst ihn zu haschen. Nicolai's Sebaldus, Lessing's
> Emilie, Wieland's Oberon sind zuverlässig nicht das leichte
> Spiel verlohrner Viertelstündchen; mancher Bogen kostete
> ohne Zweifel Wochen, und zwar dann doch vielleicht noch so

> nicht vollendet, als es diesen grossen Männern vorschwebte,
> dass er seyn könne. (III, 114 f.)

Eschenburg senses new hope for the development of the German novel since
about the mid 1770's:

> In Deutschland haben wir erst seit den letzten funfzehn
> bis zwanzig Jahren verschiedene Originalromane erhalten,
> die sich zum Theil von den ehemaligen geschmacklosen
> Werken dieser Art, wovon unsre Nation einen Ueberfluß
> hatte, eben so vorteilhaft unterschieden, als von der
> Menge mißlungener Versuche darin, womit sie noch immer
> heimgesucht wird. Die vornehmsten darunter sind von Haller,
> Wieland, Göthe, Nicolai, Frau von la Roche, Hermes, Dusch,
> Miller, Meißner, Wezel, Schummel, Jung, Müller, Musäus,
> und einem Ungenannten [Hippel]. (Theorie, 343)

To these Georg Kellner would add "Goethe's Werther and Pope's Heloise
[sic!]' because they present 'true copies of real human characters'
(Familie der Rosenbusche, IV, 225).[5] Heinrich Werther insists in Eduard
Rosenhain that every writer who influences the reading public should
follow the 'magnificent example of a Wieland, Gedicke, Biester and other
worthy men'. Only then, he argues, can one re-awaken a healthy common
sense (76).

Most novelists, like most 18th-century writers in other branches
of literature, were convinced that art must teach while it entertains.
This is the doctrine taught by Horace in The Art of Poetry:

> The poet's aim is either to profit or to please, or to
> blend in one the delightful and the useful. . . the man
> who mingles the useful with the sweet carries the day
> by charming his reader and at the same time instructing
> him. That's the book to enrich the publisher, to be
> posted over seas, and to prolong its author's fame.[6]

Accordingly, a basic narrative intent in 1790 was that of imparting a particular moral view to one's reader by means of a pleasing fiction, and it is noteworthy that writers of the period regarded English
publications as the prime models. As the Teutscher Merkur for 1790
(vol. 2, pp. 435 ff.) observes when announcing a new translation of
Richardson's Clarissa:

> Schon der bloße Nahme: Englischer Roman, hat so viel
> Vortheil für sich, daß unsre besten Köpfe sich nicht
> schämten, die Werke eines Richardsons, Fieldings,

> Goldsmiths, sogar bis auf den Witz der Ueberschriften,
> sich zum Muster zu nehmen, und unsre Halbköpfe, sie zu
> kopieren. . . . Es ist wahr, das Lesen einer Klarisse und
> Pamela ist ausser Mode gekommen. Allein, was beweißt
> [sic] die Mode für oder wider die Güte des Gegenstandes?

Oertel speaks for his colleagues in _Kilbur_ when he writes that while the
adventures in English novels are always the same, they are generally
pleasing and well-received because they are 'highly moral.' More specifically, they make their morality practical by broadening our understanding of man (II, 438 ff.). With this ideal in mind, Oertel intended
his own novel to be "nützlich, und im Allgemeinen interessant" (I, 9).
Useful truth, he writes, is the great demand that one can make of any
piece of writing (II, 426). He even contends that the proper articula-
tion of 'useful truth' makes up for many errors of style and short-co-
mings in learning (II, 426). Friedrich Mursinna urges the same point
in his Preface to _Die natürliche Tochter_. Every writer must first
strive to arouse a love of virtue and humanity; only then must entertainment and a pleasing style be a reason why the author should wish to
speak to his public (iii f.). Indeed Marianna Ehrmann informs the general reading public in _Amaliens Erholungsstunden_ (1790) that whoever is
merely fascinated by entertaining plots should simply quit reading altogether:

> Wer während dem [sic] Lesen nicht denkt, nicht urtheilt,
> sich nicht Schlussfolgen herauszieht, nicht nach Menschen-
> kenntnis hascht. . . sich blos an den historischen Anwen-
> dungen, nicht ans Räsonnement, nicht an des Verfassers
> Denkart hält, der lege ums Himmelswillen das Buch weg![7]

Every writer, Oertel notes in _Kilbur,_ should write for the education of adults (II, 440); for his own part he is quite happy to entertain
provided he can also be 'useful' (I, 239). His other novel, _Weiber machten ihn weiser,--und glücklich_, aims equally at "Unterhaltung als Belehr-
ung" (477). Christiane Naubert regards her epistolary novel _Die Familie
von Wallis_ as 'entertaining and instructive' (I, 40), Ernst Göchhausen
writes his _Büchlein_ in order 'to nurture wisdom' (163), and Friedrich
Rambach insists in _Kniffgenies_ that his basic concern is 'entertainment
and instruction' (I, 173), while Gottlob Heinrich Heinse's _Heinrich der
Eiserne_ lays somewhat more emphasis on pure pleasure--Vergnügen (I, 4).

It is surprising that only one novelist of the period, Sophie Tresenreuther, regards achieving this narrative aim a problem. This is particularly strenuous, she explains with an uncharacteristic touch of wit, if instruction is to be useful and the entertainment harmless--'if I might speak with Fielding in joining cookery with authorship' (Geist der Memoiren, II, 6).

The biographical novel has a well-defined didactic intent. Ignaz Fessler, for instance, defines the purpose of Marc-Aurel as the diffusion of useful knowledge, or the renewal of the sacred memory of meritorious men for the well-being of mankind (II,ii), and Wilhelm Heller seeks to instruct the readers of his Sokrates in 'virtue and wisdom' (267). The facts of biography or history often remain secondary to the moral lesson. Whether Christiane Naubert's hero is actually guilty of the crime of which he is accused in Alf von Dülmen, is really of no concern because "seine Geschichte ist nicht ohne gute Lehre" (44). Friedrich Hegrad summarizes the convictions of his fellow-writers regarding the purpose of novels in Felix mit der Liebesgeige:

> Unter allen Büchern sind die Romanen die einzigen, in welchen Moral anzutreffen ist. Diese sind es, in welchen wir am richtigsten den Einfluß unserer Handlungen auf das Glück und auf die Aufführung derienigen, welche uns umgeben, bemerken — unstreitig, der wichtigste Theil der Moral, und auch zugleich derienige, welcher am meisten vernachlässiget wird! (II, 166 note)

3. Typical moral views

Like most of her fellow-novelists, Christiane Naubert was convinced that one needs an infinite degree of understanding in order to sense one's own shortcomings without outside instruction (Werner, I, 59). The writer's social function was to provide this counsel. It is interesting, therefore, to review the types of moral statements which the majority of writers of the period endorse. It was a generally held view of the Enlightenment that reason could be both taught and learned, a view to which most of our authors subscribed. Thus Fessler asserts in Marc-Aurel that one must learn to be virtuous and can do so by reading his novel. By virtue Fessler understands 'a perfect reason--Vernunft--or a correct and thorough knowledge of the rules according to which one must act, together

with a facility, acquired through practice, of always conducting oneself
according to them' (I, 82 f.). Ernst Göchhausen's concept of virtue as
expressed in <u>Meines Vaters Hauschronika</u> (304) typifies views held by
writers of love stories: "Tugend ist Kampf--nicht immer <u>Sieg</u>, gegen
die Hindernisse <u>gut</u> zu seyn." Heller's <u>Sokrates</u> tries to promote the
virtues of "Mäsigkeit [sic], Rechtschaffenheit und Verachtung des Reich-
tums" (32). In Heller's view, Socrates was a most fitting hero for a
novel because he had resisted the trends of his times, particularly
"den schändlichen Geldgeiz der falschen Weisheitslehrer" (39); one wonders here if he is not really trying to debunk the contemporary novelist.
The hero of Heller's novel epitomizes these virtues; it is through him
that the author instructs his public in the ideal of human conduct.
Christian Gotthelf Salzmann's <u>Sebastian Kluge</u>, as we will see in Chapter
VI, promotes the ethics of work and prayer and 'the proper use of one's
time' (34). "Wer den Kopf auf dem rechten Flecke hat" makes good use of
his time, never suffers from need, and always gets as much money as he
needs (90). It might at first seem that Heller and Salzmann espouse
antagonistic principles; but in fact they agree. The acquisition of
money through work, prayer, and the practice of virtue is quite in order; financial speculation is wrong.

Proclamations of the ethic of work often result in bathos, for
instance in Georg Kellner's <u>Familiengeschichte der Rosenbusche</u>. Here
the affluent Adolph relinquishes his medical practice as he has no pa-
tients, and becomes a factory director in partnership with his wife.
They expand the company 'immeasurably.' How happy they were by day at
their labours, Kellner writes: "Glücklicher noch am Abend, wenn sie in
Armen sich liegen, sich wechselseitig den Schweiß von der Stirn küssen
. . ." (III, 181) Ambitions are fulfilled through labour, and labour
leads to marital bliss. Yet while ambition is often exalted in this
context, many voices forwarn the reader of the dangers of trying to
reach beyond one's social class. 'Woe unto the city-girl who fancies
herself a fine lady, and unto the townsman who tries to be a squire,'
writes Leonard Meister in <u>Neue Schweizerische Spaziergänge</u> (122).
Naubert prophesies even greater doom in <u>Brunilde</u>: 'What is the moral
that flows from Brunilde's story?' she asks on the final page of the

novel. "Readers, take it to heart and remain happily in your own sphere, beyond lurks scorn, misery, and death!' (84). Brunilde's suicidal plunge from a castle window is proof enough of that.

Social position is extremely important to these writers, and marriage is the most important institution for a stable society. 'Marriage alone assigns us an established place in the household of God,' writes Oertel in _Kilbur_: 'only through marriage do we receive a social position, become useful, and participate in the commonweal' (II, 395). Fessler explains in _Marc-Aurel_ that marriage must be based on 'reasonable, not on Arcadian principles,' for the 'fever of love' soon passes (I, 255). Albrecht agrees in _Fackland_ that marriage and romantic love have nothing in common (II, 184). Sophie Tresenreuter in _Geist der Memoiren_ offers motherly counsel to her "junge Freunde und Freundinnen": 'Not love alone, but personal worth, makes for lasting happiness in marriage' (I, 206). The contemporary reader need scarcely have asked what sorrow neglect of these principles might lead to, for the novels leave no one in doubt. We have already noted that Brunilde committed suicide. The anonymous _Die unglückliche Fürstin aus Wien_ warns us by the example of a high-born lady who disobeyed her mother by falling in love, thus ending her days in poverty and despair. Under 'torrents of tears' she laments having broken trust with her mother, whose advice was meant to spare her 'this series of misfortunes' (14). While moral counsel was largely concerned with affairs of the heart, marriage, the maintenance of home and family, common sense and the maintenance of 'true' religion, a few writers like Karl Friedrich Bahrdt in _Ala Lama_ turned their attention to matters of government by promoting the view that nothing is more beneficial for a nation than a form of justice composed of wisdom and humanity (II, 256).

4. Problems of fact and fiction

Friedrich Hegrad, as we have seen, insisted that the moral instruction which society needed could only be found in novels. Indeed a reviewer in the _Allgemeine Deutsche Bibliothek_ for 1790 (vol. 94, p.149) observed "Romane sind das beste Mittel, moralische Wahrheiten in Umlauf zu bringen, und solchen Menschen anzudrängen, denen kein Prediger beykommen kann." Moral effectiveness, most novelists seem to feel, is directly related to the ability to convince the public that their works are founded upon truth. They may in some measure have been encouraged in this view by the type of public response to literature recounted among Goethe's experiences in Italy (1786-88) when he was repeatedly greeted as the author of Werther and asked whether his novel was based on facts.[8]

Johann Christian Müller seems to suggest that the popular mind was more concerned with truth than with style or art. He explains in Frag-mente aus dem Leben und Wandel eines Physiognomisten that an author must write from solid experience and cannot depend on "ein guter Vorrath Laune" (76). Friedrich Mursinna voices the mood of the period in Die natürliche Tochter when writing that truth is sublime beyond all fiction (iii); he doubtless means that the fate experienced by heroes and hero-ines in novels must be the logical and natural outcome of their actions. This view is supported by Sophie Tresenreuter, who draws her readers' attention to the fact that all the heroes and heroines in Geist der Memoiren are punished or rewarded as a natural result of their actions (9). An author must be 'truthful,' she explains in her Preface. 'Gene-ral experience and a little knowledge of man,' she continues in deni-gration of contemporary fiction, 'give more than a paltry imagination can provide' (i, iv). Oertel agrees entirely. It is not his duty 'to portray events in a more or less romantic light,' he explains, 'since truth is his motto and the sole deity' (Kilbur, I, 330 f.) Properly handled by an imaginative writer the portrayal of truth permits the author 'to creep into the reader's heart.' Ernst Göchhausen, the artist, as he calls him-self in Meines Vaters Hauschronika, feels assured of such success:

Ach, Ihr [die Leser] schenkt ja wohl eine Thräne des Mitgefühls dem Künstler, der sich in Euer Hertz und Einbildungskraft hinein stahl! Hier ist Wahrheit, nicht Roman. Dies konnte nicht geschehen. Es geschah! (245).

Göchhausen attempted to arouse his readers' emotions through the pretence of truthfulness, that is through a degree of realism enhanced by the inclusion of the 'actual names' of those who appear in his father's chronicle. J.F.E. Albrecht approves of this technique in Uranie: "Einmal kann das kein Roman seyn, in welchem alle Personen namenhaft genannt und aufgestellt sind. Das ist entweder Wahrheit oder Pasquil" (II, 22 f.). Albrecht expresses an equal regard for truth and hopes the reader will

19

find "nichts gekünsteltes" (<u>Uranie</u>, II, 230). Thus no matter how 'strange' certain events might seem, nor whether they 'bear the mark of an invention', they are generally claimed as true (Kaffka, <u>Ruinen</u>, I, 190). The nature of 'truth' and the manner of its expression vary from work to work, as might be expected. Johann Kaffka, for example, claims his work is 'historically true' (I, 190), whereas Friedrich von Oertel insists that his main concern is philosophic truth and not fidelity to history: "es ist hier von philosophischer, nicht historischer Treue die Rede, also davon, ob unter so gegebenen Umständen das und diess erfolgen konnte und musste" (<u>Kilbur</u>, I, 6). As we will see later, Oertel's approach approximates Lessing's concept of 'inner probability' and Schiller's concept of 'inner or philosophical truth.' Thus while Kaffka tries to present certain events as facts, Oertel claims to examine the motivating forces which could have initiated the events of his narrative.

Tresenreuter had characterized the writer's dilemma of combining entertainment and instruction as 'particularly strenuous if instruction is to be useful and entertainment harmless' (II, 6), and later complains of the difficulty of discovering what goes on in the mind of real people. 'It is almost completely impossible,' she writes in <u>Geist der Memoiren</u>, 'to distinguish truth from lies and appearance from fact with any degree of certitude when accounting for the actions or thoughts of a third person' (II, 91). Her statement anticipates her readers' objection that the manuscript upon which she claims to have based her novel might not be true, and thus reflects her view of what the public expects. To her mind, the public expects to find facts in memoirs. Christiane Naubert copes with this difficulty in <u>Alf von Dülmen</u> by resigning herself to the view that "die Sache sey übrigens Wahrheit oder nicht, wir werden es nicht ergründen" (23).

Feigned adherence to truth or facts, and one doubts if it is ever more than pretence, seems of greater importance in works purporting to be histories or biographies. What the modern historical novelist would regard as the conscious ordering of narrative material for particular effects, the author of 1790 fears his public will judge as wilful manipulation of details. Perhaps out of fear of public censure, writers like Ignaz Fessler are so naively honest with their readers. At one point in

<u>Marc-Aurel</u>, for example, where Fessler records the death of Justin Mar-
tyr, he adds a footnote explaining that Justin actually died in Aurelius'
third or sixth year of government; he had 'placed the episode here because
of the context'   (III, 130 note). Oertel resorts to the same technique
in the second part of <u>Kilbur</u> when describing a certain letter he had received from a lady; 'It was here,' he notes, 'where she wrote me that
letter which for other reasons I inserted in Part One' (II, 151). A
footnote follows with the precise page of Part One where the letter is
to be found.

Writers who either seriously or playfully maintain they are telling a true story frequently claim to work from manuscripts or letters.
This technique makes it easier to feign truth and belongs to a very old
tradition which had already been parodied by Cervantes. As we will see
in Chapter II, these fictional documents have invariably been ruined by
mice, moths, and mold. But the semblance of truth is maintained nonetheless. The anonymous author of <u>Heinrich und Henriette</u> observes, for instance, that the papers he found were full of holes; he immediately confesses that he filled the gaps as well as possible, yet not so as to
transform the history into fiction: "ich gestehe, dass die Geschichte
selbst, nicht zu einem Roman umgewandelt ist" (iv f.) In Christian Sander's words, the technique of filling the gaps of an original manuscript
often amounts to a "Schneiderscherz" (<u>Salz, Laune</u>, 72 f.).

It is ultimately up to the reader to decide whether a novel is based on fact or fiction, and some writers are as forthright as Naubert in
saying so. In an incapsulated narrative in <u>Barbara Blomberg</u>, she intrudes into the frame-work narrative to comment on the tale's effect upon
its listeners:

> Die Geschichte. . . war lang und sonderbar, und gewährte. . .
> manche nicht unangenehme Zerstreuung, sie [die Zuhörer] glaub-
> ten von derselben, was sie wollten. . . Meine Leser glaubten
> hierin ebenfalls, was sie wollen, und bedenken, dass sie einen
> Roman gelesen haben (II, 440).

Novelists then, were primarily concerned with the instruction and
diversion of their readers, and this concern made them cope with distinctions between fact and fiction. The reader must first be convinced that
the books were true so that 'good teaching' might naturally follow. Not

all writers were so adamant, however, and Friedrich Rambach is the most
conservative among them. "Die Wahrheit ist," he writes in Kniffgenies,
"daß sich die Menschen bei [Puppen-] Schauspielen mit dem Leser eines Romans in Einem Falle befinden; diese wissen woll [sic], daß sie betrogen
werden, aber ihnen gefällt der Betrug, und so wie diese Behagen in den
märchenhaften Erzählungen finden, so finden jene ihren Vortheil bei einer
solchen Farce, die im gemeinen Leben aufgetischt wird: - Ursache genug,
sich in beiden Fällen täuschen zu lassen." (I, 209 f.) This is precisely
why the pill of instruction had to be sugared by entertainment; the public
read solely for diversion. None of the authors of 1790 ever confessed
that they themselves exploited this situation; they all condemned it.

5. The author and his public

One cannot refrain from asking at this point just who were the readers and why they desired the type of entertainment which novels provided.
Fessler indicts both authors and readers in Marc-Aurel by saying that
people read 'such stupid stuff' for the same reason that leads poets and
actors astray to their wonderful fictions and imaginings; they crave satisfaction of the need for new impressions: "Befriedigung des Bedürfniss-
es neuer Eindrücke" (I, 185). It is this need for the wonderful which to
his mind gives rise to 'the unnatural assemblages of plots' (I, 185).
For Leonard Meister this need for new impressions reveals society's moral
bankruptcy. People turn away from the magnificent natural beauty of the
Alps, he writes in Neue Schweizerische Spaziergänge, for the same reasons
that many a writer and reader prefers the 'heroic stage to the stage of
man.' They prefer the "theater" of high society to scenes of domestic
life and feelings for 'simple, unsophisticated' nature (37, f.). If
people would only return to the 'womb of nature,' he exclaims, one would
not miss 'that multi-coloured soap-bubble called high society' (178).
Meister later addresses the "unbefangene Blätter" that he had just written
and laments that their 'ramblings' into the outside world will not be as
innocent as his own ramblings in the Swiss countryside. Meister seeks
the solitudes of 'grove and vale,' whereas his pages, he fears, will 'prefer desk and dressing-table' (279).

Friedrich Hegrad's Felix mit der Liebesgeige portrays the type of reading public which causes Meister's sorrow. One chapter in particular presents the dramatic dialogue of two witless belles who have just been reading a novel and now address themselves to Hegrad, their author, in order to justify their way of life. Surely, they argue, an author could wish for no better reader than one who is well-read and up-to date in all the fashions and fads, especially the French ones. The allusion to French culture is equally interesting, for the French are invariably described in novels of the period as 'the most innovation-crazy, unstable and petulant of creatures' (Göchhausen, Hauschronika, 115), and as the pace setters of German society (Albrecht, Fackland, I, 42).

France and the novel bear the burden of guilt for the moral decline of Germany, and Müller von Itzehoe's parody of the novel and its public in Herr Thomas reflects the serious misgivings of his dour colleagues. Where other writers speak as prophets of doom, Müller enjoys the game of fiction by attacking the very genre in which he writes. At one point in the novel the young hero, himself aspiring to authorship, utters the 'rational and commonsense view' which has been urged upon him by his sceptical mentor. Literature and a woman's mind don't mix, he asserts. Popular literature turns women into fools or libertines and leads to unhappy marriages, spoilt children, and neglected homes. A woman must restrict her reading to the catechism and the cook book:

> Man sieht nur, wie viel Unheil schon entstehet, seit unsre jungen Weiber und Töchter sich auf das verfluchte Roman-lesen legen. Die schönen Arianen, die durchlauchtigen Kassandren, die liebenswürdigen Konstantinen, und wie das Teufelszeug weiter heisst, machen die armen Dinger zu Närrinnen oder--noch was ärgern. Das gibt dann unglückliche Ehen, verwilderte oder verzogenen Kinder, und verwahrloste Haushaltungen. . . ein junges Frauenzimmer muss ihre Lektüre auf den Katechism und das Brandenburgische Kochbuch mit der wohlunterwiesenen Köchin- und Confect-Tafel einschränken. . . (I, 186 f.).

Although Müller's facetiously coined titles refer to the still popular "heroisch-galante Romane," we may assume that they include those 'usual novels' of love and adventure that both Oertel and Werder had pilloried.[9]

We have already seen that the authors of the period had no comprehensive critical definition of the genre they cultivated, and J.F.E.

Albrecht suggests that the public was in a similar quandary. In fact he claims in _Dreyerley Wirkungen_ that there was a confusion in the public mind between 'literary products' and "schlüpfrige und zur Wollust reizende Bücher" (III, 158). The latter are ruining society, he claims, and, in Müller's phrase, make the young ladies believe they can live on moonlight and forget-me-nots (_Herr Thomas_, II, 342). Albrecht points out with amused candour that such works are undermining the church, for even young curates read lubricious novels (_Uranie_, I, 14). Most writers agree that vicarious eroticism makes novels particularly dangerous to the well-being of society, and the discussion finds its way into the critical literature of the period. A writer in the _Allgemeine Deutsche Bibliothek_ for 1792 (vol. 110, p. 597) argues, for example, that the downfall of young girls cannot be blamed on novels because most girls who lose their virtue are illiterate. But despite all the hue and cry about this aspect of fiction, many writers seemed to recognize it as an obligatory ingredient which could almost guarantee the sale of their books.[10] The love story, as we will see in Chapter III, exploited the theme to warn its readers of the dangers of romantic love, a situation that led to the ambiguous position of eroticism in novels. Yet whatever their avowed aversions to the topic, most writers attempt a lubricious scene or two. The novels of 1790 contain many episodes in which writers take a critical view of lubricious scenes and their effect upon readers, and then give examples of the very thing they supposedly abhor. Heinrich Rehkopf describes in _Franz Wall_ how a young woman is sexually aroused by reading a novel. His reasons for the scene are curious. He wants to show, we are given to understand, that novels arouse the passions; and secondly, that women who read novels are sensualists and libertines. Yet under cover of his 'upright' intentions, he achieves an obligatory scene which we might presume to have taken him a step nearer to literary success:

> Der Tag war heiss, sie hatte gelesen und war dadurch empfäng-
> lich geworden: ihren Busen hatte sie etwas gelüftet, er
> dampfte vor Gluth in dem engen Behältnisse und wallte hoch
> auf, sie selbst freute sich seiner Fülle, seines wilden
> Tobens. (I, 145)

Time and again writers speak of over-sensitive readers who are ready to weep and swoon in the vicarious delights of love's vicissitudes and

pleasures and, having given their examples, invite their readers to follow the protagonists' lead. This prompts Kellner to exclaim in affected
indignation at the trend of his times:

> . . . alle Hagel! Wozu giebt's wohl so viele Menschen
> mit Löschpapierherzen in der Welt, durch die jeder
> Firlefanz durchdringt, und einen Specktackel d'rinn
> macht, als wenn alle Teufel aus der Hölle mit ihren Pfoten's
> Schornsteinfegerhandwerk trieben? (<u>Rosenbusche</u>, III, 34 ff.)

Sophie Tresenreuter ascribes the phenomenon to an inability to 'digest'
the novel properly. "You can ruin your stomach on bread and milk if you
don't know how to chew, or overindulge, or else eat at the wrong time,"
she writes in <u>Geist der Memoiren</u> (10). Authors of 1790 seem to have felt
that the public was guilty of all these errors, particularly of overin-
dulgence and failure to chew. At any rate, the answer to the problem
did not seem to lie in producing fewer novels. 'Bad' reading habits were
said to prevail.

Oertel's <u>Weiber machten ihn weiser,--und glücklich</u> describes the
curious and not altogether unsuccessful attempt of a local lending library to correct the 'bad' reading habits of its clientele. A group of
'reasonable women of some means' had established a lending library to
'instruct the better part of the female sex.' They soon realized, however, that their readers were spending more time with 'entertaining'
works than with anything else. As 'this pained their patriotic hearts,'
they published a quarterly reader's list indicating the type and quantity
of literature which each member had read. The members, we are told, soon
felt uneasy about the incriminating evidence and gradually brought their
own interests into line with what they felt propriety demanded. By the
end of the next quarter the required 'enlightenment' had begun, and the
reading of 'entertaining books' had been reduced by 'one sixth.' They
then turned their attention to more serious objects of literature (92).
We unfortunately are not told what these 'more serious objects' were.

If one were to trust the insinuations of authors who published in
1790, one would have to conclude that their reading public consisted
mainly of impressionable youths and girls, dim-witted and love-lorn hou-
sewives, and frivolous, modish coquettes. These are the people who are
denounced and lamented in novels; authors presumably felt that the bad

novels they attack were read by silly people, while their own novels
appealed to sensible readers. They certainly have 'sensible' people in
mind when interjecting comments to their 'dear readers.'

It is instructive to compare these views of the reading public with
the subscription lists of the two novels of the period, Phillipp Lohbauer's <u>Der Tannenbauer</u>[11] and Sophie Tresenreuter's <u>Geist der Memoiren,</u>
that provide this information.

Lohbauer: Der Tannenbauer

Subscriber	No. of subscribers	Approx. %
"Fürstliche Personen"	11	5.0
Professors	8	4.0
Schoolmaster	1	0.5
Senior Officials (i.e.Oberforst- meister, Oberamtmann, Stadtrath)	45	20.0
Other Civil Servants (i.e. Post- verwalter, Stadtschreiber)	70	32.0
Merchants and Tradesmen	60	27.5
Pastors	15	7.0
Women	9	4.0
	219	100.0

Tresenreuter: Geist der Memoiren

Subscriber	No. of subscribers	Approx. %
"Fürstliche Personen"	5	8.0
Physicians	1	1.0
Pastors	2	2.0
Senior Officials (i.e. Kammerherr)	26	43.0
Other Civil Servants	8	13.0
Merchants and Tradesmen	8	13.0
Women	12	20.0
	62	100.0

One must bear in mind when reviewing these lists that a great number of
prefaces contain fervent, even fawning, dedicatory passages in praise and
adulation of the local ruling nobleman; it would therefore seem to have
been politic for the "Fürstliche Personen" to have contributed toward
publication costs. One might even regard this as an example of literary
symbiosis: a writer could attract public attention to his work by gracing
it with the name of a nobleman; the nobleman would be rewarded by having
his popular image enhanced. Fessler, for example, praises a different
statesmen in the Prefaces to each of four parts of <u>Marc-Aurel,</u> and

acknowledges each patron as noble as the hero of the novel. Of course, these are methods which Fielding had already parodied in Tom Jones (1749):

> . . . I shall always prefer the indulgence of your inclination to the satisfaction of my own. A very strong instance of which I shall give you in this address, in which I am determined to follow the example of all other dedicators, and will consider not what my patron really deserves to have written, but what he will be best pleased to read.
> (Preface)

Another point to bear in mind concerns the female subscribers. While women form only 13 % of the patrons, it is doubtful whether they would generally have had sufficient financial or social independence to play a significant role in the commercial aspects of popular literature other than through the purchases and patronage of their husbands, or else through lending libraries. The husband would subscribe at the request of his wife, who would read the book.

6. The author and the book-trade

Most publishers and novelists wanted to earn money, and recognized popular literature as a field for commercial speculation. We find an early and comprehensive debate on the subject in the dialogue between the Magister and Sebaldus in Nicolai's Leben und Meinungen des Sebaldus Nothanker (1777):

> Seb. Ich weiss nicht, was Sie sprechen. Ein Buchdrucker oder ein Buchhändler mag ein Gewerbe mit Büchern haben, aber ein Schriftsteller ist ein Gelehrter, der der Welt nützliche Kenntnisse mitzuteilen sucht, der Wahrheit und Weisheit befördern will.
>
> Mag. Ihre Einbildungskraft, mein liebster Freund, fliegt noch ziemlich hoch. Lassen Sie sich herunter und kommen Sie der Erde näher. Der größte Haufen der Schriftsteller von Profession treibt ein Gewerbe, so gut als die Tapetenmaler oder die Kunstpfeifer und sieht die wenigen wahren Gelehrten fast ebenso für zudringliche, unzünftige Pfuscher an. . . . Der Autor will gern dem Verleger so wenig Bogen Manuskript, als möglich, für so viel Geld, als möglich, so wohlfeil, als möglich einhandeln, und so teuer, als möglich, verkaufen.[12]

Friedrich von Oertel also regarded the book-trade--der deutsche Buchhandel--as the axis around which literature and author revolve. In fact, it would always remain so as long as the reading public continued to let itself be swayed by publishers' titles. The less people distinguish between the clothes and the man, he continues in the Preface to Weiber machten ihn weiser,--und glücklich, the more novels increase their capacity to make sensual impressions. Books are marketed according to "the first sensual impression" they make. Indeed it is the prevailing mood 'of our frivolous century,' the 'norm of our reading,' to judge everything by its outward appearance. It has often happened, he continues (and here we may recall Albrecht's discussion of the 'Kingstang' on planet Sirius) that the finest memorial to human knowledge was overlooked in the shops at bookfairs because the author did not apply this rule to the 'business of writing.' Oertel's publisher took a businesslike approach in suggesting the title for his novel.

Göchhausen reports that his publisher actually made him change the title of Meines Vaters Hauschronika, but gives us no clue as to what the original title might have been. His complaint is the same as Oertel's: "Wares are not sold according to their inner value, but according to the sign on the cover" (xxii f.). Christian Sander describes a similar experience in Salz, Laune und Mannichfaltigkeit. Undecided as to how he should "baptise" his book, he had turned to his publisher. The businessman regarded titles as "lighthouses for luring the public; the brighter they shine, the better." In order to illustrate this merchandising approach the publisher had shown Sander "a few volumes of very commonplace extracts from generally known travelogues by Campe." Campe, Sander comments, had gleaned the secrets of the trade and had provided his work with a subtitle indicating it was "durchgängig, zweckmäßig abgefasst." Sander himself, we are told, was urged to follow suit and expand the present title Salz, Laune und Mannichfaltigkeit by adding the descriptive phrase: "in einigen unvergleichlichen comischen Erzählungen" (I, 3 f.). But he refused to do so. He wanted to sell his book but, like many of his literary colleagues, expressed aversion to such means.

Müller von Itzehoe's essay Ueber den Verlagsraub (1791) sheds light on another important literary relationship by describing the treatment an

28

illicit edition of his <u>Siegfried von Lindenberg</u> received at the hands of
Schmieder of Karlsruhe, one of the most infamous book-pirates:

> Denn der Mensch in <u>Carlsruhe</u>, den ich doch wohl offenbar
> <u>einen</u> <u>Betrüger</u> seiner <u>Käufer</u> nennen darf. . . dieser ohne
> allen Widerspruch ehrvergeßne Mensch begnügt sich nicht,
> meine Schriften nachzudrucken, sondern er verstümmelt sie,
> und. . . läßt ganze Kapitel weg, macht Lücken von 80, von
> 100 Seiten, und unterdrückt jede Stelle, in welcher von
> der Natur und Moralität seines lichtscheuen Gewerbes die
> Rede ist; und um in alle Wege Falsarius zu seyn, giebt er
> auf dem Titelblatte seine Verhunzung für eine vom Ver-
> faßer verbesserte und vermehrte neue Ausgabe. (5 f.)

As we might expect, Müller found these methods 'morally outrageous' (80).

Writers of the period prefer to remain aloof when confronting business matters, even though forced to recognize, in Johann Christian Müller's words, that books are "Waarenartikel" (<u>Physiognomisten</u>, 99).
The best they ever seem to do is tilt at windmills, while harbouring an
ambivalent attitude to the business of marketing. Business practices
not only promoted the sale of novels, but in some cases, many argued,
prejudiced the public against the trade by making people distrust the
written word. The Preface to George Kellner's <u>Klingstein, Eine Geschich-</u>
<u>te, mit Szenen aus dem spanischen Successionskriege</u>, for example, pours
scorn upon the "commercial speculation in the choice of book-titles; in
this decade it is not better than a deceiving inn-keeper on the highway
who lures the parched wanderer with a deceptive sign, only to regale him
with suds instead of solid fare for his money." No one, he insists, can
trust a title any more. Because of this practice of deception, Kellner
insists his novel is 'really based on authentic sources' and is 'absolutely true.' The title is "nicht eine leere Floskel zum trüglichen Aus-
hängeschild" (5). Yet Göchhausen had to concede, though somewhat begrud-
gingly, that the circumstances of the day had forced author and publisher
into a marketing team--with the author as junior partner. "It is the
publishers who really direct the orchestra," he explains in <u>Meines Vaters</u>
<u>Hauschronika</u>; the writer simply has to put up with the conductor playing
a capricioso like a "Hopheysa" as soon as he has commercially assessed
his listeners. "Conductors claim to know the audience better than the
composer, and play the score any way they like; but never the right way"
(xxiv f.).

29

Having recognized that writing is as much a commercial venture as
a medium for instruction and delight, authors are faced with the problem
of sustaining the interest of their clientele. As most novels appeared
in fascicles, parts or books published at intervals, the main technique
for holding the reader was to break off the tale near the climax and pick
it up again in the continuation or sequel. Heinrich Rehkopf, for example,
concludes the first part of Franz Wall with a dramatic public execution.
The executioner is about to decapitate the hooded victim whom the reader
has recognized as the executioner's long-lost mistress. She screams
out his name in the final moment, and the book ends. Part Two, published
separately, picks up the episode at this point and immediately retards
the action to its usual slow pace.

Novelists often inform their readers that the story will be continued, in order to whet their appetite for future episodes. Sophie
Tresenreuter uses this technique to good advantage at the end of the
second part of Geist der Memoiren, where she introduces a chamberlain
who has not been seen since the early pages of Part One. Here she announces that 'what had become of the chamberlain and the puzzling circumstances of all other persons who have appeared in our book, will be
revealed and unravelled in the third part of this famous novel--at least
as far as possible' (II, 164). As we will see in Chapter II, she is
playing a Shandean game. Tresenreuter's novels are among the most 'puzzling' of the period (challenged only by Naubert, as was seen earlier);
her characters fade in and out of the narrative for even less apparent
reason than those of her colleagues. If she had gained a steady readership by the end of Part Two, her promised solution to these 'puzzling
circumstances' no doubt was welcome. Of course, there is nothing unusual in a writer hinting at what he is going to do in future volumes, nor
even in calling his story famous; Cervantes' Don Quixote offers salient
examples of the technique. But Tresenreuter's earnestness in referring
to 'the third part of this famous novel' suggests that she is trying to
entice her public with yet another device. No fashionable reader, she
seems to feel, would covet unfamiliarity with a novel thus touted in
print. Tresenreuter's novel had only sixty-two subscribers, hardly
enough to sustain publication, and her promise of clarifying the plot

'as far as possible' reflects her continued dependence upon the uncer-
tainties of the publisher and his market. Johann Kaffka reveals a similar dependence when concluding a tale in Ruinen der Vorzeit and advising
his readers that he will 'perhaps deliver more scenes' (I, 298). He is
much more reserved than Tresenreuter. While his promise offers little
encouragement to his reader, it expresses his dependence upon circumstances beyond his control. Public acclaim or the approval of reviewers, he
explains, might easily persuade him to write a sequel.

J.F.E. Albrecht even asserts in Dreyerlei Wirkungen that public
acclaim 'obliges the writer not to withhold further instalments' (II,
iii). In fact Albrecht is so certain of this acclaim and of his publisher's reliability that he promises 'to be back in 6 weeks, 3 days,
2 minutes and 21 seconds' (IV, 283). The whimsicality is as striking as
the regularity with which he produced the eight books of his novel from
1789 - 92. This regularity lends support to Heinrich Werder's assertion
in Eduard Rosenhain (viii) that public approval is of decisive importance:

> Ihr [des Lesers] begünstigendes Kopfnicken oder ihr [sic]
> verbietendes Schütteln wird entscheiden, ob sich Verfasser
> und Leser bald, oder gar nicht wieder sprechen werden (294).

Friedrich Thilo's Lebensscenen aus der wirklichen Welt, which was published at a regular rate of two volumes per year for six years (1784 -
90), is comparable in this respect to Albrecht's achievement. Thilo's
Preface to the '12th and last volume' attributes his industry to the
'general public acclaim' which made his book 'grow to twelve volumes in
length.' 'The number of volumes could easily be increased,' he adds,
'but everything must come to an end sometime' (XII, Preface).[13]

Better known authors did not need the devices which Rehkopf and
Tresenreuter used to retain the readers' interest. Müller von Itzehoe
is a case in point. He concludes Part Two of Herr Thomas with the brief
comment "Wir brechen hier ab, und zwar ohne Autorgriff" (II, 456). He
has not left 'our hero' in any situation which might 'entice the reader
to approach the next volume with curiosity.' Such an 'old acquaintance
as the Brown Man' does not need author's tricks to assure himself of 'a
friendly face on his return' (II, 456). The reference to the Brown Man
would have been readily understood by devotees of contemporary fiction;

31

it was Müller's pseudonym in <u>Komische Romane aus den Papieren des braunen Mannes und des Verfassers des Siegfried von Lindenberg</u> (1786 - 91). The success of <u>Siegfried von Lindenberg</u> ([1]1779; [2]1784; [3]1790) was sufficient advertisement for anything else that Müller von Itzehoe might write. It was common practice, as the present example illustrates, for books to be promoted by reference to an author's previous successes rather than to his name. As Harvey Thayer points out in an early study of the 18th-century German novel, "a brief consideration of the principles of book-reviewing would establish the fact indisputably that the mentioning of a former book, some hint of familiarity with the author by open or covert allusion, is an integral and inevitable part of the review of a later book." [14]

We have already noted the ambigious position of authors who voice nothing but contempt for the readers of other peoples' novels. Only one author explicitly accepts the criterion that the merit of a book should be judged by its success on the market. Göchhausen writes in his <u>Büchlein</u> that 'if my book pleases you [the readers], then it is a good book'; he promises yet another volume as a bonus "Ihr sollt dann fürder noch eins haben, mit viel schönem Schnitzwerk und Konterfey" (248). He fulfilled his promise later in the year with <u>Meines Vaters Hauschronika</u>: "Da habt Ihr dann das feine Büchlein" (iii).

Authors are not solely concerned with their reading public, but with their publisher as well. In most cases their obligations amount to meeting the publishers' marketable quota. Thus Oertel brings <u>Weiber machten ihn weiser,--und glücklich</u> to an abrupt and awkward conclusion because it has 'unexpectedly grown to a rather large volume' (476). Other examples show equally well how literary concerns are subordinated to practical considerations. J.F.E. Albrecht's Preface to the third volume of <u>Dreyerlei Wirkungen</u> explains that he would have liked to have added a fourth volume, but there was not sufficient time until the book fair (III, iii). He gives advance notice of the fourth volume, assuring his readers that it contains the latest events and will be no less entertaining (III, vii). Part Three ends so abruptly that one suspects that Albrecht simply ran out of time; indeed he tells us in his "Vorbericht" (doubtless written when he was about to send his manuscript to the publisher), that he was hardpressed by a deadline. But true to the contemporary literary practice of publicly dissociating oneself from commercial interests,he offers another reason for having concluded Part Three: "Die gerade Fortsezung jener Geschichte ist sonderbar traurig und es gehören einige Intervallen dazwischen, um sie nicht zu angreifend für die Nerven gefühlvoller Menschen zu machen." (III, 184). Albrecht's sincerity seems suspect on addressing his public once again as Part Four opens. "It is very good that the fourth part could follow the third so closely,' he claims, for through oversight while submitting the manuscript, "der rührende Schluß" of Part Three was omitted and is now included in the beginning of Part Four (IV, 3).

Tresenreuter's <u>Geist der Memoiren</u> is a prime example of tailoring a novel to meet the mechanics of publication. She shows no serious concern for literary form, but merely for delivering a given amount of printed matter that her subscribers had been promised. At the end of the fifth book of Part One Tresenreuter laments that unavoidable obstacles had caused the belated appearance of her novel; not the least of these was the heavy frost which had brought the presses to a halt. She begs forgiveness of her 'kind subscribers' and offers an expression of her 'deepest gratitude' for their patience. But so as not to 'misuse' their patience any further, she hastens to 'deliver these 15 signatures instead of the 27' which she had promised for Part One. Her publisher had given her 28 lines per page instead of the 25 which she had expected. Having thus increased the number of lines per page, she explains, the publisher had of course decreased the number of pages per volume. Tresenreuter offers to compensate her reader: she will either add the missing number of signatures to the second part of the novel by extending the narrative beyond her original plan, or else give the subscribers a third part gratis:

> Damit Sie aber nicht Ursache zur Klage wider mich finden
> mögen, werde ich entweder dem zweiten Theil die fehlende
> Bogenzahl beifügen, oder. . . den Pränumeranten einen
> dritten Theil unentgeltlich geben. (I, 215)

The readers got their third part.

It might seem an imposition to demand that a writer produce a novel under the rigors of commercial demands, but the practice of literary

massproducers like Albrecht, Naubert, and Tresenreuter suggests otherwise. One simply kept on adding more and more material until one either
met the quota, grew tired (as in Thilo's case), or public demand abated.
Müller von Itzehoe parodies this situation with considerable success in
Herr Thomas, and a survey of novels published in 1790 reveals that his
comments have more truth than his colleagues might have cared to admit.
The best bet on the market, Müller's hero explains, 'is to produce a
thick bundle of tales. If the collection should turn out a little gaudy,
one's only excuse need be that such books should have something for every
palate.' [Stutz and Sander saw the market possibilities in this, for
each published a 'gaudy' collection in 1790]. Müller's hero continues:
'If the author should not find enough useful material in his own larder
he could easily be helped out by translations and adaptations from foreign languages.' Rambach's plagiarism of Fielding's Jonathan Wild is
but one case in point. In this way one could 'stitch together a book of
considerable size,' for 'publishers do not care for the pocket format.'
If such an 'opus' finds public acclaim, it is all the more reason why a
second and third 'tome' should follow (IV, 393 f.).

Thus novelists appear to be waging a contest with each other for
the favour of a public which they both chide and cajole, and the book-
trade, in Oertel's words, is the axis about which literature and author
revolve. Johann Christian Müller's Fragmente aus dem Leben und Wandel
eines Physiognomisten presents a humorous episode which illustrates these
cross-currents. The young hero of the novel has just begun work in a
publishing house, and gains in this 'underworld' his first insight into the
'mighty republic of writers.' He is utterly astonished at the 'relationships of these men, their way of waging learned war, sending letters of
refusal, jousting to the death, and forming defensive and offensive lea-
gues.' He observes the cunning of book-sellers who steal the wind out of
each others sails, raise money, and touch up best-sellers without their
authors' hearing about it (89). 'Journals, weeklies, monthlies, and sun-
dry publications are the jousting grounds for hearty warriors'--die Tum-
melplätze rüstiger Kämpfer (363). But competitors, the reading public,
and publishers were not the only factions in the book-trade. There were
reviewers as well.

7. Authors and reviewers

Hans Ehrenzeller[15] has described critical acitivity of the day as a court of judgment to which authors would direct their attention in prefaces. Taste, he observed, was regarded as a super-individual factor, and writers expected a given work to receive a unanimous judgement from different sources. So tenaciously did Hermes hold to this view, he reports, that when different journals offered varying opinions of his Miss Fanny Wilkes (1769), he was completely taken aback. Hermes voiced his consternation in the Preface to the second edition by demanding to hear the voice of truth instead of 'all these voices'; he hoped to find truth among the public. But even worse happened to Sophiens Reise (1769/73)-- it was not reviewed at all. Hermes therefore advised his readers in the Preface to the third volume that Sophie would journey no further if she were not properly reviewed (148 f.).

Authors of 1790 prove more cantankerous than Hermes, and much less willing to grant that critics have any taste at all. They hold more to Herder's view that German critics form "eine verpachtete Bude, eine verachtete Lästerschule" which operates with false weights and measures.[16] "Vergänglich wie Recensentenstaub" is Sander's byword in Salz, Laune (42), expressing the consensus of his day. Müller von Itzehoe's Herr Thomas denounces the "Recensionkrämer und Rauchfässler" (III, 121) who are ready to publish a favourable review of anything for a price. Werder finds graphic expression for the practice of literary criticism in Eduard Rosenhain in the term "kritikakeln," a word derived with intended ambiguity from "kritisieren," from "kackeln" (to cackle like a hen), and from "kacken" (to crap). He uses the term to describe the ridiculous manner in which an inn-keeper in his novel, who regards himself as a "Kraftgenie" and a literary expert, rejects out of hand such masters as "der pöbelhafte Bürger und der zierliche Wieland" (198).

We still find some vestiges of Hermes' respect for critics in prefaces of the period, but these are mainly voiced by those who seek the reviewer's indulgence on the grounds that they themselves are not professional writers. Such is Lohbauer's approach in his Preface to Der Tannenbauer, where he offers his inexperience as justification for not having written according to "aesthetic principles." The reviewer in the

<u>Allgemeine Deutsche Bibliothek for</u> 1790 (vol 96, p. 283) kindly accepted
the excuse:

> Da der Verf. in der Vorrede um gütige Nachsicht bittet,
> wenn etwa Darstellung und Schreibart in seiner Lebens-
> geschichte nicht ganz den ästhetischen Grundsätzen gemäss
> seyn sollten, weil er kein Schriftsteller von Profession
> sey, und diese Lebensgeschichte nur auf Veranlassung
> seiner Freunde habe drucken lassen: so wollen wir die
> so häufig vorkommenden Provinzialismen nicht besonders
> rügen.

The anonymous author of <u>Heinrich und Henriette</u> also approaches the task
of authorship with considerable trepidation; he has 'learned the fate of
a recent writer' to whom the reviewers did not take kindly, and therefore begs "die sämmtlichen Herrn Kunstrichter" to deal indulgently with
him on this his first venture (ii ff.). Tresenreuter urges the readers
and critics of <u>Geist der Memoiren</u> to make a 'quiet, dispassionate judgement' of her work, as she knows too well how <u>Siegfried von Lindenberg</u>
had been dealt with when it first appeared. It was so misinterpreted,
she explains, that had paper war not replaced club-law one of her beloved
countrymen, Müller von Itzehoe, would have been a bloody sacrifice
(I, vi).

But novels of the period were not always as worthy of consideration
as their authors felt; the often terse and forthright reviews reflect the
critics' displeasure. Freiherr von Meldegg's <u>Karl von Lindenhain</u> (1790),
no copy of which seems to have survived, only warrented a single unequi-
vocal sentence in the <u>Allgemeine Deutsche Bibliothek</u> for 1791 (vol.98,
p. 134): "Wässriger, geschmackloser und gedehnter kann gar nichts er-
dacht werden, als diess freyherrliche Product." The same journal reviewed the second part of Bakel's equally unavailable <u>Origines</u> (1790) in a
single sentence (vol. 97, p. 424, 1790):

> "Es würde schwer zu entscheiden seyn, ob der in dieser
> Bibliothek schon recensirte erste, oder ob der vorliegende
> zweyte Theil dieses schlechten Werks reicher an grotesken,
> schmutzigen, plumpen Bildern und langweiligen Schilderungen
> . . . wäre."

Had we been able to obtain a copy of S.G. Presser's <u>Oko von Okowsky</u>
(1790), we doubtless would have found the task of reading it as thank-
less as did the reviewer in the <u>Allgemeine Deutsche Bibliothek</u> for 1791

(vol. 104, p. 418):

> Es kostete uns Mühe, unsrer Recensentenpflicht gemäs,
> mit Aufmerksamkeit bis ans Ende fortzulesen, und wir
> können nicht sagen, dass uns jene saure Mühe auch nur
> durch einen guten Gedanken, oder durch eine glückliche
> Erzählung und Wendung belohnt worden wäre.

No novelist of the period suggests that critics felt any real sense of
duty or obligation such as Presser's reviewer does. A survey of the
Allgemeine Deutsche Bibliothek reveals, however, that reviewers in many
cases performed the services of a writer's advisory board.[17] Promising
novelists could expect encouraging and often detailed advice on such
matters as plot, style, language, and even spelling; worthwhile novels
could expect a summary. 'Bad' works, of course, were rejected out of
hand. Reviewers' judgement of the novel of 1790 are largely sound.

In general, however, novelists regarded critics as the parasites
of the literary profession. Thus when describing the 'uses' of his book
Salz, Laune, Christian Sander intrudes the snide comment that it will,
among other things, serve a little to 'exercise and whet the acumen of
many a contributor to general and common reviews'--allgemeinen und gemeinen Bibliotheken (135).[18] Bahrdt whimsically recommends himself to
a periodical in the hopes of obtaining an appreciative review, but apologizes for not having enclosed a tip with his book:

> Schliesslich empfehle ich mich der allgemeinen Litteratur-
> Zeitung zu einer verherrlichenden Recension, und bitte um
> Verzeihung, dass ich kein Douceur beigelegt habe, sintemal
> ich eben bei der Vollendung dieser meiner Geistesfrucht
> vernehme, dass meine Frau in die Wochen kommen, und eine
> Leibesfrucht produciren wil, welches meine Börse in Ver-
> legenheit sezt. Leben und leben lassen!! (iv)

Albrecht (Dreyerlei Wirkungen, IV, 192 ff.) attacks the practice of literary criticism by providing a history of its development. Certain inhabitants of the Earth ask the inhabitants of Sirius whether their "mächti-
ge Geiseln" are as terrible as their counterparts on earth. A Sirian
writer discourses at length in terms which most of Albrecht's colleagues
would have applauded. Literary criticism began, we are told, at a time
when scholarship was particularly impoverished. 'Second-rate' scholars
had formed a tight faction in order to 'tear every vestige of honour'
from the true scholars and their writings. It grew increasingly diffi-

cult for the 'true scholars' to maintain their standards, and in the course of time many of them preferred to spend their days in carousing and flirtation (IV, 195). They skimmed the surface of knowledge, and thus could speak ingnorantly on all subjects; many were forced into obscurity. Others did not want to give the appearance of idleness and took up their studies and research once again. This time they sought out entertaining works, even if they were works of fiction (IV, 197), because their scientific works had become too boring. Thus to Albrecht's mind, frustrated scholars practised literary criticism.

Speculators in the book-trade, the Sirian continues, soon realised that knowledge did not bring in nearly as much money as wit, imagination, and lies; hence some critics became novelists. Soon nothing was sold but 'hoardes of fables, stories, and novels.' The 'true scholars' quickly realised that they too would have to speculate on the literary market if they did not want to starve to death. This was the time, the narrator continues, when the 'frenzy of criticism' gained the upper hand (IV, 197). The 'whole world' gradually realised it was being taken for a ride--auf eine ganz erschreckliche Art besch[issen] wurde (IV, 200), and reviewers' copy was 'the most insipid thing' one could read. But most ridiculous of all, Albrecht charges, were writers who maligned novelists for writing for money while they themselves 'made a nice round sum for every sheet they wrote, plagued the world with new editions, addendas and corrections, and cheated the public' (IV, 205 f.). Urged on by "Spekulanten" authors took 'huge bites out of each others hides'-- Seelenrippen (IV, 206).

The best protection under the circumstances would seem to have been the anonymity under which 62 % of the fiction of 1790 was published.

CHAPTER II

NARRATIVE TECHNIQUES AND LITERARY CONVENTIONS IN 1790

> For my own part, I am just set
> up in business, so know little
> about it--but, in my opinion, to
> write a book is for all the world
> like humming a song--be but in
> tune with yourself, Madam, 'tis
> no matter how high or how low you
> take it.
> (Tristram Shandy, Bk.IV,Ch.25)

1. Preamble

An examination of narrative technique, as Wolfgang Kayser has shown,[1] best reveals the distinctive quality of the emergent modern German novel. The fiction of the baroque period and the early 18th-century impresses one with the anonymity of the narrator and his lack of individuality and personal participation in the narrative.[2] This situation changes with the appearance of Wieland's Abenteuer des D. Sylvio von Rosalva (1764), for here a personal narrator intrudes.[3] There is now a new vitality in the language, which is often quite consciously ambiguous. No longer can the reader blindly follow the narrator's words, for he must expect several perspectives and be prepared to see through even his own role as reader. Just as the narrator slips into different postures, now as author, now as translator or commentator, so the reader himself is urged to assume different roles as an object of the narrator's game.[4] The "auktoriale Erzählsituation" as Stangel defined it,[5] dominates the fiction of 1790. As early as 1792, Schiller regarded this approach as standard practice:

> "Die Epopöe, der Roman, die einfache Erzählung
> rücken die Handlung, schon ihrer Form nach, in die Ferne,
> weil sie zwischen den Leser und die handelnden Personen den
> Erzähler einschieben."[6]

Novels in which this approach predominates have a clear affinity for a humorous or ironic world-view and for playing with the illusion of both art and life.[7] It is significant that Wieland's technique was largely influenced by Fielding, whose first novel, The History of the Adventures of Joseph Andrews (1742), had begun as a parody of Richardson's Pamela (1740).

Of all the foreign influences on the 18th-century German novel, as Peter Michelsen has shown,[8] that of Sterne was by far the most far-reaching. The first six books of Tristram Shandy, all that had been published in England at the time, appeared in Germany in 1763 ([2]1769-72, [3]1773) in the translation of Johann Frd. Zückert.[9] The difficult task of translating this whimsical and apparently formless work met with the adverse criticism and ingratitude of Zückert's contemporaries. J.J. Bode's long-awaited and lauded translation did not appear until 1774. It contained an impressive subscription list of over 600 names, including those of Goethe, Hamann, Herder, Hippel, Klopstock, Wieland, Zimmermann, Mathias Claudius, F.H. Jacobi, Gerstenberg and Schummel. The work saw two further editions and some pirated editions in the 'seventies, and formed the basis for almost every German translation up to the present day.[10]

It is significant, however, that Bode's approach led to a distortion which was not at all in the spirit of Sterne. Sterne's conversational charm and simplicity of style was lost. The reader, as Michelsen aptly expresses it, was faced with a syntactical thicket--Satzgestrüpp-- through which he had to break trail. Such is not the case in Sterne, for despite the involved syntax, there is a peculiar lucidity, an acrobatic lightness which makes difficult passages at once disconcerting and refreshing.[11] The German public, as Michelsen notes, received Tristram Shandy in an interpretation which, apart from errors in translation, was tailored to meet its own literary milieu. Even apart from syntactical changes, Bode did everything to adapt the novel to the German situation.[12]

The success of Bode's Tristram was assured by the sensation caused by his translation of the Sentimental Journey in 1768, which marked the beginning of Sterne's influence on German writers. Bode's translation of the Empfindsame Reise (as Lessing had advised him to render the title) and of Tristram Shandy exhibit similar characteristics. Both translations distorted Sterne by rendering his work in a heightened emotional

tone. Michelsen cites some striking examples: 'spirits' is rendered as
'Herz,' 'weak' as 'weichherzig'; 'it struck me' as 'mir fiel aufs Herz,'
'an elevation of spirit,' as 'eine Erhebung des Herzens'; 'sprightliness'
becomes 'ein seelenvolles Gesicht,' 'a look of kindness,' 'Blick der
Liebe'; 'fair spirit' becomes 'schöne Seele', and a 'web of kindness,'
'Gewebe der zärtlichen Empfindungen.'[13] It is clear, as Michelsen ob-
serves, that this heightened emotionality enhanced the book's appeal for
German readers. Sterne's reserve and ironic treatment of sentiment went
unobserved in Germany, and his comic illogicality was misconstrued. As
Thayer points out, "Germany had been for a decade hesitating on the verge
of tears, and grasped with eagerness a work which seemed to give her
British sanction for indulgence in lachrymose desire."[14]

The German assessment of Sterne began with the translation of his
work and was carried on by authors who tried to copy his techniques
(such as that of the self-conscious or comically intrusive narrator,
aposiopesis, whimsical suspension of plot, and digressions) and to imitate his sense of humour. J.C. Schummel's Empfindsame Reisen durch
Deutschland ([1]1771, [2]1772) is a salient example of the attempt at copy-
ing Sterne's digressive style, but in his case the digressions become
irksome distractions which frustrate the reader's sustained interest in
the novel.[15] Schummel's use of Sterne's techniques, as is the case with
most other imitators, was meant to create the impression of Shandean
humour or "Laune," a characteristic which Schummel and his contemporaries
particularly admired with Sterne.[16] In actual practice, Michelsen suggests, Schummel and his fellow-imitators were not motivated by "Laune"
itself, but were trying to implement humour as a literary principle.
The resultant artificiality caused C.E.F. Schulz as late as 1786 to decry
the inept imitations: "[die] zahlosen Heere von Sudeleyn, die ohne Welt-
und Menschen- und Sprachkenntniss, ohne Plan, ohne Verwickelung, ohne
Anfang und Ende hinfabricirt wurden."[17] With perhaps the exception of
Jean Paul, Thayer was correct in observing that Sterne's whimsicality
is a peculiarly British characteristic which defies transplanting and
that German attempts at accommodating it to their own culture perforce
led to distortions.[18] Whereas in England imitations of Sterne remained
short-lived, the Yorick-hungry German public formed a ready market for

translation and imitation, thereby helping to prepare the ground for
Shandean stylistic features in novels from Wieland to Jean Paul.

The flood of German imitations of Sterne, as Michelsen found,
reached a high point in the 1770's (thus corresponding with the peak of
Empfindsamkeit) and again after a decade of comparative quiet in the
1790's.[19] There is, however, a decided difference between the first wave
in the 'seventies and the second in the 'nineties. The first is marked by an enthusiasm which is noticeable even when the imitators are cal-
culatingly adhering to fashion and giving free rein to what Michelsen
aptly terms paroxysms of feeling and garrulousness--Gefühls- oder
Schwatzhaftigkeitsanwandlungen. Sterne's principle of subjectivity was
here picked up with a certain freshness, for German writers were convinced of the appropriateness of their technique. Imitators in the 'nineties, on the other hand, have a worn-out and run-down air about them;
even in cases of virtuosity, their work has lost all lustre and has fall-
en into mere routine. This is all the more annoying as they claimed an
originality that had long since become conventionalized.[20] The evidence
of 1790 corroborates Michelsen's views.

2. Digressions

> For in this long digression which I
> accidently led into, as in all my
> digressions. . . there is a master-
> stroke of digressive skill, the merit
> of which has all along, I fear, been
> overlooked by my reader. . . and it
> is this: That though my digressions
> are all fair, as you observe,--and
> that I fly from what I am about, as
> far and as often too as any writer
> in Great Britain; yet constantly I
> take care to order my affairs so,
> that my business does not stand still
> in my absence.
> (Tristram Shandy, Bk. I, Ch. 22)

When a witless young bell in G.C. Kellner's Familiengeschichte der
Rosenbusche discusses the popular prose fiction of her day, she turns her
attention with marked ease to the dramatic technique of Shakespeare's
The Tempest. As far as she is concerned, Shakespeare epitomizes the narrative methods of German novelists by hurling his readers time and again

42

to far distant places, and letting many years pass in a single moment.
His works, we are informed, are so improbable--so gewaltig unwahrschein-
lich--that one cannot find one's way about. There are so many characters,
and their actions are so intertwined, that one never knows which character is supposed to lay greatest claim to one's attention: ". . . es
kostet so viel Mühe, alles im Zusammenhange zu denken und das ist nicht
hübsch von einem Buche, das einen aufheitern soll" (IV, 232 f.).
Curious as it might seem, the young lady's pronouncement on Shakespeare
really does summarize the most prominent narrative features of the novel
of 1790.

The novels of the period abound in narrative leaps which bear the
reader to various places and events with no apparent causal connections.
Characters appear and disappear without credible motivation; they seem
directed solely by the author's whim. The novels are often vitiated by
the whimsical, and indeed arbitrary, introduction of wearisome digressions, yet one frequently suspects that the writers have an ironic or
parodistic purpose in mind. In practice, the term 'digression'--Aus-
schweifung/Abschweifung--is ambiguous in 1790. It may refer to subplots
or else to non-narrative departures from the theme.[21] The wide use of
the first kind of digression, characteristic of the whole tradition of
Romance from the earliest times, reveals the novel's kinship with its pre-
decessor. In some cases it is, in the words of Friedrich Hegrad's Felix
mit der Liebesgeige, desperately difficult to find all the heroes and
heroines which authors 'paint on paper.' Sheer chance motivates the action: "was fügt nicht der Zufall?" (I, 187).

Gottlob Heinrich Heinse's Heinrich der Eiserne is a case in point.
One of his principal devices is to retard the main action by introducing
digressive material. Before continuing his principal plot at critical
points, he feels he must describe new characters, shift the scene, or
reveal sub-plots:

> Ehe wir von diesen Unruhen selbst sprechen, glauben wir
> unsere Leser erst mit dem Manne bekannt machen zu müssen,
> der die Veranlassung dazu gab. (II, 272)

> Doch ehe wir erzählen, was Heinrich. . . that, . . .
> glauben wir unsere Leser zuvor. . . nach Schweden führen
> zu müssen. (II, 317 f.)

Ehe wir fortfahren, müssen wir den Lesern ein schändliches
Gewebe von Lügen und Verläumdungen entdecken. (II, 454)

Heinse's achievement lies in his ability to keep two or more plots moving simultaneously. At one point in the novel, for example, a band of
highwaymen abducts a certain Countess, whereupon a squadron of riders
under Heinrich's command gives chase. Heinse sets Heinrich and his band
in pursuit and leaves them chasing the highwaymen while he himself recounts the events that led up to the abduction: "Indes unsere Ritter den
Räubern der Gräfin nachsetzen, wollen wir den Lesern, über den Unfall,
der dieser begegnete, einige Erläuterungen geben" (I, 183). Once having
brought the reader up to date in the events leading up to the Countess'
abduction Heinse returns to Heinrich to see how he has been faring in the
meantime: "Doch wir kehren jetzt zu Heinrichen. . . zurück, um zu sehen,
ob sie [Heinrich und dessen Bande] in ihrem Forschen glücklich waren"
(I, 199). Once we learn that Heinrich has caught the robbers, Heinse
returns to the main plot. This is a technique which Fielding had parodied in Jonathan Wild, for example in the following passage:

> We will leave our hero to take a short repose, and return
> to Mr. Snap's, where, at Wild's departure, the fair Theo-
> dosia had again betaken herself to her stocking, and Miss
> Letty had retired upstairs to Mr. Bagshot. . .[22]

Part one of Heinse's novel concludes with the impending murder of
the hero--a technique, as we have seen, designed to assure the sale of
Part Two. But the second part neglects Heinrich's predicament until we
leave the Countess for a while in order to return to our hero (II, 211).
Heinse feels no need to apologize to his readers for these constant digressions, for they all contribute in some degree to the plot. But he
is the only author who is consistent in their use. His colleagues are
more inclined to appear self-conscious when making a digression and, as
we will see later, generally preface it with an apology or an explanation. The anonymous author of Heinrich und Henriette also uses the technique of multiple plots. They first develop independently, intertwine,
extricate themselves, and then proceed independently again until 'circumstances' merge them with one another. This "glückliches Ohngefähr"
always solves confusions of plot (41); and when the author confesses he
has nothing important to report about one of his characters he simply

44

leaves him alone (94). He occasionally declines the opportunity of recounting more digressive adventures so that he will not waste time:
"so wollen wir die Zeit nicht damit verschwenden" (231 f.). As we see
in Christiane Naubert's Werner, Graf von Bernburg, digressions can get
out of hand. Naubert begins the account of Werner's childhood, introduces the reader to the child Luitgard, who is 'destined' to be Werner's
love, and becomes so interested in Luitgard that Werner is almost entirely forgotten for 728 pages. She must then confess the obvious: 'Luitgard was more the heroine than the title of the book permitted, but now
that she has died, what more is there to tell?' (II, 728) In the hands
of some writers, notably Albrecht, Kellner, Naubert and Tresenreuter,
digressions result in sheer chaos, as Albrecht himself acknowledge in
Uranie (II, 13).

    J.F.E. Albrecht's Uranie is a good example of the manner in which
an author plays with his narrative. The fictional narrator of this story begins to relate a new series of incidents only to stop himself short
after a couple of pages, explaining that as he is embarking upon a very
intricate story--eine sehr verwickelte Geschichte (I, 133 f.)--it is
better to pick up the track he had left and return to the main action.
Having only explored the possibilities of a new plot he in fact returns
to his original story--and thus meets the approval of the fictional reader who interjects that up to this point we don't yet know what it is all
about--denn bis jetzt wissen wir noch nicht, woran wir sind (I, 134).
G.C. Kellner's Familiengeschichte der Rosenbusche, on the other hand,
explores the possibilities and then exploits them to the full. He concludes the second of four books, for example, by promising his readers
to continue the 'following strange complications of fate' which had involved his heroine with 'these and many other persons' and which formed
'a long chain of the most unexpected and the strangest human situations'
(II, 174 f.). Indeed the novel is so confusing that Kellner must remind
his readers of certain characters by adding a footnote whenever one of
them reappears after a lengthy absence. Thus when a certain Rudolphus
is mentioned in a conversation in Part Three, the author's footnote expresses the hope that his readers must surely remember him from Part One:
"Meine Leser erinnern sich doch, aus dem ersten Theil, dieses Mannes
noch?" (III, 80). Here as elsewhere, Kellner is imitating Sterne, but he

lacks the lightness of touch and the capacity for self-parody of his
master:

> It is so long since the reader of this rhapsodical work
> has been parted from the midwife, that it is high time
> to mention her again to him, merely to put him in mind
> that there is such a body still in the world, and whom,
> upon the best judgement I can form upon my own plan at
> present,--I am going to introduce to him for good and
> all. . . .
> (Tristram Shandy, Bk. I, Ch. 13)

Rudolphus' name means nothing to Kellner's reader, who has to search
Part One only to find the character in an obscure and peripheral role.
But he actually need not have undertaken the search, for Part Three
tells him all he needs to know. Such repetition is not uncommon, and
Albrecht even justifies it in Uranie. If any earlier material should
'creep in,' he writes, 'the readers will surely be good enough to excuse
us since many a further reminder cannot be unwelcome' (I, 145).

Christiane Naubert is equally concerned with reminding her readers
of characters who have become lost to the readers' view in her narrative.
'I hope my readers have not forgotten the Old Graf von Nordheim,' she
writes in Werner, Graf von Bernburg, 'or at least that they still remember gentle Elisabeth' (II, 689). The chances are, however, that the
reader has not been able to follow the host of characters in their pere-
grinations, for in this novel in particular, the sub-plots have become
so intertwined that the reader is as confused as Naubert herself seems to
be. She is doubtless pretending to have to think twice to get her facts
right: "Bald nachdem Werner von Bernburg und Luitgard von Meissen die
arragonische Maria von Tode rettete, ach was sage ich, noch vor diesen
Geschichten. . . wachten in dem Herzen. . . ' (II, 435). But though her
readers might have been unwilling to believe her, she might well have
spoken with Sterne:

> . . . if I should seem now and then to trifle upon the road,--
> or should sometimes put on a fool's cap with a bell to it, for
> a moment or two as I pass along,--don't fly off,--but rather
> courteously give me credit for a little more wisdom than
> appears upon my outside; and as we jog on, either laugh with
> me, or at me, or in short do any thing,--only keep your temper.
> (Tristram Shandy, Bk. I, Ch. 6)

46

Christian Sander, like most novelists of 1790, prefers the non-narrative type of digression. He finds that inserting apparently extraneous material into his narrative affords, as it were, an interpolated pause during which the reader may refresh himself by reading something new. Indeed, he writes in Salz, Laune und Mannichfaltigkeit, it is 'an ancient and not altogether objectionable fashion of writers--particularly of epic writers like Homer, Virgil, Tasso, Milton, Klopstock, Wieland and myself--to grant to the reader a little pause' (72). His discourse on the advantages of such "Ruheplätzchen" is itself such a pause he grants his reader before taking up the narrative once more.

Novels of the period abound in 'convenient opportunities' for broaching a new subject, and such chances are rarely acknowledged without being exploited. In Sophie Tresenreuter's Geist der Memoiren, to mention but one of the rare exceptions, the journey of a young lady presents many occasions on which the author could have digressed; one can scarcely travel without finding something of interest on the highway or in the inns, she observes. But she resists the temptation, for two reasons: it would not meet the requirements of her chapter heading, and her chapter is already long enough (II, 32). The refusal to digress, as we will see in Chapter V, is the prime source of parody in Heinrich Werder's Eduard Rosenhain.

When the pastor in J.F.E. Albrecht's Uranie is poring over the manuscript which has fallen from the planet Sirius, he is struck by a certain feature found in popular writings on earth. Its author, he proclaims, is similar to those of ours who start talking about air as soon as they mention balloons; and here, he adds with a touch of humour, they have quite an expansive field. The pastor does not begrudge these authors their holding forth on air and wind provided it is done so that the reader might pass his time pleasantly. If the reader's pleasure is achieved, the author is welcome to the few extra pence which the additional pages add to the few "Thaler" on which he has to live: "so kann er die paar Kreutzer Beytrag leicht zu den paar Thalern geben, von denen sie [die Schriftsteller] leben müssen" (I, 51 f.). Freiherr von Knigge exemplifies an especially irksome manner in which authors introduce tedious digressive material. Das Zauberschloss, a book whose title lures

the reader with expectations of the supernatural, presents several scenes
in which the author discusses the narrative with the fictional protagonist. Knigge, we are given to believe, has been listening intently to
Graf Tunger's account of the haunted castle, recording it verbatim while
the Count rambles on in seemingly endless digressions. Knigge soon becomes exasperated (as does the reader), for both Knigge and his readers
know that the solution to the mystery could have been revealed much earlier if Graf Tunger had not been consciously avoiding it. Here we must
recall Knigge's words near the beginning of the book that a practised
writer leaves the unravelling of the knot until the end of the book lest
the remaining signatures be left unread (48). Knigge soon loses patience
and denounces Graf Tunger as a cruel man who is teasing his readers, but
bids him carry on nonetheless: Grausamer Mann! Sie treiben Ihren Spass
mit mir--Aber fahren Sie fort! Ich höre zu! (109). Of course Graf Tunger has long since informed Knigge's readers that every one has his own
narrative technique and that his public must simply be patient: "jedermann hat seine eigene Weise zu erzählen; ich habe die meinige--Sie müssen
Geduld haben; ich kann Ihnen nicht helfen" (69). This is a variant of
Sterne's injunction to the reader of <u>Tristram</u>:

> Therefore, my friend and companion, if you should think me
> somewhat sparing of my narrative on my first setting out,--
> bear with me,--and let me go on, and tell my story my own
> way. . . (Bk. I, Ch. 6).

However, even if Knigge's arbitrary digressions are interpreted as
a parody of contemporary narrative techniques or as self-parody, they
constitute an excessive imposition on the readers' endurance. Sterne's
facile humour has been lost. Knigge's digressive technique is comparable
to E.A. Göchhausen's manner of reaching into "meine philosophische Gau-
keltasche" (<u>Büchlein</u>, 43) whenever he wants to make a fresh start.
Occasionally, also, an author will deliberately move in the wrong direction with his narrative only to stop himself short, confess his wayward-
ness, and continue with the original plot. Thus it suddenly occurs to
Kellner in <u>Familiengeschichte der Rosenbusche</u> that he is moralising and
describing characters instead of telling a story: "So eben merk ich,
dass [ich] Karaktere schildere und moralisire, statt zu erzählen. Ich
mache meinen Fehler im Augenblick wieder gut" (II, 87). Here as else-

where we note a characteristic expression of responsibility of an author towards his reader, but we must agree with Heinrich Werder's observation in Eduard Rosenhain that moralising is a rock on which many a writer founders:

> Wir haben uns bisher ganz absichtlich alles Moralisirens
> und Raisonnirens über diese erste Begebenheit unseres
> Abenteurers enthalten, weil wir aus Erfahrung wissen,
> dass mancher Schriftsteller an dieser Klippe scheitert,
> und mit seiner Moral und Kritik auf dem geraden Weg ist,
> ennüyant und langweilig zu werden, wenn er auch vorher
> noch so angenehm unterhielt und belustigte (67).

But having said this, he embarks upon twelve pages of polemics. Carl Ignaz Geiger rejects such padding in Reise eines Erdbewohners in den Mars while briefly explaining how he got sufficient hot air into his balloon to fly to Mars:

> Wie diess geschah--und wie überhaupt das Schiff, das ich
> dazu errichten liess, gebaut war: hiervon werd' ich noch
> einen besonderen Abriss, samt der weitläufigen Beschrei-
> bung veranstalten; um nicht wie irgend ein teutscher
> Reisebeschreiber, durch die Beschreibung meines Fahrzeuges,
> beinahe den halben Raum meines Buches auszufüllen. (6)

With the exception of Geiger, writers of 1790 agree that digress-ions have a legitimate place in the novel. It is by no means considered a mark of poor craftsmanship to divagate from one's plot. The digress-ion--Abschweifung--is not completely outside the plan of my writing, Friedrich von Oertel comments in Kilbur, "for I believe that I may insert any thought that comes to mind to the extent that it seems to me good or perhaps new" (II, 110 f.). Oertel's attitude suggests that nothing is 'completely outside the plan' of a writer if his whim should decide to include it. G.C. Kellner illustrates this feature well in Familienge-schichte der Rosenbusche. In the course of his narrative Kellner has occasion to make passing mention of the Moravian Brotherhood (III, 104), and a footnote informs the reader that 'perhaps a more convenient oppor-tunity' will present itself for describing it in detail. He finds this opportunity forty pages later. Before taking up the new theme, however, Kellner argues with his 'reader' about the justification for digressions. It is a recurrent feature of novels of the period that the author and his reader encounter one another at such moments in dramatic scenes of

49

the author's making. Kellner's 'reader' is dismayed at the repeated
"moralising and declamation on economy and such things," and wants to get
back to the story. But the reader is told that he is too impatient and
that the interspersed insights into man and human relationships are the
only excuse for reading a novel, and indeed for having written one as
well:

> Nun noch Etwas von der Herrenhutersekte. . .
> "Immer noch Etwas? Ist's nicht schon genug des Karakter-
> isirens, Moralisirens: Deklamirens über Oekonomie und
> derlei Sachen? Wann lesen wir denn wieder Geschichte?"
>
> Ja, lieber ungeduldige Leser! Diesmal wird Ihre Geduld
> noch ein paar Minuten auf die Folter gelegt. Doch nur
> noch auf ein paar Minuten; das versprech ich Ihnen. Auch
> können Sie ja überschlagen, was Sie nicht lesen wollen.
> Besser wär's vielleicht für Sie und für mich, wenn Sie
> nicht überschlügen.
>
> "So! Warum das?"
>
> Für Sie! Weil das Beachten der in einigen Romanen und auch
> in dieser Familiengeschichte hie und da eingestreuten Resul-
> tate über Menschen und Menschenverhältnisse Sie am besten - -
> und manche Leserinn besonders, wohl nur einzig und allein - -
> entschuldigt: dass Sie einen Roman lesen.
>
> Für mich! weil, neben der Beruhigung, dass ich hier nicht
> erdichtete, erfaselte, nein! würkliche Menschenkaraktere
> und Menschenverhältnisse schildere, besonders auch der, wenn
> gleich geringe, Nutzen solcher eingestreuten Resultate mich
> entschuldigt:
>
> Dass ich einen Roman schrieb.
>
> Also noch Etwas von den. . . Herrnhutern. (III, 144 f.)

When his digression of almost thirty pages is over, Kellner whisks
his reader away to the further adventures of his hero: "Weg nun von den
Herrnhutern; und hin bis zum Adolph und seinen Schicksalen!" (III, 173).
Göchhausen supports Kellner's views on the justification of writing novels when he comments in the Hauschronika that almost nothing would be
left of his novel if he had ripped out the whole litany of reason,virtue
and self-control: "Gern hätt' ich die ganze Litaney von Vernunft, Tugend,
Bändigung der Leidenschaften, Beherrschung sein selbst, Genuss sein
selbst. . . herausgerissen; aber dann wär beynahe nichts übrig geblie-
ben!" (318). One is reminded of Tristram Shandy where we read: "Digressions, incontestably, are the sunshine;--they are the life, the soul

of reading;--take them out of this book for instance,--you might as well take the book along with them. . . .(Bk. I, Ch. 22).[23]

Writers of fiction, as we saw in the previous chapter, harboured ambivalent feelings toward what Oertel and Werder called the 'usual novel.' Yet as far as digressions were concerned, most were trying to play the Shandean game by agreeing that, to speak with Kellner once again, it is not 'nice' of a supposedly entertaining book to create confusion. Indeed Heinse informs the reader of Heinrich der Eiserne that it would not be difficult to weave adventures and complicated love plots into his tale, were it not for his delicate conscience--unser zartes Gewissen (I, 52). Müller von Itzehoe's satirical Herr Thomas explains with amusement "es würde dem Pressbengel unsers Verlegers auf ein ganzes Jahr zu tanzen geben, wenn wir alle seine romanhaften Tollhäuslereyen hierher schrieben" (IV, 302). He therefore restricts his "Büchlein" (I, 8) to 919 pages! Leonard Meister is serious in charging his colleagues with letting themselves be diverted from a planned narrative. Just one word of sorcery, he exclaims in Neue Schweizerische Spaziergänge, and a hundred ghost stories arise (109). Although we find only one so-called ghost-story among the extant novels of 1790, Meister's point is valid as far as it describes the readiness of novelists to follow their whims wherever they might lead.

In the hands of a writer like Kotzebue, the novel becomes a child of his mischievous whim--Kind meiner muthwilligen Laune (Die gefährliche Wette, Preface). Why indeed should it be otherwise, writes Oertel in Kilbur. Whatever an author writes should be a portrayal--Schilderung-- of himself: this is far more important than whatever else he actually describes in the book. If he were merely an historian or a traveller giving information to the public, he continues, he could not cede to any whim but would have to 'seek truth with cold reason' (II, 33 f.).

3. The author-reader relationship

> Writing, when properly managed, (as
> you may be sure I think mine is) is
> but a different name for conversation:
> As no one, who knows what he is about
> in good company, would venture to
> talk all;--so no author, who under-
> stands the just boundaries of decorum
> and good breeding, would presume to
> think all: The truest respect which
> you can pay to the readers' under-
> standing, is to halve this matter
> amicably, and leave him something to
> imagine, in his turn, as well as
> yourself.
> (Tristram Shandy, Bk. II, Ch. 11)

Freiherr von Knigge observes in Das Zauberschloss that sympathy or
antipathy between author and reader play a significant role in the prose
fiction of the period and that writers sometimes exploit these emotions
in developing their plot, manoeuvering their characters, or introducing
instructive commentaries (41). Almost invariably, however, sympathy is
taken for granted. Thus Göchhausen writes in Meines Vaters Hauschronika
that the author wishes nothing better than to join his reader in a little
corner by the hearth, for they are brothers of the same flesh and blood--
[der Verfasser] wird sich gern mit ihm [dem Leser] in ein Winkelchen,
oder an seinem Feuerherd sezzen, [denn] wir sind Brüder, von einem Fleisch
und Bein (xxvii f.). He describes his Büchlein as a work consisting of
"manches Gesprächsel, mit meinen Nachbarn oder Mitwallern, über dies und
das" (v) and hopes that he will engage his reader's attention with profit.
Indeed Oertel's greatest need, as he puts it in Kilbur, is to befriend
the reader and portray this heart-to-heart encounter (II, 33 f.).
Leonard Meister sums up the general attitude in Spaziergänge: "Ich komme
nicht zur Audienz, sondern zum Besuche, nicht zum Katheder, sondern zum
Gespräche, nicht zum Patron, sondern zum Freund" (282).

Authors of the period make a practice of assuming this relationship
in their narratives and exploiting it, as Knigge correctly observes, when
soliciting the approbation or acclaim of their public. Writers like
Göchhausen pander to their reader's self-image. Thus in his Preface to
Hauschronika he enjoins all those to read his book who love sincerity

and truth, and can appreciate the ideal of perfection (XXVII). This is but one example of predisposing the reader through flattery; when other writers address themselves to intelligent, sensitive, understanding and pious readers, the presupposition is essentially the same. The novelist is intent upon drawing the reader into a pact of friendship, so that the two of them might enjoy the telling of a tale. Thus Heinrich Rehkopf involves the reader of <u>Franz Wall</u> in the description of an appealing young girl by saying that whoever has read this far would perhaps take a girl of such beauty and charm to wife and expect many pleasant things in the possession of her (43). Albrecht solicits the agreement of all those readers of <u>Fackland</u> who sympathize with the hero--die Antheil an Fackland nehmen (I, 51)--and feels assured they will regard his hero's fate as a happy one. He actually thanks the reader towards the end of the novel for the sympathy by which he has rewarded the author--den aufrichtigsten Dank für die Theilnehmung mit der sie uns belohnen! (II, 190). The anonymous author of <u>Heinrich und Henriette</u> plays with this relationship in describing his overwrought heroine. When Henriette faints on finding and reading some papers in a hidden compartment, the author turns to his reader with characteristic confidence and suggests that they should both take a close look at these important papers, but without fainting: ". . . wir wollen die Papiere fein langsam . . . durchlesen (denn es ist eine für uns wichtige Nachricht darin enthalten) und - - - - nicht in Ohnmacht sinken!" (32).

Despite occasional traces of parody, the technique of involving the reader's emotions is generally used with serious intent in 1790. Thus when the heroine of <u>Die unglückliche Fürstin aus Wien</u> dictates the story of her life to her anonymous author she offers him stylistic guidelines to enliven the narrative. Clothe the narrative in as warm a garb as you please, she pleads; whatever wells up from the heart, whatever the moment of feeling brings forth, is always more persuasive and allows the reader to gaze more deeply into the depths of one's soul. 'It ennobles my suffering and lends emphasis to my words' (14). The author took her advice. Other writers, such as G.C. Kellner, professed similar aims. In <u>Fami-liengeschichte der Rosenbusche</u>, for example, Kellner pauses after a 'moving scene' of tearful melancholy and affected wistfulness to justify his style to the reader: "Ich gab Ihnen, liebe Leser! den Ausfluss dieser Stimmung, um Sie selbst in sie zu versetzen, um es Ihnen dadurch recht interessant zu machen" (III, 7). Müller von Itzehoe advises the reader of Herr Thomas with mischievous delight: "Wir rathen Dir, aber, einige Schnupftücher zur Hand zu legen, denn der Kasus ist tragisch!" (II, 368).

It is not uncommon for emotional scenes to end with bloody tears of farewell--blutige Thränen des Abschieds (Thomas, III, 246). Indeed it is a common feature of these novels that the inability to weep is regarded as a symptom of "Seelenerstarrung" (IV, 378). The case for 'tears of gentler sympathy' was argued in the Neuer Teutscher Merkur for 1790 (vol. 3, pp. 289-301),[24] an attitude which recalls Goethe's consternation at a guest who could not weep on parting (Tagebuch, 29 Juli 1797). Some authors, like Ignaz Fessler, who is intent upon instructing his readers in matters of "moderation" and "beauty," seem ill at ease when employing emotionally stirring scenes. In an episode in which his hero, Marcus Aurelius, engages in a sentimental dialogue with his mistress, Fessler adds a footnote to justify his hero's uncharacteristic behaviour. His hero, he explains, had really only wanted to influence the rapturous imagination--schwärmerische Einbildungskraft--of his mistress (Marc-Aurel, II, 84).

While tearful scenes, as Kellner had explained, were meant to involve the reader in interesting situations, many authors preferred to leave the suffering of their protagonist to the reader's imagination. This is the case, for example, in Bahrdt's Ala Lama: "Wir überlassen dem Leser, diese rührende Scene sich vollends auszumahlen"(II, 230). Albrecht takes the same approach in Fackland when he suggests that the hero be left to cry himself out while we set off to see what has been happening at his father's home--Doch wir wollen ihn ausweinen lassen, und sehen, was im väterlichen Hause vorging (I, 27). Johann Stutz' fictional narrator in Erzählungen leaves it to the reader who has had to suffer a similar fate to imagine the speaker's emotions: "Was ich jetzt empfand, kann nur der sich denken, der jemahls ein ähnliches Schicksal erdulden musste" (149). Such approaches are designed to reinforce the confidential relationship between author and reader. The reader must be convinced of the author's purpose and sincerity by assurances of mutual trust, by his own emotional involvement, and--as we shall see in the next section--by the inclusion of corroborative evidence that supposedly authenticates the facts.

Christian Sander epitomizes the mood of a great number of his fellow-writers in their endeavour to please their readers. Despite all he claims to have suffered in time lost to his profession, and from gout, sleeplessness, poverty, and the gratitude of reviewers (as he muses in Salz, Laune) he fears that he still may not have attained 'the sweet satisfaction of his purpose.' Perhaps he has not even managed to 'elicit the slightest smile--to say nothing of a laugh--from the moist eye of his reader!' Perhaps his only consolation is "dass ich ihnen wenigstens nicht schadete!" (87). Müller von Itzehoe interrupts the otherwise humorous tone of Herr Thomas for a serious discussion of the small consolations of authorship by explaining:

> . . . dass in Deutschland kein Mensch so leicht in Gefahr kömmt, sogar mitten in einem gedrängten Kreise von Bewundrern und Lobpreisern des bitteren Todes zu sterben, als ein Mann von Genie wenn er kein andres Vermögen hat als seine Feder, und keinen andern Gönner als das Publikum in corpore. Und selbst das bischen [sic] wohlerworbenen Ehre wird ihm auf mannichfaltige Art verbittert (III, 97).

Having been merely innocuous, as Sander had implied, may well have been small consolation for novelists, yet their frankness in such matters is but another appeal to the sympathy of their friend the reader. But with due deference to their public, authors still tend to regard their own personality as sovereign. An author, in Johann Christian Müller's words, is "der da lehret, plaudert, scherzet, trompetet oder flötet," and in general does as he pleases (Physiognomisten, 85).

4. The documented narrative

> To sum up all; there are archives at every stage to be looked into, and rolls, records, documents, and endless genealogies, which justice ever and anon calls him back to stay the reading of . . .
> (Tristram Shandy, Bk. I, Ch. 14)

Writers of 1790 have frequent recourse to documents, manuscripts, and letters that supposedly authenticate their narratives. Often introduced on a whim, they on occasion contain traces of self-parody. Leonard Meister's Neue Schweizerische Spaziergänge, for instance, informs his reader in the frame-work narrative of his work that he has just been "dragged away from ancient annals and documents" (1) over which he has been poring in preparation for a story, and is now prevailed upon by two young ladies to disclose their contents. The ladies, he confesses, would simply flee if he were to conjure up dark spirits from the monkish chronicles he has been reading. Instead, he will show that nature in the Swiss Alps is the only antidote to the aberrations of popular literature and city life.

Novelists, as Friedrich Rambach confesses of himself in Kniffgenies (I, 6; II, 7), 'rummage through the rubble of yore' in search of subjects. Christiane Naubert's Alf von Dülmen, for instance, begins with a framework narrative recounting the discovery of the von Dülmen manuscript. The narrator, we are told, had dug up a leaden box which contained what can occupy our readers for a few leisure hours: "was unsere Leser in einigen Stunden der Musse beschäftigen kann"(35 f.). The story then proceeds on the basis of this supposed evidence and of other eyewitness reports. The mnauscripts contain interpolated documents as well, which give rise to incapsulated narratives. J.F.E. Albrecht insists in Uranie that his account of the realm on planet Sirius is true "denn da steht es ja trocken deutlich, und rein geschrieben, dass es sich so verhalte" (I, 3). Gottlob Heinrich Heinse uses a similar technique when he writes in Heinrich der Eiserne that he too would be groping about in trying to establish certain facts if a happy coincidence had not delivered into his hands a few rolls of parchment which had been buried in Heinrich's grave at Itzehoe: "Wir würden eben so im Finstern tappen, wie alle unsre Vorgänger, wenn uns nicht ein glückliches Ohngefähr einige Pergamentrollen in die Hände geliefert hätte" (I, i f.). He then goes on to say that he is presenting the text 'in modern German' and trusts it will meet with public acclaim. It is typical of his narrative technique that he expects fate to play more remnants of yore into his hands in the event that his readers enjoy the book.

56

The technique, in the opinion of contemporary writers, has the particular advantage of protecting the author from charges of inadequacy, for he can always refute them by saying that he was, after all, only the editor or translator of an ancient document. Thus Christiane Naubert expresses her astonishment that Barbara Blomberg's story in the novel of that name is not briefer and told in more refined language (I, 194) and insists that she cannot be responsible for Barbara's manner of speaking. E.A. Göchhausen suggests in Meines Vaters Hauschronika that his father ought to have digressed less frequently, but claims that there is nothing he can do to mend matters: "ich gebe zu, dass mein guter Vater sich zuweilen hätte kürtzer fassen, weniger Sprünge machen,--nicht so offt, und auf die nehmliche Art, sich herum tummeln können und sollen" (127). Just as Naubert apologizes for her heroine's language and style in Barbara Blomberg, so she regrets her inability to offer readers a more homogeneous narrative; but again, it is not her fault that she only has fragments in her possession (I, 199 f.). Bahrdt's whimsical Preface to Ala Lama, as we will see, parodies this editorial fiction.

The manuscripts on which so many novels of 1790 are purportedly based are invariably in poor condition. Heinse's manuscript in Heinrich der Eiserne, for instance, exhibits the principal defect that is found in the texts of his colleagues. The tooth of time has been handsomely gnawing on his parchment rolls, until they are riddled with holes. He could have followed the example of his predecessors, he adds, by 'filling in the gaps' with his own inventions, but he claims to be too conscientious a writer to do so and decides to leave the gaps as they are and trust that his approving reader will understand that the holes were made by moths and worms (I, 15). While writers like Albrecht and Naubert prefer not to patch up the 'original manuscript' which they claim to have found, others claim to have used it as a basis for an adaptation without damaging the 'essence' or 'spirit' of the source. Tresenreuter's Geist der Memoiren der Herzogin Mathilde is a good example. She claims to have edited a novel from the remnants of a manuscript that she has rescued from complete ruin and dressed up according to contemporary fashion:

> Dass ich nun. . . den kostbaren Überrest aus der mir zugefallenen geheimen Cassette des Uhr-Enkels [sic] eines gewissen Prinzen, dem gänzlichen Verderben entreisse, ihn nach

der Mode aufpuze [sic] und auf diesen Grund gebaut,
einen Roman herausgebe, wird, hoffe ich, ohne besonderen
Tadel Jeder gerne geschehen lassen, den die belles
Lettres interessiren oder nicht interessiren (8).

J.F.E. Albrecht's <u>Uranie</u> is based on an inventive variation of this
technique. The mysterious manuscript from the planet Sirius, we must
recall, is in the process of being translated by the village pastor before the reader's eyes. Hence, whenever the pastor stops translating
the tale, the reader must stop reading it--unless, as Albrecht argues,
the 'pause' can be 'filled up' with something of interest until the
pastor returns to work again:

> Allemal, wenn unser Pastor eine Pause macht, pflegen
> wir auch eine Pause in der Mitteilung unsers Manuscripts
> zu machen, denn wir müssen warten, bis er weiter übersetzt hat
> (II, 173 f.).

Not wanting to spend the time in complete silence, Albrecht avails himself of one of the pauses to speculate on airship travel--Luftschiffer-
ey-- until the pastor has picked up his pen once again.

The inclusion of letters is a convenient device for "filling in
the gaps" of an incomplete manuscript or for opening the novel to new
narrative possibilities. Freiherr von Knigge 'gathered' correspondence
from many sources in his attempt to solve the mystery of the "haunted
castle" in <u>Das Zauberschloss</u> (8 f.); Sophie Tresenreuter 'compiled'
letters and papers for <u>Geist der Memoiren</u>. Whenever she mentions the
existence of certain pieces of correspondence she presumes her readers
will not be averse to reading them: "Meine Leser sehen vermuthlich nicht
ungerne, wenn wir ihnen den Briefwechsel mittheilen, von dem wir. . .
geredet haben" (I, 122). The narrator of <u>Die unglückliche Fürstin aus
Wien</u> (anon.) corroborates the verbatim account of his over-wrought heroine by including her personal correspondence, and finds the device particularly useful whenever 'torrents of tears' (99) interrupt her dicta-
tion. The reader might well marvel at the propensity of characters in
novels for hoarding an impressive variety of letters over a considerable
number of years. They are all found ready at hand whenever the author
requires them. But no less impressive is their capacity for recalling
verbatim the minutest details in letters which have long since been

destroyed:

> Diesen Brief erhielt ich [der Autor] nicht im Original,
> und theile meinen Lesern ihn so mit, wie er mir dictirt
> [sic] wurde, denn das Original war vernichtet, wie wir
> unten sehen werden (108 f.).

The technique is used as much to produce verisimilitude as to offer
the reader insights into the private thoughts and character of the
correspondents. The latter is done, for instance, by G.C. Kellner in
his Familiengeschichte:

> Die zwei ersten Briefe. . . muss ich wenigstens sogleich
> mittheilen, weil sie die Denkart der beiden Freundinnen,
> besser, als irgend eine andere Schilderung, meinen Lesern
> ins Licht setzen. (I, 96).

Christiane Naubert's Alf von Dülmen best represents the views of 1790
on the advantages of the epistolary technique: ". . . der Feder sey
überlassen, was der Mund nicht auszusprechen vermag; da kann die müde
Hand doch so oft ausruhen, das Auge sich so oft satt weinen als es will,
ohne dass euch die Erzählerin lästig oder langweilig würde. (221)
Letters often reveal emotions rather than actions. The correspondence
between Henriette und Karoline in Kellner's Familiengeschichte, for instance, is invariably expunged by the flow of tears that drench the
pages:

> --Sie werden aus meinem Kritzeln nicht klug werden.
> Die Thränen stürzen mir in einem Strom auf's Papier hin,
> und verwischen allemal das Wort wieder, wenn ich's eben hin-
> geschrieben habe (III, 259 f.).

The emotionality is most intense in this novel when Emilie is writing
a secret letter to her lover and suddenly hears her husband's footsteps
approaching; she rushes about hiding the writing materials, yet continues
to pour out her fears during the last anxious moments:

> Stille! Die Hausthüre klingelt. Ha! er kommt schon die
> Treppe herauf. Geschwind, geschwind, Schreibzeug und
> Brief weg! Sieht er, dass ich schreibe, so muss ich ihm den
> Brief zeigen. Allmächtiger Himmel! Was würd' er anfangen,
> wann er die Klagen läs! (I, 107)

She continues in this manner for two more paragraphs before stopping.
Albrecht is here as serious in his use of the epistolary technique as

Richardson was in _Pamela_ (1740). Indeed only Johann Christian Müller and Müller von Itzehoe, as we shall see in Chapter V, saw the humorous possibilities that Fielding had explored.[25]

As Becker points out in her study of the novel of 1780, everyone writes letters in all circumstances--for instance, young lovers who live in the same house. Thus J.F.E. Albrecht's young lover in _Dreyerlei Wirkungen_ informs his lady (and of course the reader as well) of the delights he has enjoyed with her: "er arbeitete eine Epistel an das schöne Fräulein. . . . Er schilderte darin die Freuden der verflossenen Nacht" (I, 146). Müller von Itzehoe parodies both the situation and the love letter itself in _Herr Thomas_ when his hero writes such a letter, an "Epistolam theologico-homiletico-eroticam" (I, 66): "Statt zu schlafen elaborirte er in der folgenden Nacht eine erotische Epistel voll homiletischer Eleganz und orientalischer Simplicität" (I, 65).

The practice of documented narratives is ridiculed in Albrecht's _Uranie_ when the fictional translator of the mysterious manuscript that has fallen to earth comments on the scribe in the distant planet who is always at pains to substantiate his statements, and still only manages to limp along through his narrative, "unser glaubwürdiger Autor, der alles so gern aktenmässig belegen will, und allenthalben hinkt und anstösst" (I, 198). Albrecht ist not far from the mark in describing German novels of the period. Yet no matter how laboriously they express their views, or however digressive or retarding the action might be, all novelists seem assured that their readers (like the attentive listeners in Christiane Naubert's _Barbara Blomberg_, will simply have to hear the tale to the end (I, 161).

5. Prefaces

> All my heroes are off my hands;--
> "this the first time I have had a
> moment to spare,-- and I'll make use
> of it, and write my preface.
> (_Tristram Shandy_, Bk. III, Ch. 20)

Prefaces of novels published in the early 18th-century arose out of the concerns and uncertainty of the novelist, who lacked confidence both in himself and in his public.[26] It was the custom to justify one's

style, point of view, and even one's reason for writing. Hans Ehrenzeller regards the gradual disappearance of the preface as a sign of the
writer's social emancipation. The influence of Sterne and of his German
imitators, which culminated in Jean Paul, as Ehrenzeller observes, transformed the convention into a purposefully whimsical literary motif. It
is significant therefore, that only 18 of the 35 first editions dealt
with in this study contain prefaces. Of these, eleven are either serious commentaries on the author's approach to his work or apologies for
his shortcomings; the other seven are purposefully whimsical.

Turning to samples of the first type, we find E.A. Göchhausen's
Preface to Ein Büchlein zur Beförderung einfältiger Lebensweisheit explaining to his "liebe gute Leser" how the book has been written, and
that he expects them to bring their common sense to bear upon it: "Ich
rechne freilich billiger Weise darauf, dass er [der Leser] den Sinn
eines Biedermanns mitbringe; denn geben kan ich den keinem Menschen"
(iii). His Preface to Meines Vaters Hauschronika also expresses the
view that common sense is necessary for a proper understanding of his
book which, he adds, is both entertaining and instructive: "Ist übrigens
allerley nützlicher Lahr [sic] und viel guter Ding drin, und wohl hie
und da ein Schwank. . ." Ignaz Fessler prefaces the second volume of
Marc-Aurel by begging indulgence for his work and trusts his reader will
judge his intention rather than his achievement: "so hoffe ich wenigstens in Rücksicht dessen, was ich leisten wollte, duldende Nachsicht
für das, was ich leisten konnte" (II, ii). He sets forth his aims and
justifies his choice of theme:

> Wäre meine Feder so stark, als mein Wille gut ist; so könnte
> dieses Werk. . . Marc-Aurel, dem Muster der Fürsten, ein
> bleibendes Denkmal seyn, welches dasjenige noch weit über-
> träfe, das ich schon lange in meinem Herzen zum Besten der
> Menschen gesetzt habe . . . Marc-Aurel lebte für die Tugend
> und für das Glück der Menschen. Dies ist im kurzen die
> ganze Geschichte seines Lebens.

Karl Philipp Moritz, whose Preface to the first volume of Anton
Reiser (1785) had explained that this psychological novel could also be
called a biography, because it is largely based on observations from real
life, addresses the reader of Part Four (1790) in much the same vain as
Göchhausen had done in the Hauschronika: "Dieser Teil enthält auch

einige vielleicht nicht unnütze und nicht unbedeutende Winke für Lehrer
und Erzieher sowohl als für junge Leute. . . ." His "Vorbericht" to
Andreas Hartknopf. Eine Allegorie (1786), however, contains only a single line--Der Buchstabe tödtet, aber der Geist mach lebendig--and Part Two
of the novel, Predigerjahre, has no preface at all. Friedrich von Oertel's Preface to Part One of Kilbur--Vorrede zum ersten Theil-- explains
the general purpose of his work; the introduction to Part Two--Vorerinner-
ung zum zweiten Theil--presents his views on human development, discusses their importance, justifies Part One, and explains his reasons for
offering his ideas to the public in the present form. J.F.E. Albrecht
explains in the Introduction to Dreyerlei Wirkungen that he writes to
show on the basis of facts what the political life of Germany is actually
like.

G.C. Kellner's introduction (An den Leser) to Klingstein. Eine
Geschichte, mit Szenen aus dem spanischen Successionskriege has the sole
object of justifying his choice of title. He inveighs against the commercialism of book-titles that attract the public through appealing
catch-phrases and assures his reader that, despite appearances, "das
Büchlein selbst trägt zwar auf jeder Seite. . . das Gepräge der Wahrheit." Friedrich von Oertel was similarly motivated when he wrote the
Preface (Apologie meines Titels, und Vorrede zu dieser Schrift) to
Weiber machten ihn weiser,--und glücklich. Despite its title and the
fact that it is "dressed up" as a novel, he claims his work is really a
biography: "Biographie, nicht Roman, ob sie gleich hier unter dem Kleid
desselben, und unter diesem hier gewählten Titel erscheint." It had not
sold well when first published in 1787-88 under the unprepossessing title
Geschichte meiner Kinder- und Jünglingsjahre, in psychologischer Rücksicht [Halle, bey Friedrich Christoph Dreyssig] and his new publisher
had persuaded him to change the title for the edition of 1790. Sophie
Tresenreuter has quite different reasons for being defensive. She explains in the "Vorbericht" to Geist der Memoiren that her 'fellow coun-
tryman's' book Siegfried von Lindenberg (the second edition of which had
actually appeared nine years earlier, in 1781) had been misinterpreted
by a prejudiced public. She therefore explains that her Preface aims to
help the reader form a dispassionate judgement:

> Die erste Pflicht eines Autors ist Unpartheilichkeit
> . . . Für die zweite Pflicht eines Autors hat die Ver-
> fasserin dieses Romans es gehalten: wahr zu seyn.
> . . . Der eingeschränkte Wunsch der Verfasserin fordert
> ausserdem nichts, als dass dieser kleine Vorbericht
> jeden Leser zu einem ruhigen, kalten Urtheil vermöge.

In his "Vorbericht des Herausgebers" to Volume Three of Die graue Mappe
(1791), which is really the author's Preface, as Haken's claim that he
is merely the editor of the book is the usual make-believe, J.C.L. Haken
apologizes to the reader for having published a third volume when he had
only planned two. He promises a fourth volume in response to public demand. 'Two full years' were to pass before Part Four (1793) was published, during which Haken claims to have been counting on his readers
continued patience (IV, Preface). Friedrich Thilo makes excuses for
having written twelve volumes of Lebensscenen over the past six years
and assures his reader that he was only acting in response to public
acclaim (XII, Preface). G.C. Kellner is the only author who provided
his novel with an epilogue rather than a preface. He concludes Molly
und Uranie with some final words "An die Leser" describing the genesis
of the work and discussing other books he has written.

Other novels take the Preface less seriously. Thus the anonymous
author of Heinrich und Henriette informs us that according to contemporary custom it would be a great crime to write a book without a preface.
This has its advantages he adds, for whoever wants to write a thick book
can easily fill a few signatures with a Preface that contains absolutely
nothing. His own Preface, we are assured, has a real purpose, namely
to explain how his story arose:

> Nach der heutigen Sitte würde es in der That ein grosses
> Verbrechen seyn, ein Buch ohne Vorrede zu schreiben. Nun ist
> es zwar eine ganze feine Sache, für einen, der nun gerne ein
> dickes Buch schreiben will,--denn wer sonst Lust dazu hat,
> kann mit leichter Mühe einen oder etliche Bogen mit einer
> Vorrede anfüllen, welche lauter--Nichts enthält--der Zweck
> dieser Vorrede aber soll blos [sic] dahin gerichtet seyn, dass
> ich ganz kurz die Ursache der Entstehung dieser Geschichte
> angeben will. (i f.)

Müller von Itzehoe's Preface to Herr Thomas is devoted in large
measure to ridiculing the digressive genealogies so frequently found
in popular literature. He later parodies the convention of the Preface

63

(and himself as well) when his young hero writes an introduction to a
book of his own, but does not know how to continue. 'One can easily shake half a dozen sheets of declamation out of one's sleeve' he laments,
but once the introduction is done, one has to follow up with the book
itself: "Aber nun sollte, wie sich gebührt, auf die Einleitung zum Buche
auch das Buch folgen" (III, 157). In E.A. Göchhausen's view--it takes
him eight pages to make the point--'short prefaces are the best short
things on earth' (Büchlein, viii). Heinrich Werder parodies the convention in his satirical novel Eduard Rosenhain by entitling his introduction "Statt der Vorrede." He too muses for eight pages, comments on the
contents of his book, which he claims has 'thus been dedicated in the
best form' and, stealing a phrase from Wieland's Don Sylvio, explains
that the reader will meet his 'unauthoritative opinion' at every turn in
the novel. Kotzebue changes the traditional title of the "Vorrede" into
"Meine väterliche Instruktion für diesen Knaben," the 'young lad' in
question being, of course, the book itself, the child of his mischievous
whim.

Bahrdt's Preface to Geschichte des Prinzen Yhakanpol, a work published under the pseudonym "Magister Wromschewsky" and relating the travels of a foreign prince who goes to Europe in search of the best religion, anticipates his readers' doubts as to the appropriateness of his
narrative technique. The preface justifies the digressive journey of
the hero and lampoons theological education with its emphasis on dogma-
tics and polemics. The effectiveness of the Preface lies in its self-
parody:

> Der Leser dieses Buches dürfte vieleicht die Frage auf-
> werfen, warum der Magister Wromschewsky, zu dessen Buch
> ich eine Vorrede zu schreiben ersucht worden bin, seinen
> Prinzen zwei Jahr auf Reisen geschickt, und in so weit-
> läufige und mühselige Untersuchungen verwikkelt habe,
> da er ihn ja auf einem weit kürzern Wege hätte zu seinem
> Ziele führen können. . . Aber man hat absichtlich den
> weiten Weg gewählt, weil es höchst heilsam scheint,
> die langweiligen Jugendjahre mit etwas hinbringen zu
> lassen, was doch immer einen indirekten Nuzzen erzeugt. . .

Bahrdt signs the Preface with his other pseudonym, "H. Hofstede,
Grossinquisitor."

The whimsicality of which Ehrenzeller's study speaks finds its

fullest expression in the four-page Preface (Vorrede) which Bahrdt inserted between pages 308 and 309 of the first volume of <u>Ala Lama</u>. This
is the trick that Sterne played in <u>Tristram Shandy</u> and <u>A Sentimental
Journey</u>. The book, Bahrdt informs us, has not been translated from some
other language, as he suspects his readers to have assumed, but from
German. He admits that this sounds rather strange and explains that he
will not be able to solve the puzzle until the year 2442, when the original will be found. This "autorschaftliche Deklaration" of having
translated his work, he explains with the authority of tradition and convention, will exonerate him from responsibility for the errors or impro-
prieties of the original:

> Dieses Buch ist nicht aus dem französischen, nicht aus dem
> englischen, nicht aus dem spanischen, nicht aus dem
> italienischen,--nun?--auch nicht aus dem arabischen,
> türkischen, ätheopischen--übersetzt, sondern--aus dem
> Deutschen.
>
> Das klingt sonderbar, werden die Leser sagen. Ja
> freilich und noch sonderbarer wird es ihnen vorkommen,
> wenn ich sie versichern muss, dass ich dieses Räthsel
> nicht eher, als im Jahre 2442 werde lösen können.
> Denn erst in diesem Jahr wird das Original zum Vor-
> schein kommen, welches ich hier übersetzt habe.

As might perhaps be expected, only satirical writers saw the possibilities for whimsy in the Preface.

6. <u>Chapter headings</u>

> This chapter, therefore, I name the
> chapter of THINGS--and my next chap-
> ter to it, that is, the first chapter
> of my next volume, if I live, shall
> be my chapter upon WHISKERS, in order
> to keep up some sort of connections
> in my works.
> (<u>Tristram Shandy</u>, Bk. IV, Ch. 32)

Whereas in 1780 only comic novels were divided into chapters, the
technique predominates in all types of 1790. Here chapter headings
serve generally as a table of contents to inform the reader of the action
that is to follow and warn him of scenes that might be upsetting or that
he might care to omit as boring or inconsequential. Like author-intru-

sions and prefaces, chapter headings were used both for serious and whimsical purposes. The influence of Fielding and Sterne is obvious.
Christian Sander, as the title of his Salz, Laune und Mannigfaltigkeit, in comischen Erzählungen suggests, is motivated by Shandean whim [Laune] to write a 'rather long' story which has been 'divided into chapters to make it easier reading' (7). His first chapter heading, is more than it purports to be and describes for whom the story is intended and what it is to achieve:

Kapitel I, Inhalt

Dieses Mährchen, Leser, ist ein wenig
                                        lang,
Drum theil' ich es in kleine zehn
                                Kapitel.
Erhabner tönte zwar: Gesang;
Allein der Autor fürchtet grosse
                                Titel.
Um jungen und um alten Kindern
Die Müh des Lesens zu vermindern,
Steht vornan, zur besondern Zier,
Ein kurzer Inhalt, so wie hier:

. . . ich erzähle euch itzt von einem simpeln Bauer ein
simples Abenteuer so simpel, als ich es vermag. . .
Traute Leser, mir und jeder deutschen Seele verständlich
will ich euch, wo möglich, einen und allenfalls auch
ein Paar langweilige Augenblicke zu verkürzen suchen. . .(8)

No other writer is quite so simplistic; but then, few have Sander's sense of humour.

A survey of representative chapter headings will give sufficient indication of their form and tone. Whether the purpose of the headings was serious or humorous, writers had no difficulty in achieving their aim: headings were signposts that made reliable predictions--Sterne's chapter on "whiskers" actually did follow his chapter on "things." Thus Sander's Salz, Laune rightly forewarns us of "Fortsetzung und Ausschweifungen" (370), while Sophie Tresenreuter's Geist der Memoiren abounds in headings in which she promises to fulfill her obligations to the reader, and then does. She confesses in others that she has been whimsical where the reader might consider her arbitrary, and warns her reader when she is about to offer her opinion on certain subjects. A collection of her chapter headings would form a compendium, as it were, of headings pre-

vailing in the period. All seem to have been inspired in some degree by
Fielding: "Welches wie ein Reise-Journal anzusehen ist" (I, 86); "In
welchem der Autor seinen Grillen aufs neue gar sehr nachhängt" (I, 181);
"Meinungen von mancher Art" (III, 17); "In welchem der Autor erfüllt was
er zu Ende des vorigen Capitels versprochen hat (III, 42)"; and "In welchem die Gutherzigkeit des Schriftstellers, dem Leser nichts zu wünschen
übrig läßt" (III, 181). Müller von Itzehoe correctly, and doubtless in-
advertently, warns us in Herr Thomas of a boring chapter--ein langweiliges Kapitel (II, 392), while another heading informs us that the chapter
contains enough material for a whole folio volume--Welches Stoff zu einem
Folianten enthält (III, 7).

J.F.E. Albrecht prepares the reader of Dreyerlei Wirkungen for
increasing complications of plot--"Immer tiefere Verwikelung in diesem
Labyrinth" (III, 37)--while another heading informs us that the author
is going to retrace his steps to finish important episodes (IV, 103).
Friedrich Rambach prepares the reader of Kniffgenies for a chapter of
which he is particularly proud and which he regards as his masterpiece.
"Ein Kapitel, worauf wir ausserordentlich stolz sind, und welches wir
in der That als unser Meisterstück ansehen" (I, 65). This, of course,
has been lifted directly from Fielding's Jonathan Wild: "A chapter of
which we are extremely vain, and which indeed we look on as our chef-
d'oeuvre . . . ."[27] A chapter heading in Heinrich Werder's satirical novel Eduard Rosenhain braces us for what in his view is the essence of the
popular novel: "Wunder Plunder,Magnetismus, Prophetismus, Wunderkuren
zeigen seines Fingers Spuren" (278). Indeed, the German writers of 1790
seem to have adopted Fielding's view in Joseph Andrews ("Of Divisions
in Authors") "that it becomes an author generally to divide a book, as it
does a butcher to joint his meat, for such assistance is of great help to
both the reader and the carver" (Bk. II, Ch. 1).

With Fielding's text clearly in mind, G.C. Kellner is the only
author who does not resort to chapter divisions and indeed who even argues
against carving a book into portions:

> Die Mode, ein Buch, das an einander hängende und in einander
> eingreifende Menschenschicksale in erzählenden Schilderungen
> darstellt,durch Kapiteleinteilung in Portionen zu zerschneiden;
> die Mode scheint dem Originalmuster aller Darstellung, [der]

... (147), and later that it is ...

As a consequence he does not even try. Friel

... confusion and ...

Natur eben so untreu, als die Mode, sanftabgerundeten, mit
weichen, unmerklichen Uebergängen verbundenen Glieder
ventil des menschlichen Körpers durchaus abgeschnittene
Kleidungsstücke mit insektartigen Einschnitten zu unter-
scheiden (Familiengeschichte IV, 242).

This question arises in a division entitled 'A chapter for those who are
sufficiently fond of their health not to want to ruin it with trivia'
(IV, 242)--the only division in this novel of over a thousand pages.
At this point in the book Kellner resorts to a grotesque type of humour,
feeling that the reader has been warned by the heading. The chapter
itself deserves mention only because of its extraordinarily offensive
subject. It tells the story of a servant girl who had unwittingly slept
with her mouth open. A spider had walked in and gained access to her
stomach and intestines, resulting in vomiting and hallucinations.
Kellner describes the spider withstanding the onslaught of gastric jui-
ces, feeding on the food in the victim's stomach, and growing to the size of a saucer. Bloody bowel movements could not pass the beast, which
the poor girl eventually retched out on the bedroom floor.

Writers generally conclude their chapters with the same sort of
whimsy with which they initiate them. Probably Sterne served as a model,
e.g., when he writes: "I forthwith put an end to the chapter,--though
I was in the middle of my story". (Tristram Shandy, Bk. II, Ch. 4).
Particularly frequent is a feigned concern not to bore the public. When
the hero of Felix mit der Liebesgeige retires for the night, for example,
Hegrad turns to his readers to explain that he himself is tired and concludes the chapter because sleep might be creeping up on the reader as
well: "und da vielleicht einem oder anderm meiner Leser hier gleichfalls
der Schlaf anwandeln könnte, so will ich zu grösserer Bequemlichkeit
dieses Kapitel schliessen" (I, 157). J.F.E. Albrecht draws a chapter
of Uranie to a humorous close by having the fictional translator of his
manuscript reject the text in sheer disgust. The exasperated pastor puts
down his pen and slams his fist onto the table, thereby awakening his
wife, who had fallen asleep while listening to the tale. At this point
Albrecht intrudes into the narrative and offers his readers a much-needed
break:

> --Und ich will auch in der That, sagte der Pastor, und
> schlug auf den Tisch, das Buch nie wieder ankucken. . . .
> Die Frau Pastorin erwachte durch den Schlag, denn sie
> war. . . eingeschlafen, und damit es unsern Lesern nicht
> auch so gehe, wollen wir schnell schliessen! (I, 96 f.)

Sander, who claims that he skips details to prevent the reader from
becoming bored, fears in Salz, Laune that his praise of sleep may have
been too effective: "Doch vielleicht preise ich hier den Schlaf so wirk-
sam, dass du, mein Leser, bereits schlummerst" (36). Sophie Tresenreuter
reflects the same concerns as her colleagues (Geist der Memoiren, I, 187)
and reveals in her "Fourteenth and final chapter"--a heading set in heav-
ier bold-faced type than is used elsewhere--that she too has found her
narrative somewhat tedious and trying (I, 199). "God did not create you
for the tortures of boredom," writes Kellner in Familiengeschichte der
Rosenbusche (III, 242); he thus expresses a major concern of all his
colleagues. Their anticipation of the reader's boredom is sufficient
cause to shift scenes, end chapters, and beg forgiveness for having
robbed the reader of his day (Die unglückliche Fürstin aus Wien, anon.,
205).

7. The convention of humility

> "Til then, it is not in my power to
> give further light into this matter,
> or say more than what I have said
> already--
> (Tristram Shandy, Bk. I, Ch. 2)

Inexperience and lack of skill are the excuses which authors of
1790 offer for their presumed lack of achievement. This is of course
the age-old rhetorical device of humility. In the German novel of 1790,
however, confessions of inadequacy occur so frequently and are so stereotyped that the original poignancy of the device is lost. Becker found
similar evidence of this variant of the "Unsagbarkeitstopos" in the novel of 1780.[28] A few examples will suffice to illustrate this feature.

Ignaz Fessler introduces Marc-Aurel by admitting that if his pen
were as strong as his will is good (I, i), his work would be an enduring
monument to the real Aurelius. The anonymous author of Heinrich und
Henriette laments that his pen is too weak to describe Henriette's sad-

ness (147), and later that it is even too weak to describe her joy (166).
As a consequence he does not even try. Friedrich Hegrad uses this convention to effect a transition. Thus in an episode in which the heroine
of Felix mit der Liebesgeige faints in a crowd, he informs his reader
that the confusion and bewilderment of the scene could only be portrayed
by the 'brush of a skilled painter,' and not by 'the weak pen of an un-
practised writer;'[29] thus he passes on to another scene: "wir wollen
also den Vorhang herablassen und zu einer anderen Szene übergehen"
(II, 140 f.). The next scene poses similar problems, for he attempts
to describe an episode which has neither action nor dialogue. No sooner
does he begin when he realizes how difficult descriptive writing is; he
consequently changes the situation once more and offers a dialogue after
all, because: "eine stumme Szene ist abermals sehr schwer durch Worte
zu geben, und so will ich. . . eigentlich da anfangen, wo die Unterredung
selbst einen förmlich ordentlichen Gang zu nehmen anfing" (II, 141).

J.F.E. Albrecht finds mute scenes equally difficult. When the
young hero of Fackland escapes from the arms of his wanton mistress
and runs home to his mother with tears of remorse, Albrecht asks who can
possibly describe such mute rapture: "wer vermag stumes [sic] Entzücken
zu schildern?"(I, 195). Such a scene, writes the anonymous author of
Kabale und Liebe, "lässt sich freilich nur empfinden, nicht beschreiben"
(151). Kellner calls on the readers of Klingstein to use their own imagination when his words are unable to 'paint' the scene: "Darstellen
muss sie [die Szene] sich die Fantasie meiner Leser. Worte vermögen hier
nicht zu mahlen" (138). Sophie Tresenreuter too would wish her readers
to have a lively imagination, for as she writes in Geist der Memoiren,
she feels 'utterly incapable of protraying the mixture of pain, fearful
modesty, affected whimsy, and gentle yet masculine bearing' of one of
her characters (I, 117). What more need she have added in portraying
him? When she asks how to 'describe the results of this horrible event'
in Werner, Graf von Bernburg (II, 724) or how to 'portray the chain of
events' in Alf von Dülmen (527), one fears that she--like many a collea-
gue--is expressing a very real quandary.

The manner of using such conventions to reveal one's real or pre-
tended literary concerns is reminiscent of Fielding and Sterne. All that

has gone into the making of a piece of fiction stands on display in the finished novel. In some cases this is characteristic of an author's attempt at whimsicality, but the majority of authors seem to be in earnest. This impression may be due to their actual lack of skill or to having misunderstood their models. Blanckenburg's comment of 1774 that in the hands of Yorick imitators, good humour (die gute Laune) gave rise to adventuresome distortions in both thought and style,[30] still seems to hold true in 1790. Sterne can still delight us after having "got through these five volumes" of Tristram Shandy by explaining: "What a wilderness it has been! and what a mercy that we have not both of us been lost, or devoured by wild beasts in it!"[31] By contrast, the German author of 1790 creates such a wilderness of misunderstood whimsicality that it threatens to overwhelm both him and his reader.

CHAPTER III

THE NOVEL OF LOVE AND ADVENTURE

Preamble

The central motif which runs through the romance tradition from the Baroque heroic novel to the Prüfungsroman of 1780 is that of virtue threatened by an evil world.[1] Love plays a dominant role in the development of the hero of the Prüfungsroman, and seduction is a hazard which the virtuous upper-class protagonists of this type of novel have to negotiate if they are to reap the rewards that Providence bestows.[2] In opposition to this idealized world which portrayed heroes and heroines as they ought to be instead of as they actually are, a new type of fiction, the erotic novel, arose in the mid-1780's.[3] Lubricious scenes abounded in these novels, but were rarely presented for their own sake. The portrayal of characters ruined by indulgence in forbidden sexual practices was meant as a deterrent. Johann Bernhard Basedow, the noted pedagogue and founder of the Dessau Philanthropinum, had actually recommended that boys and girls in their early teens read erotic novels in order to witness the 'horrifying results of sin'.[4] The resulting combination of vicarious eroticism and moral instruction led to an ambiguity in moral narrative literature,[5] for as a writer in the Allgemeine Deutsche Bibliothek for 1791 (vol. 102, p. 421) noted: "die Romandichter geben oft dem ungeübten Wollüstling die feinsten Systeme der Verführung an die Hand, indem sie die unerfahrene Tugend für [sic] die Fallstricke des Lasters warnen wollen." Eschenberg caught this ambiguity and cautioned against it in his Theorie:

> Solche Romane. . ., worin das Laster empfohlen und die
> Wollust verführerisch geschildert wird, sind äusserst
> verwerflich. Und überhaupt muß man aus der Lektüre dieser
> Art nur beiläufige Erholung, nie aber einzige oder
> herrschende Beschäfftigung [sic] machen (338)

But as we found earlier, few novelists of 1790 would have considered their work complete without including a modicum of eroticism. They knew that their public expected it and on occasion exploited this

expectation by using the mere promise of erotic scenes as bait to hold
the reader's attention or to arouse his interest in a sequel. The
salacious scene that is found in most novels of the period is designed,
in J.F.E. Albrecht's phrase, to make the onlooker's mouth water (Fackland, I, 178). Drawing upon a limited assortment of obvious props, the
novelist's stock-in-trade usually also includes 'torrents of tears during
long and painfully sweet embraces' (Kellner, Familiengeschichte, IV,
208). Most scenes, however, stop short of complete consummation. Albrecht, for example, skips over the 'Duodrama' at the climax of a love
scene on planet Sirius in Dreyerlei Wirkungen because 'we have the same
thing on earth' and he does not want to paint a lubricious scene':

> Wir übergehen den weiteren Inhalt und die Beschreibung
> des Duodramas, weil in der That auf unserm Erdplaneten
> dergleichen sich auch, nur unter andern Titeln befinden,
> und wir keine schlüpfrige Scene. . . mahlen wollen"
> (I, 136).

J.E. Stutz' tale "Die beiden Freundinnen" in Erzählungen exemplifies the
horror with which most heroines experience the prelude to the lubricious
scene. Here a young lady informs her friend of her passionate struggle
to save the 'innocence of her heart' from the ardent advances of the
young man she loves:

> Auf einmal entstand in mir ein Klopfen, bange und strafend,
> wie das Bewusstsein einer Freveltat. Schaudernd sprang ich
> auf, und riss mich aus den Armen meines Geliebten; Weg von
> mir, Verräther! rief ich, fast meiner Sinne beraubt, noch
> ist die Unschuld meines Herzens unbefleckt, noch dieser
> Busen unberührt. (159)

Yet her struggle is in vain, for she loses her 'innocence in the tumult
of love' (170) and announces her pregnancy a paragraph later. No writer
is so boldly defiant of Albrecht's principle of decorum as Franz Kratter,
whose Das Schleifermädchen aus Schwaben exploits the prurient interests
of his readers in an attempt to warn them of the moral danger they court.
It is the only extant novel of 1790 that approaches pornography.

Heinrich Werder's Eduard Rosenhain and J.F.E. Albrecht's Fackland
come closer than most to Kratter's unrestrained realism, but they too
stop short of describing sexual intercourse. Thus Werder begins to
describe his hero's delights in bed with a prostitute but quickly "draws

the curtain for this scene" (235), while Albrecht's wanton coquette
throws herself onto the bed and pulls her lover into her arms, only to
have the scene end because "Die Sache ist zu schmutzig!" (II, 133).
Friedrich von Oertel remarks in Kilbur that one ought not portray 'lusty,
sensuous or horrid' characters in a novel, for there are people whom an
author can only portray with a trembling hand, and before whom one
blushes in the name of humanity, fearing its just censure (I, 341).
Indeed, ". . . es giebt Materien, für die die Feder sich entsezt [sic],
aber eben aus dieser fliesst unser meistes Elend, Kränklichkeit, Lebens-
überdruß, Melancholie und jene Abneigung für die Ehe, die immer weiter
sich ausbreitet, obgleich leztere [sic] auch noch an politischen Fäden
hängt" (II, 171). He might have added that the frequency of suggestive
scenes was one of the main reasons for the disrepute of the novel as a
genre.

Of course, this kind of sexual behaviour has no place in ordinary
domestic circumstances, since 'love' and marriage were held to have
nothing in common. Nor indeed do the novels reveal 'chaste and sacred
love of moonlight nights in the Alps' which Leonard Meister proclaims as
the right of 'natural' man in Spaziergänge (58). The love which figures
in love-stories belongs, in Meister's words, to the hurly-burly of civi-
lisation--Gelärme der Welt (58)--in princely manors and courts and in
corrupted cities. Other evidence ot 1790 supports Meister's view that
love is the tool of the politician, the ruin of innocent girls, and the
profession of the coquette.

The nine extant novels of love and adventure published in 1790
handle love themes in essentially the same way as the novels that only
occasionally dabble in lubricious scenes, except that such scenes are
generally more frequent. These novels of 1790 have two elements in common with the elevated Prüfungsroman: the episodic structure and the trials
of virtuous characters. Heroes and heroines are pursued by lascivious
squires, Counts, highwaymen and caliphs, virtue is rewarded and vice
punished, wicked characters turn from their evil ways (often on their
deathbeds); sexual restraint, if not total abstinence, is extolled.
They differ markedly, however, in one important aspect. The middle-class
milieu predominates. Aristrocratic lovers, who traditionally form the

74

focal point of the Prüfungsroman, are represented only in the anonymous
Heinrich und Henriette. Seven others depict middle-class lovers, and one
(Die unglückliche Fürstin aus Wien, anon.)recounts the misfortunes of a
princess who loved a commoner. One anonymous novelist seems to have understood this shift of focus as partly due to class differences in the
concept of virtue. For the middle-class, he suggests in Kabale und
Liebe, virtue is synonymous with continence, or even with one's moral
stamina to resist being ravished; for the nobility, he explains, virtue
is synonymous with concupiscence (155). Novelists do not always seem to
agree that their readers would learn more by example than precept. They
find ample opportunity to counsel them on the qualities which make for a
harmonious marriage, even, in one case, to the point of obliquely pre-
scribing the frequency of sexual intercourse.

We may now turn to an account of the individual works themselves.

[Franz Kratter:] Das Schleifermädchen aus Schwaben (1790)

> Ein Mädchen von glücklicher Anlage
> zur Tugend, von guten Grundsätzen,
> und einer gesunden verständigen Er-
> ziehung, ist nicht so geschwind zu
> verderben, als man glaubt. (II, 190)

Edifying examples, Kratter informs us, are the soul of moral education (I, 23). Young Hannchen Reiter, the heroine of his novel, enjoyed
a home life which abounded in examples of solid middle-class values.
Her father, master-grinder Hans Reiter, had become one of the richest
citizens in Swabia 'by the work of his hands and the sweat of his brow'
(I, 3) and had married 'a lovely pious maiden' whose life centered on
domestic activity (I, 11). In mutual concern and love they enjoyed 'the
most contented, the happiest, and the most enviable marriage' (I, 18).
Everything which Hannchen saw and heard in her parental home consisted
of 'order, harmony, activity, moderation, noble neighbourly love, sensible frugality on the one hand and gentle generosity on the other' (I,
23). There is little doubt that the author endorses these exemplary
domestic qualities. Kratter recognizes, however, that good upbringing
and a harmonious family background alone do not make the man; circumstances, human relationships and fate often exert the most ruinous influences on one's heart and mind. If this were not so, he explains, the

reader might expect great things of our promising young heroine:

> Machte die Erziehung allein den Menschen, hätten nicht
> Umgang, Verhältnisse, Schicksale oft die widrigsten,
> verderblichsten Einflüsse auf Herz und Verstand, was
> könnten sich meine Leser nicht alles von diesem
> hoffnungsvollen Mädchen versprechen? (I, 24)

The novel portrays 'edifying examples' of Hannchen's experiences
beyond the educative influence of the home, and her encounters with those
who exploit her awakening sexuality. Hannchen was indeed so lovely that
her beauty might well be blamed for her experiences; she was attractive
to 'the man of feeling' (I, 25). Kratter sketches the sensuous lines of
her physical charms and, as so often in the novel, is fascinated by the
elasticity of her breasts. He doubtless expected a similar fascination
on the part of his readers:

> Hannchen war eine Brünette, von etwas starken, auffallenden
> Zügen. . . Ihr edler, liebreicher, etwas wollustig gewölbter
> Mund lächelte die unversiegbarste Freundlichkeit. Ihr
> voller, runder, kraftvoll aufathmender Busen verrieth auch
> durch den Zwang seiner Fesseln den gefährlichen Reiz einer
> seltenen Elastizität. (I, 26 f.)

We are informed that her mind was completely equal to the charms of her
body (I, 27). She was a perfect example of feminity--intelligent and
physically attractive. But she was also a woman of imagination; she
loved things that were out of the ordinary, liked to read adventure
stories and had a feeling for the "romantic" aspects of nature. For
such a soul, Kratter warns, nothing can be more dangerous than over-
exaggerated concepts of virtue and sanctity (I, 30).

This assertion sheds light on the ambiguity of the eroticism in
Kratter's novel. He portrays sensuous scenes in order to expose their
moral dangers, but at the same time he cannot espouse a rigid concept of
virtue. For this reason there is no real cause-and-effect relationship
in his novel according to the old formula of virtue rewarded and vice
punished. Kratter attempts to titillate the reader by showing how the
heroine enjoyed her sexual experience, and then promptly superimposes a
moral by telling him that the experiences were bad. An equally important
consideration is that Kratter's statement on over-exaggerated concepts
of virtue and sanctity enables him to embark on a favorite sport of

contemporary novelists: the harangue against the evil influence of the priesthood and the Church.

Hannchen's adventures begin on hearing a sermon on the merits of virginity: "So viel Unsinn auch das Ding enthielt, so galt es doch, verfasst und deklamirt, wie es war, für ein seltenes Stück Meisterarbeit einer Kapuzinerpredigt." (I, 32) Our heroine learns that through the virtue of virginity she can become an angel in the flesh, and a chosen bride of Christ. A single impure thought, as the priest intoned, and one's virginity is irretrievably lost (I, 32). A question which immediately comes to Hannchen's mind is what is meant by 'impure thoughts,' for up until her sixteenth year she has led an innocent life, knowing only the ambivalent feeling of her awakening sex-drive:

> Indessen war das, was in Hannchens Herz bis ins sechzehnte Jahr einer eben schuldlosen als fröhlichen Jugend vorgegangen, weiter nichts, als ein zweideutiges dunkles Gefühl des Geschlechtstriebes, der nun sich zu entwickeln im Beginnen war; ein wollüstiges, süsses Behagen beim Selbstbeschauen ihres Körpers, ohne eigentlich die Bestimmung seiner Reize errathen zu können; ein schnell aufsteigendes und eben so schnell vorübergehendes ängstliches, unerklärbares Verlangen beim Anblicke einer wohlgebauten Mannsperson. (I, 34)

Kratter pursues his own fanaticism against 'the fanaticism of the priesthood' with its 'ruinous influence on the peace of the soul and the harmony of the family' by sending Hannchen to confession to examine her thoughts.

The dialogue in the confessional box probes the recesses of her soul, for the priest (clearly out of prurient interest) must know everything to a nicety--ich muss alles haarklein wissen (I, 37). Is she a virgin? Has she been fingering herself? Does she experience erotic fantasies? Does she find men attractive? It is thus, Kratter bursts forth in a harangue, that youthful innocence is perverted and false morals are disseminated (I, 43). In his view, the confessional affords the best opportunity for the sensual priest to take advantage of a woman's weakness, while healthy young priests who are forced into celibacy will feel the 'tickle of the flesh' all the more intensely in such close proximity to subservient women (I, 47). We need not follow the additional pages of text on this subject, except to point out that Hannchen learns from the priest how to masturbate and to enjoy 'impure thoughts':

> Aber wie macht man es, wenn man mit sich selbst sündigen
> will? -Man denkt an Mannspersonen, an Entblössungen, an
> Sachen, die man mit ihnen in Geheim thun möchte; man
> tastet sich an; man hat wollustige Empfindungen dabei!
> (I, 54).

Hannchen enjoys the results of her instruction.

Kratter intrudes at this point to explain that while he has perhaps portrayed a vice with all too alluring colours, the pleasure is only
momentary. This chapter, he adds, could be dangerous only if the reader
were not acquainted with the horrible results of the action. We are in-
vited to read the ensuing account 'with an attentive soul'; merely pon-
dering the consequences will almost overcome the dangers:

> Ich habe dir vielleicht, lieber Leser, ein Laster. . .
> mit zu reizenden Farben geschildert. Lass diesem
> Laster immerhin seine augenblicklichen Reize!
> Bist du mit dem Entsetzlichen seiner Folgen nicht
> bekannt, so könnte dir dieses Kapitel gefährlich
> werden. Lies das folgende mit aufmerksamer Seele,
> und denke darüber - und deine Gefahr ist so viel
> als überwunden. (I, 55)

Hannchen masturbates for seven nights until she is exhausted. Her
mother discovers what her daughter has been about and in a melodramatic
dialogue forces her to confess. The dismayed heroine is taken to a
doctor noted for having cured a boy and girl in their very early teens
who had masturbated to the point of chronic lethargy (I, 60). The doctor
moralizes for several pages and explains that 'sinning with oneself'
leads to paralysis of body and soul (I, 62), blood poisoning (I, 63),
and to a life poisoned to its innermost marrow (I, 65). Curiously enough,
the remedy for such sexual problems is the same type of advice presented
in some character novels of the period for middle-class professional
success. Fulfilment of one's obligations to one's social class and useful work dispels idle thoughts by day and makes one too tired to sin at
night:

> Wer die Pflichten seines Standes aus redlicher Absicht
> erfüllt, thätig die Stunden des Tages zu nützlichen
> Geschäften verwendet, dem bleibt unter Tags keine Zeit
> übrig, an unanständige Sachen zu denken; und er schläft
> die Nacht hindurch immer einen ordentlichen, ruhigen,

keuschen Schlaf. (I, 68)

Hannchen's physical charms develop with each passing day (I, 70) and make her irrepressibly attractive to the neighbourhood boys. The postmaster's son develops a curious perversion by ogling her through the bedroom window as she examines her naked body (dutifully described by Kratter) before the mirror. He espies a blood-letting basin full of blood that he assumes to have flowed from her 'round lily-white arm' (I, 76), plunges into the room to swallow the blood ecstatically by the handful--ach es ist so kostbar, so süsse, so unvergleichlich! (I, 77)-- and is 'engulfed by love' (I, 81). Kratter assures us that the lad's reason suffered more than his body (I, 79). Other scenes and adventures of dubious taste follow, such as Kratter's description of Hannchen learning from lubricious novels how to languish in the nude and to enjoy libidinous delights. Once again the postmaster's son bolts through the window out of sheer ecstasy: this time he is dragged off to prison for attempted rape. (I, 89)

Soon other characters are introduced, who eventually make love to Hannchen. Thus we read the story of Strehler, the Chaplain who was deflowered--entjüngfert--at the age of 16 by the young wife of a jealous, emaciated 60 year old man' (I, 124). The experience made him a hypocrite for life, for his pious demeanour hid a lascivious heart. He has moved the confessional booth to his bedroom, finding it a more salutary base of operations (I, 138). As is to be expected, no girl held such powerful attraction for his lasciviousness as Hannchen (I, 140). The lubricious scene which ensues, one of many in the novel, may serve as an example of Kratter's technique.

> Strehler hielt Hannchen noch immer mit seinem Arme fest
> umschlungen, und machte mit der andern Hand unvermerkt
> die Busenschleifen los. Hannchen starrte ihn mit
> trunkenem Blick an. . . Die Wange glühte, der Busen
> athmete heftig auf und nieder, das ganze innerliche
> Mädchen bebte in zitternder Bewegung. -Liebes, herrliches
> Geschöpf! Dein schwarzes seelenvolles Auge, Dein süsser
> wollustathmender Mund, Dein voller, heftig emporwallender
> Busen, Dein schöner schlanker, ganz nach dem Model wahrer
> Regelmässigkeit gebildeter Körper, alles in Dir stimmt
> überein, den fühlenden Mann zum Genuss der Liebe hinzu-
> reissen, ihn mit unnennbaren Seligkeiten zu überströmen.
> -Er sank mit ihr auf den Hügel. Das schwache Mädchen

> unterlag, und fühlte sich im taumelnden Uebermass der
> Wonne seliger, als jemals. . . (I, 168-179)

She lets him have his will and finds the experience 'inexpressible'
(I, 171). Presumably even the contemporary reader himself might just
have found Kratter's "horrid results" thoroughly delightful.

After many similar episodes, we are told that the mad young Berger,
the postmaster's son, has refused to repent of the blasphemies he purportedly shouted on being carried off to jail from Hannchen's bedroom,
but is rescued by Hannchen and a group of rebellious students. Hannchen
enjoys her sex-life with Pastor Strehler until she finally exposes him
as a hypocrite and proclaims the moral truth she has learned: Reason
and virtue are an innocent girl's sole weapons against the wiles of
seduction (I, 256). Her father sends her away to an aunt in a large
city, and Hannchen bids farewell from the deck of a ship as Book I ends.

Part II is concerned with the heroine's experience in a large city,
where her aunt tries to change her into a "lady": "Man [wollte] das
schwäbische Bürgermädchen in ein grosstädtisches Fräulein umschaffen
. . ." (II, 23). Risqué underclothing, transparent negligés, and liaisons with lascivious priests and aristocrats lead to the same situation
we witnessed in Part I. We learn in all this that Hannchen remained
steadfast in her middle-class values: "Hannchen bewiess [sic] hier die
noch unverdorbene Denkungsart eines gut erzogenen schwäbischen Mädchens,
dessen edles Herz nie sich zur grosstädtischen Niedrigkeit herablässt
. . ." (II, 110). However, the erotic 'stormy scene' (II, 116) of the
naked Hannchen lying on the bed in the arms of the Canon of the Cathe-
dral would seem to disprove Kratter's contention:

> Der Domherr zog zitternd die Busenschleife auf, und ein
> Busen enthüllte sich vor seinem Blicke, der einer Venus
> zum Model des ihrigen gedient haben würde. Ein elek-
> trisches Feuer zuckte ihm durch alle seine Empfindungs-
> nerven; hoch schlug sein Herz; die Leidenschaft wüthete ihm
> durch die Adern, er bemeisterte sich, wie ein hungriger
> Raubbär seiner Beute, mit gierigen Händen ihres Busens. . .
> (II, 113 f.)

One wonders after having read two volumes of this sort of thing whether
Hannchen was called the "Schleifermädchen" solely because she was the
daughter of a grinder (Schleifer) or because the laces of her bodice

80

(Schleifen) were always being feverishly undone by passionate males. Etymologists will of course choose the former, but the reader of this novel might entertain some doubts.

The only novelty in the second part is the heroine's introduction to the Order of the White Lily, a secret society for the practice of group sex (II, 135-77). Hannchen becomes an initiate and is undressed by two ladies who cover her body 'with hot kisses', which fill our heroine with new-found ecstasy: "Welche Reize!" The room in which the so-called festival of nature takes place abounds in erotic pictures among which the participants pose and preen themselves in the nude and play enchanting games. When the games are done all lie naked in the arms of the partner of their choice and enjoy ritualistic sexual pleasures. Kratter finally instructs his readers that the secret society which he has so clearly depicted transgresses all laws of decency and morals (II, 179).

Towards the end of the book Kratter explains that what we have been experiencing in this novel is not love but sexuality. Love, he continues, is something quite different: "Liebe ist das Bedürfnis schöner Seelen" (II, 220). To love and be loved without being primarily motivated by sexual impulses, he explains, to be one with the beloved through a sense of commitment, to have one soul for two hearts, is a pure love most heartily to be desired. As Hannchen was beginning to feel this kind of love (albeit without being particularly motivated to do so) Kratter returns her to her father in the small Swabian town, where he gives her in marriage to the once deranged Berger. Like their parents (I, 18), the young couple were the joy of the town, and lived a happy tender marriage in the harmony of mutual tenderness (II, 348).

The disparaging review in the <u>Allgemeine Deutsche Bibliothek</u> for 1791 (vol. 98, p. 137) may be cited in full as an apt concluding commentary on Kratter's salacious pedagogy:

> Es ist fast nicht zu begreifen, wie ein Mann, der, seiner
> Schreibart nach zu urtheilen, wohl fähig wäre, würdigere
> Gegenstände zu bearbeiten, sich verzeihen kann, niedrige
> Ausschweifungen und Scenen der gröbsten Wollust und Völlerey
> mit so lebhaften Farben zu mahlen, dass ein schamhafter
> Mensch kaum ohne Erröten gestehen darf, dass er diess
> Buch gelesen habe. Weiter hat es denn auch kein Verdienst,

als dass darinn (so viel wir uns auf dergleichen verstehen)
diese Scenen treu dargestellt, und pöbelhafte Menschen,
groteske Charaktere und niedrig komische Situationen mit
viel Wahrheit geschildert sind. Die liebenswürdige Heldin
dieses Romans kömmt indessen, nachdem sie alle Schulen durch-
gelaufen ist, doch noch mit Ehren an einen Mann, und wir
wünschen dem Heldenpaare Glück, ohne es zu beneiden.

Anon.: Heinrich und Henriette oder Die traurigen Folgen eines
raschen Entschlusses. Eine Robinsonade.

This novel, which closely resembles the early Greek prose romances,
recounts the trials and adventures of Heinrich and Henriette, two inno-
cents in love. The author explains he cannot say with certainty to which
social class Henriette belongs because her old mother observed a stubborn
silence with respect to their family background: "Vielleicht erfahren
wir in Zukunft einiges davon und wir werden sodann die Neugierde unsrer
lieben Leser mit vielem Vergnügen zu befriedigen suchen" (2 f.).
However even at the end of the tale we can only surmise that Henriette
was of noble origin, for this assumption is central to Heinrich's 'sudden decision' that sets both lovers on their incredible travels.

A lecherous squire who spent his youth in rakish living and revel-
ry (10) encounters Henriette on his estate and demands that she immediately satisfy his sexual appetite. Henriette, whose 'virtue' is thus
threatened by the squire's 'vile intent' (5), defends herself 'heroically' and is cast into a dungeon, there to remain until she accedes to his
wishes. Heinrich, the squire's servant, falls in love with Henriette
during her imprisonment and eventually runs away with her. No sooner
are they free of the 'monster' when they are dragged off by highwaymen,
rescued by soldiers and rewarded by the death of the squire--all in the
space of a few pages. Providence is shown to care for virtue and to
punish vice when the judge awards the squire's estate to Henriette as
compensation for her ordeal:

> So sorgt die Vorsehung für die Tugend; und so bestraft
> sie den Lasterhaften. Je länger und ungestörter sie einen
> Bösewicht in seinen Sünden dahin leben lässt, desto schneller
> und härter sind auch gewiss die Strafen, die ihn alsdann
> treffen (24).

This is the basic point of the novel, and the plot continues accordingly.

Although Heinrich is deeply in love with Henriette, he is overwhelmed by
the social disparity between himself and his noble lady, and leaves the
estate in despair, a decision 'which was the basis for all the suffering
and misfortune' (27) which the two lovers encounter. Henriette, who had
planned to reveal her 'powerful passion'(28) to her lover is most dis-
traught at his departure. However, buoyed up by the discovery of hidden
papers which prove that Heinrich is really a Count, she sets out in hot
pursuit.

The reader must now follow two plots, as the author alternates between hero and heroine. Thus we must leave Henriette to her travels
while we hasten in pursuit of our dear Heinrich: "geschwind unserm lieben Heinrich nachreisen" (41). After we have thrilled at length to the
hero's fortunes, his acquaintanceship with an officer, together with the
latter's love and life, we are turned back to seek Henriette in Paris:
"Wir wollen sie aber reisen lassen und in Paris unsre liebe Henriette
aufsuchen. Wer etwas von derselben hören will, der lese das folgende
Kapitel!" (63). Here the poor girls searches in vain for her lover although Heinrich is close at hand. Though her search may be in vain, her
resistance to numerous attacks on her virtue is most successful and we
leave her in 'good hands' (78) while we join the elusive Heinrich once
more.

Heinrich is truly buffeted by fortune. Made wealthy through the
death of the officer, he falls into bad company, is imprisoned, sent to
Arabia, and becomes a slave in the Caliph's garden. Through the mysterious aid of a fellow victim, he escapes and sails on to further adventures,
while Henriette barely survives the honourable but despised advances of
a Marquis. Heinrich's further adventures include shipwreck, a Robinsonade on a desert isle, chance encounters with concomitant tales of love
and adventure, rescue, and the surprising revelation of his marriage to
a certain Adelaide who had, however, died in childbirth. Finally he returns to Germany, a rich man. A young student whom he rescues from a
band of robbers collapses into Heinrich's arms when he offers him half
his fortune for news of Henriette. On loosening the lad's neckpiece to
give him air, Heinrich discovers a young woman "ein Frauenzimmer... und
in dem Augenblick lag sie an Heinrichs Busen" (240). The novel ends
happily with marriage, domestic bliss, and the blessing of children:

Sie lebten übrigens sehr glücklich. Henriette gebahr
nach zwei Jahren eine kleine Gräfin und beyde Aeltern
erreichten ein hohes Alter. Henriette starb in ihrem
acht und sechzigsten Jahre und Heinrich folgte ihr bald
nach. Sie hatten viel Freude an ihren Kindern erlebt,
die noch ietzt beyde eine Zierde des Landes sind, in
welchem sie wohnen. (243)

The reviewer in the <u>Allgemeine Deutsche Bibliothek</u> for 1791

(vol. 102, pp. 412-13) explained that there could hardly be a stranger

tissue of improbabilities. He claims that it is impossible to follow

the hero and heroine in all their adventures, complains that the work is

carelessly written and tedious, and in quoting Horace's <u>Ars Poetica</u>,

advises the author not to take up writing again until he has reflected

upon the demands of the craft:

Ein seltsameres Gewebe von Unwahrscheinlichkeiten und Aben-
theuern zu Lande und zu Wasser, als diese neunzehn Kapitel
enthalten, kann es wohl nicht leicht geben. Schlag auf
Schlag, gerathen der Held und die Heldin dieser Geschichte,
aus einer Verlegenheit in die andre, und machen es dadurch
dem Rec. unmöglich, ihnen hier immer genau zu folgen.
Die Leser mögen sich also mit diesem kurzen Auszuge be-
gnügen, und wenn sie noch Lust haben wollten, mehreres zu erfahren, das Buch selbst zur Hand Nehmen. Der V. bittet in
der Vorrede die Kunstrichter, glimpflich mit ihm zu verfahren,
aber auch das glimpflichste Urtheil wird ihm sagen, dass er
sich nicht eher wieder gelüsten lassen möge, einen Schritt
in die Schriftstellerwelt zu wagen, bis er reiflich erwogen,
quid valeant humeri, quid ferre recusent.[6]

[G.C. Kellner:] Familiengeschichte der Rosenbusche. Aus authentischen
Quellen

The reader who trusts the title of this novel and expects a history

of the Rosenbusch Family based on authentic sources will be disappointed.

It lacks continuity and resolution of the plot and offers no unifying or

sociological perspective. Kellner does not show how the members of the

family develop, but crowds his narrative with the lives of many indivi-

duals thrown together by chance encounters. The work becomes less and

less disciplined as it progresses, and the first three parts seem to

possess few significant links with Part Four. As Kellner published no

less than three novels in 1790, it is perhaps little wonder. The situa-

tions and events in Part One are related by means of third-person narrative, dramatic dialogues, descriptive scenes and letters, pieced together by the ingratiating comments of an omnipresent author. The remaining parts contain less action, consisting mainly of descriptions of states of mind and heart as revealed by monotonous dialogues and documents. Kellner claims to have changed his approach so that the readers might enjoy vicarious sentiment (III, 7).

Kellner's description of one of his many sentimental episodes characterizes the whole novel:

> "[die] sonderbare Verwicklung des Schicksals Karolinchens
> mit diesen und noch vielen, vielen andern Personen, die
> durch das Leben dieses liebenswürdigen, obgleich etwas
> schwärmenden Mädchens eine lange Kette der unerwartet'sten
> und seltensten Menschenschicksale durchführt. . ."
> (II, 174 f.).

Kellner runs the gamut of the novelist's stock-in-trade: heroines who are all innocence, purity and virtue (I, 62) caught in the clutches of lascivious courtiers, women who 'tyrannize even the wisest men' by 'fanning the flame of all-powerful love' (I, 163), chronic melancholy, a hero who longs for death in battles as compensation for unrequited love (II, 13), exchanges of misunderstood correspondence (II, 115), conniving highwaymen (II, 165), utter confusion--Wirrwarr (II, 203), poison-pen letters (III, 211), and the all too common 'streams of tears" (IV, 208). Everyone weeps, sighs, swoons, loves, gets lost and is found again. Kellner fills over a thousand pages with lachrymose sentimentality and awkwardly contrived lubricious scenes, all of which he presumes his reader to have experienced sometime in his life (II, 17). Perhaps with good reason, therefore, Kellner redefined his 'history' as a 'novel' (III, 145) but feared his readers might dub him a pedlar of trivia: "Ja, meine Leser! . . . Schelten Sie mich keinen Kleinigkeitskrämer" (III, 129). Our plot summary will perforce be as disconnected and confusing as the original, but will have the advantage of brevity.

The novel opens with an account of the life of Dr. Wilhelm Rosenbusch, a general practitioner living in idyllic circumstances and "fern von französischhöflicher Falschheit und Zweischneidigkeit des Charakters" (I, 7). A long awaited son and heir is born, in whom the good doctor sees traits of genius. In time the boy leaves home for university and

eventually becomes a physician. He marries Emilie Goldbach, the epitome
of virtue, "Unschuld, Sittenreinigkeit und Tugend" (I, 62), who has fled
lascivious court circles and inherited a small fortune. Adolph spends
considerable time away on medical calls, leaving Emilie to correspond
with a friend at court and to describe her marital bliss. She is so
horrified by the experience of child-birth and the responsibilities of
motherhood that she rejects her first-born, Lorchen, placing her in the
care of a nurse. A second daughter, Karoline, is born two years later,
but Emilie can now face motherhood. Family life of love, tears and
happiness continues. During one of Adolph's lengthy absences Emilie
writes 'a long letter' (I, 195) to her friend, telling of her twin sister Auguste, who was forced to marry General Klingstein--the hero of
another novel Kellner published in 1790.[7] Auguste was inconsolable for
months until her child was born and Klingstein went to war, but then enjoyed the misery of her lonely existence. Incapsulated letters introduce
us to other characters and events. Thus we read Klingstein's personal
papers in which he reveals his unhappy marriage, and explains his involvement in the Wars of the Spanish Succession (I, 217). Correspondence
of a certain Graf Leopold enables Adolph to locate his sister-in-law
Auguste, whom he has not yet met, bring her to his happy home, and recount to her his marital bliss. Fearing she will disturb her sister's
happiness, she slips away into the night disguised as a coal miner, but
is traced to the home of a real coal miner who had found her exhausted
in the woods. The two sisters are enraptured with each other, and Auguste promises not to spend her days in tears.

'Four weeks later' (II, 1) Auguste's over-emotional attachment to
her sister has destroyed the family. The sisters have become "Schwärmer-
innen" (II, 13) carried away by a sentimental concept of friendship.
Spurned by his wife, Adolph decides to become a regimental surgeon and
longs to die in battle, though he faints at the thought of blood. The
sisters' discussions of their dream-home in a charming grove now dominate
the novel. Auguste soon dies, whereupon the author interjects a paean
to the serene life the two sisters had led:

> O! ihr zarten, zur süssesten Engelharmonie vereinten
> weiblichen Herzen! Ihr baut da das kunstvolle Meister-
> stück der sittlichen Weisheit: ununterbrochene Seelen-

heiterkeit; ununterbrochenen Genuss eines inneren
Seelenglücks. (II, 100)

Overcome by her sister's death, Emilie locks herself in her room and
smashes furniture, ranting and raving for three days.

Adolph's messenger arrives and begs Emilie and her friends to visit
the army camp. Distrusting the messenger, who looks like satan incarnate
(II, 115), a servant extorts a confession from him and discovers that
armed riders are awaiting in ambush. Everyone stays safely at home. A
second messenger arrives with a whole bundle of letters: one from Graf
Leopold to Adolph's former teacher Professor Müller, begging him to save
the Rosenbusch household from the approaching French troops; another to
Müller lamenting what would happen if he did not save the household; a
third letter from a certain "Räuberhauptmann Rolling" to his imprisoned
colleague, containing plans for escape and a plot to take revenge on
Adolph by razing the Rosenbusch household; and finally a letter from the
imprisoned robber to Rolling, explaining that he is now ready to escape
and take revenge. At the moment of crisis, we learn that Emilie is un-
accountably dying, but is trying to stay alive until she has learned
whether Lorchen has died and whether the cause was dysentry (II, 70).
Emilie dies of shock on learning of the advancing French forces. The
author now explains his plans for the next volume, promising to show the
influence of the French siege and the resultant battle upon Adolph,
Müller, Eleonore, Karoline and Lorchen (II, 174 f.). His promise, as one
might expect of such a preposterous work, is not fulfilled.

Part Three opens instead with a view of Emilie's corpse:

Da liegt sie, mit Leichentüchern umwunden, hingestreckt auf
hartem Stroh, die Hülle, die vor einer Stunde noch die
schönste Seele bewohnte. Seele mit den zarten, heil'gen
Gefühlen! Wohl Dir. (III, 8).

Adolph meets General Klingstein for the first time and divulges the contents of a packet of letters, thus repeating what the reader has already
learned. He meets a lovely young widow in church who looks like Emilie.
After gazing at her 'tearfully and with sacred emotion' (III, 109),
Adolph marries her and returns to the army. Adolph and his Minna later
become factory managers and then inherit a mysterious fortune.

Young Lorchen has meanwhile become aware of her growing sexuality and has been associating with lower-class girls, longing to gratify her impulses: "heimlich lechzend nach der Befriedidung jener Triebe" (III, 253). However a series of letters expounds the virtue of continence. Kellner inserts more peripheral information about the lives of other characters, explaining: "ich sehe noch gar nicht das Ende der langen Kette von Empfindungen und Schicksalen, die ich noch von der Rosenbuschischen Familie. . . zu erzählen habe" (III, 262 f.). Karoline writes that she is in love with her step-brother (the child of Minna's first marriage), expressing the ethereal purity of their relationship:

> Wir denken so gar an nichts Arges, sprechen von nichts
> als von Gott, und der Natur, und davon, daß wir uns
> lieb haben; und manchmal giebt's freilich auch einen
> Druck der Hand, einen Kuß: aber ist denn das Sünde?
> (III, 305 f.)

At the beginning of Part Four, Karoline arrives at the house of her aunt, who luxuriates in the same sentimentality as Emilie and Auguste. We need not summarize the scenes of happy melancholy in which this volume abounds. Lorchen leaves home and works in a fashion shop, where she is equally tender and "melancholischzärtlich" (IV, 187), while Karoline becomes a lady-in-waiting. Finally Lorchen discovers that she is pregnant and the novel ends abruptly when Karoline appears with Lorchen's lover and learns of her condition. They both reject the unwed mother-to-be and 'run away ashamed and confused' (IV, 390).

Only the most devious reasoning can relate this conclusion to anything that preceded it. At best, we might assume Kellner to have formulated his message at the beginning of Part Two:

> Liebe ist die stärkste, die süsseste, die göttlichste
> aller Empfindungen. Dann folget unmittelbar Freundschaft.
> Liebe verbreitet über alle andere Empfindungen einen Reiz,
> der sie weit über die Schönheit erhebt, die sie an sich etwan
> schon haben. Liebe verschönt, verstärkt die Freundschaft.
> Aber verschmähte Liebe giesst Eckel [sic] und Tod in alle
> andere Empfindungen. (II, 12)

[G.C. Kellner:] Molly und Urania. Novelle. Mit einem Dialog: Ueber die Schöpfung aller Welten und aller Geister, die sie bewohnen und ihre Schönheiten geniessen.

According to the Epilogue, the inspiration for this work came to Kellner's mind as he pondered 'the beauties of heaven during starry nights, united observation and speculation, invented a cosmogony, and dressed it in a semi-oriental story' (265 f.). The actual story is an entertaining account of love and adventure that forms a frame-work for the philosophical dialogues of two of the protagonists. Kellner halts the narrative abruptly after sixty-nine pages, inserts one hundred and fifteen pages of dialogue on such topics as the nature of Being and the development of philosophy from the Greeks to Leibniz, and then picks up the thread of his tale in a chapter entitled "Fortsetzung und Schluß der Novelle." The final episodes cover eighty-five pages. While the Epilogue admits that the story is fictitious, it is curious to note Kellner's meticulous concern for maintaining the impression of a factual account. He has graced the text of his Chinese episodes, for example, with some thirty-three extensive footnotes explaining various aspects of Chinese culture and history. The layman must accept his apparent scholarship as proof of his intimacy with the facts. The author later apparently authenticates his account by speaking of a certain traveller who substantiated all the events recounted in the tale.

Kellner's love story is not only a vehicle for his speculations, as he explains in Chinesische Hieroglyphen (265 f.), but also for instructing his readers in 'practical morals' by portraying human character.

The plot runs as follows:

Kjen Long, Emperor of China, whose sublime wisdom has spread as far as Europe, despairs of ever finding a suitable wife until Molly Dunkershill appears at the Chinese Imperial Court. The orphaned daughter of a rich Londonderry merchant, Molly had been placed in the care of a lascivious guardian and had 'reached the heroic decision' (4) to escape to an uncle in Malabar. Her ship having been attacked by Turkish pirates, Molly had been captured and repeatedly sold as a slave from one master to another right across Arabia and Persia, until she had been bought by the Emperor of China. To all appearances she is just as fresh

and virginal on arrival in China as she had been before her adventures
began. The Emperor falls in love with her, but gives her time to master
the Chinese language, so that she can be his intellectual partner as
well. This takes about two months. For the next seventeen years they
enjoy such an ideal union that Kellner recommends it as a model to all
the 'girls and youths' (18) who are reading his book. Kjen and Molly
would have intercourse only once a week, and 'love the perfections of
each other's soul':

> Mädchen und Jünglinge! Soll die Liebe, von der Ihr Euch
> die süssesten Freuden des Lebens versprecht, kein Wolken-
> bild seyn. . . so liebt wie Molly and Kjen Long. . .
> Sie sahen sich nicht immer; lagen sich nicht ewig im Arm;
> weihten oft in einer ganzen Woche nur einen Abend der Liebe;
> und zwar gerade dann, wann eben beide sich unwiderstehlich
> zu einander hingezogen fühlten; . . . Sie liebten. . . nur
> ihr wahres Ich: das heisst: die Vollkommenheiten der Seele. . .
> Selten wurd' ihre Liebe sinnlich. (18 f.)

A daughter, Jenny, is born to them and is secretly brought up as a European, yet with enough Chinese culture to suffice for an Emperor's
daughter. When the Emperor dies, Molly and Jenny depart for Londonderry
with Hoang Ti, a trusted servant. On reaching Europe they free their
servants and adopt European clothes. They purchase a huge home on the
Isle of Wight, where Jenny meets Coelistin, a student of philosophy and
astronomy who quickly becomes her fiance. The four live together in the
house and enjoy a secluded intellectual life. It is here that the 115
pages of dialogues are inserted, which have no significance for either
plot or characterization.

When the story is resumed, Hoang Ti reveals himself as a cunning
villain with a 'black soul,' whose patient dissembling has concealed his
political and sexual ambitions. He has received an offer to become se-
nior mandarin to the new Emperor, recommended by his vast experience and
an imputed liaison with Jenny, the former Emperor's daughter. He steals
her money, murders Molly, abducts Jenny and Coelistin, and sets off for
Peking. His plot is uncovered aboard ship, the captain releases the two
young lovers from their cabin, and after a hasty tribunal, Hoang Ti is
sentenced to death. By his own choice he dies "after the manner of
Seneca" by bleeding to death in a tub, begging forgiveness for his evil

ways. Jenny and Coelistin finally arrive in Calcutta and settle down to love, study, reflect, and 'communicate the most important results of their study to their fellow-men' in East India, "zur Aufklärung ihres Verstandes und Veredelung ihres Herzens" (258). Kellner is careful to explain that they live on the income from their books and the interest on their money.

The reviewer in the Allgemeine Deutsche Bibliothek for 1791 (vol. 105, pp. 130-31) did not comment on the incredibility of Molly's journey to Peking. Indeed he regarded the account as a good narrative, even if occasionally somewhat artificial and contrived. Hoang Ti's sudden transformation, for example, he found ill-prepared and unexpected. He also regarded the 'didactic dialogue' which has been 'inserted into the novelle' as successful even though the spontaneous spiritual harmony of the two young lovers was 'not quite according to the usual course of nature at first encounter.'

Kellner employed the same literary approach in his Chinesische Hieroglyphen [1791; see bibliography], a work which he hoped might have moral as well as aesthetic value:

> Kaum war sie [die Erzählung Molly und Uranie] unter der
> Presse; so fühlt ich mich auch schon wieder zur praktischen
> Moral und zur Darstellung von Menschencharakteren hinge-
> neigt; und machte einen Versuch, die wichtigsten Grundsätze
> der Moral in Chinesischen Erzählungen [auch?] nach des P.
> Du Halde Nachrichten und Litteratur von China bearbeitet,
> so anschaulich zu machen, dass die Erzählungen neben mo-
> ralischem, auch noch aesthetischem Werth hätten. (Hiero-
> glyphen, pp. 265 ff.) [8]

Anon: Kabale und Liebe, eine Hofbegebenheit von einem Ungenannten.

This novel, which recounts the trials and rewards of virtue in the political arena, consists of twenty-six letters exchanged between three intrigants. Each letter recounts past events, together with reflections and details of amorous and sentimental scenes. Whenever the emotions become very intense or when the protagonists soliloquize, the method of presentation changes; the narrative is replaced by monologues and dialogues on love and intrigue which the letters report verbatim. The first letter is written by an 'experienced uncle,' who has been ousted from a

'voluptuous court' by a corrupt government. He has sent his 'youthful
nephew' Karl to the court, in order to overthrow the Minister by means
of a love intrigue with a Countess, a woman 'created for the enthusiasms
of love' (13).

The uncle's first letter to Karl explains the 'great intentions
which have summoned the young man from the peaceful quietness of the
country' and describes the dangers implicit in the undertaking. The
greatest danger lies in the fact that "die Begriffe von Tugend bei einem
Staatsmanne verschieden von denen seyn dürfen, die ein Bürgerlicher davon hat" (2). The uncle advises his nephew that the art of politics is
akin to that of the gardener who uproots the weeds and nurtures the
beautiful flowers. The Countess is just such a flower, upon which the
scandalous Minister and the over-weening Prince are utterly dependent.
The fatherland is languishing under the tyranny of the government.
Whereas all was well when the uncle was in power, the people, whose labours support a self-indulgent and frivolous court, are now oppressed.
The uncle's views are uncompromisingly explicit:

> Der Minister ist eine Blume, oder wenn du lieber willst,
> ein Unkraut, das ausgerissen und an die Sonne gelegt
> werden muss, damit er verdorre, und auf keine Art mehr
> Wurzeln fasse. Die schöne Gräfin ist aber auch eine
> Blume und zwar eine sehr reizende verführerische Blume.
> Betrachte noch die vielen Schönheiten, die neben ihr an
> diesem Hofe blühen. . . und sieh zu, ob ich zu viel thue,
> wenn ich besorge, deine Jugend mögte sich dem Gärtner
> ähnlich werden lassen. (2 f.)

The nephew is cautioned to be extremely wary of the role of love in
politics. If he uses love as a political tool without becoming its
victim, "Unsere Unternehmungen können sich mit dem Beifall der Tugend
schmeicheln" (5). To the uncle's mind at least, this is as it should be:
"die Tugend selbst [muss] krumme Wege gehen, wenn sie dem Laster begegnen
und es in die Flucht schlagen will" (7). As the Countess herself is to
remark once she has recognized her evil ways, virtue makes us firm and
secure (213).

In a series of replies, in which he often encloses letters he has
received from the Countess, the nephew keeps his uncle informed of his
progress, reporting discussions verbatim and describing the details of
his erotic exploits. Love scenes and discussions of the delights of

love form by far the greater part of the novel. Love is considered the
prime ingredient, if not the sine quą non, of political endeavour. The
whole government is in the grip of the Countess because, as the author
admits, love is the basis of her intrigues and her politics (30).
Karl does not spend long at the court before he finds himself the object
of the Countess' amorous advances, and decides, in consultation with his
uncle, that you can only fight love with sex. He informs his uncle of
his plan as though he were addressing the Countess herself: "Schöne
Gräfin du hast mein Herz und meinen Kopf durch Liebe irre führen wollen;
ich werde dich durch die Reize der Wollust in Verwirrung sezen" (84).

Karl plays his role so well that he almost overplays his hand.
At first he insists upon safeguarding his virtue, even when sexually
aroused by the naked Countess who lies panting on the bed before him.
Yet he soon falls in love with her. The uncle delights in his nephew's
'political' talents and urges him to go the limit in enjoying 'the sweet
natural impulses which the Creator himself placed in our hearts' (122).
Following his uncle's advice and the dictates of his own heart, he makes
love to the Countess in the bedroom by night and in the post-chaise by
day. She is so overwhelmed by his 'virtue' and 'true love' as well as by
prospects of a 'chaste harmonious marriage' (155), that she promises to
renounce her promiscuous ways and her political intrigues. Yet she and
Karl continue to 'struggle the sweet struggle of love' (155) out of wed-
lock.

The Countess gives Karl all the government records and advises the
Prince of the abuses of his rule. Through her intercession the Prince
reinstates Karl's uncle, whose intentions the Countess regards as nothing
other than noble (203), as regent. She now turns from her former ways:
"Ich arbeite jetzt für die Liebe und die Tugend" (205). To all appearances, therefore, she has rejected the statesman's concept of virtue in
favour of those of the middle-class, yet even after her confession she
begs Karl to remain at court as her lover. Karl, however, is so revolted
by political life that he takes her away from 'the disgusting noise of
the city to the refuge of love, the beautiful country' (219). The moral,
if indeed there is one, consists in the repudiation of the evils of
city-life-- a theme of the character novel--and in the rejection of

politics as a debasing and dehumanising craft--the theme of many a satirical novel. But the main emphasis of the story rests upon amorous encounters for their own sake.

Curiously enough for the modern reader, the reviewer of <u>Kabale und</u>
<u>Liebe</u> in the <u>Allgemeine Deutsche Bibliothek</u> for 1791 (vol. 102, pp. 97-
99) remarks that the story betrays an author who has observed life at
court and was perhaps actively involved in it. Unfortunately, he explains, many citizens in the smaller provinces of Germany might notice
parallels between their own political leaders and the story:

> Diess ist der Innhalt gegenwärtiger eben nicht romanhaft
> aussehenden Geschichte, die in Briefen zwischen dem Oheim
> und Neffen, und zwischen diesem und der Gräfin erzehlt [sic]
> wird, und die einen Verfasser verräth, der in der Nähe des
> Hofes, vielleicht gar als selbst mithandelnde Person genau
> beobachtet zu haben scheint. Leider dörfte mancher Bürger
> in den kleinern Staaten Deutschlands, in der Schilderung
> des Fürsten S. 8 nur allzugut getroffene Züge aus dem
> Bilde seines getreuen Landesvaters erkennen: "ein zwei-
> deutiges Mittelding von Stärk' und Schwäche. . ."
> Man glaubt sich, indem man diess liest, wirklich nach
> St. oder M. versetzt.

[Heinrich Rehkopf:] Franz Wall oder der Philosoph auf dem Schafot (1790)

Rehkopf's book recounts the adventures of the son of a farmer noted
for his uprightness and commonsense, a quick-witted lad who would have
followed in his father's footsteps if he had not been endowed with a
fiery temperament. Because he could not accept the 'purposeful instruction' of his 'sensible father' (1), but was always interested in 'the
whys and wherefores' (2), Providence was to lead him 'along dark paths'
and make him in turn a physician, a theologian, a lawyer, and finally,
after many tests and trials, an executioner, or as the title announces,
the 'philosopher on the scaffold' (143). The narrative moves at the whim
of an omniscient author who frequently intrudes to address both his hero
and his reader. He rescues his hero from each successive difficulty
until the rewards of self-restraint can finally be demonstrated.

Franz Wall is trained to become a farmer until the age of twelve.
A certain Baron is impressed with the lad's fine qualities and undertakes
to send him to school and care for him if he will work 'industriously'.

His teachers discovered his excellent potential (5), and after a few
years he 'left school with a knowledge that gave promise of his becoming
a useful and great man' (5 f.). By the age of eighteen he had 'the
noblest heart and the most fervent feeling' (6). It is at university
that his trials begin: he becomes involved with gambling students and
falls in love with Henriette Wagenheim, a nymphomaniac who offers him
all the pleasures a young student could wish. Wine and love set his
blood aflame (3). When the lovers are fatigued by the exertions of love-
making they sustain their delight and excitement by reading novels together, preferring moving or stormy passages, "eine rührende oder stür-
mische Stelle" (70). The moral of the love story is evinced in a scene
where Franz discovers that his mistress is pregnant. In a melodramatic
moment, his dying father begs him to turn away from the 'slippery brink
of ruin' and be 'steadfast in the struggle of virtue' (79).

Franz leaves the pregnant Henriette and gives up the study of
medicine in favour of theology. His reasons are largely economic, for
we are informed that it is cheaper to become a theologian than a physician. When he returns to his hometown for a visit, he finds himself a
father. Meagre financial resources force him to postpone marriage until
he has studied law; he exhorts Henriette to be faithful while he attends
university. What follows constitutes the 'sad' part of the story:

> Ob [Henriette] aber hielt, was sie versprochen, und ob Franz
> nun genug gelitten hatte, durch harte Führungen vom Mediciner,
> zum Theologen und von diesem zum Juristen übergehen zu
> müßen, macht den traurigen Theil unsrer Geschichte aus, den
> wir nunmehr bearbeiten müßen (98).

Franz' decision to leave Henriette proves to have been hasty, for
he chances upon her in a compromising situation with his former university friend, Braunfels. (We later learn that Henriette became pregnant
from this encounter as well.) Franz assaults his friend, is consequently
imprisoned (120), and whiles away many a leisure hour reading Young's
Night Thoughts (129). On release from prison he starts a fight with some
soldiers and is ambushed and beaten in revenge. The dismayed author intrudes into the narrative at this point to illustrate for his youthful
readers the fate of wayward living:" Zertreten und zerschlagen, ohne
Sinnen und in seinem Blute lag der arme Wall auf dem Rasen, eben der

Jüngling, der schon in seiner frühesten Jugend an Kopf und Herz alle
übertraf" (136). Fortunately, he is found by a 'good honest executioner'
(138) and confesses the 'confused and sad path' he has been following.
His confession of error marks the beginning of a 'happy and satisfied'
year-and-a-half as the adopted son of a worthy man. The executioner dies,
leaving Franz a fortune (142). Having closely observed his foster-
father at work, Franz now finds himself appointed executioner in his
stead. His first professional duty is to execute a woman accused of in-
fanticide; while awaiting the victim's arrival, our 'philosopher on the
scaffold' reviews the vagaries of his past life. Just as he is about to
bring down the axe he recognizes the hooded victim as Henriette--and
Part One ends.

Part Two immediately continues the brief action. The real murderer
of Henriette's child makes a hasty death-bed confession just in time to
save her. Franz, feeling some responsibility for Henriette's well-being,
but unwilling to marry her because of her promiscuity, tries to re-inte-
grate her into society by finding a suitable husband for her. She eventually marries an honest town-clerk and becomes a useful member of society. Meanwhile Franz has fallen in love with the mayor's daughter and
comes to enjoy "reine Liebe statt der sinnlichen" (222). He postpones
marriage long enough to accompany a Polish prince to Switzerland and then
back to Poland, where he becomes involved in political intrigues. Here
he manages to save the life of the Polish regent in a scuffle, but to no
avail, for the regent is eventually murdered anyway. Franz recognizes
one of the murderers as his old friend Braunfels, the seducer of Henriette. Braunfels confesses his wicked past and warns Franz to flee before other assailants kill him. Franz escapes, arriving at the home of
his betrothed just when she is playing an aria entitled 'Joy of Man,
Omnipotent Love' (261). They marry and live happily ever after.

The terse and pointed review in the Allgemeine Deutsche Bibliothek
for 1791 (vol 104, p. 417) correctly describes the novel as a miserable
composition:

> Studenten-Scenen und Liebschaften; das sind die gewöhnlichen
> Gegenstände, welche unsre neuern Romanschreiber uns dar-
> stellen. Herr Wall schwängert auf Universitäten ein Mädchen,
> die ihm aber untreu wird. Er bringt einige Leute um, rettet

einem Paar andern das Leben, wird einmahl Soldat, dann
Scharfrichter, dann Hofmeister, dann Reisegesellschafter,
dann Liebling eines Fürsten, verlässt endlich den Hof
und heyrathet.--Eine elende Composition!

J. F. E. Albrecht: Fackland oder Schaden macht klug (1790)

Albrecht's novel recounts the amorous exploits of Fackland, a picaresque hero who is drawn into erotic escapades because of the inconstan-
cy of his character and the whims of fate. Albrecht informs his readers
repeatedly that it is a rigorous fate that enmeshes the hero in liaisons
with high-born ladies and with whores, but there is no evidence of such
causality. Narrated in the third person with rare author-intrusions and
occasional letters, the episodic narrative is clearly designed to demonstrate the contention of its title: the hard knocks of experience make
one wiser. Although Albrecht contends that the tale does not end because
it has been broke off by the hand of fate, but because it is only known
up to this point (II, 187), another explanation seems more likely. He
actually concludes the tale because Fackland has paid for his sins and
has mended his ways. The book seems a feeble imitation of Tom Jones,
but lacks its model's psychological insight, engaging characters, and
mastery of language.

The author claims to demonstrate a principle:

> . . . den aus Erfahrung gemachten Grundsatz, daß Kinder des
> Ehebetts den Stempel der Dummheit--Wirkung einer schläfrigen
> Behaglichkeit ihrer Aeltern--auf die Welt brächten, indeß die
> Kinder einer schönen Mondnacht, oder eines sich selbst ver-
> gessenen Augenblicks, durch feine Bildung und feuriges
> Temperament, für die Vorwürfe der Welt schadlos gehalten
> würden (I, 4 ff.).

Such a pronouncement in the early pages of the work was doubtless
designed to awaken the reader's interest. Christian Sander's story
"Die unverhoffte Erbschaft" in the collection Salz, Laune takes the same
point of departure:

> Denn Kindern, die bloß aus Gehorsam gegen Eid und Pflicht,
> in der kühlen Dämmerung zwischen Schlaf und Wachen erzeugt
> werden, wie oft fehlt es denen an Allem, was Ridolfo im
> Ueberfluß besaß. Aus dem heissen Quell der Liebe fließt
> in ihre Geschöpfe jene vis vivida, welche Helden und Genies

> bildet; aus dem kalten Borne der Convenienz ergießt sich
> in die Adern ihrer Kinder nur Wasser. (107) [9]

Fackland's illegimate birth foreshadows his later amorous adventures. By the age of six the lad has grown far too unruly for any teacher to handle. His father wants him to be trained by a strict task-
master, while the mother dotes on him and engages a gentle widow as tu-
tor. Fackland is finally sent away to school, but is expelled for having
spied upon the headmaster and his wife during their marital pleasures.
The father dies, leaving his young wife and unruly son all his money.
Fackland now becomes wilder than ever, and his mother feels she needs a
man. A family crisis arises when a professor who is boarding with the
young widow begins to play the role of husband and lover and tries to
have Fackland disinherited. The sixteen-year old Fackland has by this
time become a gambler, driven on by pride, vanity and ambition. The
author intrudes at this point to explain that the hero's youthful errors
were the result of frivolousness, excess, and lack of a friend. His
heart was sensitive to every impression (I, 52).

He one day surprises his mother and the professor in a 'herculean
embrace,' and can thus blackmail them for money. Next he meets a woman
at a costume ball who seduces him. Conditions at home become increasingly oppressive; Fackland, whose self-confidence has increased since he
lost his virginity, is happy to be sent away to a boarding school again.
Although the school turns out to be rigidly authoritarian, the boys break
the monotony by having affairs with the scullery-maids, by sneaking into
town for whoring and drinking, and by occasional forays into homo-sexua-
lity. Fackland is expelled as an incorrigible trouble-maker, whereupon
his mother decides that the only hope for him lies at university. Here
the young man gambles, drinks, and incurs debts while receiving financial
support from home. When the professor openly advocates disinheriting the
boy, the mother breaks with him.

On his way home for a visit Fackland meets a 'sweet lovely lady'.
He lavishes gifts and money upon her only to find out that she is a
whore. Continuing home utterly penniless, he encounters the woman who
had seduced him at the age of fifteen. Fackland is now twenty-four and
somewhat wiser; she is older and uglier. At a critical moment in a love
scene, he breaks free of her passionate embrace and runs home to the

safety of his mother's arms.

In the second part of the novel, Fackland advances from private tu-
tor to ministerial secretary. He becomes a tyrant and gets involved both
with a love-starved widow of rank and with the Minister's wife. He falls
in love with the Minister's cousin and is victimized by 'tyrannical female coquetry' (II, 62). His new mistress arouses his ardor in the woods,
lures him to the critical point of passion and then scorns his advances.
So great is the shock to his ego that he leaves town to become the secretary of a legation (II, 113). At this point the narrator intrudes his
structural principle: "das Schicksal, das sich wider ihn verschworen hatte,spielte ihm den Streich, daß je erfahrner er selbst wurde, um so klü-
ger war das Weib, in dessen Netze er fiel" (II, 114). Fackland now becomes involved with a nymphomaniac: "ein derber starker Fleischlumpen. . .
nur für die gemeine Wollust gemacht" (II, 116). However, he finds relief
from the exertions of passionate love in a platonic relationship with the
Minister's wife. Kellner clearly intends her as the kind of friend (I,
52) who can guide him along the straight and narrow path. She dies after
imploring him in a letter to give up his past and 'be a man' (II, 151).

Fackland becomes so depressed on the death of his friend that he
joins the army. Although by nature not inclined to military life, he
is soon promoted to Lieutenant. After distinguishing himself in a battle
in which his right arm is crippled, he is promoted to Captain. Soon,
however, he reveals his true nature by disobeying orders to execute a
captured French officer, whom he later helps to escape. Eventually he
leaves the army to return home, a broken and lonely forty-year old man.
But even now he has still not gained full control over his passions.
While walking through the woods his senses are aroused by a sixteen-year
old girl whom he attempts to rape. Her brother rescues her just in time
and beats him soundly, but, as Fate would have it, the brother is none
other than the French officer whom Fackland had saved. The three become
reconciled, and their reconciliation grows into deep friendship. Fackland eventually proposes marriage, but the girl refuses on the grounds
that she is still too young to give up her freedom. She promises to marry him in the future if only he will wait patiently. The novel ends with
a redeemed Fackland realizing the 'pure joy' of friendship with a sweet

young girl, and of domestic quietude among friends. Perhaps, the author concludes, Fackland and the girl might even be married by the time the reader has finished the book.

> Welche schöne Gruppe für empfindsame Seelen--er und sein
> Mädchen, vielleicht schon seine Frau. . . Welche herrliche
> Gesellschaft, selbst im Grabe! (II, 187 f.)

The reviewer in the <u>Allgemeine Deutsche Bibliothek</u> for 1790 (vol 97, p. 429) described the novel curtly and aptly. It is a boringly detailed and extremely insignificant life-story of a person who could hold no interest for the reader. He drew attention to the concrete portrayal of erotic adventures, but did not seem particularly disturbed by them:

> Der äusserst unbedeutende Lebenslauf eines Menschen, der, wie
> er da geschildert ist, gar nichts an sich hat, das sich Leser
> für ihn interessiren könnten. Auf Schulen und Universitäten
> macht er dumme Streiche, wovon man hier die langweiligsten
> Details lesen muss, wird Hofmeister, dann Sekretair, hat in
> jeder dieser Perioden viel Liebesabentheuer, die zum Theil
> auf sehr materielle Weise beschrieben werden, und nimmt nach-
> her Kriegsdienste, da ihm ein Arm lahm geschossen wird.

Anon.: Die unglückliche Fürstin aus Wien (1790)

This is the only novel which consistently warns its readers of the dangers of romantic love by sustaining a mood of misery and suffering. The confession of the destitute Viennese princess, who has lost friends, money, and social status as a result of her faith in romantic love, is meant to offer proof of how little we poor mortals are in control of ourselves (7). The narrator informs us that unfavourable winds had caused his ship to lie over in Lübeck while enroute to Reval in 1782. A stranger had approached him, with the explanation that he was sent by an unfortunate woman who had been so impressed with his writing that she wanted to dictate the story of her life to him as a warning to others. The narrator was at first hesitant to undertake the task: "Es ist nicht reizend, das Leben Unglücklicher darzustellen, um so weniger, wenn man mitfühlend bei ihrem Unglück ist, wie ich es seyn würde" (2). He nonetheless agreed to the offer and was taken outside Lübeck in a carriage to the 'unfortunate' princess.

She was a woman of rare beauty (4) whose voice was like angelic

100

harmony (5). Indeed the narrator is astonished to find 'such a divine
object in such a miserable little town' (5). The 'unhappy' tale is told
both by the princess and a stranger (whom we later recognize as Melian,
her former lover) who is suffering exile with her. Relatively little
attention is paid to the plot, for the most important feature of the novel is the description of remorse. Fate, we learn, had changed the princess's life. Once entitled to live in a palace, she must now dwell in a
hut while trying to hide from the world. Despite 'all applied philosophy', she can neither live with herself nor bear the thought of her de-
basement:

> Was der Mensch Schicksal nennt--ein Etwas, unter welches,
> wie ich wohl sehe--alles sich schmiegen muss, hat mich
> zum Gegenstande eines ganz besonderen Lebenslaufs genommen.
> Berechtigt in einem Pallast zu wohnen, muss ich in einer
> Hütte leben. Bestimmt unter den ersten glänzenden Weibern
> als eine der Ersten zu erscheinen, muss ich mich vor allen
> zu verbergen suchen, und wünschte es vor mir selbst zu
> können, denn Trotz aller angewandten Philosophie, bin ich
> nicht im Stande, den Gedanken meiner Erniedrigung zu
> ertragen. (6)

She begs the author to have the patience to listen to a long tale of
sorrows (7) and provides him with writing materials. She cannot tell her
name, she explains, for that would sully the honour of her family (9).
Scarcely has her story begun when she bursts into tears, and her former
lover follows suit:"ein Thränenstrom stürzte aus seinen Augen" (12).
The root of her misfortunes lies in her disobedience to her mother, whose
advice she ought not have neglected:

> Hätte ich damals das Zutrauen zu meiner Mutter nicht beyseite
> gesezt, so hätte ich die ganze Reihe von Unglücksfällen mir
> erspart und das Opfer der paar süssen Jahre, die ich in der
> Täuschung, Liebe sey Glück, zubrachte, wäre gewiss nicht
> einmahl in Anschlag gekommen (14).

The 'unfortunate princess' and Melian recount their tale as though
they were alone, while the chronicler silently takes notes: "Wir spre-
chen als ob wir allein wären" (15). Yet the author weeps with them at
the frailty of human flesh. They had fallen in love and had enjoyed a
sexual relationship. What was dangerous about their love was that it was
becoming more and more romantic, "romantischer" (68). She forgot virtue

(106), simply because she had fallen in love (181). The reader's presumed delight in the heroine's amours is overshadowed by the sense of danger they court. So great is her remorse that the princess, her former lover, and the narrator himself weep at every description:

> Hier brach sie in einen Thränenstrom aus. O meine Mutter, rief sie. (31)

> Melian weinte mit ihr, und meine [des Geschichtsschreibers] Seele ward . . . äusserst erschüttert. Ich liess selbst einige Thränen fallen. Die Fürstin bemerkte es, und drückte mir teilnehmend die Hand. (73)

> Ein heisser Thränenstrom stürzte aus meinen Augen. Der liebreiche Melian sah es, nahm meine Hand, drückte sie freundschaftlich, sah mir theilnehmend in die Augen, und weinte mit mir. (177)

An emotional highlight of her confession, doubtless intended as a didactic tour de force, is the description of the death of the princess's mother, whose advice she had not heeded. All her errors of omission and filial neglect now burden her to the point of despair. Even now, she explains, choking with sobs, she would love to gaze into her mother's coffin and proclaim her own impending death:

> So starb leider die beste aller Mütter. . . und könnte ichs noch--nur noch einmahl über diesen Sarg hinsehen, und hinüber rufen: Mutter! Mutter! ich komme bald! (68)

The princess finally tells how she was rejected by her father and family, disinherited, and spurned by society. The message which she wishes the author to proclaim to the world (205) is that one must not let oneself be carried away by love. The author promises not to publish her story before her death in order to protect the innocent. He consoles her with the remark that we are all, after all, only mortal (205).

The narrator explains that in accordance with the princess' wishes the manuscript lay untouched for several years until a stranger unexpectedly asked to speak to him alone. The stranger is of course none other than Melian, who has come to conclude the tale. We are informed that the princess had received a letter from home saying that her father was dying and longed for reconciliation. She had gone to him and found him suffering from an 'illness in the soul' (211). On his death the princess had become deranged. Once, thinking that her father was merely asleep in his bed, she had caressed his corpse as it lay in the coffin just prior to burial (278). Then she had collapsed, ending her days in madness (285). Having concluded the account, Melian went his way and was never seen again (288).

Both the novel and its author got short shrift in the <u>Allgemeine Deutsche Bibliothek</u> for 1792 (vol 106, p. 153). The reviewer was obviously correct in his rejection of the improbable fantasies which the author had conjured up:

> Die unwahrscheinlichsten, unmöglichsten, unnatürlichsten Begebenheiten, die nur ein schiefer, phantastischer Kopf in fieberhaften Anfällen zusammenträumen kann, sind hier in einen Roman gebracht, von dem man wahrlich ohne unverzeihlichen Zeitverlust keine genaue Gliederung liefern kann. Man braucht nur einige Seiten in diesem Buche zu lesen, um unser Urtheil billig und gerecht zu finden.

Friedrich Hegrad: Felix mit der Liebesgeige (1790)

In Hegrad's novel, love 'overcomes all obstacles, scorns all danger, regards neither social position nor riches, but seeks fulfilment, peace and bliss in itself' (I, 49). The reader is supposed to learn from this tale what love can accomplish (I, 49). The novel's distinctive feature lies in its Shandean self-parody. The principal characters are young Felix, a lad "edlen Herzens und guten Humors" (I, i), and his beloved Antoinette, "das sanfteste unverdorbenste und liebenswürdigste Geschöpf unter der Sonne" (I, 4). Chance occurrence is the prime motivating factor in all the episodes and events, and indeed, as Hegrad exclaims on one occasion: "was fügt nicht der Zufall?" (I, 187). The story of Felix and Antoinette is largely told by Felix himself as he sits by the fire-side with an acquaintance or two:

> Wenn die beiden Freunde nun so vertraulich beisammen am Kaminfeuer sassen, und ihre Pfeife. . . rauchten, oder ein Glas Punsch ausleerten, und ihr Gespräch bald auf diess, bald auf jenes fiel, und Felix dann auf seine Begebenheit mit Antoinette kam, da traten gewöhnlich dem Zuhörer sowohl, als dem Erzähler Thränen in die Augen, und sie legten beide ihre Pfeifen auf einige Minuten bei Seiten, und blieben stumm, bis sie sich wieder sammelten, und ein anderes Gespräch anfiengen" (I, 101).

Besides presenting the oral narrative, Hegrad 'gathers' the correspondence exchanged between Felix and Antoinette, inserts an occasional
comment, and creates the impression that Felix' conversations quite ar-
bitrarily wander where they will. The effectiveness of Hegrad's self-
parody depends upon his feigned acceptance of the narrative conventions
of the love story such as confusing plot and fortuitous events, as well
as upon comments which his fictional readers interject into the novel.
Secondary love-plots are woven into the tale to such an extent that we
sometimes lose all trace of the principal lovers. But this, as a female
reader of _Felix_ complains, is the very lack of realism one expects of a
novel: "aber da sehe mir einmal Eins hin, und suche die Helden und Hel-
dinnen auf, die uns diese Herren auf das Papier hin malen! Sie zu finden möchte wohl verzweifelt schwer halten" (II, 18).

The novel opens with Felix' compulsive decision to see 'what things
are like in God's wide world' (I, 1). Whoever will perfect himself must
travel, he explains, and 'this is especially true for men, who for the
most part become virtuous through experience alone. Women, on the other
hand, are virtuous by taste' (I, 6). Thus Felix takes leave of his
sweetheart, Antoinette, after having aroused her deepest emotions with
the 'divine music' of his viole d'amour: "Ach! der schöne Busen der
Leidenden hub sich so mächtig" (I, 11). After much wandering and many
adventures (which according to Hegrad were of no great account) Felix receives letters from Antoinette imploring him to rescue her from a forced
marriage. He vainly suggests rescue plans by mail until the problem
eventually solves itself. Antoinette recounts the events in a letter to
Felix. The young man she was to have married was actually in love with
a girl from the lower classes, and had run away from home in defiance of
his father's wishes. This 'mad idea' (I, 56) of marrying for love leads
to the revelation of yet another love story. The rich father had fallen
in love with the same peasant girl and planned to break up his son's forbidden engagement by marrying him off to Antoinette. Antoinette and the
young man decide not to marry under these circumstances. This plot soon
fades from the letter, and Antoinette herself disappears from Part One.
Then, much to the chagrin of the fictional readers of Hegrad's novel,
Felix is informed by post that Antoinette has "passed away" (I, 72).

Surely, the fictional readers complain, it is unreasonable that the author should have her die (II, 20). But of course, retorts another, she will certainly come back to life again. Resigned to the untimely death of his beloved, but hoping that she might yet be alive, Felix travels to many parts of Europe, where he plays his violin, reads novels (which Hegrad 'excerpts') and converses until new possibilities for love tempt his virtue. One fictional reader finds the plot foolish: "In der That, eine närrische Geschichte! . . . Liebesbriefe und Geschenke, wie vom Himmel herab!" (I, 50). An encounter with a woman who looks like Antoinette follows. After various uneventful journeys with a companion who has long been seeking his lost beloved, Felix chances upon the real Antoinette in a theatre in Vienna.

A chapter entitled "Zwei Ohnmächten" (II, 139) unites the astonished and bewildered lovers, unravels the mysterious paths which hero and heroine have taken and, by revealing an intrigue which had led to the false announcement of Antoinette's death, interposes yet another love story into the tale. The reunion is crowned with "Thränen, Küsse, Umarmungen. Ein Schauspiel für die Götter" (II, 146). By this time Felix' companion has also found his long-lost sweetheart, and the novel ends with a chapter entitled, "Zwei Hochzeiten, und eine Beurlaubung" (II, 149). If we can trust the judgement of the fictional readers of Hegrad's novel, the ending is just what the contemporary public would have anticipated: "denn mit einer Heurath endet sich doch der Roman gewiss" (II,20).

The novels of love and adventure we have reviewed are the weakest extant works of fiction published in 1790. They are vitiated by crass distinctions between vicious and virtuous people, by a complete dependence on stock types and situations, and by a sentimentality verging on bathos. Contemporary reviewers, we have noted, were unimpressed. It would seem, indeed, that the reviewer's disdainful judgement of the unavailable Karl Rosenheim und Sophie Wagenthal, auch ein Beytrag zur Kenntniss des Menschenherzens (Meissen, 1790), as published in the Allgemeine Deutsche Bibliothek for 1792 (vol 106, p. 152), was an apt assessment of the whole class:

Plan, Ausführung und Schreibart sind gleich gemein.
Welch ein Unsinn!

CHAPTER IV

THE HISTORICAL NOVEL

Preamble

It is generally maintained that the German historical novel arose
at the beginning of the nineteenth century under the direct influence of
Sir Walter Scott. One can, of course, find novels with historical themes
very much earlier, but they tend to be excluded from the genre, on the
ground that the specific nature of their heroes was not derived from the
characteristic features of the age they portray.[1] Georg Lukács points
out that Scott understood historical authenticity as the quality of the
inner life of his characters and as the ethos peculiar to a given age.[2]
Historicity in fiction he understood as the creation of characters whose
personality and inner motives were historically authentic.[3] In this respect, Scott was indebted to the realism of Defoe, Smollett and Fielding.[4]
Recent English critics tend to support Lukács' findings by suggesting
that Scott's fiction became the prototype of the historical novel and
established the characteristic features for the genre: historical accuracy of costume and milieu, immediacy of characterization and social
mood.[5]

For the period of 1790, however, these criteria cannot be applied.
The concept of the historical novel as a distinct genre was only gradually being formulated in Germany, and its beginnings found to coincide
with the revaluation of historical methods that took place about the
middle of the 18th century.[6] For example, Graf Heinrich von Bünau and
Johann Jacob Mascou were making significant contributions to the improvement of historiography and anticipated to a considerable degree what was
to become the characteristic feature of historical writing. Bünau promoted the principle that the historian should represent all the circumstances of a given event faithfully, even as Mascou was concerned that a work
of history be kept entirely free of fiction; he distinguished clearly between genuine historiography and reports or chronicles in which fiction
was mixed with real events. As early as 1726 Mascou insisted in his

Geschichte der Teutschen that it was not the task of the conscientious
historian to make a novel out of history: "aus der Historie einen Roman
zu machen." Johann Friedrich Burscher made essentially the same point
in his Abhandlung von Fehlern der Geschichtsschreiber (1754). The
historian must speak the truth as he himself knows it and must describe
events exactly as they happened. Burscher adds the criterion of impartiality and insists that a historian who turns his hand to fables and
fairy-tales is sinning against an office that requires neither more nor
less than the recording of actual facts. Views such as these were
gradually finding acceptance in the popular writings of the day.[7] This
resulted in the public's growing awareness of the aims of historiography
and gave novelists further reason for taking a stand on whether or not
their narratives were true.

During the latter part of the 18th-century many scholars were
attempting to define the proper concern and content of history. Ernst
Martin Chladenius noted in his Allgemeine Geschichtswissenschaft (1752),
for example, that the new science of history consisted of accounts of
"sogenannte Händel. . . neue und sonderbare Taten. . .wichtige Geschäfte
. . . eine Reihe von Begebenheiten".[8] Taking a similar approach, the
Leipzig historian Hansen explained in his lecture "Von der Theorie der
Geschichte" (1765) that history could not be regarded as a science simply
because it was, to his mind, nothing but a series of events, and was
without any general principles.[9] Most 18th-century scholars, however,
insisted that history was in fact a science.

In his editorial preface to Allgemeine Reichshistorie (1769),
F.D. Haberlin explained that historical writing constituted a collection
of material whose underlying principle was chronological order,[10] an idea
more fully developed in August Ludwig Schlözer's introduction to Vorstellung der Universal-Historie (1772); here it is argued that the historian's task is to point out the relationships between events by judiciously selecting and editing his data.[11] Didactic effectiveness, as Johann
Christoph Gatterer explains in his Allgemeine historische Bibliothek
(1767), depends upon illustrating these relationships: "der höchste Grad
des Pragmatischen in der Geschichte wäre die Vorstellung des allgemeinen
Zusammenhanges in der Welt".[12]

One must understand the views of Schlözer and Gatterer in terms of
the Enlightenment concept that regarded epochs as stages in the progressive perfection of human culture--a concept which, as D.H. Hegwisch observed in his Preface to Allgemeine Übersicht der deutschen Kulturgeschichte
bis zu Maximilian dem Ersten (1788), led to distortions in historical
presentation. To his mind, culture was rather the result of a series of
chance causes in which, of course, the aspirations of both individuals
and social classes were involved. The argument for the progressive perfection of culture led to the prejudice of regarding the eighteenth century superior to any previous era.[13] In no other science, he explained
in Neue Sammlung kleiner historischer und literarischer Schriften (1809),
was the power of conventional prejudices so rampant, so deeply rooted,
and so enduring. As an example of such prejudice he cited the contemporary view that the Middle Ages was a period of barbarism, ignorance and
superstition.[14] It is significant that in 1790 this prejudice forms the
basis of the historical novel of Gottlob Heinrich Heinse and the short-
stories of Friedrich Schlenkert. Schlenkert's opening description of
medieval Germany in "Graf Albert von Babenberg," in the collection Altdeutsche Geschichten romantischen Inhalts (1790), reflects the extent of
this bias:

> Es war eine traurige Zeit in Teutschland. . . So viele Grafen
> und Markgrafen, Freiherren und Dinasten — so viele kleine
> Tirannen! so viele Burgen und Vesten — so viele Raubnester
> und Zwinger für Niedergeworfene! unaufhörliche Befehdungen,
> gewaltsame Uiberfälle [sic] gegen die Fehdrechte, Bedrükkun-
> gen, Beraubungen, Todschläge, Mordbrände — das königliche
> Ansehen geschwächt, die königliche Gewalt vernichtet, die
> Geseze [sic] ohne Kraft, das Recht in der Faust — die Un-
> wissenheit und der Aberglaube unter Bischofshüte, Chormäntel
> und Mönchskutten versteckt, als unumschränkte Alleinherrscher
> auf dem Throne, den Bannstrahl in der einen, das Schwert in
> der andern Hand, Vernunft und Wahrheit unter die Füße ge-
> treten. . . dies ist der schwache Schattenriß von Teutsch-
> lands Gestalt, Aussehen und Verfaßung im Kleinen, als man
> schrieb das Jahr Neunhundert nach Christi Geburt! (303 f.)

We saw earlier that in order to serve their didactic aims novelists
of 1790 were inclined to claim that their narratives were factual. They
tended to defend themselves against anticipated charges of having contrived incredible narratives and frequently asserted that their works had
at least some basis in truth. This situation posed the question of the

relationship between reliable objective historiography and fictional
historical narrative. Exploration of this problem in French literature
and criticism, as Kurth explains, exerted an early influence on German
thought. Vivienne Mylne[15] points out that during the seventeenth century
the French "novel tended increasingly to lay claim to some of the credit
and privileges of history" (20), and that "history and the novel came together over their potential effects on the reader" (22). Historians and
novelists alike assumed responsibility for moral instruction, and 18th-
century French novelists regarded it as their business to convince their
reader of the value of a particular moral view by winning the reader's
belief in the 'truth' of their story. In general practice, as Mylne
finds, writers used the term 'true' to mean 'based on fact'. She observes a trend in the eighteenth century from "novels which claim to be
literally true (and are often wildly implausible). . . towards works laying less emphasis on their supposedly factual origin, and displaying instead more concern for everyday standards of probability and possibility"
(10). To her mind, the French achievement during the latter part of the
century lay in realistic characterization.

German techniques seem not to have been so highly developed. Indeed Kurth suggests that Lenglet-DuFresnoy's De l'usage des Romans (1734)
and de la Salle d'Offrémont's Histoire de Sophie de Francourt (1768) were
particularly important for German practice because they contrasted factual reports and prose fiction. Lenglet-DuFresnoy considered the historical novel superior to historiography because, in his view, the novelist
had the advantage of being able to resort to principles of poetic justice;
he could achieve a didactic effect by showing virtue rewarded and vice
punished.[16] J.J. Engel in Über Handlung, Gespräch und Erzählung (1774)[17]
seems to have brought a new term into German discussions of historiography when speaking of "unpragmatische Geschichtsschreiber" (185 f.) as
those who describe a sequence of actions and events without revealing
their motivating forces. Historians, he explained, must write 'true
practical history' (187); they must be 'pragmatic' (188) by revealing how
events actually developed. Drawing upon this terminology, Johann Joachim
Eschenburg's Entwurf einer Theorie und Literatur der schönen Wissenschaften (1783) actually regarded novels as "pragmatische Geschichtserzählun-
gen".[18]

Eschenburg's revised and enlarged Entwurf einer Theorie (1789)
offers illuminating observations on the subject in a chapter on historical style ("Historische Schreibart," pp. 345-54). There are rhetorical
rules for the preparation of true historical narratives, he claims, but
because history has such breadth of scope the application of the rules
is as varied as the subjects treated. The salient characteristics required of an historical writer and his work are honesty, love of truth,
impartiality, acumen, reliability, freedom from all passions and fantasies, knowledge of the history of statecraft, a healthy philosophy, and
an intimate acquaintance with the human heart. Individual occurrences,
circumstances and events form the basic elements of history; other events
and their consequences may be inferred.

Eschenburg seems to argue that historical writers need not restrict
themselves to the reporting of facts. Just as a philosopher may properly
find it advantageous to explain his general truths by means of historical
examples, so the historian is allowed, and may even be required by his
purpose, occasionally to introduce judgements and reflections on the
events in his narrative. Without reservation, he adds, a historical writer is not to be forbidden digressions and excursions. But whatever the
extent of digressions and interjected reflections, an historical work
must be ordered--either chronologically or according to what he calls the
'inner relationships of events.' He insists in italics that historians
prepare a plan of their narrative, an idea which, as we will see, a critic suggested to the popular historical novelist, Christiane Naubert, in
1791. Insistence on a planned narrative finds support in an article in
the Neuer Teutscher Merkur (1. Stück, 1790, p. 228) which argues that
historical writing must cease being 'an aggregate of indefinite, completely unrelated observations' and approach 'the systematic form from which
it is now so far removed.'

Eschenburg also implies that historical writers are free to use
their imagination, even to the inclusion of speeches and conversations
which the protagonists might only presumably have held. We recognize in
such statements his inclination to distinguish between two overlapping
types of historical narrative: the "wahre Geschichtserzählung" or historiography, and the "Geschichtserzählung" or historical novel. In fact

110

he tacitly alters the long-accepted rule of Horace's poetics by explaining that historical writers may focus either on entertainment or instruction: "die Absicht des Geschichtsschreibers mag Unterhaltung oder Belehr-
ung seyn." But whichever approach one takes, the most meticulous observation of unity, and concentration of all occurrences and circumstances
in a single viewpoint remains his essential requirement. In his view,
factual and fictional works seem to differ in one basic point of style
only: the style of the 'actual historical writer' [i.e. historiographer]
distinguishes itself from the 'actual rhetorical and poetical style'
[i.e. that of the historical novel] "durch einen gemäßigtern und kaltblü-
tigern Ton" (349).

By 1790 reviewers were conversant with the term "Geschichtsroman"
although novelists themselves did not use it. In the Allgemeine Deutsche
Bibliothek for that year (vol 94, p. 445) one writer offered a definition
when speaking of "der neuen Gattung historischer Romane, wo Geschichte
zum Grunde liegt, die aber durch Hinzudichtung mancher Umstände erweitert
wird und verschönert." By 1791 the terms "Geschichtsromane" and "historischer Roman" seem to have become accepted parlance in this journal (vol
104, p. 188), although another review of the same year (vol 104, p. 141)
notes that the 'currently popular historical style' of novel is a 'hybrid.' The same reviewer, exasperated both by the new type of novel and
Schlenkerts Altdeutsche Geschichten romantischen Inhalts, observed:

> Herr S. hat schon mehrere zum Theil sehr korpulente Romane
> in der jetzt gewöhnlichen, und so Gott will, beliebten
> historischen Zwittermanier geschrieben. . . Die drey dia-
> logisierten Erzählungen. . . sind so kahl, so unbedeutend,
> daß es wahrlich nicht der Mühe lohnte, sie aus der Geschichte
> längstverflossener Jahrhunderte herzuholen.

An article in the Allgemeine Deutsche Bibliothek for 1791 (vol 104,
pp. 409-14) is very instructive in this connection, for it explains the
problems which this hybrid narrative form caused. While the new 'class
of historical novels' was very popular, it was not greeted with enthusiasm in all quarters of society as critics had apparently complained of
the 'inexcusable indulgence with which this genre of writing' was becoming current. Instead, they wanted a few novels 'of the genuine type'
written by experienced writers in order to supplant "diese Bearbeitungen
der Geschichte," which, the reviewer agreed, bear some similarity to

the 'ausgestorbenen Haupt- und Staatsactionen.' But the most unfavorably
disposed--according to the anonymous writer in the <u>Allgemeine Deutsche
Bibliothek</u>--were the professional historians who feared that the attempt
to render history 'more pragmatic' might be injurious to the 'faithful
portrayal of historical facts.' They feared as well that writers of
this 'genre of novels' would so misuse historical sources in search of
motifs that all certainty would disappear, "oder wenigstens Wahrheit und
Dichtung so vermischt werden würde, daß die Geschichte dadurch nothwendig
verlieren müßte." Such a situation, the article continues, would so
confuse students of history who were not conversant with the facts that
they would not be able to distinguish between genuinely historical
(ächthistorische) and fictional (romantisch-historische) narratives, a
descriptive term which seems to have been in current use by 1800.[19]
Moreover it was feared that novels would make the serious study of history distasteful. The author of the article agrees that there is much
truth in these reproaches, but argues that historians go too far in their
objections. He recommends certain procedures which historical novelists
might adopt in order to obviate 'the well-founded laments of historians.'
Novelists should follow the lead of many dramatic poets by indicating
their sources and pointing out those areas where they have taken particular liberties. This should be an easy matter, he adds, for such novels
are not usually based on many facts:

> Auch liesse sich den gegründeten Klagen der Historiker sehr
> leicht dadurch vorbeugen, wenn die Verf. solcher Romane,--
> wie es so mancher dramatischer Dichter [tut]. . . die Facta,
> woran sie ihre Dichtungen gereiht, entweder in der Vorrede,
> oder, damit die Wirkung nicht geschwächt würde, am Ende,
> ganz kurz erzählten, welches leicht geschehen könnte, da der
> eigentlichen Factorum, die bey solchen Romanen zum Grunde
> liegen, gewöhnlich nur wenige sind, besonders, wenn der Verf.
> sich nur auf die Puncte einliesse, bey denen er sich Freiheiten
> verstattete.

Christine Touaillon has observed that the younger generation of
historical novelists, such as Christiane Naubert (writing since 1785) and
Leonhard Wächter (writing since 1787), differed from their predecessors
in not wanting to teach either history or statecraft through the medium
of prose fiction. Their methods, neither strictly scientific nor freely
inventive, are characterized by their compromise between three approaches:

where factual accounts served as a source, they were used conscientious-
ly; where no reliable accounts were available, they resorted to historical tales; where there were gaps or inadequacies in both these sources,
the novelists fell back on invention. Yet whatever method they used, it
is characteristic that they discussed their techniques (a procedure perhaps learned from Fielding) and had a ready justification for them.

Four of the six extant novels of 1790 that deal with historical
themes designate themselves, by title or subtitle, as "Geschichten".
All deal with characters and events from the Middle Ages. Four of them
portray aristocratic protagonists, while one (Naubert's Brunilde) recounts
an 'anecdote of bourgeois life.' J.A. Bergk remarked in 1799 that such
works falsify truth and distort history, but suggested reasons for their
popularity.[20] To his mind, they set us back into an age rich in adventures, and show us customs and ways of thinking that are far removed from
the present and also have a touch of the romantic and the heroic about
them. The current opinion that 'fidelity, honesty and boldness were
germane to knighthood' attracts the reader's imagination and gives him
'the illusion that men of the Middle Ages not only possessed greater
physical strength but also a nobler and more sublime way of thinking.'
He adds, by the way of definition, that historical novels contain partly
true history and partly invented incidents, and as was the opinion of
reviewers in 1790 are hybrids--ein Zwittergeschlecht.[21]

This is the basic feature of what may be called 'the historical
novel of 1790.' It is, in short, a genre of prose fiction which treats
history as a repertory of characters and events that may be used to
authenticate moral views or to epitomize ideal human types. Under the
often tenuous pretence of historical precision, it deals with genuinely
or purportedly noble characters of political or social significance.
We do not find that inner probability that Lessing required of tragic
poets (Hamburgische Dramaturgie, 19. Stück, 1767), nor the inner or philosophical truth which Schiller felt must dominate in the novel or in
other poetic forms.[22] Neither do we find close attention to the 'inner
relationships of events' that Eschenburg advocated, nor the verisimilitude characteristic of Scott. The historical novel of 1790 is entirely
lacking in psychological insight, frequently modernizes its heroes

through either ignorance or disregard of the milieu it claims to describe, and tends to present sterotyped heroes typical of the romance. What
emerges from a survey of these novels is the curiously ambivalent attitude which novelists seem to bear toward their craft. One suspects that
they are paying token acknowledgement to the historiographical principles
mentioned earlier, but are really much more interested in presenting a
pleasing didactic fiction.

[Gottlob Heinrich Heinse:] Heinrich der Eiserne, Graf von Hollstein
[sic] Eine Geschichte aus dem vierzehnten Jahrhundert. (1790)

> Es wird Euch, theure Leser nicht unbekannt seyn, dass in der
> Geschichte des Mittelalters Finsterniss und Verwirrung herrscht.
> Heinrichs des Eisernen Geschichte ist nicht mehr aufgeklärt,
> als die Geschichte der mehresten seiner Zeitgenossen.

Having began his History with the traditional gambit that the Middle
Ages are inferior to the age of Enlightenment, Heinse resorts to conventional techniques by claiming an advantage over his predecessors. He
would be 'groping about just as much in the dark if a fortunate quirk
of chance had not delivered a few rolls of parchment' (i) into his hands.
These rolls, he maintains, had been found many years ago in Heinrich's
grave in the convent at Itzehoe. Heinse thus poses as the editor and
translator 'into modern German' of 'ancient documents' that contain 'information about Heinrich and the characters who are enmeshed in his
history.'[23] Like most of his colleagues, Heinse seeks his reader's approval and explains that if the present volume should meet with acclaim
and 'fortune should once again wish to play similar remnants of yore into our hands' he and his readers might perhaps meet one another again.

Heinrich der Eiserne suffers from lack of continuity, but this,
the 'approving reader' is asked to believe, is the fault of moths and
worms. 'The tooth of time has been gnawing handsomely on the parchment
rolls' with the result that 'gaps have arisen here and there' (15).
Though Heinse suggests he 'could follow the example of many of our predecessors by filling in the gaps with his own resources', he insists he
is too 'conscientious to add anything to the original source' (15).

Heinse's claim that there were as many as ten different accounts
of Heinrich der Eiserne may indeed be correct; we find two such variant

114

accounts, for example, in facing columns of Zedler's encyclopedia.[24]
According to one of these accounts Heinricus was Landgrave of Hessen, the
eldest son of Landgrave Otto and Countess Adelheid von Ravensperg. He is
said to have been named 'der Eiserne' because of his great physical
strength and the force he used to constrain his subjects and neighbouring
princes on becoming head of government in 1323. Fear of offending him
was so pronounced that a proverb arose: "Hüte dich vor dem Landgrafen zu
Hessen / wenn du nicht wilt werden aufgefressen." Zedler notes that he
died in 1376, and gives no credence to the then current view that he lived to the age of 104 years.

Zedler's second account has more in common with Heinse's novel.
This particular Heinrich, eldest son of Count Gerardus the Great of
Holstein, was called the Iron,"der Eiserne", because of his strength and
intrepid courage. In 1340 he accompanied his father to Jutland where the
latter was murdered. [Perhaps Heinse was correct in maintaining that
'the documents are silent about Heinrich's early childhood and say little
about his youth' (15), for Zedler makes no mention of these periods.]
He avenged his father's death. Immediately thereupon King Woldemarus III
of Denmark confirmed Heinrich's possession of the Danish holdings of
Fünen and Jutland and of areas of Seeland which his father had held in
fief. Heinrich tried to exchange Jutland for Schleswig, but Woldemarus
did not approve. Heinrich later fell out with the Danish throne, but let
his brother Nicolaus carry on the disputes in his name, and proceeded to
Sweden to assist King Magnus in his extraterritorial claims. Next Heinrich travelled to England, to the court of Edward I [sic], in whose service he fought in the battle of Crecy (1346) and later in the siege of
Calais. His bravery earned him Edward's favour, but gained the envy of
the English nobles. Zedler notes that the jealous English nobles un-
leashed a lion in Edward's court one early morning, hoping it would kill
Heinrich der Eiserne. However, he spoke to it, made it lie down before
him like a pet dog, placed a wreath on its head and shamed the nobles by
daring them to remove it. King Haquinus of Norway, son of King Magnus
of Sweden, had meanwhile spurned Heinrich's sister Elisabeth by refusing
to marry her; Heinrich therefore left the English court to seek revenge
in Sweden, refused the Swedish crown which was offered him, and was later

persuaded by Pope Urban VI to assume command of the Papal Army in Avignon. His journey there in 1378 was in vain, as the papal generals did not wish to be deposed and the Pope himself lent no support to the undertaking. He died in 1381, Zedler concludes, leaving three sons from his marriage to Anna, daughter of Duke Albrecht the Lion of Mecklenburg.

Heinse inserts brief summaries of the historical period at key points in the plot. This affords the reader a clear indication of what is fiction and what is supposed to be fact. His explanatory sketch of the historical background to the opening scenes describes Gerhard, the father of Heinrich der Eiserne, as one of three regents ruling Denmark on behalf of young King Waldemar [sic]. Holding Schleswig and several other Danish provinces in fief, Gerhard lived happily for two years until the Danes recognized that he was more despotic than their former king Christoph who had been expelled from the realm and was now seeking support in Germany. Kaiser Ludwig der Baier admonished Gerhard and appointed the Dukes of Saxony, Pommerania and Mecklenburg to judge him (2). Gerhard would not submit to the ruling and warned Ludwig that he would defend his rightful position by war. These details, Heinse explains on concluding his summary, are all that are needed to introduce the period in which Heinrich's story begins. He will not speak of the ensuing war as he is not inclined to describe 'bloody scenes of battle' even if they could have been documented. The 'description of bloody scenes would afford the dear reader but little pleasure.' In speaking thus he betrays the prevalent prejudice against the Middle Ages:

> So viel, um den Zeitpunkt, wo Heinrichs Geschichte beginnt, herbeizuführen. Wir sind nicht gesonnen, die Geschichte dieses Kriegs zu schreiben, auch würde es Euch, theure Leser! wenig vergnügen, Schilderungen der blutigen Scenen zu lesen. . . Laßt uns einen Vorhang ziehen vor diese Greuel der Vorzeit, und Gott danken, daß Aufklärung unsre Regenten und Grossen, und uns selbst menschlicher gemacht hat, als es ihre und unsre Väter im vierzehnten Jahrhunderte waren (3).

The early pages of the novel contain melodramatic dialogues between Gerhard 'a man whose ruling passion of ambition left no room for love,' and his wife Elisabeth, who suffers from premonitions of his murder at the hands of the Danes. Elisabeth wants him to flee with his family to escape the danger she fears, while Gerhard continues his domination of

Denmark. We later learn that Gerhard has won the battle against Ludwig which Heinse had refused to describe, but had been almost killed in the attempt. It is at this point that the actual narrative of Heinrich's exploits and the description of his 'courage and heroic temper' (16) begins. Hearing that his father's life has been endangered in battle, young Heinrich takes leave of the Duchess who has been instructing him in the gentler aspects of knighthood; 'gallantry towards the fair sex, as those of my readers versed in history will know, was as necessary as courage if one was to lay claim to the name of a Knight' (17). The ensuing dialogue between young Heinrich and the Duchess is typical of the stilted tone which dominates such scenes:

> Pflicht gebeut mir, Euch zu verlassen, und glaubt Ihr wohl,
> Frau Herzogin, dass diess so leicht ist, um nicht, wenn man
> Euch sieht, unschlüssig zu werden?

> Vortrefflich, lieber, gelehriger Zögling! Ich freue mich,
> dass mein Unterricht so schön von Euch belohnt wird--ant-
> wortete ihm die Herzogin lächelnd--Fürwahr, Ihr werdet keiner
> von den Rittern werden, die blos durch Tapferkeit sich Ach-
> tung erwerben. Doch hättet Ihr jetzt immer mir ohne Umschweif
> entdecken können was, wie Eure Mienen zeugen, Euer Herz presst.
> Wohin ruft Euch Pflicht?

> Zu meinem Vater, um an seiner Seite zu kämpfen und Gefahren
> von ihm zu entfernen, die ihm begegnen könnten. . . Mein
> Arm wird stark, und Gerhards Sohn ziemt es nicht, müssig zu
> sitzen, wenn sein Vater blutet. (I, 20)

Briefly, Heinse's tale recounts how Heinrich became a knight, charmed the ladies, fell in love, engaged in battle, and eventually married. He first accompanied his father to Denmark, but 'found no nourishment for his adventurous spirit' (27) because the country was enjoying an interlude of peace. Indeed apart from Elisabeth's prophetic dreams, only the appearance of the mysterious Brigitte, who foretells Heinrich's fame as a warrior and national leader, gives an inkling of greater things to come. She reappears in disguise some 300 pages later, when her prophecy has been fulfilled. Characteristically, Heinse claims that his inclusion of the Brigitte-scenes is based on documents (I, 41).

The narrative is at first almost entirely lacking in the kind of action and intrigue that the contemporary reader would have expected in the account of a medieval warrior. Indeed the narrator himself antici-

pates his reader's disappointment by explaining that it would not have
been at all difficult to 'weave a web of adventures and complicated love
affairs' into the present account if his 'delicate conscience did not
demand that he remain true to his sources.' They 'will find more according to their taste in the continuation':

> Bey dieser Gelegenheit können wir nicht ermangeln, denjenigen
> unsrer Leser, welche vielleicht dies Büchlein mit der Ver-
> muthung ergriffen, darinnen ein Gewebe von Abenteuern und
> verwickelten Liebeshändeln zu finden und sich bisher in ihrer
> Erwartung getäuscht sahen, die Versicherung zu geben, dass
> sie in der Fortsetzung von Heinrichs Geschichte mehr für
> ihren Geschmack finden werden. Es würde uns nicht schwer
> geworden seyn, auch in den bisher erzählten Theil derselben
> welche zu weben, wenn nicht unser zartes Gewissen uns ge-
> boten hätte, unsern Ueberlieferungen treu zu bleiben.
> (I, 51 f.)

Heinrich spends two quiet years at home in Holstein before he
learns that his father has been murdered in Denmark. Heinrich and his
brothers prepare to avenge his death, attack the Danish castles at the
cost of two thousand Danish lives, and eventually capture the murderer,
who is broken on the wheel. Once peace has been restored in Denmark he
becomes involved in wars with Hamburg and Lübeck. The narrator now interrupts his account to 'include a little digression about Edward III of
England' (I, 64). The digression includes descriptions of the English
court and dialogues of courtiers on matters of knighthood and love. When
Heinrich arrives in London, he gains fame as a knight and earns Edward's
esteem and the jealousy of the English nobles. Heinse does not use Zedler's 'lion episode' but tells us instead that:

> Erzählung von den Turnieren, die noch [d.h. in 1790!] an dem
> englischen Hofe gehalten und wie und an wen die Dänke ausge-
> theilt wurden, würde unsern Lesern wenig Unterhaltung gewähren,
> ob schon manche unter ihnen nach den Küssen schöner Damen,
> die die letztern begleiteten, lüstern seyn dürften. Ver-
> dienstlicher und nöthiger dünkt es uns, ihnen eine Gallerie
> von Menschen aufzustellen, die sie bald näher werden kennen
> lernen (I, 75).

Hence the narrator offers superficial character sketches of Edward III,
the Countess of Henegau, Edward Prince of Wales, the Countess of Salis-
bury, the Count of Lancaster, and the Bishop of Durham (I, 80 ff.).
We are next informed that King Edward and Heinrich have joined for-

ces on the Continent and have won many battles. Indeed it is the English, and not the Germans as in Zedler's account, who dub Heinrich "der Eiserne" for his bravery and daring (I, 103). The narrator remains true to his principle of refusing to describe battle scenes, but, as one would expect in a romance, introduces a love affair between King Edward and an unidentified Countess. The sterotyped emotionalism of the dialogues unintentionally verges on parody:

> Die Gräfin: . . . Warum musste ich an Euren Hof kommen!
> Warum ist mir der Gedanke an Trennung von
> Euch so peinigend! Aber brich du immer armes
> Herz! ich muss scheiden, will aus den
> Armen der Liebe fliehen, jetzt da es noch
> Zeit ist. . .

> Eduard: . . . Ihr windet Euch vergebens, Geliebte, diese
> Arme lassen Euch nicht eher, bis Ihr mir ver-
> sprecht in meinem Lager zu bleiben, um das
> Glück Eurer Liebe in vollem Masse zu geniessen.

> Die Gräfin: Eduard, missbraucht nicht Eure Gewalt über mich!
> . . . Fordert mein Leben, es sey Euer, aber meine
> Ehre, o Eduard was ist ein Leben ohne Ehre. . .

> Eduard: Unnöthige Bedenklichkeiten! . . . Wollt Ihr nun
> bleiben, Gräfin?

> Die Gräfin: . . . Ich bleibe! . . . So nimm mich denn ganz
> hin, theurer geliebter Eduard, und schütze mich,
> schütze das Weib, das wenn es auch alle Schwächen
> hat, an Stärke der Liebe gewis von Keiner über-
> troffen wird. (I, 106 ff.)

Tedious dialogues and 'a fragment of a conversation' between a certain Karl and King Edward dominate the following pages, until the narrator tries to liven up his narrative with a love-scene between, of all people, the Bishop of Durham and a court coquette called Cöleste.

> Ehe wir fortfahren, müssen wir dem Leser melden, daß der
> geistliche Herr den ungeistlichen Streich begangen hatte,
> sich in Cöleste zu verlieben. Eine Ewigkeit für einen
> Liebenden--ganzer acht Tage! hatte er schon geseufzt,
> ohne einen Kuß als Minnesold. . . zu finden (115).

Then follows a lengthy dialogue between the lovers until the Bishop embraces her and gets his kiss: "[er] beschwor sie mit aller Beredsamkeit der erotischen Mimik: Nur einen Kuss von diesem Rosenmunde!" (I, 121).

When the narrator returns to his titular hero, we find a very bored Heinrich whiling away his time in King Edward's camp during the siege of Calais (I, 123). He is attacked by jealous English knights whom he and his friends either kill or wound. This incident leads to lengthy dialogues in which Heinrich complains to King Edward of the treatment he has received at the hands of supposed allies (130-141). The intrigues of Edward's wife increase the ranks of Heinrich's English enemies, while the coquette Cöleste uses the Bishop to spy on the Queen's behalf, paying him with moments of love. Calais finally capitulates to the English besiegers (I, 155) and Heinrich becomes involved in rescuing a certain Countess who has been kidnapped by robbers. At this point, Heinse's novel disintegrates into a romance with multiple plots of adventure and intrigue, and the rescue by gallant knights of women in distress. Heinrich gains even greater renown as a chivalrous knight and audacious warrior, and is wooed by foreign kings and princes who would have him lead their armies.

Towards the end of the first volume, Heinrich and his band become lost and are warned by a stranger not to take shelter in a nearby castle, as it is ruled by a treacherous Baron. Heinrich disregards the warning, is robbed of his weapons and threatened with death. Part One ends with a meagre attempt at gothic horror: "Verrätherey! schrie Heinrich mit fürchterlicher Stimme. Der Burgbesitzer trat jetzt in das Zimmer und lachte" (I, 202).

Part Two does not begin where the first part ended, but opens with a conversation between a recently rescued Countess and a knight. Finally it 'occurs' to the narrator that he has left his hero 'in a situation which must have made all readers concerned about Heinrich's fate' (II, 211; continuous pagination from Part One). We now learn that the owner of the castle ist Eustache de Saint Pierre, who during the siege of Calais was made to stand for hours with a noose around his neck until King Edward had freed him and his five fellow-citizens. As Heinrich had fought at Edward's side during the siege, Eustache had wanted to revenge himself by making him stand in fear of death for two hours with a noose about _his_ neck. Having done so, he releases Heinrich, whereupon the two men become firm friends. After many further battles and deeds of heroism Heinrich's thirst for fame is slaked: "Sein Durst nach Ruhm war gesättigt" (II, 317).

Up to this point, Heinrich has always gone to war to gain earthly

goods--um irdische Güter zu erwerben (II, 471)--but now has an opportunity for having his sins forgiven by fighting for Pope Urban VI against
Clement VI. He soon realises, however, that this is a pointless war, and
returns home to spend two years in seclusion. 'Nothing worth telling
happened in this period' (II, 489). The novel concludes with the aged
Heinrich dying peacefully, lamented by all who knew him. He leaves his
countrymen the memory of 'a great man and worthy ruler,' and his body is
placed beside the coffin of his wife in the family vault of the Convent
of Itzehoe (II, 489).

Heinse's novel was not reviewed when it first appeared, though the
second edition (1791) drew a very terse commentary from the Allgemeine
Deutsche Bibliothek for 1793 (vol 115): 'Perhaps the author would have
been more successful if he had given us a historical fragment of the life
of Heinrich the Iron. His novel is too cold; whenever he tries to create a moving scene we remain unmoved.' The reviewer seems to have felt
that Heinse had fallen between two chairs: he had neither written a good
novel, which would have demanded stirring scenes of love and adventure,
nor had he provided an objective historical account, but had unsuccess-
fully attempted to combine the two in what other reviewers called the
hybrid form of the historical novel. One need only think of the mystifi-
cations caused by prophetic dreams and prophecies, the emphasis on idealized heroes, the stereotyped love intrigues, together with the multiple
and often confusing plots, to recognize that Heinrich der Eiserne--de-
spite its setting against a specific historical background and its array
of actual or credible historical occurrences and personalities--is essentially a romance.

Christiane Benedicte Naubert: Introduction

Naubert began publishing her novels anonymously in 1785. In the
next ten years, the most prolific years of her career as a writer, she
published thirty-five historical novels in fifty-three volumes. A reviewer in the Allgemeine Deutsche Bibliothek for 1791 (vol 104, pp. 188-
90) commented on this mass production when introducing her Werner, Graf
von Bernburg:

> Schon wieder ein vollwichtiger Knabe aus dem fruchtbaren
> Schooße der ungenannten Muse, die in einer Zeit von kaum
> drey Jahren _funfzehn_ bis _sechzehen_ Produkte ihrer Zeugungs-
> kraft, männlichen und weiblichen Geschlechts, in die Welt
> gesetzt hat. Jede Niederkunft scheint, statt sie zu schwä-
> chen, ihr neue Kräfte zu geben, und wenn man den jüngstge-
> bornen Kindern schon nicht nachrühmen kann, daß sie sonder-
> liche Vorzüge vor ihren ältern Geschwistern verdienten,
> so sind sie doch auch in keinem Betracht schwächlicher,
> oder schlechter. Ohne Metapher -- Die Fertigkeit des unbe-
> kannten Verfasser, Romane zu fabriciren, sucht ihres Gleichen,
> und übersteigt fast alle Vorstellung. Gegen ihn ist der
> fingerfixe Pariser Mr. Retif de la Bretonne ein bedächtiger
> Scribent. Hat er diese seine Geschichtsromane nicht in
> mehrern Jahren ausgearbeitet, und nur erst in dem angegebe-
> nen Zeitraum so rasch hintereinander abdrucken lassen, was
> aber gar nicht wahrscheinlich ist: so begreift man nicht,
> wo er die Zeit nur zum Niederschreiben hernehmen kann?

The reviewer may have been aided in attributing all these works to a
single author by their similarity in style and narrative technique, and
by the fact that they were all published by Weygand of Leipzig. Yet this
still left room for doubt. Meusel, for instance, attributes Naubert's
Alf von Dülmen to Gottlob Heinrich Heinse (Das Gelehrte Teutschland, III,
171). Admittedly, the reviewer commented, invention and organisation
usually caused this author no great trouble, for in none of his novels
was there a firm plan, central interest or main character to which everything else was subordinated.

According to Touaillon,[25] Naubert used historical data in four
distinct ways: either as the main element of a novel, as a side interest
in the narrative, as a background, or as a source for a few motifs. Her
approach was to choose first an historical work from which she derived
the basic outline of her story, the significance of its action, and the
chain of events and circumstances. This work was a source for 'learned'
quotations which she used as trimming for her novel. In those novels
whose action took place in the more remote past she tended to restrict
herself to a single source work. Touaillon suggests this was due to the
scarcity of historical documentation for the earlier periods. The later
the historical events portrayed in her novels, the greater number of
source works Naubert claimed to have consulted. From the standpoint of
the modern historical novel, Touaillon explains, the majority of Naubert's
works can only be described as pseudo-historical, as the historical

features only form 'the outer trappings' and have little to do with action and character.[26] The evidence of Naubert's fiction of 1790 supports these findings. Her novels, as Touaillon observed, tend to be similar in their general characteristics; this is no less true for complications of plot. Only the action of <u>Brunilde</u>, the briefest of her narratives, need be summarized.

[Christiane Benedicte Naubert:] <u>Brunilde. Eine Anekdote aus dem bürger-lichen Leben des dreizehenden Jahrhunderts (1790)</u>

    This novel recounts a 'single anecdote' (23) from the reign of 'Duke Friedrich of Austria, the last of the Babenberg line' (81).[27] As usual, Naubert does not point out the moral until the end of the narrative, consistently maintaining her pretence of historicity. Her text is footnoted throughout with supposedly learned annotations, and she insists that historical concerns are the main attraction of her narrative. Like many subjects which Naubert chooses for her novels, the tale of Brunilde is obscure:

> . . . die kleine Geschichte, meine Theuern, die ich euch
> jetzo mittheile würde unter tausend andern verloren und ver-
> gessen worden seyn, wenn sie nicht Veranlassung zu in die
> Auge fallenden Revolutionen geworden wär, wenn sie nicht einen
> Fürsten aus seinem Reiche getrieben, und ihn endlich
> einen schmählichen Tode entgegen geführt hätte (3 f.).

Brunilde's History reveals itself very quickly as a thinly disguised romance.

    Emperor Friedrich has begun to tax the robber barons and destroyed the castle of Adelmar von Kuenring. Nikolaus Seifried, a jewel merchant and former victim of Kuenring, passes the smouldering ruins of the castle and finds a young woman in rags, upon whom he takes pity. She confesses to being Kuenring's daughter Hedwig. Seifried keeps her identity secret and removes her to a convent, where he frequently visits her. Though he has travelled throughout Europe and has access to all the courts, he has been unable to find a woman worthy of being his wife; he chooses Hedwig, who marries him on condition that they move to Vienna. Brunilde is the issue of this marriage; as she was born with the best attributes of both parents, she 'could be called perfect.' We learn that Vienna was a dangerous city in those days because it was controlled by the oppressive force of Duke Heinrich of Austria and Hedwig's brothers. Hedwig grows ashamed of her family name; she resents the fact that, while born into the nobility, she has become the wife of a merchant, and is beginning to hate her husband.

Many men were living incognito in Vienna at this time, among them Ottokar of Moravia, whose mistress happened to be Hedwig's sister Kunigunde. Kunigunde visits her sister, who soon accompanies her to all the social functions. Ottokar borrows large amounts of money from Seifried to finance his pleasures and thus brings the merchant into ruin. He dies, beloved and bewailed by all the populace, while his widow is hated.

After years of mourning, Hedwig, who still desires self-aggrandisement, tries to marry her daughter to Duke Friedrich, or else to make her his mistress. The cunning and ambitious mother coaches her daughter in the wiles of the coquette so that she can plead with the Duke to have her mother raised to the nobility once again. Subsidiary plots reveal more of Hedwig's story and the rascality of her brothers. Brunilde marries an ordinary clerk for love, but at a castle party Hedwig helps the Duke seduce her. She leads her daughter down a dark passageway and Brunilde 'awakens in the Duke's arms.' History, we are told, speaks of the means which Friedrich used to 'achieve his vile ends, but the end of the event is too shocking for the narrator to tarry long over it.'

Brunilde's husband tries to avenge her, but is cut down by the Duke's swordsmen. The only solution to the problem of Brunilde's disgrace is suicide, so she casts herself out of the castle window. The populace rises up in revolt and vanquishes the Duke's minions. He flees for his life. Years later, the Duke returns to rule Vienna with imperial honours; his role as seducer of Brunilde is long forgotten. But one day while hunting, the Duke is found by Brunilde's brother, who 'thunders forth' her name and strangles him. Like her other novels, Naubert's Brunilde is an object lesson in social behaviour. Social ambition, we were informed at the beginning of her story, is not an 'illness' peculiar to the 18th century; it can also be documented in the remote past:

> Die Sucht der kleinen, es den mittleren Ständen gleich zu thun, und das thörichte Bestreben dieser, sich in die Sphären der Grossen zu drängen, scheint keine Krankheit

zu seyn, die dem achtzehnten Jahrhundert ausschliesslich
eigen ist; auch in der grauen Vorzeit finden wir Spuren
derselben (3).

As the history of Brunilde is a vehicle for her moral view she concludes
her tale by warning us to stay within our own social sphere:

Die Lehre, die aus Brunildens Geschichte fliesst?
. . . bleibt gern in eurer Sphäre; jenseits derselben
lauert auf euch Beschimpfung, Elend und Tod. (84)

The reviewer of this novel in the Allgemeine Deutsche Bibliothek
for 1971 (vol 102, p. 99) summarized the plot (presumably because he regarded the novel as worth while) and concluded by remarking that the anecdote was interesting, and well narrated; he summarized the obvious moral
that 'the vanity of marrying beyond one's social level often has sad consequences.'

[Christiane Benedicte Naubert:] Werner, Graf von Bernburg (1790)

Die Geschichte, sagt ein Schriftsteller des vorigen Jahrhunderts, ist eine seltsame Matrone, zu stolz oder zu
bescheiden mit Reizen zu prangen, welche den ernsten Blick
der Wahrheit nicht aushalten können; die Sage eine junge
muthwillige Dirne voll Begierde zu gefallen, und unbekümmert
wo sie ihren Schmuck erborgt, wenn nur ihr Zweck erreicht
wird.

Da ich euch, meine Leser, ganz offenherzig bekenne, daß
nicht die erste, nur die andere, ein wenig von ihrer ersten
Schwester unterstützt, bey diesen Blättern meine Leiterin
seyn soll, so wißt ihr, was ihr von denselben zu erwarten,
und in welchen Stunden ihr sie zu lesen habt. . .(3)

Having been duly warned in the opening lines (or perhaps, rather, encouraged) by the fact that this 'history' is actually a novel, the reader
is expected to settle back to enjoy an account of an historical event so
'confusing' and so much a 'puzzle' that 'most writers only mention it
lightly in passing' (26). Too confusing, she doubtless means to say,
for a real historical account, for one realizes very quickly that the
work properly belongs to a genre for which confusing puzzles are of the
essence. Even a glance at representative chapter headings accentuates
the kinship of this particular historical novel with the traditional romance: "List wider List" (40), "Sehr verschiedene Scenen" (112),

"Ränke" (140), "Fragmente" (196), "Weitläufigkeiten" (300), "Verrätherey" (348), "Nachholungen" (434), and "Alte Bekanntschaft" (598). The 'thread of the History' is in fact 'spun along to such an extent' (413) that, as we noted in an earlier chapter, Naubert herself occasionally seems to have forgotten what has taken place. Touaillon found this a common occurrence in Naubert's novels and attributed it to a failure to re-read the manuscript. While this may have been true, considering her massive output, there is also a likelihood that she was trying to create the atmosphere of a live story-teller. Thus while seeming to have forgotten what has transpired she occasionally expresses the fond hope that her readers might not entirely have lost sight of the events of her narrative (689).

But whatever her reasons for this feature, it is difficult to remember the host of tearful separations and joyous reunions which the lovers in her story undergo. The changes of fortune are too wilfully motivated for an historical account. Luitgard, the author writes, would simply have had to become Werner's wife if fate had not intended it otherwise (88). The lovers are the victims of a thousand ambiguous events-- tausend zweydeutige Handlungen (181)--and suffer "Wunden, Krankheiten, Gefängniss, Hunger, Elend und tausendfache Todesgefahr!" (669). The author becomes so absorbed (or rather carried away) by Luitgard's fates that she never really deals with the life of Werner, her titular hero, until Luitgard's domination of the novel ends with her death 728 pages later! Naubert apparently realizes all too late what has been happening, and anticipates her reader's reproach:

> Luitgard, meine Leser, war, wie ihr [sic] mir vielleicht
> vorwerfen werdet, mehr meine Heldin als der Titel dieses
> Buchs erlaubte; sie ist dahin, was habe ich euch noch zu
> sagen? (728)

There is really nothing more for her to relate than how the lonely Werner dies heroically in a battle which, characteristically enough, is quite unrelated to anything that has gone on before. (753)

Werner has all the marks of a romance, but Naubert assures us that it is not entirely of her 'own making, but is based on the legend of Luitgard and Erich the Unknown, which is so intimately connected with the

history of the hero that we cannot speak of the one without the other'
(3). Naubert feigns historical precision by supporting her account with
lengthy and detailed footnotes, but despite her pretence at scholarly
accuracy concedes that the legend has been perhaps 'somewhat distorted'
(4) by the passing of seven centuries.[28] But whether the legend is distorted or not, Naubert argues, it is not so divested of all probability
that it would be unworthy of retelling (4). Much later in the novel we
read:

> Wir gestehen, dass diese nicht allein sehr mögliche sondern
> auch sehr wahrscheinliche Dinge sind, ohne darum sie als
> gewiss einzugestehen. (313)

In other words, while the account may not be historically sound in terms
of documented facts, it is sufficiently close to the facts to be worthy
of the reader's serious attention. Yet in a different sense of the word,
'history' is also regarded as a body of human knowledge to which the
novelist can rightfully contribute. In this particular case Naubert's
history of Werner and Luitgard is "ein Beytrag zur Geschichte miss-
lungener menschlicher Anschläge" (758). This concept of 'history, as
we will see in Chapter VI, is particularly relevant to the character
novel. Friedrich von Oertel's Kilbur, for instance, is subtitled: "ein
Beitrag zur Geschichte des sittlichen Gangs menschlicher Natur".

The reviewer in the Allgemeine Deutsche Bibliothek for 1791 (vol
104, pp. 188-90) cannot agree with a colleague who in the previous year
(vol 96, p. 138) had praised Naubert's 'flowing language and precise observation of costume.' To his mind (and ours) Naubert 'very often seems
to forget completely that the period of her story falls in the Middle
Ages,' and attributes attitudes and expressions to her characters 'which
derive from the last half of the 18th century.' The reviewer of 1791
feels that this 'disturbs the illusion extremely unpleasantly and largely destroys the advantages which could be created' by placing 'the scene
in past centuries, into which the imagination of most readers is lured
with such pleasure.' Although the reviewer found the language to be
often very careless, he explained with perhaps a touch of irony that he
enjoyed the 'product' and wished the author well for the future. His
closing words of advice are to organise and trim: "mehr Plan, mehr Ein-

heit, mehr Kürze, mehr Sorgfalt für die Sprache!"

[Christiane Benedicte Naubert:] Barbara Blomberg, vorgebliche Maitresse
Kaiser Karls des Fünften. Eine Originalgeschichte in zwei Theilen (1790)

The opening lines of Naubert's book prepare us for a swiftly moving account of an historical figure. The year is 1546. An enraged
Charles V tears up a mysterious document, pieces it together again, tries
to read it, seals it in an envelope, and hands it to a servant without
comment. What can it all mean? No sooner is the question broached in
the reader's mind than Naubert retards the plot she began with such vigour and confesses her ignorance of Charles' purpose. She assures us,
however, that she will spare us the 'retelling' of a multitude of equally puzzling scenes in the future: "so verschonen wir ihn [den Leser]
mit Nacherzählung einer Menge eben so räthselhafter Auftritte" (I, 8).
Many pages later she comments that this first scene has never been quite
clear to her (I, 70).

Though the opening scene initiates no action, Naubert must clearly
have felt that it established an historical point of departure from
which the legend of Barbara Blomberg could be developed. In the next
episode Barbara herself arrives, unannounced and unexpected, at the court
of Charles V, and tells the story of her life. By claiming to 'retell'
the events, Naubert leads the reader to believe that she has some reliable source other than mere legend.Details of the legend, she asserts,
are "bey verschiedenen Gelegenheiten zweydeutig" (I, 15); hence she ac-
commodates them to her own understanding of the facts. But once again,
we are not informed of her criteria for historical truth. Apart from
occasional references to "einige Geschichtsschreiber" (I, 15) whom she
claims to have consulted, the historicity of the tale remains unsubstan-
tiated.

The purported reason for having written this work was to correct
certain misconceptions which 'history' had ascribed to her heroine.[29]
According to Zedler's encyclopedia, "Barbara Blumbergin" was born of a
good Regensburg family. It was believed for a long time that she was
the mistress of Charles V and the mother of Don Juan of Austria. Zedler
also reports an opinion that Barbara was really only a scape-goat and

that rumours of her liaison with Charles had been spread among the people
to protect the name of a princess who was the real mother of Don Juan.
There is no doubt, Zedler continues, that the Emperor summoned Barbara
to sing for him when he was in low spirits in Regensburg. (In Naubert's
account she does not sing to the Emperor at all, but recounts her life
to the courtiers). Don Juan always regarded Barbara as his mother and
for this reason highly recommended her to Philip II, who summoned her
to Spain in 1578 on the death of Don Juan 'in order to strengthen the
world in this delusion.' She was then sent to the royal convent of St.
Cyprian in Mazote, where she died in 1582.

Barbara's popular image was formed by 'puzzling' and 'ambiguous'
accounts written in ignorance of the evidence Naubert claims to possess.
Her superior knowledge is based on an inscription on the very piece of
bark which the Barbara of her novel shows to her avid listeners to authenticate her tale at the court of Charles V (I, 162). This is not her
only piece of purported historical evidence. Where she disdains to in-
trude into her text to reveal 'the truth about these seemingly puzzling
things' (I, 80), she resorts to scholarly footnotes. Some of them are
as long and involved as separate episodes in the life of the protagonist.
They are intended to convince by sheer weight of the evidence they feign,
but often dissuade one from reading them for fear of losing the tenuous
thread of the actual narrative. One footnote asks "meine Geschichts-
erfahrenen Leser" (I, 143) whether it might not be necessary to remind
them of certain circumstances for the sake of greater clarity, and then
proceeds to discourse at length.

The reader's justifiable doubts as to the historicity of Naubert's
book find expression very early in the words of those fictional ladies
who listen to Barbara's story at court. They do not quite know how to
take her: "Ich weiss nicht, was ich von ihr [Barbara] denken soll" (I,
161). She is either a person of 'extraordinary fates, or of the most
frightful powers of imagination and the greatest boldness' (I, 161).
They are astonished at a person who could invent such things and still
have the courage to present them as truth: "Solche Sachen zu erfinden,
den Muth zu haben, sie uns als Wahrheit vorzubringen" (I, 161). They
suspect her of being a fiction-monger--Phantasiekrämerin (I, 161).

Naubert, as we have noted, is convinced that 'history is wrong,' and attempts to solve the 'puzzle' (I, 54) which tradition had formed. Because her historical sources are inadequate, she explains, she cannot always recount as much as she would like about the strange events concerning Charles' court and Barbara's life because "wir besitzen leider nur Bruchstücke von diesem Abdruck wahrer Hofsitte"(I, 200). 'Courtly customs' form the substance of Barbara's life story, and the reader of romances is scarcely astonished to learn what they include: love and intrigue, separations and reunions, adventures, ship-wrecks, and amorous Arabian despots. Curiously enough, despite her professed intention of correcting history, she admits complete unfamiliarity with conditions at the time of Charles V. She is quite unabashed in her assumption that they were scarcely inferior to the tastes and preoccupations of her own day (I, 46). The milieu she describes is little more than a convenient approximation.

Barbara Blomberg's problem, Naubert informs us, was that she did not know she was beautiful. Her innocence made her fall 'into the snares of malice' (I, 54). Friedrich Schlenkert's description of the Luitgard in the short-story "Graf Werner von Walbeck" (Altdeutsche Geschichten romantischen Inhalts), alluded to earlier, focusses on the same characteristics. His Luitgard is also a woman of rare beauty and irresistible charms (132). As Werner, her lover, says to her: "Wer eure schöne Gestalt, eure süße Gebehrde, euren himmlischen Liebesreiz zum ersten Mal erblikt, eure Zauberstimme zum ersten Mal hört: der muß hingerissen werden zur Bewunderung und Liebe" (133). Her flaw, and Barbara's as well, lies in 'her ignorance of her attraction for men.' Naubert agrees that this is what got her own heroine into so much trouble. Both Barbara and Luitgard share the fate of those stock-types who have to suffer because they are steadfast in their love of virtue: "darum wird sie Viel leiden müssen und vielleicht bis zur Verzweiflung gepeinigt werden" (Schlenkert, 194). Luitgard's lament would be equally appropriate for most of Naubert's heroines:

-Bin ich nicht das unglücklichste Geschöpf auf Gottes Erdboden?--auf immer vielleicht getrennt von meinem Verlobten, hingerissen aus den Armen der besten edelsten sorgsamsten Mutter, der Gewalt eines Vaters--ach! dessen unersättliche

Ehrsucht und Gewinnsucht die einzigen Triebfedern aller
seiner Handlungen sind, ganz überlassen, und preisgegeben,
verhandelt, verkauft. . . (Schlenkert, 231).

The story Barbara Blomberg tells at the court of Charles V is the
ideal contrivance of the incapsulated narrative, for both she and her
listeners have 'time for the longest of tales' (I, 162). Having assumed
the role of editor, Naubert dissociates herself from responsibility for
narrative style. Hence she has, for instance, 'no idea' why Barbara
would not have shortened or passed over certain events of her story (I,
194). Abductions, encounters, and adventures are retold time and again
with new characters and places. At one point Naubert is frank enough to
admit that she has been retelling what she had 'already told ten times
before' (I, 337). (It is doubtless situations such as this which led to
Touaillon's assumption that Naubert never re-read her manuscripts).
Barbara enthralls her 'audience' throughout Part I until she must at last
leave Charles' castle and her 'wonder-struck listeners' (I, 396).

Part II is no different from the first. It continues "unerschöpf-
lich in Geschichten dieser Art" (II, 123). Naubert agrees at the end of
Part II that the "Geschichte" has indeed been long and strange; yet it
has afforded Barbara's listeners "manche nicht unangenehme Zerstreuung"
(II, 440). They believed just what they wanted to believe, Naubert concludes. The readers should do likewise, bearing in mind "dass sie einen
Roman gelesen haben" (II, 440). The reviewer in the <u>Allgemeine Deutsche
Bibliothek</u> for 1790 (vol 96, pp. 437-449) was pleased to have found 'a
good piece of work'; indeed it was 'a fairly good German original novel'
which warranted a plot summary of over ten pages:

> Es däuchte uns gut, nach so viel schaalen Producten dieser
> Art, (die aber, weil sie doch gewissen Leuten die Zeit ver-
> treiben, nicht minder gelesen werden) ein gutes Stück Arbeit
> vor uns zu sehen, das uns die an's Lesen gewandte Zeit ver-
> galt. Als ein ziemlicher guter deutscher Originalroman ver-
> dient es wohl, dass wir den Inhalt epitomiren. . . .
>
> Der Verf. scheint Schillers Geisterseher gelesen, und hier
> und da etwas von dessen Manier angenommen zu haben. So wie
> dort der Armenier, stößt einem hier überall die alte Sybille
> auf; doch wird ihre Gabe an Weissagung nicht erklärt, wie die
> vom Armenier. Die Schreibart in diesem Roman ist sehr gut.
> Manches Unwahrscheinliche in den Begebenheiten wird durch den

> Vortrag auf gewisse Art weggeschmeichelt; und die Dunkel-
> heit einiger Perioden kann durch eine nochmalige Revision
> leicht gehoben werden.

The reviewer's comment that Naubert appears to have read Schiller's Der
Geisterseher and to have imitated something of his style is gratuitous·
Having singled out the figure of the sorceress as a likely derivative of
Schiller's Armenian, he discredits his own case by adding that they real-
ly have little in common.

Christiane Benedicte Naubert: Alf von Dülmen. Oder Geschichte Kaiser
Philipps und seiner Tochter. Aus den ersten Zeiten der heimlichen
Gerichte. (1790)

The narrator of Alf von Dülmen has taken it upon himself to edit
the History recorded in certain documents purportedly found by Count
Palatine Ruprecht. The legend of Ruprecht's discovery of the von Dülmen
manuscripts and letters form the frame-work of the story. The manuscripts and the ensuing incapsulated narrative and dialogues are claimed
as the historical substance. The account abounds in credible names,dates
and places that give the impression of historical expertise. But as
we have found in Naubert's other novels, the milieu is again little more
than a purposefully vague approximation. We shall review the opening
pages of the novel in some detail, as they document Naubert's technique
of authentication. The plot itself is of little importance, as it follows the vagaries of the traditional romance.

The frame-work narrative begins with a scene entitled "Eingang
1383:"

> Auf einer einsamen Reise, deren Ursache und Endzweck die
> Sage zu melden vergessen hat, kam Pfalzgraf Ruprecht, mit
> dem Zunamen der Bärtige, in eine Gegend, welche unser Ur-
> schreiber, der seine Gegenstände überhaupt hier und da
> geflissentlich in Dunkel zu hüllen scheint, ebenfalls unge-
> nannt läßt (5).

The mystification of these opening lines accords well with the contemporary view that the Middle Ages were a period of darkness and confusion.
Ruprecht seeks shelter in the home of a commoner named Thomas Knebel, and
the two men converse. That a nobleman should sit at table with a commoner, we are told, was rather rare about "das fünfzehende Jahrhundert, an

dessen Gränzen sich diese Geschichte zutrug" (12).

The narrator explains further that 'in the German Empire of that time the power of those secret avengers, whom my readers will have encountered elsewhere, had assumed the upper hand' (17). Everything came before their court of judgement and nothing could escape their power. After this historical excursion Ruprecht and Thomas Knebel find their conversation interrupted by a crash of lightening, which shatters the so-called von Dülmen column (19). Of course, the reader is as curious as Ruprecht to hear what this column is, and Thomas tells the tale as he had heard if from an old peasant: "Hört, was ich euch von diesen Dingen sagen kann, so wie ich es beym Ankauf dieser Gegend aus dem Mund eines alten Bauern. . . erfuhr" (20). The first purchaser of the house, we learn, had been approached by a servant, who had handed over the keys of a dungeon in which a man had been held for forty years. The owner found the prisoner to be Alf von Dülmen, a childhood friend who died two days later. The narrator intrudes at this point to explain that we will never know whether this event is true or not: "die Sache sey übrigens Wahrheit oder nicht, wir werden sie nicht ergründen" (23).

Ruprecht retires, preoccupied with the 'ancient history of which the present owner [Thomas Knebel] had only delivered incomplete fragments.' The story, 'as Thomas had told him, was of Alf von Dülmen, who had died in excommunication without blessing or sacrament' (26). Ruprecht falls asleep and has a vision of 'a male figure full of majesty and dignity' (27) who turns out to be the ghost of Alf von Dülmen, prophesying that Ruprecht will one day be Emperor. Next day Thomas takes Ruprecht on a tour of the castle grounds and, pointing to some of the rubble of the old ruins, offers him a clue to the mystery:

> Die Steine decken nicht nur die Asche eines Menschen,
> der bey seinem Leben denen die ihn liebten, wichtig seyn
> mochte, nein, wahrscheinlich verschliessen sie Dinge, an
> welchen noch der Nachwelt gelegen ist und die euch [Ruprecht],
> der einst Kaiser seyn wird, besonders wichtig seyn müßen (31).

This statement astonishes Ruprecht, who immediately recalls the spectre's words during the dream. Ruprecht and Thomas have by this time reached the obelisk known as the von Dülmen column and read the inscription. Its words are recorded to authenticate the narrative:

> Evert von Remen setzte dieses Denkmal der Schuld und der
> Unschuld seines Freundes Graf Adolfs +++ -Grabe tiefer, du,
> dem der Arm des Himmels diese Höhle öffnete, und bist du aus
> dem Fürstenstamme desjenigen, welcher unschuldig für Kaiser
> Philipps vergossenes Blut büssen musste, so wisse, dass du
> einst Kaiser seyn wirst, die Wage der Gerechtigkeit richtig
> wägen, und ihr Schwerd [sic] mit Schonung strafen zu lehren.
> (34)

The 'arm of heaven' mentioned in the inscription is of course the lightening bolt that had struck the obelisk during Ruprecht's conversation
with Thomas. The two men dig beneath the obelisk and discover a leaden
box: "Es ward geöffnet, und das darinn gefunden,was unsere Leser in
einigen Stunden der Muße beschäftigen kann" (35). Ruprecht takes the
manuscript with him, becomes Emperor ten years later, and causes the
narrator to reflect on the authenticity of his source:

> Die Begebenheiten bey des von Dülmen Säule schien er ganz
> vergessen zu haben. . . und sie sind erst lang nach seinem
> Tode, vielleicht, als wofür wir nicht stehen können, durch
> die Tradition ein wenig verfälscht ans Licht gekommen. . .
> (38).

The actual History of Alf von Dülmen begins at this point. It is
documented with such pieces of correspondence as, for example, were purportedly exchanged between 'Pope Innocent III and Emperor Philipp in
1198' (57), as well as such items as a legal declaration of 'Emperor
Otto IV.' (296). The account culminates in the protagonist's 'confessions
to posterity in the year 1210' (344-50). One of many footnotes acknowledges the author's indebtedness to "die Fabulisten der grauen Vorzeit,
denen wir die umständlichsten (obgleich eben nicht die wahrscheinlich-
sten) Relationen von diesen geheimnißvollen Dingen schuldig sind. . ."
(452)

Very early in the narrative we learn that the historical accuracy
or authenticity of the events are of no real significance. No one cares
any more whether Alf von Dülmen was actually guilty or innocent of the
charges of murdering the Emperor which led to his 40-year incarceration,
"aber seine Geschichte ist nicht ohne gute Lehre" (44). Indeed, who
could conclude that 'fire and sword are the proper means for converting
those who have gone astray' (325) after having read the confessions of a
victim of circumstance living in despair (465), and 'tossed between mad-

ness and melancholy' (467). Naubert has constantly substantiated her history with documents, confessions, eye-witness accounts and letters, yet even when the tormented von Dülmen himself has discussed matters with his chroniclers, the events remain an 'eternal puzzle' (510). This same von Dülmen acquits Naubert of any historical responsibility: "Wie werde ich die Vorgänge schildern, die nur noch wie Traumbilder vor mir über schweben?" (527). There need be no doubt as to whether this narrative is anything more than a fiction with a moral.

The novel seems to have escaped critical commentary until 1793, when its second edition (1791) was reviewed in the Allgemeine Deutsche Bibliothek (vol 115, pp. 392-94). After having summarized the plot (presumably as a mark of approval) the reviewer remarked that this novel was attractively written and would long since have found its devotees. Curiously enough, he observes that the work 'keeps fairly close to the chronology.' Chronology, we must recall, was the distinctive principle of Haberlin's historiography. The reviewer finds, however, that the dream sequence and other prophecies in the novel are too far-fetched and improbable--allzuromanhaft und unwahrscheinlich--and objects to the 'profanation' of Papal decretals, the crass portrayal of evil, and the 'characteristically beautiful portraits of princesses.' As was the case with Heinse's Heinrich der Eiserne, it would seem that this reviewer was uneasy about the accommodation of romance elements to the historical narrative.

[Sophie Tresenreuter:] Geist der Memoiren der Herzogin Mathilde von Burgund: Aus den Begebenheiten verschiedener Personen aus dem zwölften und dreizehnten Jahrhundert (1789-90)

This novel requires very brief mention as it exhibits all the features found in Naubert's historical novels--including neglect of her heroes.[30] As noted earlier, Tresenreuter claims to have 'edited a novel' from the valuable remnants of a secret coffer, and to have 'dressed them up according to contemporary fashion' (I, 8). By her own admission, she prefers the costume of the 18th century (I, 26) to that of the period she pretends to describe, and makes only a pretence of authenticating her

narrative. She aims 'to be true' (I, iv) and 'useful' (I, vi) by showing
that all her heroes and heroines are punished or rewarded as a natural
result of their actions:

> Dinge, die ihrem Herzen, ihren Sitten, ihrer Art zu handeln
> schädlich werden könten, meine geliebten Leser, sollen Sie
> wissentlich nicht in meinem Buche antreffen. . . . Sehen Sie
> gütigst darauf, daß alle meine Helden und Heldinnen durch
> die natürliche Folge ihrer Handlungen bestraft oder belohnt
> wurden. . . . So werden Sie, glaube ich, von selbst auf die
> Spur kommen, daß frohe Thätigkeit, ruhige, treue Erfüllung
> unserer Bestimmung, Genuß des Gegenwärtigen -- einzigwahres
> Gluk des Lebens ist. . . .(9)

In practice, however, this 'novel about princes and aristocrats' (I, 10)
is contrived to show 'young readers' (I, 11, et passim) and 'mothers and
aunts' (I, 39, et passim) that the morals and actions of the upper classes have always influenced society adversely. She exhorts her middle-
class readers to hold fast to 'quiet domestic joys' (I, 11).

Tresenreuter peppers her pages with trite counsel: 'Longing for
festivities is among the nastiest feelings' as it detracts from the joys
of 'staying at home, cooking, spinning, and sewing' (I, 37); young girls
and good mothers should have a 'modest bedroom' (I, 119); a young wife
'will always be assured of her husband's esteem' if she is a 'sensible
housekeeper' (II, 57). Supposedly historical accounts and vignettes of
self-indulgent, sensuous aristocrats are designed as a foil for preaching
middle-class morals. The author might well have been pleased had the
review of Haken's prose features Die graue Mappe in the Allgemeine
Deutsche Bibliothek for 1792 (vol 108, p. 484) applied to her:

> Von Seiten der Moralität ist an allen Erzählungen nichts
> auszusetzen, und wer nur lieset, um sich zu unterhalten,
> und ohne zu genau auf den angewandten Grad von Kunst Acht
> zu haben, dem können wir einige ganz angenehme Stunden. . .
> versprechen.

CHAPTER V

THE SATIRICAL NOVEL

Preamble

Satire played an unprecedented role in the novels published between 1760 and 1790.[1] Based during this period on models provided by
Cervantes, Fielding, and the fool-novel of the 17th and 18th centuries,
it influenced the forms and techniques of the whole genre by applying wit
and humour to problems of didacticism.[2] Jörg Schönert suggests that a
drastic change occurred around 1790 when these derivative works were
'pushed into the background' by a new type of novel characterized by
humour and romantic irony.[3] As all novels of the period contain at
least a latent tendency towards social criticism,[4] developments in satirical literature cannot be categorized in chronological stages according to definitive canons of style. Besides, the most important stylistic devices in 18th-century satire were already well established in the
satire of classical antiquity.[5] Gilbert Highet remarks that the original
Latin word satura, meaning "motley' or "hotch-potch," describes a form in
which "the satirist tries always to produce the unexpected, to keep his
readers guessing and gasping."[6] Writers of romances had traditionally
kept their readers "guessing and gasping" by contriving complicated love
plots and adventures, one of the principal features that led Schönert
to surmise that the novel was the obvious literary form to assume the
function of the classical satura. He contends that the satirical novel
is the focal point for examining the extent to which the novel as a genre
freed itself from the rules of Horace, established its own laws, and
followed the demands of 'autonomy' which aesthetic theory is advocating
for art by 1790. He admits that concrete analyses are still necessary.[7]
The evidence presented by the satirical novel of 1790 offers no support
to Schönert's view on the special significance of the genre and the altered character of satire. Indeed we have already seen that purely
aesthetic concerns were secondary to the necessity of pleasing a broad
reading public and dealing with commercial considerations.

The principal model for the German satirical novel after 1760 was
Fielding,[8] whose approach shows that despite its "many variations,
satura is basically an imitation of a realistic situation."[9] Satirists
prefer subjects which are "concrete, usually topical, often personal.
. . . . This fact involves one of the chief problems the satirist has to
face. To write good satire, he must describe, decry, denounce the here
and now."[10] The satirist's effectiveness depended upon his ability to
pillory the object of his attack by exaggerating and distorting facts,
whereas the historical novelist strove to impart his moral views by
claiming historiographical precision. Fielding's The History of Tom
Jones. A Foundling (1749) exemplifies this interest in realistic situations. (Schönert found that this type of realism prepared the ground
for the satirical novel,[11] and we have seen that Lukács regarded it as a
major influence on the historical novel). Fielding claims in the Preface
that in writing "this history" (i.e. "this true story") he did not want
to draw upon himself "the suspicion of being a romance writer." He believed that "it is much easier to make good men wise, than to make bad
men good," and "employed all the wit and humour of which I am master in
the following history; wherein I have endeavoured to laugh mankind out of
their favourite follies and vices."[12] No German writer of 1790, however,
achieved Fielding's "shrewd, dynamic analysis of human psychology."[13]

Flessau's study of the novel of social criticism places the 18th-
century satirical novel into a meaningful context by regarding it as a
kind of 'moral novel,' a term that is not used in most bibliographies,
literary histories, or encyclopedias. It is not even mentioned in the
more recent studies of Greiner and Becker.[14] Flessau has adopted
Adelung's definition of "moralisch" as meaning "socially oriented,"[15]
and argues that most moral tales and novels (which reached their highest
achievement around 1800[16]) have this orientation. Their constant theme
is human society and its ethical, legal, economic and social problems.
Such 'moral' literature tries to improve its readers by showing heroes
who have fallen into difficult straits because of social conditions,
stupidity or thoughtlessness.[17] Flessau notes, however, that although
no specific literary form or genre called The Moral Novel has yet been
established, we can identify four main types of moral (i.e. socially
oriented) novel according to their dominant function or orientation:[18]

the "Staatsroman," exemplified, for instance, by Christian Friedrich
Sintenis' novels extolling humane princes who work for the well-being of
the citizens while the citizens work for their prince; the "Bewährungs-
roman" or "Prüfungsroman" (as defined by Becker[19]), which abounds in in-
credibly virtuous characters who triumph over all the temptations of the
world; the "Familienroman," which instructs the reader in the happiness
to be found in domestic life and regards the family as the healthy antithesis of courtly life; and finally a fourth group, which satirically
attacks presumed or actual weaknesses of the nobility.

The humour and satire of this fourth type, as is the case with
satire in general, derive from wilful exaggeration and distortion of
reality and the presentation of absurd situations.[20] Flessau finds that
the literature of social criticism presents distorted views of contemporary conditions. Its authors do not pay attention to historical events,
the particular is generalised, and the exception is portrayed as the
rule. Even when authors mention historically relevant events such as the
French Revolution, the superficiality and vagueness of their allusions
afford us no insight into the actual political and social problems involved. The readers are presented with clichés such as, for example,
that all centres of government are dens of iniquity and that true humanity can only be found in a pastoral existence.[21] The five extant political satires of 1790 substantiate these findings.[22]

Flessau ascribes the general vagueness of satire to the author's
fears of censorship.[23] This was doubtless an important consideration,
and it is noteworthy that J.G. Müller in his Preface to Siegfried von
Lindenberg ([1]1779, [2]1781, [3]1784, [4]1790) recommends in an ironical tone
that satire and political writing be permitted as an outlet for suppressed political passions.[24] Schönert agrees that fear of censorship dissuad-
ed novelists from precise satirical attacks and notes that writers could
never be certain of publishing a book acceptable throughout Germany,
simply because the laws governing censorship varied widely from state to
state. The book trade depended upon mass circulation and no writer could
afford to offend either the censor or his public.[25] Also, the readership
was so heterogeneous that a writer ran the risk of alienating large
groups if he took a well defined stand on specific topical issues.[26] No

matter how critically authors regard what they consider to be the dehumanising and debasing craft of politics, they never doubt the sovereign's or ruling prince's right to rule. Their ire is largely spent on mistresses, court coquettes, political favouritism and priests. Beaujean observes that this fact remains unchanged even after the success of the French Revolution.[27]

Satirical writers of the latter part of the 18th century were gradually turning from periodicals to the novel as a vehicle for their views because the novel was commanding an increasingly large public.[28] At the same time, the gullibility of this public and the absurdities of popular fiction are important targets for satirical novelists of 1790. We see in Müller von Itzehoe's Herr Thomas, for instance, a ridiculous hero who parodies the genre by being purposefully forced through all the conventional antics of love and adventure; Heinrich Werder accomplishes the same aim by refusing to let the hero of Eduard Rosenhain act as convention expects of him. Johann Müller's Fragmente, an attempt at writing a contemporary Don Quixote, satirically portrays the life-story of an aspiring vatic aesthete. It is in these parodies of the novel itself that we find traces of the new novel of 'humour and romantic irony' at which Schönert has hinted.

[J.F.E. Albrecht:] Dreyerlei Wirkungen. Eine Geschichte aus der Planetenwelt, tradirt und so erzählt (8 vols, 1789-92)

Posing as the editor of a translated manuscript, Albrecht recounts a tale of political intrigue in a strange distant planet 'in the present century'. The events are so comparable to 'individuals and incidents' in Germany that 'they deserve to be made known' (I, 7). His "Büchlein" of well over 1800 pages is supposed to prove on the basis of facts (I, 5) that darkness and barbarism are mankind's companions in political endeavour: "Finsternis-Barbarey-tiefes Dunkel! Ihr seyd die Gefährten der Menschheit" (I, 3). Albrecht's chapter divisions, alternately labelled "Finsternis" and "Aufklärung" throughout the book, reflect his view that politics follows an unchanging cyclical pattern of evil followed by good, with no apparent basic improvement in social institutions:

> . . . weil Aufklärung zwar licht gebiert, Licht aber wieder
> verlöscht, und finsterer es werden lässt, als es vor war.
> Das ist der Zirkel der Unvollkommenheiten, lieber Leser,
> und wenn wir uns nicht Vollkommenheit als ein daseyendes
> Muß vorstellen könten [sic], so müßte der Zirkel uns alle
> rasend machen. (3 f.)

He writes his novel to illustrate his contention that hypocrisy, dissi-
mulation and egoism in political manoeuvring are the downfall of that
ideal 'philanthropic political virtue' which the aging Duke on the strange planet had tried to establish. The Duke had ruled with great wisdom
in the knowledge that man's happiness consists in his natural freedom
(I, 7) and that laws exist solely to permit harmonious human relationships (I, 17). He embodies Albrecht's concept of what it means to be a
human being:

> Menschseyn: Fühlen, daß man andre glücklich machen könne,
> wissen, man könne es durch sich, einsehen, daß außer uns es
> Dinge gebe, für die wir in der Welt sind, und daß diese alle
> nicht um unseretwillen blos [sic] da sind, sich einen Wirkungs-
> kreis um sich her denken, überzeugt seyn, man sey ein Rad
> in dem großen Triebwerke der Natur, und störe das Ganze des-
> selben, wenn man sich nicht in demselben fortbewege. . . .
> (20 f.)

Albrecht expounds his repetitious views on the mechanics of statecraft and political one-upmanship throughout the novel, but nowhere more
clearly than in Part One (1789) during a harangue against the guile of
political leaders: "So wird Frömmigkeit zum Dekmantel [sic] der Bosheit,
Güte zum Schilde der Heuchelei, Gerechtigkeit zum Stichblatt der Falschheit gebraucht" (I, 205). This view is strikingly similar to that in
Fielding's satirical The Life of Jonathan Wild the Great ([1]1743, [2]1754)
which regarded politics as the epitome of baseness:

> With such infinite Address, did this truly GREAT MAN
> know how to play with the Passions of Man, and so to set
> them at Variance with each other, and to work out his own
> Purpose out of those Jealousies and Apprehensions, which
> he was wonderfully ready at creating, by Means of those
> great Arts, which the Vulgar call Treachery, Dissembling,
> Promising, Lying, Falsehood, etc., but which are by
> GREAT MEN summed up in the collective Name of Policy, or
> Politicks, or rather POLITRICKS. . . . (29)

In the first two volumes of his novel, Albrecht seems primarily concerned with telling a tale, though he introduces lengthy discourses on politics, the theatre, and freedom of the press. In Part III, which is no more than a loosely structured factory-product, capable of being prolonged indefinitely, his plot disintegrates. The style of the third part is uneven, its parts imbalanced; it contains inordinately lengthy essays and polemics on freedom of speech, on politics and intrigues, on Jewry and usury, international finances, literature, the occult; it indulges in peripheral schemings and cabals which have no apparent connection with the main plot. All this clearly demonstrates the truth of Albrecht's prefatory remarks that he was rushed by a deadline to meet the book-fair: "die Zeit zur Messe war zu kurz" (III, vii).

The plot is just as lean in Part IV, in fact most of the volume consists of attempts to inflate an almost non-existent narrative. Albrecht's facetious comments on writers in the distant planet who are better off marketing their products by bulk than according to literary merit seems one of the few indications of his capacity for self-irony. He continually begs his readers' forebearance for his rambling digressions, which range from discussions on contraband in luxury articles to a discourse on the raising of pedigree sheep, from a disjointed monologue on actors and acting, to a denunciation of land speculation. The remaining volumes are similar, and it is only in the seventh volume (1792) that we learn the significance of the title, Dreyerlei Wirkungen. Albrecht explains that the number three was once sacred on the planet Hidalschin, but that with time it came to represent hypocrisy. Instead of three upright men coming together to reach harmonious decisions on political and religious matters, "3" became the mark of deceit and intrigue: "Die multiplizierte Zahl blieb, aber der rechte Sinn ging verloren" (VII, 188).

Except for private judgements, Albrecht explains in 1789 (III,iii), he has no idea of the 'fate' which his book met at the hands of the reviewers. With five volumes yet to be published, he informed his readers he would continue with further publication despite such apparent lack of critical response. He viewed his decision to finish the task he had begun as a matter of conscience. He points out, however, that if his readers were not really interested in the subject itself, they must have been attracted by his manner of narrating: "es müsste denn seyn, dass Ihr [die Leser] nicht so viel Interesse an der Sache selbst, als an

unserer Art sie vorzutragen gefunden hättet, und in dem Fall wird euch
diese Fortsezung [sic] allerdings willkommen seyn" (III, 2). The novel
seems to have escaped critical attention entirely, and we can therefore
not judge its impact. A resumé of the main plot, rescued as it were
from the tangled skein of the larger narrative, will give a sufficient
taste of his novel.

The hero is a young Prince, heir to the lands of his father, a
Duke who epitomizes the benevolent despot. Fritz Beliwald, son of the
Duke's energetic, righteous and devoted advisor, encourages the Prince's
sexual instincts and leads him to forsake his principles for the delights
of prostitutes and court coquettes. Mme. Mind, the sensuous mistress of
many pleasure-seeking politicians, involves the Prince in her ambitions
to attain a high position in the Court, while the equally ambitious
Beliwald aids and abets the liaison. The Duke becomes in easingly concerned about his son, sends him away from the influence of the court,
and then proclaims Albrecht's views on the fate of all political states,
which fluctuate between barbarism and enlightenment: "Aus Barbarey in
Aufklärung, aus dieser in Barbarey" (I, 113).

The Prince enjoys some months of undisturbed pleasures with Mme.
Mind away from the court. Meanwhile the President, Fritz Beliwald's
father, has taken the industrious and ambitious young Lebenzow into his
household. The product of a 'courtly education,' he is master of subterfuge. Lebenzow quickly befriends Beliwald and becomes the lover of the
President's wife, a jaded beauty who seeks release from the sexual frustration caused by a husband who has been overly attentive to his professional duties and is now weakened by advancing years. The old President is constantly deceived by his wife and the political scheming of
young Lebenzow, whom the Duke denounces as the most candid rascal on the
face of the earth (I, 153). As the upshot of Lebenzow's scheming, the
President sends his own son on a foreign expedition so that he can no
longer influence the future ruler.

Fritz Beliwald thus spends several years abroad while we follow
Lebenzow's liaison with the President's wife. Lebenzow shows his ver-
satility by having Mme. Mind beguile the Prince into sexual excesses,
while he himself fulfills his own lascivious obligations. Suddenly we

learn that the President's last remaining domestic joy is his only daugh-
ther. On receiving a letter from the richest Count in the land asking
for her hand in marriage, the President rushes jubilantly to his wife's
chamber only to find her in bed with young Lebenzow. So great is the
shock that the old man dies on the spot. The ambitious wife now finds
her political position endangered by the passing of her influential husband, summons her son back from his expedition and presents him to the
Duke as a completely changed man. She then promises her daughter in
marriage to Lebenzow. The Duke, however, does not approve the marriage,
and the newly arrived Fritz Beliwald suggest a scheme to his mother to
get the girl pregnant. They could thus force the Duke to approve the
marriage in order to save the honoured name of the late President. This
is no sooner said than done, for both Lebenzow and the daughter are obe-
dient servants in such matters. As a consequence, Beliwald now appears
as 'a light in the firmament of politics.'

When Mme. Mind informs the Duke of her relationship with the Prince
and of her desire to marry him, the Duke refuses consent and obliges
her to take a husband pro forma to keep her out of trouble. She marries
the governmental secretary, thus adding a new force (and subsidiary plots)
to the cabal. Beliwald advises Mme. Mind to become the Prince's closest
confidante, since he realizes that her charms are fading and that she
will not always be a satisfactory mistress. Subsidiary plots cluster
about her intrigues to obtain the Prince's confidence. Beliwald founds
a secret society (purportedly modelled after many he had seen in foreign
lands), proclaims its tenets of equality and brotherly love, and invites
the Prince to follow the custom of foreign monarchs by joining as a subordinate member. Thus the Prince falls victim to misplaced trust and becomes increasingly subservient to the influence of the intriguers and
their feigned affection for him. The Prince remains under their influence until he falls in love with Heloise, the very quintessence of good upbringing and virtue, who is soon regarded as a threat to the strategems
of the secret society.

All schemes and subsidiary plots now aim at removing Heloise from
influence by forcing her to become the Prince's mistress. Political
success continues to depend on sex. Lebenzow and Beliwald plan Heloise's

144

downfall and Mme. Mind's removal from power and influence. Meanwhile the
Duke dies and the Prince becomes ruler. All the schemers and dissemblers
now cluster around him in praise and glorification. The ruler promises
to uphold his father's principles of government, but succumbs to Beliwald's wishes to have the members of the secret society as advisors.
Beliwald is appointed private advisor and undertakes to trap Heloise in
an ethical quandary by convincing her that the ruler's passion for her,
if unrequited, will lead to dire consequences for the whole nation. It
is her duty to sacrifice her virtue for the common good. Through the
subterfuge of the ruler and Beliwald, the posturings of other schemers
who regard Heloise as a future influential courtier, and through the force
of public opinion aroused by Beliwald, the virtuous Heloise consents.

Lebenzow has meanwhile been appointed to the government and, having
long disagreed with the former Court of Opinion (Meinungsgericht) which
had decreed 'the natural right of freedom of thought,' is authorized to
draft a new "Meinungsplan." Under the guise of proclaiming unity and
concord, the new legislation reverses the principles of the deceased
Duke. The immediate result is increased oppression and misery for the
people, censorship for the press and pandering and favour-mongering at
court. However, a trusted advisor to the former Duke soon makes surrep-
titious advances to Heloise, wins her confidence, and begs her to reveal
the true condition of the realm to her master. At her bidding the ruler
starts an investigation. The cabal now regards Heloise as an extreme
threat to its political security and attempts to cause a rift between her
and her master. Heloise remains above all intrigues while the Ruler is
once again involved with Mme. Mind and Beliwald. In time, however, the
Ruler begs Heloise' forgiveness for his shortcomings and entrusts himself
to her guidance. Heloise reveals the true state of the nation and all
former advisors of the old regime are recalled to set matters right.
Lebenzow is forced out of the realm, Mme. Mind is banished, Beliwald is
removed from office, and the whole land returns to its former condition
of freedom and happiness. Yet the condition is doomed to be of short
duration, for new cliques are formed and the ousted insurgents regroup
and infiltrate the system once again. Thus episode upon episode expounds
Albrecht's view that Enlightenment gives birth to light, but light is
again extinguished and becomes darker than before (I, 3).

The conclusion of Volume VIII (1792) summarizes Albrecht's concerns and expresses his view that his novel has been a successful didactic work:

> Wir haben nicht umhin gekont, liebe Leser, auch dieses annoch
> von den dreyerlei Wirkungen mitzutheilen, und hiermit das
> Buch zu schliessen, welches in Hadalschin so viel Aufsehen
> machte, und auch auf unsrer Erde seine Wirkung nicht verfehlte.
>
> Es thut uns nur leid, dass wir es mit einer Finsternis
> schliessen müssen.
>
> Allein was wäre auf dieser Erde, was nicht finster und unvoll-
> kommen wäre? Und wahrlich, Finsterniss scheint fast noch
> mehr Eingang jetzt zu finden als Licht.
>
> Ob Ihr in dem Büchlein vom Glauben mehr Licht erhalten werdet,
> wissen wir nicht, wagen es auch nicht zu hoffen, sondern
> erwarten euer Urtheil (VIII, 165)

There are some passages in the novel that may allude to the French Revolution, but these references are so vague that it is impossible to base firm conclusions on them. The next novel is clearer on this point.

[J.F.E. Albrecht:] Uranie. Königin von Sardanapalien im Planeten Sirius/ ein Werk Wessemi Saffras des genannten Weisen, aber eines Thoren unter seinen Brüdern/ verdeutscht von einem niedersächsischen Landprediger (1790)

This novel, which also seems to have escaped critical attention, is a thinly disguised satirical account of the French Revolution up to the October Days of 1789. The leading personalities and events of this period provided the novelist with a rich source of possibilities for sa-tire: an inept and indecisive king, an energetic and politically aggres-sive queen who was easily deceived by the flattery of place-seekers, and priests whose power resulted from the Church's great temporal endowments and its preponderant role in the civil administration. Albrecht's plot is heavily dependent upon the traditional devices of love and intrigue, as exemplified in Dreyerlei Wirkungen, and in the anonymous Kabale und Liebe, eine Hofbegebenheit (Ch. III). Hence he takes special interest in Louis XVI's impotence and consequent marital problems as well as in the affairs Marie Antoinette is supposed to have had in order to provide an heir, and only marginally acknowledges a faulty financial structure as

146

the chief weakness of France's pre.-revolutionary government. After devious intrigues, the plot ends with an episode based on the events of
6 October 1789, when Louis XVI returned to Paris from Versailles, where
he had been forced to sanction the Declaration of the Rights of Man and
Citizen adopted by the National Assembly on 26 August 1789. Albrecht
favoured the Revolution for moral, not for political reasons. To his
mind, as we will see, it turned the royal household from its wickedness
and made the king a human being. The following summary will highlight
the novel's structure and reflect its bias.

On a certain morning which Albrecht assures us will be the most
important of earthly days--der wichtigste aller Erdentage (I, 13)--two
plowmen come upon a mysterious book, which they hurriedly take to a
learned vicar, an authority on hieroglyphics, only to find him poring
over Kant's Critique of Pure Reason: "er sass bey Kants Kritik, und wollte reine aber auch schwärmerische Vernunft lernen" (I, 14). Thus begins
the decyphering of Uranie, which Albrecht himself finally 'edits.' The
vicar discovers from the Preface to the manuscript that it was written
on the planet Sirius, 'in the year following the Great Revolution.'
Wessemi Saffra, the Sirian chronicler, writing in fear and trembling, explains that while untoward political conditions prevent his manuscript
from being published on his own planet, it will prove to earthlings that
things are not any worse on earth than elsewhere (I, 28). The planet
Sirius is, in fact, "eine irdische Hölle" (I, 146). Queen Uranie [Marie
Antoinette] is one of the most dissolute trollops: "eine der verworfen-
sten Alltagsweiber, weit unter die Klasse jedes Freudenmädchens herab-
gewürdigt" (I, 146); the King [Louis XVI] is "ein schwacher, unsteter,
schwankender Mann, ganz von ihr bethört, ganz ihren Schlingen überlassen
. . . Sklav eines jeden der ihn nur lenken will" (I, 146); his ministers
and advisors [i.e. the Swiss financier Jacques Necker] are 'scoundrels of
the first magnitude,' his relatives are whoremongers, his soldiers are
'children'; Uranie's retinue are all whores without exception: "schänd-
liche Weiber-Huren ohne Ausnahme" (I, 147). Like the palace in Dreyerlei
Wirkungen, the Residence [Versaille] in Sardanapalien [France] is 'an
abyss of perversion and a hell of foul deeds' (I, 212).

The work is composed of three narratives: Wessemi Saffra recounts the political intrigues on Sirius while addressing himself to his readers on earth; the vicar transcribes the work into German while discussing it with his wife and drawing analogies; Albrecht adds editorial comments and reveals aspects of private life in the vicarage. As Albrecht explains, 'whenever the pastor takes a rest from his translation we tend to pause in our communication of the manuscript, for we obviously must wait until he has translated further' (II, 173). These 'pauses' afford ample opportunity for Albrecht's comments. It is as though the reader were peering over the shoulder of three narrators at once. The pastor regards Wessemi as an indefatigable bore, digressive, and bearing 'some similarity with our own authors who speak of air as soon as they see a balloon' (I, 51). Wessemi Saffra explains that he is not restricting himself to chronological order in Uranie's life (I, 106) and that it is a very complicated History (I, 133). Indeed he is so concerned with reporting the intrigues of Sirius accurately that he occasionally recounts different versions of a given incident (I, 173). This technique makes Wessemi Saffra, in the pastor's view, a credible author who authenticates everything with piles of documents, (I, 198). We find frequent traces of self-irony like this throughout the novel. On one occasion the pastor shares the reader's perplexity in trying to pick his way through the confusion of Saffra's narratives and challenges the reader to find a way out of the labyrinth if he can: "Finde dich einmal Leser aus diesem Wirwar" (II, 13). While all three authors are concerned with recounting the tale in the first part of the novel, they seem less interested in it in the second, where digressions and interjections preponderate. In writing the plot summary we have accepted Albrecht's challenge to find our way out of the confusion.

It is the custom on Sirius, as it is on other planets, we are told, that royalty only marry royalty, in order to keep the blood pure or, as Albrecht interjects, so that generations of kings and rulers become worse and finally dwindle altogether (I, 32). Another factor contributing to political upheaval is that the religion of Sirius has always been used as a scourge in the hands of those who wanted to come to power (I, 37). Young Uranie [Marie Antoinette] was born [1755] to a 'virtuous and pious woman [Maria Theresia] who was so concerned for her daughter's piety that

the young girl was put too much into the care of [Jesuit] priests. Very
early in life Uranie displayed a penchant for sexual delights, and the
'religionists, these skulking scoundrels who have less genuine religion'
than anyone else (I, 54), exploited her feelings, 'sowed the seeds of
passion,' and turned the 'angel into a little devil' (I, 55). She became
a sinful woman. All this took place at a time when the whole planet was
involved in war and in social unrest. The licentious Uranie was soon
married off [1770] to the impotent king [Louis XVI] of Sardanapalien, but
because she belonged to the [Roman Catholic] religion which forgave sins
she set forth to her new realm in 'chastity, purity and virtue' and was
duly received as a virtuous Queen.

The realm soon abounded in rumours that Uranie was a lesbian who
could not have children; as a consequence she set out to prove the rumours wrong by consorting with, among others, a young man [the Swedish
Count Axel de Fersen?] who was 'no friend of spirituality, but loved all
flesh' (I, 118 f.). She bore a child [in 1777, the year Louis was purportedly cured of impotence[30]]. The perspective shifts at this point in
the novel when Wessemi Saffra expresses the Sardanapalian [French] view
that a king's successor need not be his own offspring ('for who can prove
with mathematical certainty all the whimsies of nature'); it is enough
if the Queen produces the child. Albrecht joins the discussion, wishing
that this view were held on earth. On returning to the plot we learn
that Uranie's intrigue soon gave her complete control of the king. She
demanded (and was granted) the same liberties she had enjoyed in the
realm of her birth. Conditions in Sardanapalien swiftly deteriorated because of intrigues in love and politics, corrupt administration, squan-
dering on the part of the nobility, speculations in foodstuffs, and poor
fiscal policy. The narrative contains a wealth of treachery and lechery
of which Uranie is considered the instigator.

The castle which had been built to protect the 'happy and peaceful
inhabitants of the city against attack and the rage of enemies' was turned into an 'object of horror, inhumanity and barbarism' (I, 212). The
whole country was 'infected' with secret societies, intrigues, quack phy-
sicians, and charlatans; as the pastor observes, it should be 'the sovereign's first concern to root out' such influences from his lands (II,2 f.).

149

The greatest and most prevalent evil among rulers, he concludes, is that
they pay much more attention to what is happening abroad than at home
(II, 21). [It is correct that France's involvement in war and colonial
expansion largely contributed to the fiscal crisis in the pre-revolutio-
nary period]. Sexual perversion and self-seeking political expendiency
led Sardanapalien into economic ruin, and the king finds it easier to
replenish his treasury by exporting the produce of his land to richer
countries than by selling on the home market. Through Uranie's guile he
becomes a leech--Blutigel des Landes (II, 57)--who wants to rule 'without being the father of the people, the caretaker of laws or the watch-
man over humanity' (II, 58). The king's position is similar to that of
his counterpart in Dreyerlei Wirkungen: he is unaware of what is happening in his realm, of the poverty and of the oppression of his people.
When he finally tries to rally his financial resources to put his country
in order his advisors lie to him and Uranie refuses to curtail her expend-
itures. The main fault, we are told, lay with: "die Kapitalisten. . .
die selbst das Mark des Landes in Händen hatten" (II, 76). When the
country is on the brink of collapse a new National assembly [10-17 June,
1789] is formed consisting of the 'religionists, the nobility and the
people' (II, 115), i.e., the Three Estates. The populace sees no hope
against such odds and fends off certain starvation by attacking the gra-
naries, looting, and becoming as greedy and as hungry for power as their
tormentors.

This civil disorder culminates in the 'great dreadful day of the
taking of the state prison' [La Bastille, 14 July 1789]: "der Jubeltag
des sardanapalischen Volkes, eines Volkes was nach einem Schlaf von Jahr-
hunderten aufwachte, sich fühlte, sich erkannte" (II, 138). They storm
the prison, attack the palace and form their own national assembly. Yet
they wish to destroy only Uranie and her vile cohorts, but want to save
their king. He vows to support the national assembly, when a promising
young national hero [Lafayette] returns to the land amidst jubilation to
act as advisor to the government. Uranie's friends desert her in the
fray.

Wessemi Saffra, the Sirian chronicler, grows jubilant at this point
and proclaims the event as a 'great instructive day' for the 'Monarch of

Sardanapalien' who 'descended from his throne to humanity; may he ascend
the throne as a fellow human being' (II, 186). Uranie undergoes a complete change of character and becomes 'good', while the king and the
royal family are feted by the populace. However a new slate of ministers
causes new intrigues; the king is attacked once more, his guards are
slaughtered by insurgents, and he is stripped of all authority. He ends
his regal career as a king in name only: "Er behielt nichts mehr als den
Namen der Majestät" (II, 226).

Albert Goodman's account[31] of the fateful 6 October 1789 would
suggest that Albrecht was closely following events at this point in his
narrative. Albrecht was also correct in regarding Louis as a king in
name only, for he henceforth held office not by divine right, but by
virtue of French constitutional law. Albrecht's concluding 'editorial'
comments make three assertions which his narrative does not really bear
out: 1) a republican government is impossible because too many people
want to make a name for themselves in politics; 2) political writings
are ruining the populace; 3) there is no better form of government under
the circumstances than a monarchy (II, 229).

Wessemi Saffra 'recapitulates' his views on authorship at the end
of the work and trusts that the reader will not think his work 'contrived'
(II, 230). Indeed, he adds, it is an author's duty to 'state as true all
that has revealed itself to him as true, for only thus can the good be
brought to light' (II, 231 f.). Albrecht has taken this Sirian scribe
at his word and has parodied the conventional techniques of the discovered manuscript in his opening editorial remarks. The basis for believing
that the recorded events on planet Sirius are true, he explains, is the
indisputable evidence of our manuscript (I, 3).

The work concludes with the pastor's speculations that Uranie must
still have been alive when the account was written, for otherwise the manuscript would have had to be entitled "Leben und Tod": "Das ist eine
schöne Pastatee [sic] wenn man da sitzt, und weiss weder Kix noch Kax.
Komm, Frau, wir wollen zu Bette gehen" (II, 238). Readers of Albrecht's
novels were never to know 'how the story ends,' for he apparently never
returned to the theme of the French Revolution. His closest approach was
the superficial treatment of political intrigue in the continuations of

<u>Dreyerlei Wirkungen</u>, with its alternate scenes of 'darkness' and
'enlightenment' (I, 3).

[Carl Ignaz Geiger:] Reise eines Erdbewohners in den Mars (1790)

    Geiger claims to have written his book for thinkers, and not for
the unreflective types who, he feels, usually read novels and travelogues
(33). Yet to his mind earth had been so thoroughly dealt with in conventional travelogues that there scarcely remained anything which had
not already been treated from every possible point of view (5). Thus he
journeys to Mars, and in the sense of Terence's "inspicere tamquam in
speculum, in vitus omniam Suadeo, atque ex aliis sumere exemplum sibi"
(which is inscribed on the title-pages of Müller von Itzehoe's <u>Siegfried</u>
<u>von Lindenberg</u> and <u>Herr Thomas</u>) holds up a mirror in which his readers
can see the world as it is and as it might be.

    Now, the motif of the imaginary journey[32] had long been a popular
vehicle for mingling truth with fantasy, but the question of possible
models for Geiger's work remains a difficult one, though one can trace
the theme as far back as the myth of Icarus. Perhaps his most influential sources were the baroque travel fantasies whose central motif was
the voyage to the moon. The most successful of these was Bishop Francis
Godwin's <u>The Man in the Moon</u> (1638), which Grimmelshausen had adapted
from a French translation as <u>Der fliegende Wandersmann nach dem Monde</u>
(1659). Whereas these works centered upon sheer fantasy, Cyrano de
Bergerac's satirical moon-novel <u>L'autre monde ou les états et empires</u>
<u>de la lune</u> (1657) took account of natural science. The novels of Godwin
and Cyrano de Bergerac were very popular around 1700. The 'voyages ima-
ginaires' and Robinsonades became more political in the 1780's as the
sheer fun of imaginary voyages was gradually replaced by satire. Strong
elements of realism were added to the theme when the Montgolfier brothers
made their first hot-air balloon ascent in 1783. By 1785 the balloon had
conquered the English Channel. Behind this enthusiasm for balloon travel, as Hermand points out, lay a longing for freedom and a yearning to
raise oneself above earthly misery that reflected the revolutionary feelings of these years.

    Geiger's <u>Voyage to Mars</u> describes a journey to four political states, the dictatorships of Papaguan, Plumpatsko and Biribi, and the ideal state of Momoly. He explains that his first task on returning to earth was to write down 'this remarkable account' for his 'fellow-citizens in order to convince them that Nature and Simplicity alone can make men happy' (86). He expresses the 'pious wish' that he might be 'useful' by helping 'truth, supported by example and experience, to gain admission' into his country (54). But lest his readers accuse him of bias, he extols the power, esteem and wealth (54) of his homeland, having assured the Martians that their visitors from Earth are esteemed men of good social standing (26). His 'defence' of Germany is of course a veiled attack; the Martians are greatly amused by Geiger's account of the customs and practices on Earth and think that earthlings are 'crazy' (24).

Geiger is attentive to realistic detail in describing his voyage and differs from convention by avoiding lengthy descriptions of 'furnishings, fashions and finery' (33). He briefly alludes to the problem of air travel and the difficulty of obtaining sufficient hot air for the balloon, comments on the breakage of his milometer, which prevented accurate measurement of the distance travelled, and describes the difficulties encountered in communicating with the Martians, who spoke a hotch-potch of corrupt Latin. Thus they had to seek out priests to act as interpreters. Details such as these and brief descriptions of houses and cities on Mars are all Geiger needed to lend his account an air of realism. His declared interest is in ideas rather than in comparisons between objects on Mars and Earth.

Geiger devotes the first part of the book to a satire on Christianity. He and his companions land in the State of Papaguan, an orthodox theocracy controlled by jealous, intriguing priests whose actions repudiate the Christian ideals they supposedly represent and who prey upon a superstitious people. Only the 'present ruler,' one of those fathers of the nation that so many writers of the Enlightenment dreamed of, tries to assert himself against the power of the Church. Hermand sees here certain allusions to Joseph II, whose Edict of Tolerance (1781), dissolution of the monasteries (1782), and abolition of serfdom (1785) had even gained the favour of the Freemasons. The travellers are received by one of the chief priests, who explains the mysteries of their religion. Each day the priests make sacrifices 'to the Lord of the Heavenly Hosts,

the Being of Beings, the Creator of Heaven and the World' (14) by 'eating
the invisible God' (15). These are 'holy secrets' which 'no man may
doubt if he does not wish to invite the revenge of his God upon his head'
(16):

> --Die Religion befiehlt, zu glauben--und diess ist der
> zureichende Grund, gegen den die Vernunft sich zu empören
> nicht wagen darf (16).

The Papaguan faith is based upon their belief in a God who revealed himself in mortal flesh. 'Five hundred years have elapsed since certain of
His friends saw God in human form on earth'; a footnote informs us
that a Martian year is three and one-half times as long as an earth year,
thus we are to conclude that 1750 years have elapsed since the last epi-
phany. The earthlings are told that no one has seen this God since that
time, though 'some of His friends bequeathed documents in a large book
which records His deeds and sayings. To doubt this book is a sin, for it
is infallible; priests alone have power from God to interpret it' (17).
The priest describes the Virgin Birth (18), bursts into a rage when the
earthlings object that there is no evidence of such an occurrence, and
extols the ineffable love of God, who sacrificed His Son ('who was really
himself') for the redemption of future generations of man by condemning
Him 'to the most horrible death' (21). Since that time the only means of
redemption lies in 'certain ceremonies in which our heads are washed with
water' (22).

Stupified and outraged, the earthlings accuse the Martian priest
of uttering tasteless lies which make God 'into one of the most wilful
and malicious tyrants' (22), whereupon this priest of ineffable love in-
cites a mob to stone the blasphemers to death (23). The voyagers are
cast into prison, where they ponder 'the crass contradictions and insipid
nonsense' which the priest had revealed as the 'secrets of religion.'
They 'cannot comprehend how one could possibly hold all these figaments
of a crazed brain to be sacred and venerable' (24). The next day they
are brought before an ecclesiastical court where they are condemned 'to
be burned alive without mercy' (26) for their unbelief. Geiger defends
himself by repeating all that he had recorded earlier of the priest's
conversation and recounts in dispassionate tones his disbelief in the
'truth' "dass er [Gott] der Sohn einer Weibsperson sei, die mit ihm,

ohne Zuthun eines Mannes. . . schwanger geworden" (27). Fortunately for our travellers, the ruler vetoes the will of the priests and releases his prisoners as ignorant men from another world. He explains to the earthlings that priests justify every evil deed 'by quoting passages from a book which they pass off as divine and infallible' (37). He is poisoned by the priests, but just before his death he recommends the earthlings visit Momoly, 'the most remarkable part of our world' (39). Geiger flees this 'ghastly' place "wo die Priester ihren Gott fressen, und ihre Fürsten morden!!"(49).

In the second account Geiger turns his attention to pointless wars. He may be thinking specifically of Prussia or of the Turkish War 1788/89, which involved Joseph II with Catharine II, but there is insufficient evidence to be sure. When the travellers arrive at Wirra [Confusion] the capital of Plumpatsko, a state under martial law, they are immediately imprisoned for not having passes. They must either join the army or suffer fifty strokes of the cane. As the author remarks, God may know which is worse, to fall into the hands of the priests or the soldiers, for both castes seem to exercise a kind of despotism (51). The gaoler informs them that the ruler of Plumpatsko had become involved in a war in order to 'work off his ire on foreign flesh' and was in love with a 'foreign queen' (53). His troops are dying abroad of cold and hunger and the army at home is seeking both money and men. No traveller is safe, and even children are torn from the arms of their parents. The captive earthlings curry favour with their gaoler by explaining that 'the power, esteem and wealth' (54) of earth could be his if he helped them to escape and accompanied them to earth. They slip out of prison by night and sail in their balloon past the realm of Biribi where military despotism is just as prevalent as in Plumpatsko (56). As they soar past Biribi their former gaoler describes it as a land ruled by a simpleton who is tied to the apron strings of priests:

> Das Land ist entnervt, wie das unsrige [Plumpatsko]; der
> itzige Regent ist ein Schwachkopf, wie der unsrige; der noch
> überdies von Pfaffen gegängelt wird. Erst kürzlich hat er
> es wieder durch ein öffentliches Edikt bewiesen, das allen
> gesunden Menschensinn zu ersticken sucht, und puren Pfaffen-
> unsinn schwatzt. (57)

As Hermand suggests, this is probably an allusion to Bavaria under the rule of Herzog Carl Theodor and, more specifically, to the _Illuminaten Edikt_ drawn up by Pater Ignaz Frank.

After a further day's journey they arrive in Washangau in the realm of Momoly, a harmonious and natural state in which the inhabitants hold everything in common. "Momoly" may be a pun on "Mother Colony," i.e., the State of Massachusetts, while Washangau alludes to Washington, which was founded in 1790. The fact that Philadelphia, the first capital of the United States, is given as the fictional place of publication lends support to this interpretation. In this realm there are neither 'gates nor guards.' Boys and girls copulate in public as naturally 'as one passes water' (60). Money, luxury and wealth are unknown. Of course the voyagers from Earth are not entirely satisfied with what they find here, arguing, for example, that it is 'scandalous' to have intercourse in public and that decency requires man to do so surreptitiously and only after certain ceremonies have made the union socially acceptable. The Elder of Washangau, who is their guide, finds their views ridiculous and argues: "Ist eine Sache sündlich: wie kann sie durch alle Cärimonien [sic] der Welt nicht sündlich gemacht werden?" (69)

The Elder explains to his astonished and suspicious visitors that belief in God is a matter of free will based upon personal conviction, for to believe otherwise is 'bestial and slavish, and therefore unworthy of rational and free man' (65). 'Conviction is not the result of coercion and laws,' but of 'the free use of Reason, this noble gift of the deity which alone raises us above other animals' (65 f.). He urges the earthlings to love Nature, which leads none of its creatures to ruin, though it seeks vengeance when suppressed. The Elder's polemics end in a cry of anguish: "O Menschen! wie könnt ihr doch elend genug sein, Euch von der Natur zu entfernen" (72).

Geiger and his fellow travellers are persuaded that their own political constitution with its 'misconstrued Enlightenment and refinement of manners' is actually a condition of 'slavery to unnatural laws, deceit, greed and despotism' (79 ff.). Geiger's 'heart was so full' that he could not utter a word during the trip back to Earth, yet he finally burst forth in unrestrained praise of the ideal realm of natural man:

O drei und viermal glückliches Land! rief ich endlich
voll Begeisterung aus: das keine Pfaffen, keine Aerzte,
keine Soldaten und--keine Könige hat ! ! ! ! (83 f.)

The value of this work for the literary historian lies in its highly
condensed manner of presenting most of the elements found in the politi-
cally-oriented novel of 1790. Hermand, who reprinted it in 1967, regarded it as a relatively successful synthesis of satire and utopia. The reviewer in the Allgemeine Deutsche Bibliothek for 1791 (vol. 104, pp. 187-
88), however, was perhaps more correct. He commented that this type of
satire had been overworked by that time to such an extent that only an
uncommonly high degree of wit and whimsy could give it some appeal and a
semblance of novelty--qualities which are lacking in Reise eines Erdbewohners in den Mars:

Die Spöttereyen und Klagen über Religionsgeheimniße,
Priestertyranney, Militärdespotismus usw. sind schon
unzählichemal und fast mit denselben Worten da gewesen. . .
Auf solche abgenutzte Tiraden bildet sich mancher schaale
Kopf Wunder was ein, und doch sieht man nur zu deutlich,
daß sie nichts dabey denken, und selbst nicht wissen,
was sie wollen.

[Karl Friedrich Bahrdt:] Ala Lama oder der König unter den Schäfern,
auch ein goldener Spiegel (1790)

Sten G. Flygt has pointed out Bahrdt's tendency to cast his ideas
in the form of fiction even in his autobiography and in his New Testament
studies, and found the same inclination in Ala Lama and Yhakanpol.[33] Yet
polemical purposes predominate over his interest in writing entertaining
fiction. Bahrdt's indebtedness to his former associate Wieland is apparent in the subtitle to Ala Lama, but whereas Wieland's Goldener Spiegel
oder die Geschichte der Könige von Scheschian (1772) is in the form of a
fantastic oriental romance containing precepts for rulers who would go-
vern according to enlightened principles, Bahrdt's companion piece is
merely a vehicle for satirical attacks on objects of his displeasure,
ranging from his own wife to Joseph II's Edict of Toleration (1781). The
strength of his novel rests upon the same elements of love and intrigue
that we observed in the Novel of Love and Adventure. A chapter title of
a typical episode informs us, for example, that one of the principal

characters 'finds the path to the throne in the labyrinths of love' (II,
103). Situations such as this, which we know already from Albrecht's
Dreyerlei Wirkungen, reflect Bahrdt's views on the mechanics of politics.
His attitude to the Church of Rome scarcely differs from Geiger's attitude to Christianity in general, for in Ala Lama's kingdom priests, prostitutes and corrupt ministers divest the king of his power while a court
coquette saves the honour of God:

> So rettete eine Buhldirne die Ehre des [Gottes] Bohama.
> So spielten Pfaffen mit Religion und Staat. So ward ein
> König, erst mit einem Hunde, dann mit etwas Lausegold,
> und zulezt [sic] mit einer Priesterhure unterjocht. (I, 172)

The plot is briefly this: Bahrdt portrays himself as the wise
minister of state under a benevolent ruler who sets out to reform his
tiny kingdom. The chief reform concerns the power of priests, who had
corrupted the original simple belief in an impersonal numinous force.
A man had invented a god and then become the priest of his own creation.
Other seekers after privileges used the same ruse until finally, through
proliferation of oracles and temples, the people had forgotten their invisible deity and had begun to worship the God Bohama under various car-
nal guises. Political intrigues were soon based upon theological quib-
bling, so that while one sect ascribed three noses to the god (for smell-
ing out the industrious, the peace-loving, and the courageous), another
ascribed a fourth nose to him through which he could not smell. Although
Flygt notes no connection between Bahrdt and Sterne, Bahrdt may have
drawn on the theological dispute between the Nosarians and the Antino-
sarians in Tristram Shandy.[34] The benevolent ruler and his wise minister
survive numerous intrigues and theological disputes and finally free the
state from ecclesiastical chicanery. Bahrdt's 'king among the shepherds'
becomes the happiest and most beloved monarch of a land whose prosperity
(like that of Geiger's Washangau) derived in large measure from its lack
of priests and theologians:

> So ward Ala Lama der geliebteste und glücklichste Monarch
> und sein Land ward das bevölkertste, reichste, blühendste
> Land unter Gottes Sonne und--zugleich das merkwürdigste unter
> allen Ländern der Erde, als ein Land--ohne Priester und
> Theologen! (II, 383)

[Karl Friedrich Bahrdt:] Geschichte des Prinzen Yhakanpol, lustig und zugleich orthodox-erbaulich geschrieben von dem Magister Wromschewsky (1790)

This book was published under the pseudonym of Magister Wromschewsky, a writer who, we are told, had 'solicited' a Preface from 'H. Hofstede, Grossinquisitor,' another of Bahrdt's pseudonyms. Having assumed the dual role of narrator and apologist, Bahrdt attempts to present certain features of contemporary Europe as seen through the eyes of heathens. Yhakanpol, heir presumptive to a remote land governed by a wise king and four equally wise and noble priests, is anxious to see for himself what the best form of government might be. He is joined in his quest by another prince, who wishes to discover the best religion. The irony of the situation, as Flygt explains, is that they try to find in Europe what they already possess. Their route is devious and digressive. But this, 'H. Hofstede' informs us in the Preface (vii f.), has been planned by Magister Wromschewsky so that 'the sad experiences' which the prince undergoes will 'confirm him in true wisdom and defend him from further curiosity for new things.' The narrator informs us now and again that he cannot give us all the details one might expect of a travelogue because, to cite but one example, the sources of the history upon which he draws are incomplete: "Die Reise der Durchlauchtigsten Wanderer ging jetzt gerades weges nach der Schweiz, ob zu Fuss oder mit Extrapost, kan ich nicht sagen, weil die Quellen der Geschichte mich verlassen, aus welchen ich schöpfe" (192). One gains the impression, however, that he is not as interested in telling a tale as in propounding his views.

The royal travellers have disastrous experiences with prostitutes, rakes and quacks in England, are aghast at the power of money in Holland, and are overwhelmed in Cologne by the absurdities of Catholic worship. Religion and esoteric philosophies remain the principal objects of Bahrdt's attacks, and his approach differs little from that in Ala Lama. Thus when the princes arrive in Basel they encounter Lavater's Physiognomik and Aussichten in die Ewigkeit (parodied in other novels of the period), become involved in silly escapades with dilettantes who are convinced of the infallibility of Lavater's works, and eventually visit Lavater himself, whose ideas Bahrdt pillories as silly beyond ridicule.

They return to Germany, and on hearing Pastor Goeze's sermons in Hamburg, are cured of the illusion that the perfect religion might be found in Europe. Yhakanpol has a certain lightness of touch which is absent in Ala Lama, but polemics, ridicule and invective remain Bahrdt's principal tools.

The fact that Yhakanpol obtained a 22-page review in the Allgemeine Deutsche Bibliothek for 1792 (vol 110, pp. 119-141) is due to Bahrdt's notoriety and not to the literary merit of his book; his identity was easily recognized, as was his intent of overwhelming his opponents with the acidity of his own opinions:

> Wenn sich gleich der Verf. dieses Buches nicht genennt [sic]
> hat, so ist er doch durch mehr, als ein demselben ausgeprägtes
> charakteristisches Merkmal kennbar genug; denn man darf hier
> nur wenige Blätter lesen, um Bahrdt's laute Fusstritte zu hören.
> (120)

Whoever can ignore the personal invective and vulgarities, the reviewer concedes,will find the book entertaining enough:

> Wer sich über die ewigen Anzüglichkeiten, über die höchst
> eckelhaften persönlichen Ausfälle und gehäufte literari-
> schen Indecenzen hinwegsetzen kann, der wird bey diesem
> Buch, wenn es ihm bloss um Unterhaltung und Zeitkürzung
> zu thun ist, seine Absicht nicht verfehlen.

[August von Kotzebue:] Die gefährliche Wette. Ein kleiner Roman in zwölf Kapiteln (1790)

> "Wer ein Weib hat, jung, schön,
> zärtlich und geistvoll: dreimal
> glücklich der, so lange es ihm
> nur nicht einfällt, ihre Treue
> auf eine untrügliche Probe zu
> stellen."
> (G.C. Kellner, Chinesische Hiero-
> glyphen, 1791, p. 261)

Kotzebue's "kleiner Roman", the 'child' of his 'mischievous whim' (iii), is a "muthwilliger Scherz" (7) which puts the middle-class marriage to the kind of test against which moralists like Kellner had warned. Kotzebue's humour is sharp and to the point. He even includes himself among the objects of his satire, when he explains the principle of his tale:

> . . . wenn es mir vergönnt wäre, die Gardinen aller Ehe-
> betten in ganz Europa, die meinige nicht ausgenommen,
> mit dreister Hand vor euern lüsternen Bliken [sic] aufzu-
> ziehen, ihr würdet finden, daß auch das sanfteste, beste
> Weibchen oft links will, wenn ihr Gespann sich rechts
> dreht, und so umgekehrt (30).

The dangerous wager which the title of the novel promises attempts to
prove that he is right.

   Three young ladies seek shelter in Master Friedrich's cobbler's
shop while returning home during a heavy storm. Each of them claims to
lead the happiest domestic life and to have the most faithful husband.
Each is convinced she is more attractive than the others. The cobbler
suggests a wager to show which one of them is telling the truth; their
vanity urges them to accept. Each contestant is to give her husband a
gift with express instructions not to show it to anyone under any circumstances. Master Friedrich assigns to each of them the husband of
another, allowing them four weeks to seduce him and to deprive him of
that special gift, which would then serve as proof of conquest.

   Amalie Balg's hum-drum life has convinced her that her husband is
faithful, yet she is endowed with sufficient 'maidenly imagination' (19)
and has read enough novels like Siegwart to understand that life could
be different. Her husband is an astronomer who has never been particularly interested in love-making. He spends all his time watching 'venus
and its satellites, so that he forgot his own Venus and her satellites
altogether' (20 f.) Amalie gives him her gift and the couple retires to
bed:

> Darauf legte das zufriedene Ehepaar in süsser Einigkeit
> sich schlafen. Seine langen Knochenfinger nisteten in
> ihrem Schoose, und mussten ihr Ersaz [sic] gewähren für
> Alles, was sonst vielleicht an ihm zu kurz war. Amalie
> träumte von schalkhaften Entwürfen, den Advocaten Schwefel
> ins Nez zu loken, und Magister Balg von einem neuen System
> der Sonnenfleken. (22)

   Henriette Schwefel's husband is a gruff fuss-pot, a lawyer more
concerned with his files than with anything else. Sybille Flink's husband is a hen-pecked customs inspector, a 'hardy chap whose eyes sparked
with lasciviousness' (31). Each of the characters is a traditional
middle-class type hiding behind a facade of respectability.[35] Using

these fixed types and informing the reader that it is: "ein kizliches Unternehmen. . . einen Mann ins Garn der Liebe zu verstriken" (79), Kotzebue contrives typical episodes of love and intrigue. Each of Kotzebue's cardboard characters succeeds in winning her prize and all meet in Master Friedrich's shop on the appointed day: "O es war lustig, wie immer eine der andern es im Lachen zuvor zu thun suchte, und der verbissene Aerger auf der höhnisch verzogenen Lippe die lächelnde Wange Lügen strafte" (89). Each one had won and lost.

Now, many novels of the period counsel their female readers on the appropriate behaviour should they ever find themselves deceived in love. In Sophie Tresenreuter's Geist der Memoiren, for example, the woman is advised to affect blindness until her husband (or whoever the culprit may be) is himself displeased with his affair and returns home. When this happens, Tresenreuter explains to her readers, the 'repentant sinner' should not be banished after a stern lecture as heaven itself demands nothing but repentance. She exhorts her readers to exercise their 'innate goodness,' to act 'nobly,' and to spare the husband's vanity. Tresenreuter's concluding words of advice would seem to be the very sort of thing which provoked Kotzebue's 'mischievous joke':

> Der Mann, der zu Ihnen zurükkehrt, ist nicht frei von dem mächtigen Eindruk weiblicher Reize; er findet vieleicht oft noch andere schöner, wie Sie, das Glük ihrer Gunst auf einige Zeit angenehm; Sie allein aber haben für ihn so unendlichen Werth, dass er nicht von Ihnen getrennt, leben kan; er kan, glauben Sie mir, jede vergessen, jede verlassen, nur--Sie nicht! (I, 18 f.)

The worldly-wise Master Friedrich argues that possession of the gifts is really no proof that they were won through seduction and grants each contestant a private hearing behind locked doors in order to ascertain the facts. The hearing is the culmination of Friedrich's (and Kotzebue's) roguish plan: each woman must pay him the same price she paid for the gift or else have her husband informed of the adultery. Pride and vanity make them pay on the spot; Amalie Balg, for one, pays 'with pleasure thrice-double and would have paid more if Master Friedrich had not set limits to his demands' (94).

The moral of Kotzebue's 'true story' differs little from those propounded by serious writers like Sophie Tresenreuter; the ironic twist lies in the examples which demonstrates its truth:

> Aus dieser wahrhaften Geschichte mögen meine schönen Leser-
> innen die Lehre ziehen, <u>dass Eitelkeit oft eben so weit und
> irre führt, als Liebe, und dass eine Frau die Macht ihrer
> Reize nie ungestraft zum Gegenstande machen darf</u>. (96)

[Johann Gottwerth Müller (von Itzehoe):] Herr Thomas, eine komische
Geschichte vom Verfasser des Siegfried von Lindenberg (1790)

Müller's work is a parody of the 'usual' novel; two principal
characters fulfil what literary convention requires of them, while the
supporting characters do not. Indeed the protagonist's family is so
"unromantisch," that is, so unlike the types one finds in novels, that
they 'didn't even give their young daughter a gorgeous name.' They simply
'dispatched her with the name Margaretha, which gives poets a free hand
to allude to pearls and goose-pimples' (I, 39 f.). It is fortunate,
Müller informs us, that he is not writing a novel, for otherwise he would
have to banish the girl from his book because of her name (I, 40). His
'little book,' as Müller facetiously calls his four-part work of 919 pages, recounts the life of one Ferdinand Thomas. Although, as we noted
in an earlier chapter, his plot is 'supposed to move forward as straight
as an arrow, it would be silly to deal with the son without having portrayed the father' (I, 8). Of course, Müller has no intention of 'moving
straight as an arrow,' for he makes such extended use of digressions in
order to parody the convention of the involved genealogy that he almost
loses his reader in the process. He devotes Part One to a "Liebes- auch
Ehe- und Wehestandsgeschichte" (I, 244) in which Ferdinand's father becomes a quack doctor of medicine after having been forced to give up
theology for financial reasons.

Müller also parodies convention by insisting throughout that he will
limit his digressions. He does not wish his book to become a 'batch of
nonsense' (I, 49). In an apparently lackadaisical approach, though copy-
ing Fielding's phrases, he prods himself along whenever it is 'high time'
to get his 'rhapsodic history' moving (II, 303) and explains that without
further loss of time he will 'take the knot of our story in hand and continue to unravel it' (III, 9). He concludes the work with whimsical ab-
ruptness: "Weil doch so wohl unsere Leser als wir ein wenig zu Odem

kommen müssen, so verlassen wir unseren Helden lieber hier" (IV, 463).
The work abounds in the customary instructive digressions, polemics,tales,
adventures and love affairs, because Müller realises (with an eye to
the opening pages of <u>Tom Jones</u>) that a novel must have something for every palate: "dass in einem Buche dieser Art für mehr als Einen Gaumen ge-
sorgt werden müsse" (IV, 393). The whole point in letting his main plot
bog down is to parody the techniques of "alberne Romane" (IV, 266) which
he consistently regards as a blight on society (II, 331). Adopting the
motto of Rousseau's <u>La Nouvelle Heloise</u>, Müller explains that his book
is based on contemporary mores (J'ai vu les moeurs de mon temps, et j'ai
publié ce Livre. III, title-page). He also espouses La Fontaine's view
in explaining that every scandal-monger is really a prophet who requires
a response from society if good is to prevail:

> Tout médisant est Prophète en ce monde. On croit le mal
> d'abord: mais à l'égard du bien, Il faut que la vûe [sic]
> en reponde. (I, 179)

The strength of Müller's satire depends more upon his attacks against
the social customs, the literature, and the reading habits of his day
than on what his characters actually do or say. Indeed, he regards it
as "Pflicht des Schriftsteller. . . [den Lesern] ein Wort ans Herz zu
legen" (II, 330).

Doctor Thomas and his son Ferdinand are typical characters of contemporary fiction. Their lives are guided by what they have learned
from novels. Because they confuse fiction and reality their imagination
is 'fired up with oriental images' (I, 76), and they become more deeply
involved in the 'wretched frenzy of reading novels' (II, 337). Young
Ferdinand is actually living a novel, and the author comments on the
utter ridiculousness of the result. Yet his points are often belaboured
with such earnestness that his humour palls. Repeated episodes of love
at first sight are followed by saccharine sentimentality, bouts of melancholy, and further amorous encounters. The episodes are narrated in a
way which illustrates the intent of Müller's subtitle, 'a comical story':
the hero takes a good trouncing, falls head-first into a manure pile and
is thoroughly covered with things which a gentleman would only describe
by circumlocution (I, 59).

When Müller finally focusses his novel upon young Ferdinand's life
we learn that his innocence has been subverted by high society. The
young ladies have taught him to play parlour games and 'to his misfortune
have inoculated him with their wretched frenzy for reading novels, a
pestilence which did not particularly harm their nervous system, so over-
grown with talcum and grease, but which was very dangerous' to the hero
(II, 337). A new world of 'experience' lay before Ferdinand:

> . . . die asiatische Banise, Cleveland, der Mirakuloso
> Florisanti, die siebenmal unglücklich und einmal glücklich
> ausgeschlagene Ehe, die liebenswürdige Europäerinn Konstantine,
> die schöne Georgianerinn Rethima, Aramena,Pamela, manche Robin-
> sonade. . . (II, 339)

With the exception of the Robinsonades, Richardson's _Pamela_ and
Prévost's _Cleveland_, this 'pestilence' of novels consists of baroque
romances. The only indication we have that this type of fiction still
enjoyed popularity is the fact that Sophie Albrecht published a shortened
version of Anton Ulrich's _Aramena_ (1969 - 73) in 1782-86, which was reprinted in 1790.[36] All of these works, Müller explains, showed Ferdinand
'aspects and powers of the heart which he would otherwise scarcely have
perceived' (II, 319). As a result, he began to take an interest in girls
and 'made up his mind to fall in love as soon as possible' (II, 339).
He made no progress with the girls in town, however, simply because they
had never read any novels. Ferdinand remained undaunted and continued
his search:

> Ihm wars lediglich um den Roman zu thun. Er wollte eine
> Gebieterin für die er seufzen, für die er sich abhärmen
> könnte, die ihm am Tage die Eßlust und des Nachts den Schlaf
> raubte, die ihn die ganze Schule durchmachen ließe. . .
> In dieser Noth machte er sich einsweilen selbst eine
> Geliebte wie er sie sich dachte, und Verse auf sie, mehr als
> ein Pferd tragen kann. Er spann ihr Haar aus Seide und Gold,
> beperlte ihren Mund, bepurpurte ihre Wangen, und mausete
> Floren alle Rosen um ihre Lippen darum zu bilden.
>
> Uebrigens aber ließ er es ihr an nichts gebrechen, was eine
> Romanprincessinn haben muß, besonders war sie ein Ungeheuer
> an Tugend und Zucht, das weiß der Himmel! (II, 344 f.)

The love story is not the only butt of Müller's satire. Equally
ridiculous in his view are those novels which pretend to instruct one in

virtuous living under the guise of a pleasing fiction. Thus while it was deplorable that preoccupation with novels wasted Ferdinand's time and put foolish notions about love into his head,Müller claims with an ironic twist that reading novels sometimes had certain characteristic benefits:

> . . . . dafür aber gab sie [die Romanlektüre] seiner Phantasie einen erhabenen Schwung, veredelte sein Herz, lehrte ihn Freundschaft, Uneigennützigkeit, Hülfbegierde, Grossmuth, Unerschrockenheit, Standhaftigkeit, Wahrheitsliebe, Gerechtigkeit und Tyrannenhass, und pflanzte jenes tiefe Gefühl menschlicher Würde und Adels in seinen Busen, welches wir Stolz nennen, und allein mehr werth ist, als der ganze Schwall von Gesetzen die sich mit Rad und Beil bewaffnen müssen, um nur nicht ausgelacht zu werden. (II, 348)

This compendium of moral advantages gained by reading novels reflects the hopeful aspirations and assertions of practically every novelist who published in 1790, for, as we have seen almost all were convinced that the long-maligned novel could teach. They felt that fictional examples were more efficacious than precepts. Presumably even the satirical novels of Albrecht and Geiger, with their injunctions against tyranny, seemed to Müller as presumptuously ridiculous as the histories, biographies, and exemplary tales which were rolling off the presses and glutting the book-fairs. Novels, to his mind, were falsely regarded as a panacea for the ills of society. Readers should seek out the specialist for their special needs, Müller explains with mischievous delight and not expect a novel to do everything:

> Ergo lasse ich die erbaulichen Betrachtungen unterwegs, und verweise Euch auf die dicken <u>Erbauungen für Jedermann</u>, wo jeder von Euch, sey er Handwerker, Poet, Tagelöhner, Hofmeister, Französinn, ja Landesvater oder Hebamme, seine kompetirende Dosis Erbauung nur gerandezu unter seiner eigenen Rubrik im Register aufsuchen darf. (II, 369 f.)[37]

Müller interjects such ironical polemics throughout the novel and is never content to let his hero's actions speak for themselves. Ferdinand assumes foppish ways (which offer Müller numerous occasions to attack contemporary fashions in clothes), speaks in 'clichés and hackneyed erotic phrases' (II, 379), and is more often than not a bathetic figure: "Gern hätte er eine Thräne heraufgepumpt: aber seine Eisternen waren lens (d.h. sie gaben kein Wasser)" (II, 396). In a chapter entitled "Ein sehr langweiliges Kapitel" the unrequited Ferdinand is jilted by one of his many loves and receives her garter as a memento of their former bliss. Here Müller launches into a parody of Goethe's _Werther_ and asks his readers to contemplate the bliss of suicide by garter-band:

> Werther nahm seinem Gehasi die Donnerbüchse _mit Entzücken_ ab, als er hörte, Lotte habe sie ihm gegeben. Sie sind, schrieb er, durch Deine Hände gegangen, _Du_ hast den Staub, davon geputzt, ich küsse sie tausendmal, Du hast sie berührt - und so weiter, wie es im Wertherbüchlein des breiteren zu lesen stehet. Was meynet Ihr, wenn der arme Schelm eines ihrer Strumpfbänder hätte habhaft werden können!-O! man sage was man will, es ist Himmel auf Erden, sich mit dem Strumpfbande einer Geliebten zu erhenken!--Zwar hab ichs nimmer versucht, aber -- ich gebe es männiglich zur Probe. (II, 392 ff.)

The author refers the reader in a footnote to the page of "Göthens Schriften" (1787) where the passage from _Werther_ occurs and fills the following nine pages of text with the 'worthless' verses which Ferdinand subsequently wrote to his beloved Maria: "nun taugte der Singsang freylich den Henker nicht" (II, 401). Ferdinand continues in his 'romantic effusiveness' (II, 422) until he inexplicably changes character, casts off his ridiculous costumes, foregoes his romantic moods and manners, and sets off to university to begin a new life.

In Part Three (1791) Müller 'takes the tangled skein of his story in hand and continues to unravel it' (III, 9). We learn that Ferdinand has arrived at university and is boarding with his paternal grandfather. This is a prime occasion for the old man to recount the story of his youngest son (Ferdinand's uncle), who had been apprenticed to a merchant and had fallen into evil ways. Müller lets the old man continue at length and exploits the opportunity of lamenting the great freedom given to apprentices to do what they like on Sundays. Not being acceptable to 'good society,' they squander their time by drinking and whoring. The uncle eventually joins the Austrian army, serves the country well, and returns home a battle-worn hero, only to be posted to an inobtrusive garrison. Here Müller complains about countries which exploit the strength and vigour of their young men, even overlooking their scars and deformities when they can be used for battle, but which will not allow the scarred hero to appear on parade. When Müller finally returns to his titular hero we are informed that Ferdinand's "herrschender Hang zum Verseschmie-

den und Romanlesen" (III, 41) has given him delusions of grandeur. He
believes he is a creative writer. Poets, to his mind, are the ultimate
beings in creation:

> Ein Dichter war nach seinen Begriffen ein Wesen von höherer
> Natur und Art. . . mit einem Wort: das Non plus ultra der
> Schöpfung; atqui er war ein Dichter: ergo - war das übrige
> Menschengesindel puluis et umbra; das ist gedolmetscht: Staub
> unter seinen Füssen, und, um doch etwas zu seyn, der Schatten,
> der nur dazu diente, sein Licht zu erhöhen. (III, 41 f.)

While Ferdinand indulges in such delusions, Müller decries this
state of mind which makes complete fools of young men and 'in no way
forms their understanding and taste' (III, 48 f.) His attacks on insipid
novels, novelists who 'gossip novels before the public'--vor dem Publikum Romane bavardiren (III, 100)--and on 'review mongers'--Rezensions-
krämer (III, 119)--who bestow praise for a price dominate the work at
this point. The only worth-while works to Müller's mind are Nicolai's
Sebaldus Nothanker, Lessing's Emilie Galotti, and Wieland's Oberon.
After a brief pause to 'catch his breath' (III, 135), Müller describes
Ferdinand's plans for reforming the German language by compiling a work
in which all foreign words are rendered in German. "Tinte" thus becomes
"Schreibsaft" in the new "Kakographie." Ferdinand's literary endeavours,
however, still come to nought and the polemics of Part Three conclude as
drearily as they had begun.

The fourth and final part of Herr Thomas is concerned with Ferdinand's continued efforts to fall in love as a novel-hero should and with
his stubborn attempts at writing love-poetry and novels. Müller ridi-
cules these literary forms by 'excerpting' from Ferdinand's creations.
After the reader has been regaled with some seventy pages of his "Poly-
hymnia" (IV, 276) on unrequited love, he is treated to Müller's critique,
which lampoons the 'half-truths' his hero's 'romantic soul' produced:

> Der Schluss [der Polyhymnia] war eine halbe Lüge, der nur
> in Absicht seiner romantischen Seele (es wohnten offenbar zwo
> Seelen in dem Herrn Ferdinand), wahr seyn konnte; denn was
> seine Allerweltsseele betrifft, die wusste sehr gut, dass
> man nicht glücklich sey, wenn man bedauert wird. (IV, 276 f.)

Müller overworks his satire. At one point, for instance, he lets his hero confess the obvious truth that: "Teufelszeug von Romanen hat mich

irre geführt!" (IV, 363). Indeed any foreigner who reads German novels
in order to understand the state of the nation and the character of its
inhabitants, Müller explains, will conclude that the whole of Germany
is a madhouse. We are already familiar with his comment that the writing of novels in German is too rarely the serious occupation of mature
experienced men (IV, 378). Now he asserts that the German public was
beginning to regard 'foreign products' as decisively superior to native
works, and that people who wanted to be educated or who claimed to be
educated were reading almost no German literature, and were right in
leaving it alone (IV,440). The problem, in Müller's view, was that there
was no longer a proper medium for teaching a sound philosophy of life
because institutions such as churches, schools and universities were
suspect. Novelists and dramatists were trying to fill the gaps, but many
of them simply did not understand what they are about:

> . . . leider hat die Philosophie des Lebens noch keine Kanzel,
> unter den Herrn Romanschreibern und Komödienmachern, denen es
> einsweilen zukömmt sie zu lehren, sind eine Menge, die selbst
> eben nicht viel davon zu verstehen scheinen! (IV, 461)

[Heinrich Werder:]   Eduard Rosenhain oder Schwachheiten unsers Jahr-
zehends (1790)

Werder's work is an anti-romance in which the author takes pleasure in exposing the absurdities of popular fiction: "jene Sündflut von
schaalen Moderoman, womit das ehrsame deutsche Publikum halbjährlich in
Contribution gesetzt wird (2). Novels are one of the main 'weaknesses of
our decade' which the title promises to portray. Werder rebuffs them
'along with many other peculiarities that help to characterize the spirit
of this decade' (ii). He seems to have been well aware that it is almost
superfluous to parody certain works for some seriously intended books are
already so close to being absurd that the slightest shift in perspective
will make them become exquisitely ridiculous.[38] Whereas Wieland had parodied the French baroque romance in Don Sylvio von Rosalva by leading
his hero on the most extravagant quixotic adventures and flights of fancy, Werder's hero does everything which the hero of a romance is not supposed to do--or rather, he does nothing at all. In his dull-witted and
unimaginative way he is the anti-hero par excellence, except for an

ironic twist at the end, which we may reserve to conclude the account.

In its simplicity, the plot is worthy of a protagonist who is neither a 'usual nor an unusual novel-hero' (iii): it is the "pragmatische
Darstellung" (iv) of Eduard Rosenhain's journey to Berlin and Leipzig,
in which he experiences nothing of any importance and does nothing of any
great account. This, Werder seems to be saying, is what really happens
when real people take a trip; the extraordinary things that are supposed
to happen to extraordinary people are simply not real. The novel abounds
in suggestions of what an inventive novelist might do or even ought to
do with his hero at critical stages of the journey, but once the author
has pronounced "meine unmassgebliche Meynung" (v), an expression
and a technique drawn directly from Wieland's Don Sylvio von Rosalva,
virtually nothing occurs at all. In keeping with its parodistic intent,
this is the only novel whose 'plot' is narrated in the subjunctive.

Because Eduard Rosenhain is an anti-novel, it contains nothing
which one might traditionally expect; nor, for that matter is the protagonist buffeted by fate like the usual hero:

> . . . der Held meines Buchs [kann] durchaus nicht wie ein
> gewöhnlicher oder ungewöhnlicher Romanenheld handeln. . .
> Es sind daher keine freygeisterische Grundsätze, keine
> Spöttereyen über die christliche Religion, kein Ausfall
> auf die Landesregierung, keine Anweisung Gold zu machen,
> kein Unterricht, wie man unschuldige Mädchen verführen
> soll, noch sonst etwas darinn zu finden, woran sich heut
> zu Tage die feine und aufgeklärte Welt zu belustigen pflegt.
> Unser Rosenhain ist kein Genie, hat in seinem ganzen Leben
> nicht ein Fünkchen jenes unnennbaren göttlichen Feuers in
> seiner Brust gespüret, welches jeden Querkopf fähig macht . . .
> aus dieser sublunarischen Welt in die idealischen Aetherge-
> filde empor zu schwingen. Er hat sich nicht erschossen,
> nicht erhenkt und nicht ersäuft. . . Er ist aus Liebe nicht
> rasend geworden, hat im Mondschein keine empfindsame Elegien
> gedichtet, keine Luftbälle erfunden. . . kein Abendmahl ver-
> giftet. . . und kommt daher ganz unschuldig zu der Ehre,
> sich bey lebendigem Leibe gedruckt zu sehen (iii f.)

This compendium of Rosenhain's disqualifications appears in the prefatory
remarks to the novel, which Werder has ironically entitled in parenthesis
"(Statt der Vorrede)."

The first scene offers Werder 'the best opportunity in the world'
to let his 'poetic talents shine forth, if our father Apollo had only

170

granted him a modest quantity' of them (2). But like Rosenhain, Werder himself does not have the slightest potential to be a poet (3 f.). For this reason both Werder and Rosenhain remain comically unmoved by the beauties of nature and offer very prosaic observations about them. As 'improbable as it might seem to our readers' (8), Rosenhain was an ingenuous lad of twenty who was completely ignorant of the world (10). Yet (not unlike the hero of the Bildungsroman) he ponders what the future might hold for him and tries to feel some kinship with the natural forces about him. But the 'voice of Nature' speaks only though the groans of an empty stomach and disturbs his contemplation: "Itzt aber liess sich die Stimme der Natur so vernehmend in seinem Magen hören, dass er im ganzen Ernst auf die Befriedigung derselben denken musste"(13). No other hero of the period perceived Nature in quite that manner. Werder insists on being honest about the realities of life instead of placing his hero in situations that the readers might find improbable (15).

Rosenhain becomes the protegé of an alchemist, an excellent opportunity for Werder to 'explain the great phenomenon of the nonsensical addiction to miracles and secrets which clouds the light of Enlightenment in our philosophical century' (20). But the dull-witted Rosenhain observes the arguments and counter-arguments with a fixed and uncomprehending stare (36). Under similar circumstances the typical hero would have delved into the mysteries of alchemy and might even have pursued some esoteric way of life. As we will see in Chapter VI, the hero of two early Bildungsromane would have preferred these private contemplations to the apparent irrelevancies of public school education. Rosenhain too actually left school, 'those greenhouses of scholarship' and 'scholarly prisons' (44), but for rather different reasons. Schools had nothing to offer to a simple lad who merely wanted to live an ordinary life.

Werder's novel is as digressive as most novels of the period, pausing at every opportunity to discourse on the significance of the characters whom his hero encounters. No sooner is Rosenhain taken home by the alchemist than he meets the alchemist's wife, a character who in other novels would probably have exerted some occult or moral influence upon him. (By comparison we need only think of the fateful encounters in

Moritz' Hartknopf, which are invariably 'meaningful.') Yet this philosopher's wife 'was neither a Xantippe nor a Clarisse from the factory of Richardson and Company, neither an angel nor a devil from the ideal world of novels, but a good, upright, and able domestic housewife' (48). Rosenhain joins the family for lunch and is placed next to the alchemist's daughter. The reader 'who has been initiated into the inner mysteries of the present-day love trade' or who has read 'a few sheaves of popular novels or comedies or tragedies' (38 f.), will suspect that this situation is the 'best material for luring a few voluptuous tears from the eye of our sensitive readers.' It could earn for its author the "Ehrentitel eines Menschenbeobachters, Menschenkenners, Menschenfreundes, eines gefühlvollen mitleidigen Schriftstellers" (49). Whoever does not believe that the scene lends itself exceedingly well to exploitation in fiction, Werder explains, should examine "den weltbekannten Elendsstürmer Carl von Carlsberg," or see what happened to the hero of Heinrich Stilling who in two minutes time fell mortally in love with a girl whom he could not even see (49).[39] Werder's ridicule of the supposedly supernatural powers and effects of love in Heinrich Stilling, Siegwart, and Die Leiden des jungen Werthers deserves to be quoted in full, as it typifies his attitude to the 'usual' novels whose heroes are:

> . . . wie Heinrich Stillingen auf seinen Wanderjahren, der
> binnen zwey Minuten sich auf Tod und Leben in ein Mädchen
> verliebte, die er noch dazu nicht einmal ansehen konnte,
> weil sie eben krank war und im Bette lag, das hinderte ihn
> aber nicht, binnen zwey Minuten war der Bund auf ewig geschlossen.
> Er meynt zwar, das sey nicht mit rechten Dingen zugegangen,
> und schiebt die Schuld ganz ehrlich auf übernatürliche Gnaden-
> wirkungen; allein andere Erfahrungen haben doch gelehrt, dass
> so etwas auch Leuten begegnet sey, welche nichts von einer
> übernatürlichen Gnade wissen wollten. Es kann vielleicht
> auch daher kommen, dass sich Heinrich Stilling besser auf
> Augenkuren als auf Liebesangelegenheiten verstand. Denn sey
> nun übrigens wie ihm wolle, so wird doch Niemand läugnen,
> dass bey Rosenhain der Fall eben so gut als bey Heinrich
> Stilling möglich war. Es hätte ihm auch allenfalls wie
> weiland Siegwart weinerlichen Andenkens gehen können, oder
> wie Werthern blaugestrakten [sic] Andenkens oder - oder -
> Sie sehen, meine Leser und Leserinnen: es würde uns keine Mühe
> kosten, noch ein paar Alphabete mit solchen Oders auszufüllen,
> wenn wir damit nur um einen Schritt weiter kämen. Allein es
> wäre doch alles vergebliche Arbeit, denn von allen den mög-
> lichen und beynahe wahrscheinlichen Dingen ist hier nichts
> geschehen. (48 f.)

Indeed none 'of all these possible, almost probable things' happens. Ferdinand simply sits down to lunch and eats with a hearty appetite. 'Was he perhaps so cold and insensitive merely to spite his sensitive readers?' (50). Werder replies to his own question that it was just as well Rosenhain did not fall in love, for otherwise the readers would have had to hear "was schon hunderttausendmal gut und schlecht gesagt und erzählt, besungen, beweint, bedudelt und beheult ist" (51).

Immediately after lunch Rosenhain retires to the alchemist's study, where he is assigned the task of translating a book written in Arabic. Despite the fact that Rosenhain has never studied any foreign languages he completes his task in fourteen days. He is 'astounded' to find that the work contains nothing but the 'simple continuation of the world-renowned and famous adventures of the above-mentioned Caliph in war and peace, in the harem and on the hunt' (58). Werder interjects that 'the Arabian biographer lacked nothing in fitting out his little book according to the taste of the times with fairy stories and oriental tales, so that one might suppose his work were as representative as the <u>Anekdotensammlung von Friedrich dem Einzigen</u>[40] is in our own day' (58 f.). Rosenhain finds no trace of the 'truth' which the alchemist had assured him lay hidden in this work. But the alchemist remains convinced that 'in this little piece of writing great and important secrets lie hidden'. 'Although the outward arrangement of words' gives no clue, the secrets must be 'sought out' by closer study (62). Rosenhain is thus initiated into a method of literary criticism which reaches its conclusions by 'studying the essence right out of the text' (62).

Leaving his hero at his impossible task, Werder pauses to inform his reader that he had 'intentionally omitted all moralising and rationalising about this first event of our adventure' because experience has shown that 'this is a rock upon which many writers founder' (67). There follow twelve pages of polemics against such things as "Schwärmerei", superstition, and fashions. The 'united efforts of all writers, teachers, and other enlightened and public-spirited men are by no means sufficient' to rid the country of such aberrations (69). He has, however, one suggestion: 'Every writer, particularly he who influences a part of the reading world, should follow the magnificent examples of a Wieland, Gedicke, Biester and other worthy men, so that he might reawaken common sense'(76).

Werder returns to his hero to find him still poring over the 'simple, adventurous and often boring continuation' of the same Caliph, who 'does many manly deeds, releases a half-dozen charmed princesses, romps about with giants and enchanted dragons, and increases the wealth of his treasure-house and harem with the aid of a fairy' (80). The alchemist, however, finds Rosenhain a very shallow student; it must be obvious, he argues, that there lies hidden 'in this oriental tale very important insights into the inner being of the world and into the connections between the powers of nature which, however, could only be discovered and comprehended by masters with perfected knowledge' (80). Leaving the alchemist to recount how he became such a profound master of human knowledge, Werder turns to polemics against speculation and hypotheses:

> Ueberhaupt ist unser Jahrzehend ausserordentlich reich an
> Hypothesen, und das Schlimmste dabey ist, daß die Hypothesen-
> macher so fest von der Wahrheit und Würklichkeit ihrer
> Hypothesen überzeugt sind. . . (127)

Having made no progress in understanding the oriental tale, Rosenhain sets forth to Leipzig. This is not a usual novel, Werder informs us again, and therefore asks his readers to consider the possibilities which this second episode offers for making the book more pleasing for the 'fine ladies and gentlemen' who like to kill time with popular fiction:

> Um uns den schönen Damen und Herren aus dieser Classe von
> Lesern gefällig zu zeigen, könnten wir unserem Rosenhain,
> seine vorhabende Reise nach Leipzig, durch manche eingewebte
> Episode, durch manche Fährlichkeit zu Wasser und zu Lande,
> durch Verirrungen, Verwicklungen in Liebesbegebenheiten,
> Krankheiten, neue Bekanntschaften und mehr dergleichen Pro-
> dukte einer feurigen Einbildungskraft so schwer machen, daß
> es höchst wahrscheinlich in diesem ganzen Bande das Ziel seiner
> ersten Auswanderung nicht erreichen würde (147 f.)

Werder now recounts in the subjunctive mood how his hero might be whisked off by recruiters to join the army, end up in Turkey fighting the Infidels, be severely wounded and taken to Constantinopel where he would meet his uncle, who had run away from his wife and daughter. The wife would have been raped to death by marauding bands and the daughter would have been imprisoned in the Sultan's harem. Rosenhain would then be a slave in the Sultan's garden and fall in love with his cousin, who would be rescued by Rosenhain and the uncle, so that they all could escape together. Werder

regales his readers with virtually all the possibilities of the popular
romance at once: Rosenhain would find himself whale-fishing near Green-
land, the girl would live among the Indians in America, and the uncle
would spend his days harvesting tea in China. After many separations and
further chance meetings, all would meet again by chance at the Leipzig
Easter Fair. But in Werder's novel, Rosenhain simply goes to Leipzig--
though he does, after all, have a strange encounter.

He meets an innkeeper who explains what it means to be an original
genius. A genius, he discloses, is "ein Mensch der aufgeklärt ist . . .
Ein Schenie [sic] schiert sich um die ganze Welt nichts, thut sich um
keinen Menschen was bekümmern, und lebt frei und aufgeklärt, wenn auch
die ganze Welt das Maul darüber hängt, oder die Nase rümpft" (189 f.).
The tiresomely comic illogicality of the innkeeper is too imprecise for
our hero. He begs examples of this phenomenon and asks which books he
should study 'to become thoroughly acquainted with German literature in
a short time.' He is advised to read 'above all, Germany's two greatest
geniuses' Goethe and Schiller (197). Through their works alone can Rosenhain master the "Kraftsprache":

> Aber Gott im Himmel, was ist so ein Trauerspiel von Sophocles,
> Aeschylus, oder wie die Kerls heißen, gegen die Räuber
> von Schiller und gegen den Götz von Berlichingen von Göthe (198).

The innkeeper attacks 'the graceful Wieland', 'the plebeian Bürger', and
proclaims Bahrdt as the only smart fellow in matters of religion: "ein
ganzer Kerl. . . der Schenie hat" (198). Werder adds a footnote to beg
forgiveness of these 'worthy men' [Wieland, Goethe, Bürger] for having
used them as an example of how the "Schenievolk" judges their works. In
Werder's own opinion, Wieland, Goethe and Bürger 'are sublime beyond all
censure, and are the honour of our German language.' He assures his
readers that the episode in which the innkeeper expounded his opinions
was warranted, as 'there are unfortunately a great number of frivolous
people like the innkeeper who criticize in his glib manner' (198, note).

In one of the final scenes of Rosenhain's journey to Leipzig, he
almost relinquishes his role of anti-hero on finding himself locked in a
prostitute's room in Berlin. Quickly realizing that the young man has
never had an experience like this before, she leads him through the usual
antics one finds in lubricious scenes. Indeed 'our hero felt in such

embarrassment that the tricky situations Don Quixote and Don Sylvio got themselves into are as nothing' (230). The scene is a successful parody of the typical lubricious scene, even to the point of 'drawing the curtain' at the point of no return. The parody is in fact so effective that the author seems to halt his satirical portrayal and attempt the type of realism so often essayed by his colleagues. Rosenhain wakes up next morning in bed with the girl, and 'after flirting about in bed for a brief half-hour' (237), they have breakfast together while she relates the story of her life. She had been drawn into prostitution by having read novels! The hero of one of these novels, for instance, was to her mind a paragon of virtue: "ein solches Ideal von Güte, Schönheit und Sanftmuth, wie nur irgend in den Hirnkasten der Romanschreiber existiren kann" (241).

Werder concludes his novel by leaving his hero in Berlin instead of having him continue on to Leipzig, and without informing his reader whether he returned to 'healthy reason' after his encounter or continued his "Schwärmerey und Wundersucht." Indeed he concludes, 'it is sad that the author must leave his hero quite contrary to the custom of his colleagues in such an ambiguous state of mind; but even in the world of authors fate commands with unlimited power, and we can do nothing but patiently follow the whim of this wilful lady [fate] in order to see what measures she will take' (294). Werder promises to meet his readers once more if they will only nod approval and agrees not to venture into print again if they censure him.

The 'fate' which 'commands in the world of authors' was doubtless nothing less than the exigencies of the book-market itself. The reviewer in the <u>Allgemeine Deutsche Bibliothek</u> for 1792 (vol 106, p. 159) found Werder's intentions good but the results very boring. Although his book is one of the better extant satirical novels of 1790, the reviewer explained that 'the principles to which this story serves as a vehicle' could be found better and more powerfully expressed in numerous other works. The novel is dismissed out of hand somewhat unfairly:

> Man kann es in der Welt herzlich gut meinen, und doch dabey sehr langweilig seyn; davon giebt dieser gute Herr Rosenhain ein Beyspiel. . . Die Geschichte des Herrn Rosenhains [ist] sehr gedehnt und uninteressant, die Grundsätze aber, welchen,

diese Geschichte zum Vehiculum dient, [sind] unzählichmal
anderswo kräftiger und besser gesagt zu lesen. . . Da auf diese
Weise die beyden Haupterfordernisse zu einem guten Buche, näm-
lich Wichtigkeit des Inhalts und Werth der Einkleidung, diesem
Produkte fehlen; so würde es überflüssig seyn, sich auf eine
Kritik der Schreibart einzulassen.

[Adolf Freiherr von Knigge:] Das Zauberschloss oder Geschichte des
Grafen Tunger. Herausgegeben von Adolph Freyherrn von Knigge (1790)

The satire of Knigge's novel derives from his intentional frustration of the reader's expectations by refusing to get on with his tale.
His wilful suspension of plot by means of wearisome digressions whose sole
purpose is to retard the action makes for irksome reading. Indeed, the
title "Das Zauberschloss" with its intimations of either horror or fantasy was doubtless one of those 'lighthouses for luring the public' which
Christian Sander bewailed in his Preface to Salz, Laune. But the opening
fifty pages, which prepare the reader for his unexpected disillusionment,
are actually very promising. Knigge informs the reader that he met a certain Count Tunger on a journey to Tungerhausen. They immediately became
close friends--such spontaneous attraction, we are told, plays a considerable role in contemporary novels. It was here that he first became acquainted with the 'history' of the Count's haunted castle. Knigge next
explains the method he apparently followed in gathering the facts and
circumstantial evidence of his account, and thus reveals the form and
style his novel will take. On returning home from his trip, Knigge corre-
sponded with Tunger and thus acquired documentation of all the events
which the Count had mentioned orally. Although Knigge does not pose as a
scholar trying to solve puzzles in ancient documents, he displays all the
marks of the sleuth on the track of documentary authentication. He seems
to be feigning compliance with the historiographical principle of describing events as they really happened. Tunger's reports were then supplemented by the accounts of witnesses. His untimely death a few weeks later
motivated Knigge to gather all the outstanding information from local reports, witnesses, letters and documents. Knigge sometimes appears in the
novel as a biographer in his own right, and sometimes lets Tunger speak
for himself: "Zuweilen werde ich in meinem Namen als Biograph auftreten,

zuweilen ihn selbst erzählen lassen." (8 f.).

Knigge first speaks with the townsfolk of Tungerhausen and learns
that ghosts and spirits are said to haunt the Count's castle. Travellers
who stay in the castle overnight are rumoured to be mysteriously maltreat-
ed. Knigge himself spends a night in the castle and treats his readers
to the spooky paraphernalia of creaking doors, rattling chains, and strange
midnight noises. He broaches the question of these weird events when
he meets Tunger next morning, but apologizes to the reader for having to
withhold the details of the 'ghost story.' He apparently did not discover them himself until a year later: "es wird ein wenig spät an die
Gespenster-Geschichte kommen, weil diese erst in den Aufsätzen vorkam,
die er mir ein Jahr nach unsrer Trennung schickte" (47 f.). The real
purpose in withholding the information is blatantly explicit: 'a practised
writer does not untie the knot until the end of the book' lest the inter-
vening pages be left unread (48). This is precisely what Knigge does.
We do not return to the subject of the haunted castle until over 230 pages
later. In the meantime the reader is asked to be patient while Knigge
submits a verbatim report, in chronological order and with interpolated
documentation, of Tunger's account of his own life. In this manner the
reader is to become a better judge of the significance of the haunted
castle. The editor tries repeatedly to get the Count to reveal the mystery of the castle, but only receives excuses as to why he cannot:

> Es hängt aber diese Sache [des Zauberschlosses] so genau mit
> der Geschichte meines eignen Lebens zusammen, dass ich bey
> dieser den Anfang machen muss, um Ihren [Knigges] Wunsch in
> Ansehung jener zu befriedigen. Fassen Sie daher Geduld! Wir
> wollen zuweilen eine Abendstunde auf diese Weise verplaudern
> und den Rest sollen Sie schriftlich mitgetheilt bekommen (54 f.)

"Verplaudern"--killing time with idle chatter--is the Count's forte.
Exasperated with Knigge's repeated efforts to persuade him to return to
the theme, he insists (as we have seen) that 'everyone has his own way of
telling a tale' (69). When he abruptly concludes one of his tedious accounts, thus rescuing his chronicler from further tales of his rebellious
youth, he explains that novels are full of such insignificant scenes:
"aber seyen Sie froh, dass Sie so davon von der Fortsetzung gekommen sind.
Füllen doch unsre Romanschreiber ganze Bände mit [solchen] unbedeutenden

Scenen unter Schulknaben und Studenten an!" (90). Again Knigge tries to draw him back to the haunted castle, only to find himself (like the willing reader) the helpless audience of a cruel narrator: "Grausamer Mann! Sie treiben Ihren Spass mit mir--Aber fahren Sie fort! Ich höre zu" (109). Tunger recounts his life 'without restraint,' inserts aphorisms and snippets of penny-philosophy, and concedes at one point that his account may have been too detailed: "Sehen Sie, mein Freund! das war meine Art zu denken und zu handeln, die ich Ihnen ohne Rückhalt vielleicht ein wenig zu weitläuftig geschildert habe!" (204). However, his admission is qualified in a revealing footnote which betrays the intent of Knigge's clumsy satire:

> Wen übrigens solche anatomische Zeichnungen, vom menschlichen Herzen weniger interessiren, als Liebes-Abentheuer, Studenten-Scenen, Hexen-Märlein u.d.gl., der lasse dies ungelesen und erhole sich in den neuen Original-Romanen der Teutschen und andern geistreichen Sammlungen dieser Art, womit uns jede Messe reichlich versorgt.(204)

The mystery is finally explained with austere brevity (210 f.). The castle had once been a monastery containing passages built into the hollow walls, thus providing access to all the rooms. After Tunger had purchased it, he and his servants used to roam through the passages at night, observing their guests in order to study human nature, judge human actions, punish the evil and reward the good. This is the typical explanation of the mysterious in the fiction of the period.

Knigge's book is the only extant novel of 1790 which even attempts to tell a ghost-story, but the few paragraphs of thinly contrived gothic horror it offers are not a serious attempt in the field. One suspects that Knigge was trying to play with his readers in a Shandean manner, and one cannot escape the conclusion that he was convinced of his success. However, the imitation is crude and the results are meagre.

[Johann Crhistian Wilhelm Müller:] Fragmente aus dem Leben und Wandel eines Physiognomisten (1790)

> Es giebt Familienphysionomien der Schicksale, so wie es Familienphysiognomien der Gesichter und Charaktere giebt. . .

Es liesse sich über dieses Thema ein
feines physiognomisches Büchel zur Beförderung der Menschenkunde elaboriren,
das ist gewiss. . . .
(Müller von Itzehoe, Herr Thomas,
III, 7 f.)

Müller's novel is the fictional autobiography of the foundling
Kasper Flip, who ponders the course of his life from waif to disenchanted
physiognomist to domesticated husband. Interspersed with dialogues and
essayistic commentaries on the Enlightenment, human relations, literature,
and the book trade, and frequently retarded by incapsulated biographies
of its major characters, the narrative exploits most of the techniques
we have come to expect in the popular novel. Yet it is not just a satire
on the follies of popular fiction. It is, as the title implies, a parody on the major work of Kaspar Flip's namesake, Johann Kaspar Lavater's
Physiognomische Fragmente zur Beförderung der Menschenkenntnis und Menschenliebe (4 vols, 1775-1778). Written in imitation of contemporary
autobiographies, Müller's work contains "physiognomische Irrungen im
Kleinen" (ii f.) which portray Flip's 'translunary flirtation' with Lavater's thought and the hero's subsequent 'physiognomic adventures' (282)
as the ardent apostle of the new science. He ultimately debunks it as an
unfortunate and trival fad (333).

Lavater was a prime target for satire as his life and work emphasiz-
ed irrational and mystical modes of thought. He believed that the in-
scrutable and transcendental could be apprehended in visible signs and
forms, and that we could apprehend man's inner being by observing his
outward appearance. He would have us perceive a man's soul by contem-
plating his silhouette. This belief was based on the biblical truth that
God created man in His image, a view that stands as the motto of his
Essays. . . for the Promotion of the Knowledge and Love of Mankind.[41]
Though to Lavater's mind physiognomics was an empirical science,[42] his
book was actually a devotional work (Erbauungsbuch) whose author felt he
had been chosen to struggle for truth and who wanted to impart his insights and reflections.[43]

Though Richard Newald suggests that Lavater's influence upon intellectual history reached its peak in 1774,[44] the evidence of contemporary
literature seems to indicate that his influence continued until at least

as late as 1794, when Johann Caspar Armbruster published his pedagogical
work entitled <u>Johann Caspar Lavaters Regeln für Kinder durch Beyspiele</u>
erläutert. <u>Zum Gebrauch in Schulen und im Privatunterricht</u>.[45]
Novelists of 1790 still consider Lavater's ideas a force to be reckoned
with. Friedrich Heller, in <u>Sokrates</u> (I, v), regards Lavater's <u>Physiog-</u>
<u>nomische Fragmente</u> as a serious work of contemporary importance. Georg
Kellner's <u>Familiengeschichte</u> (I, 8 f.), Müller von Itzehoe's <u>Herr Thomas</u>
(III, 7 f.) and Dr. Bahrdt's <u>Yhakanpol</u> (192 ff., et passim) parody it.[46]
Certainly, Johann Müller's effectiveness as a satirist was equally de-
pendent upon topicality.

Müller distinguishes himself from other satirists of the period by
his deftness in playing with the absurdities inherent in his subject. He
creates a flesh-and-blood hero whose ridiculousness stems from his consistent attempts to carry Lavater's esoteric thought to its logical conclusion. Müller builds a fictional society around his impressionable
hero by exploiting the ambiguity of Lavater's public image; rationalists
reject him while pseudo-mystics and dilettants adore him. Yet in his
tendency to highlight the obvious and to labour motifs, Müller reflects
the shortcomings of the other satirists of the period. His work however, remains the best extant satirical novel of 1790.

Kasper Flip, who has been 'vegetating' (2) in a foundlings' home,
is apprenticed to a painter and experiences a vital turning-point in his
life when retouching some faded rococo angels in a local church. 'It
was here that the first ray of physiognomics burst forth in his imagination' (8). He notices that 'painting could be the mother and daughter
of physiognomics' and he is deliberately absurd in observing that a
physiognomist--Gesichtsforscher (8)--would need as much imagination as a
painter who wants to make a faithful copy of an original. Like the hero
of a <u>Bildungsroman</u> he soon realises that he must acquire 'deeper knowledge of the human race' by sallying forth into the world (10). Equally
characteristic of some heroes of this genre is his feeling of destiny.
He is 'marked' to become a portraitist: "Dass ich zum Gesichtsmahler
gestempelt wäre, bezweifelte ich nicht weiter" (11). Flip feels a surge
of chaotic power in his inner being:

> . . . so empfand ich jedennoch in meinem Innern, wiewohl
> noch etwas chaotisch gemischt, eine dem Kraftgenie eigne

> specifische Schwere, und jede elastische Kraft und furcht-
> baren Drang, wodurch sich in unsren aufgeklärten Zeiten ein
> solches Menschenkind wie eine Raquete [sic] empor hebt (15)

The urge to master all published human knowledge (26 f.) sends him into
the service of a book-binder. Two years of reading and excerpting make
his 'head richer and more filled up with each passing day' (45). The
young man rejects the book-binder's advice to accept the ethical and social responsibilities of a wife and home, as 'the thought of settling
down to the limitations and monotony of such a life with its sorrows and
joys' does not accord with his 'inclination for freedom and scientific
independence' (47 f.)

Puffed up with 'pendantic self-sufficiency' (55), Flip leaves the
bookbinder's shop and writes a book on how to become a self-made scholar.
Müller parodies the writer's trade by having his hero conclude his book
simply because he is destitute. Showing no regard for literary form,
Flip tosses off a conclusion, promises his readers a second volume, and
slinks away to a famous publisher:

> Ich arbeitete Tag und Nacht. Am dreyzehnten Tage, als
> meine Mundprovision, mein Geld und das Oel in meiner
> Lampe aufgezehrt waren, schloss ich mein Manuskript. . .
> versprach einen zweyten Band, und schlich damit nach
> dem Gewölbe einer berühmten Buchhandlung. (58 f.)

His first work having been rejected, Flip produces another one, which
he pads with 'a few important chapters on trust in Providence, hope,
brotherly love, good intentions, etc.,' that he feels will promote sales
'in our enlightened age' (69), but fails again to find a publisher. He
returns to his garret to work on other literary products, lacking nothing
for his professional development but an uninterrupted flow of ideas and a
good supply of whimsy: "nun fehlte zu einer glücklichen Autorvegetation
nichts weiter, als ununterbrochene Gedankenfülle und ein guter Vorrath
von Laune" (76). In particular he plans a book on 'literary solitude'
(77), an especially apt topic for the suffering aesthete he feels himself to be.

By the time the joys of literary solitude have palled, Flip encounters Thomas Well, a scholarly proof-reader in straitened circumstances. The episode marks another important pivotal point in the pro-

gress of Müller's hero, who obtains an equally menial position with a
publisher. A new and unexpected world meets his eyes: intrigues among
authors viciously vying with one another, wrangling and skullduggery between writers and publishers, commercial speculation in literature, and
book-piracy. Flip gradually loses his "Autorenkitzel" (101) and 'spends
a few years in semi-literary vegetation' (102). He concludes in retro-
spect that he ought to have been ashamed of the "Geniefabrik" (106) of
his apprenticeship to literature.

Flip's main interest, however, remains the pursuit of physiognomics. This was the field in which his 'imagination spied about' in the
hope of apprehending 'the sublime and rare impress of the human spirit'
(107). His sketches and silhouettes of famous men, particularly of Moses Mendelssohn, make him famous in high society, though artists malign
him as an empiricist (108).[47] Accepted into refined society, he falls
victim to the 'luring voice of vanity and folly' and is transformed
through closer acquaintance with 'luxury and refinement of manners'
(109). Flip spends a year "in einem Künstlertaumel"(110) enjoying the
adulation of his clientele. He finally rejects their perverted values
and returns to his accustomed obscurity, convinced that the episode
would have been better spent in acquiring knowledge of man and hearkening to the advice of a friend (111). All he could 'salvage from this
shipwreck' was a 'small bundle of experiences' (115). Müller parodies
the role of Providence in popular fiction when old Thomas Well mysteriously inherits a fortune. This 'reconciles Flip again with fate, which
rewards the upright man' (119). But such rewards soon fall Flip's way
as well. He studies Winckelmann, Sulzer and Hagedorn (albeit from a
physiognomical point of view) and is 'rewarded' for his upright living
by winning 3000 Thaler in a lottery.

Thomas Well presents Flip with a book that is destined to alter
his life: Lavater's Physiognomische Fragmente zur Beförderung der
Menschenkenntnis und Menschenliebe (131). Flip immediately indulges in
a paean to the sublimity of this 'physiognomical Talmud' (132) that is
'the infallible key to humanity' (138), and foregoes a trip to Italy in
order to 'luxuriate' in the Fragmente "wie ein deutscher Zecher"
(141).[48] He moves to Well's new estate, puts his lottery winnings into
Well's safekeeping (who profitably invests them), and devotes himself

single-mindedly to writing the present 'physiognomical' autobiography
(160). Müller reports that Flip was unaware at the time that 'physiognomics was only shooting wild sparks out of his imagination' though he was
intent upon 'helping to build it up into a true and real science' (162).

Flip's study of Lavater's profile forces him to the conclusion
that Lavater himself has not the slightest trace of the physiognomist in
him (168); Bahrdt's prince Yhakanpol had come to the same conclusion.
Shaken by this discovery, Flip recalls Lavater's dictum that 'scarcely
one good physiognomist is to be found in ten thousand men' (163).[49]
While Müller's point is that physiognomists do not exist at all, his
illogical hero concludes that Lavater is a sublime rarity. He begins to
systematize Lavater's unsystematic fragments and literally showers both
Well and the local pastor with his own derivative hypotheses: it must
be possible to develop a physiognomical language of art--physiognomische
Kunstsprache (151); physiognomics embraces the whole of Nature (173);
one should be able to develop 'economic physiognomy'--eine ökonomische
Menschen-Physiognomie (191). He who possesses 'physiognomical genius'
possesses a special organ for perceiving the mysteries of the universe
and discovering the depths of the human soul; this organ is the 'physiognomical organ' (199). Flip tries in vain to dispel his friends' 'mistaken' opinions that this new science is mere 'smoke from Pandora's box'
(196). Its advocates, he insists, embody the highest synthesis of the
philosopher, the natural scientist and the Christian (194). Yet both
Thomas Well and the vicar remain staunch in their view that it is really
"eine possierliche Wissenschaft". (192)

Desiring confirmation of his apostleship of physiognomics, Flip
pens a fawning letter to Lavater, asking whether children sired 'sub
rosa' are marked by a special physiognomical sign. (We may recall
Albrecht's claim in Fackland that illegitimate children have 'fine
breeding and a fiery temperament,' and Sander's contention in Salz,
Laune that from 'the hot source of love flows that vis vivida which forms
heroes and geniouses.') Flip waits for two years without reply and is
eventually thrown back upon his own 'scientific' resources. Undaunted
by Lavater's apparent disinterest, Flip examines himself with his 'innate
physiognomical sense" until he finally obtains the most reliable facts
from the director of the foundlings' home in which he spent his early

life. His father, he learns, was a candidate of theology who had had an
affair with an actress; the 'fruit of this theologico-theatrical interlude' (344) was Kaspar Flip. He is thus delighted to 'untie the bond of
his anonymity' and to find himself the 'result of the strangest associ-
ation of two human beings, of which one was a worker in the vineyard of
the Lord, and the other a queen of the stage' (236). The fusion of two
creative souls in his breast 'proves' that he was destined from his
mother's womb to be a physiognomist (243), and that he is the heir to
their 'physiognomical perfections' (244). Flip has now all the evidence
he needs to prepare his own magnum opus. His book parodies the major
works of both Lavater and Basedow, for he decides to step forth 'not with
ponderous fragments, but with a physiognomical primer: "mit einem
physiognomischen Elementarbuch" (263).

Thomas Well dies, leaving his daughter Florian (whom the reader
has not yet met) with a handsome dowry in the care of the vicar. Flip
is forced to give up his theorizing in order to deal with the realities
of life. He learns estate management under the vicar's tutelage and
develops a platonic relationship with Florian, one of those 'rare figures
who seem to proceed from the age of the most perfect Greek beauty and
symmetry' (430). Indeed, she is a paragon of feminine perfection who
reads Xenophon, Hume and Rousseau in the original, 'soared into the
heights with Newton, into the depts with Kant, was astonished at Vol-
taire's wit and his filthy heart, and strolled hand in hand with Plutarch' (436). Kasper and Florian are like 'two friends who had drifted
on a board to the shore of a happy isle where one draws joy and fulness
of life from the other' (443). In fact they seem to anticipate the Romantic concept of love by feeling with a single organ: "so empfanden
wir, wie durch ein Organ" (444).

Flip receives an unexpected and startling letter from Florian
begging him to marry her to prevent her immanent confinement in a convent. Pistol in hand, Flip rushes to her side to find her weeping in the
arms of an officer, who turns out to be her long-lost father. He has
just been released from service in America. The vicar reveals that Florian had been conceived 'sub rosa' on a battlefield. She is not merely
an illegitimate child whose 'physiognomical sign' drew her to Flip, but

a Countess as well. The young couple marry and settle into domestic bliss. Müller's crowning touch of satire is Flip's explanation of the process by which Florian became his wife. The marriage was not 'the infallible result' of his 'physiognomical hypothesis that love-children are intimately connected by some sort of invisible bond' after all:

> Sie [Florian] ward mein Eigenthum nicht aus der ohnfehlbarer Folge meiner physiognomischen Hypothese: dass die Kinder der Liebe durch irgend ein unsichtbares Band mit einander verschwistert sind, sondern durch jenen Erfahrungssatz: 'Wem das Schicksal günstig ist - dem wird bescheret ein tugendsames und kluges Weib.' (460).

Müller has thus broken the whole illusion upon which his parody was based by revealing the truth of a very prosaic reality.

CHAPTER VI

THE CHARACTER NOVEL

Preamble:

It is generally acknowledged that the 18th-century German novel
gained ground at the expense of Christian devotional literature, yet attempts to demonstrate precisely how this happened leave many questions
unanswered. Rudolf Jentsch' statistics on book production[1] show that
novels did in fact partly replace Erbauungsliteratur on the book market
between 1740 and 1800, a period which is strikingly coincident with the
rise of the professional writer.[2] We may assume that the readership of
both types of literature remained the same.[3] Though Marion Beaujean
points out that moral instruction remained the basic purpose of prose
fiction even when it used freer narrative techniques than before, we have
seen that in 1790 this was often mere pretense. Didacticism, whether
feigned or genuine, is common to all prose fiction published in 1790 and
we have seen that, among theoreticians, historiographers were urging
greater subtlety in its application. Some historians argued that the
"pragmatic" approach of revealing the motivating factors behind events
was more realistic and hence more instructive than the usual episodic
narratives. Certainly, the professed aim of most novelists was the communication of 'practical morality', and they too seemed to feel that moral effectiveness was directly related to the ability to convince the public that their works were founded on truth. This is particularly important in the case of biographical accounts, as a critic in the Allgemeine
Deutsche Bibliothek for 1791 (vol 99, p. 152) points out when reviewing
Albrecht's Neue Biographien der Selbstmörder (1790):

> Biographie sollte doch wohl billig, und kann auch nichts
> anders seyn, als Geschichte; pragmatische, immerhin auch
> darstellende, nur aber doch nach historischen Angaben
> darstellende Geschichte des Einzelnen.

The Character Novel of 1790, a type which makes a genuine attempt
at edifying the reader and offers insights into the hero's personality
and development, comes closest to implementing the aims of the pragmatic

narrative. Indeed some contemporary writers of this type of fiction
would seem as well to have followed the lead given by the theory of biography. Johann Joachim Eschenburg, for instance, sheds light on the
Character Novel of 1790 by distinguishing between the general purpose of
the historian and that of the biographer (Entwurf, 1789, p. 331): historians focus on actions, whereas biographers are more concerned with the
full characterization of the persons involved in the actions. Biography
is the narrative of the fates, actions and characteristics of a single
notable person. One must choose such persons as prototypes, he explains,
whose rank, achievements, or especially remarkable changes of fortune
are particularly interesting.

The presence of moral instruction in the character novels of 1790
becomes even more revealing than in other types of fiction when we examine the range in didactic techniques and ethical persuasion which they
exhibit. They encompass sententious preachment of sectarian views, the
demonstration of middle-class morals by means of exemplary anecdotes and
figures, fictionalized devotional biographies, and the revelation of a
protagonist's inner biography in the form of the Bildungsroman. It is in
this range itself that one might suspect a key to the transformation which
seems to have taken place as novels replaced devotional works.

This transformation is characterized by a shift from the dogmatic
pronouncement of Christian ethics to the confession of a highly indivi-
dualized ethos; that is, a shift from Erbauung to Bildung. Erbauung, we
may recall, is that Christian edification of the individual which devotional literature fostered by means of moral tales, parables and exhorta-
tions, whereas Bildung was understood in Enlightenment thought as the
synthesis of aesthetic, moral, rational and scientific education.[4] The
Bildungsroman, or novel of character development, is as much concerned
with portraying the development of its protagonist as with furthering the
Bildung of the reader himself.[5] If we assume that there can be a transition from Erbauung to Bildung, we will recognize the change as a process
of secularisation.[6] Five major factors seem to have contributed to the
process: developments in devotional literature and secular literature
themselves, the secularisation of pietism, the rise of the professional
writer, and aestheticism. We will single out the salient features of
these developments before surveying representative character novels

of 1790.

In its medieval beginnings, devotional literature[7] was almost ex-
clusively designed for the use of clergy and Holy Orders. With the rise
of mystical sermons in the late medieval period, however, longer tracts
evolved as extensions of sermons. The clergy's declining interest in
speculative mysticism led to the introduction of a moralising tendency
into a literature that was now being directed more to the spiritual
edification of the laity. The most important work of the time was Thomas
à Kempis' Imitation of Christ, which traces the gradual progress of the
soul to Christian perfection, its detachment from the world, and its
union with God. While many works followed this pattern, others urged the
examination of one's conscience with admonitions of repentence, confession, and penitence. A popular term for this type of Erbauungsliteratur
was Spiegel or Speculum; it was a 'mirror' of the reader's conscience,
and it is significant that we find the term occurring in this same sense
in the prose fiction of 1790; this is the case, for example, in E.A.
Göchhausen's Meines Vaters Hauschronika, which is described, among other
things, as a "Spiegel zur Selbstbeschau" (504).

Luther provided models for devotional literature in the first half
of the 16th century. His interpretation of the Lord's Prayer (1518),
"Kurze Form der zehn Gebote, des Glaubens und des Vaterunsers" (1520),
"Betbüchlein" (1522), and catechism laid the foundation for a new epoch
in the genre. His translation of the Bible, with its clear and persuasive style, became the most poignant of domestic devotional works. Daily
devotion in the home continued to be fostered during the Reformation by
Hausbücher which were directed to the broad needs of the laity as a whole.
New forms arose in the post-Reformation period, however, which concerned
themselves with particular social classes and different situations in
life. Thus there arose counsel for youth, brides and married couples,
and Consolations (Trostbücher) for times of need, distress, sickness and
death. The characteristics of the genre, namely depth of religious experience and unsophisticated directness of expression, continued to derive from Luther's personality and his singularly graphic style. Devotional literature aimed at sustaining the Christian household in the face of
religious and confessional vicissitudes.

The appearance of religious biography in the 17th century was a contributing factor to the gradual secularisation of literature. The several versions of Martin von Cochem's _Das grosse Leben Jesu_ (1681-1707), for example, moved with each succeeding publication toward greater subjectivity of inward experience. The ground for this change had been prepared by Johann Gerhard's _Meditationes Sacrae_ (1606), which described the soul's journey of purification unto _unio mystica_ with Christ, and Jacob Böhme's _Der Weg zu Christo_ (1624). It is through such works of the baroque period that devotional literature began to give way to prose fiction.

When formulating his rules of poetics in _Buch von der Deutschen Poeterey_ (1624), Opitz explained that literature was in the first instance nothing other than a covert theology for the edification--erbauung--of wise men in the fear of God and for good moral learning.[8] This view of the morally instructive character of literature prevailed for over a hundred years and was re-emphasized in Gottsched's _Versuch einer Critischen Dichtkunst_ (1730). Gottsched held that the invention of a "fable" was crucial for all literature, including the novel. His principle was first to select an instructive moral proposition and then to invent a plot which would illustrate the proposition and make it both striking and concrete.[9] E.A. Blackall offers an additional perspective on didacticism in the novel in noting that by the time of Gottsched ". . . the moral weekly has come to include character sketches and little narratives which come so close to the novel in subject matter that it is no surprise to find the novel taking over this style."[10] Certainly, as Marianne Spiegel found, moral weeklies assumed the place of devotional literature for middle-class readers, and in the early 18th-century were held to be the only serious reading material. She suggests that it was through moral weeklies that devotional literature first became secularized, thus preparing the ground for the character novel.[11] Helmut Germer[12] notes that the moral weekly may well have been the immediate forerunner of the Novel of Education (_Erziehungsroman_) and cites Ch. F. Timme's Preface to the fourth part of _Faramonds Familiengeschichte_ in Briefen (1779;[2] 1782):

> Zu einer anderen Zeit würde ich meine Sammlung brauchbarer
> Wahrheiten in die Form der moralischen Wochenschrift gebracht
> haben, aber heutzutage liest das Publikum nur noch Romane und

Schauspiele.

Germer might equally have cited the episode in <u>Sebaldus Nothanker</u>
[Zweiter Band, Viertes Buch, 1775], in which Nicolai discusses who is at
fault for the clergy's loss of esteem:

> Daran sind wieder die neumodischen [heterodoxen] Theologen
> schuld, die sich selbst die Mittel benehmen, womit man die
> Laien im Zaum halten muss. Sie schwatzen immer viel vom
> Nutzen des Predigeramts und vergessen das Wesen des Predigt-
> amts hierüber. Sie geben sich selbst als die nützlichen
> Leute an. . . die der Staat verordnet hat, Weisheit und
> Tugend zu lehren. Eine rechte Würde! Weisheit und Tugend
> dünkt sich jetzt jeder Wochenblättler oder Romanschreiber
> zu lehren![13]

It is difficult to escape the conclusion that German writers were gradually becoming aware that devotional literature was losing its appeal for a
wide general readership, and that the moral gap, as it were, had to be
filled by the secular author. But as soon as he did so, as we will see,
he could not avoid introducing secular views.[14]

Samuel Richardson, remarkable for his psychological observation of
character, is the acknowledged founder of a new type of novel[15] in which
the principles of bourgeois enlightenment were expressed, and Schöffler[16]
has suggested that protestant devotional literature may have been in part
responsible for having moved Richardson in the direction of the new novel
form typified by his <u>Clarissa Harlowe</u> (1747-48). There seems little
doubt that his postscript to the novel found general agreement in Germany.
Richardson had written:

> In this general depravity, when even the pulpit has lost great
> part of its weight, and the clergy are considered as a body
> of <u>interested</u> men, the author thought he should be able to
> answer it to his own heart, be the success what it would,
> if he threw in his mite towards introducing a reformation
> so much wanted; and he imagined, that if in an age given up to
> diversion and entertainment, he could <u>steal in</u>, as may be said,
> and investigate the great doctrines of Christianity under the
> fashionable guise of an amusement; he should be most likely
> to serve his purpose;. . .[17]

This novel, as its title page explained, was intended as a warning of
"the Distresses that may attend Misconduct both of Parents and Children
in relation to Marriage." A translation of <u>Clarissa</u>, judiciously adapted,
as a reviewer observes, to render it still more interesting for German

readers, appeared in Germany in the years 1788-90.[18] The clergyman
Hermes, author of Sophiens Reise von Memel nach Sachsen (1769/73) and a
leading representative of the moralising tendency of Richardson, records
being advised of the growing obsolescence of 'preachers', who would
eventually have to become novelists if they wanted to continue in an
effective role.[19] Although critical opinions of the didactic function
of novels varied widely as late as 1780, there was general agreement at
that time that a novel should expound morals.[20] It is still frequently
argued in 1790, as for example in Friedrich von Oertel's Kilbur (II, 438
ff.), that novels can and should make morality practical by extending our
knowledge of man.

The pietistic autobiography, a natural outgrowth of pietism, was
also of major significance for the development of the character novel,
and hence also of the Bildungsroman. These autobiographies, particularly
Philipp Jacob Spener's Pia Desideria (1675) and August Francke's Segens-
volle Fusstapfen des noch lebenden Gottes (1709), assumed the characteristics of devotional literature, and in so doing, lent further support to
the secularizing influence of personal experience which was finding expression in biographies of the 17th century. Pietistic autobiographies
influenced the development of the psychological and sentimental novel and
culminated in the "Bekenntnisse einer schönen Seele" in Goethe's Wilhelm
Meister. Haferkorn[21] suggests that purely psychological criteria gradually began to predominate over religious reflection in those autobiographies
of pietistic and rationalistic origin. The line of development, in his
view, runs from J.C. Günther to Albrecht von Haller, Gellert, Hamann,
Lavater, Jung-Stilling, and ends in the works of Moritz. The shift in
accent in works of the devotional tradition, that is, from sermons to
devotional books and allegories, then to biography and autobiography, reflects the changing concern of each generation as its primary focus shifts
from the Christian God to the Divine, then to the world, and finally to
the Self. As Arnold Hirsch observed, we witness the secularization of the
religious path of salvation.[22]

Fritz Stemme's valuable study[23] has traced the transition from re-
ligiously motivated (pietistic) self-analysis to a purely psychological
literature. The crisis of faith most characteristic of pietism was an

overriding uncertainty, and Stemme documents this feeling with Francke's sermon of 1687, which expressed his monstrous realisation that he lacked faith. Francke's struggle to regain the faith became the model for his followers. This Praxis Pietatis, or the way of personal piety, was the technique of devotional self-analysis that in time gave rise to Erfahr-ungsseelenkunde. Pietism regarded the goal of this religious struggle for faith as 'rebirth.'

Karl Holl[24] has indicated three basic features of the pietistic religious crisis, which illustrate pietism's inclination away from re-ligious orthodoxy and toward the type of secularized and psychological view expressed in the Bildungsroman at the end of the 18th century: an ascetic attitude which renounces the world for the things of the spirit, a deepened sense of personality in Christianity which makes the indivi-dual mind the measure of all things, and opposition to the established church and spiritual authority. But as Stemme has further shown, the main thrust toward the secularization of pietism was given by Spener's assertion that faith could be present in man even when not directly ex-perienced. The 'awareness' of faith was the direct result of belief and dwelt in the 'soul'; Spener understood this in strictly psychological terms. This capacity for expressing religious faith in psychological terms was the ground in which the secularized literature of spiritual quest (Bildungsroman) found its roots. The way was clear for the secu-larization of faith in the form of contemplative introspection (Erfahr-ungsseelenkunde) as soon as it had been conceded that faith could appear in its psychical effects alone.

Perhaps quite unconsciously pietism had therefore virtually legiti-mized large-scale individualisation of religious feeling and had suggest-ed the view that, in the final analysis, faith was bound to feelings; their strength and intensity 'proved' its presence. In its early stage of development, psychological self-analysis and Erbauung was justified as a means to the longed-for spiritual rebirth, but later introspection and longing became ends in themselves. As a result of the increasing practice of self-contemplation, spiritual phenomena extraneous to the strictly con-fessional context were drawn into the orbit of self-examination, thus laying the ground for the life of 'eternal becoming' that is expressed in many romantic novels. Seen in this light, we can regard Jacobi's

<u>Die Winterreise</u> (1769) as the beginning of a new development, which can
be traced in the psychological novel (<u>Seelenroman</u>) of the latter part of
the 18th century through Goethe's <u>Werther</u> (1774), Jacobi's <u>Allwill</u> (1776),
Moritz' <u>Anton Reiser</u> (1785-90), and Tieck's <u>William Lovel</u> (1796 f.)[25]
As Stemme points out, Moritz rejects religious motivation in favour of
psychological contemplation and therefore represents the highest achievement of the secularization process.

The secularization of literature was not entirely due to changes
in religious or philosophical viewpoints, however. It was also brought
about by a change in attitude toward the craft of fiction itself. Until
the middle of the 18th century, literary activity was widely held to be
founded upon learnable rules and tended to confine expression to traditional ethical values. But the rise of the professional writer from
1760-1800 reflects an entirely different approach. Writers became increasingly concerned, in Haferkorn's words,[26] with subjective originality, unregulated spontaneity, and the intimate confession of personal
views. Their craft was marked by 'the subjective formulation of artistic
truth.' Yet their independence as writers was paradoxically dependent
upon their ability to win public acclaim, and we have already seen how
most professional writers of 1790 were obliged to accommodate themselves
to commercial considerations. Public acclaim, we may recall, was in turn
dependent upon the writer's skill in satisfying the popular need for
entertaining narratives about domestic life and moving tales of love and
adventure. It would seem therefore that a secure method of pleasing the
public without sacrificing artistic integrity was to sublimate and intel-
lectualize the novel of adventure.[27]

Blanckenburg's <u>Versuch über den Roman</u> (1774) is important for the
emphasis it places on the novel's potential for revealing the inner biography of the hero, as well as for its claim that one may thereby bring
the human being closer to realising its own potential for perfection.[28]
Blanckenburg is apologetic about having dealt with a genre which is intended 'for the entertainment of the masses' (vi) but notes that novels
can affect morals by influencing taste. In his view, the novel can be
made 'a very pleasing and instructive pastime, not only for idle women,
but also for the reflective mind'--für den denkenden Kopf (vii). This

194

change in the character of the novel may be brought about, he argues, by making the novel itself a reflective work: "Das Innre der Person ist es, das wir in Handlung, in Bewegung sehen wollen, wenn wir bewegt werden sollen" (58). This new view of the nature of the novel reflects an altered attitude toward didacticism in prose fiction. Blanckenburg contends that as the novelist shows us possible people in the real world, the reader can develop himself by becoming engaged in the individual process of development (Bildung)of real people in a concrete world. In other words, the reader is educated by experiencing the inner world of viable fictional characters and then by applying this insight to his own immediate milieu. He could thus gain 'general anthropological insights'.[29] Blanckenburg goes even further by suggesting that this process of vicarious Bildung is basically education for the ideal of humanity:

> Er [der Romanschreiber] wird uns nämlich das, was wir billig
> zuerst, und vor allem Andern seyn sollten; das, was Jahr-
> hunderte und Zeiten uns immer mehr und mehr machen,--er
> wird uns lehren Menschen werden. (460)

This view of the didactic function of the novel in man's apprenticeship for Humanity finds a striking echo in Wilhelm von Humboldt's fragment, "Theorie der Bildung des Menschen" (1793), which epitomizes a completely secularized Bildung:

> Die letzte Aufgabe unsers Daseyns: dem Begriff der Menschheit
> in unserer Person, sowohl während der Zeit unsres Lebens,
> als auch noch über dasselbe hinaus, durch die Spuren des
> lebendigen Wirkens, die wir zurücklassen, einen so grossen
> Inhalt, als möglich zu verschaffen, diese Aufgabe löst sich
> allein durch die Verknüpfung unsres Ichs mit der Welt zu
> der allgemeinsten, regsten und freiesten Wechselwirkung.[30]

There seems to be every evidence to support Walter Muschg's view that the professional writer is the final link in the secularization of literature.[31]

The order in which the character novels of 1790 will be discussed is an expedient designed to highlight the type of transition which took place during the secularization of devotional literature. There is no suggestion that they reflect a trend in themselves, as the argument for a literary trend of this nature within a single year would be specious even if the sequence in which they are presented did happen to coincide with their actual order of publication. While the range in narrative perspective and moral views evidenced by the ten character novels of 1790 suggests that practically all the foregoing developments are making themselves felt in the prose fiction of that year, it is noteworthy that only one writer propounds strictly sectarian views on moral education. E.A. Göchhausen's Volksbücher proclaim the sure faith of the common-sense Christian and decry the Enlightenment with its emphasis on free-thinking, fashions, social life, and individual freedoms, which to his mind are weakening the influence of the Church. He tends to preach rather than narrate. Though his works are not, strictly speaking, novels, but fictional anecdotes and vignettes connected by moralising commentaries rather than a plot, it is important that they be considered here to illustrate the kind of book that the actual character novel replaced. Other writers placed considerably more emphasis on plot, and it is interesting to find in Christian Salzmann's Sebastian Kluge a fictional biography that is little more than an extended exemplary anecdote. Salzmann does not stress Christian charity with its renunciation of worldly goods, but uses the idiom of the Christian faith to transmit modes of action designed to bring about better adjustment to the secular form of life with its economic demands. Success in business is proof of God's grace. The hero of Wilhelm Heller's Sokrates, on the other hand, epitomizes reason, moderation, and virtue (I, 3, 32, et passim), and the work was planned as a timely offering to contemporary society, which, in the author's view, had fallen upon evil times (I, 71). Heller would have liked his work to be a "Parallelbiographie" of Christ and Socrates (I, 268 f.). At the other end of our scale stand K. Ph. Moritz' Andreas Hartknopf. Eine Allegorie (1786) and Andreas Hartknopfs Predigerjahre (1790), which portray the inner biography of a secularized Christ-figure. In Schrimpf's view,[32] the character of this work as a secularized Bible story (sekularisierter Evangelienbericht) determines both its structure and language. Robert Minder regards this novel as turning away from extroverted socially oriented writings to the introverted private experience of an aesthetically transfigured mysticism.[33] Indeed, August Langen's exhaustive study suggests that Hartknopf may be regarded as the first symbolical novel in German literature.[34] It turns away from such

middle-class values as success and domestic happiness in favour of the
free revelation of the author's own personality, and proclaims the private and often esoteric world-view of the vatic aesthete. The following
descriptive commentaries will illustrate this range in detail. However,
as Moritz' novels are now widely known and are the subject of very recent
critical studies, they will not be re-assessed within the limits of this
study, even though they are, by our definition, novels first published
in 1790.

[Ernst August Göchhausen:] Ein Büchlein zur Beförderung einfältiger
Lebensweisheit unter verständigen ehrlichen Bürgern und Landleuten (1790)

   This "Volksbüchlein" (231) addressed to the author's "Liebe einfältige gute Gesellen" (248) is a piece of didactic prose fiction designed
to nurture wisdom (163). Characteristic of Göchhausen's approach is his
claim that wisdom can only be nurtured among readers endowed with solid
common sense and a natural disposition to see things aright:

       Ich rechne freilich billiger Weise darauf, dass er [der Leser]
       den Sinn eines Biedermanns mit bringe; denn geben kan ich den
       keinem Menschen. (iii)

He regards himself, of course, as just such a pious and uncomplicated
fellow--ein frommer Biedermann (248). The preface sets forth the broad
aims of his book and explains with disarming frankness that his work (in
Fielding's idiom) 'dishes up' scenes, commentaries, occasional chats with
his neighbours and fellow pilgrims about matters of enduring significance:

       Aber manche kleine Lebensscene, manche meiner Bemerkungen,--
       deren jedoch keine Euch hindern soll die seinige für richtiger
       zu halten. . . manches Gesprächsel, mit meinen Nachbarn oder
       Mitwallern, über dies und das, was immer geschah, und immer
       geschehen wird, . . . das, und dergleichen Dinge, will ich
       Euch auftischen. (v ff.)

   One can hardly speak of characters in this work, for no individuals become engaged either in adventures or domestic scenes. Stock-types
such as farmers, townsmen, and pastors discourse with one another and
express points of view representative of their social station. The main
burden of moral instruction falls upon the many Exempelchen which form the

substance of the book. The unifying feature of the work is Göchhausen's personality: he intrudes into the narrative to address the reader and even enters into conversation with the creatures of his imagination. He has a ready retort for any figures who do not share his views and parries their objections by whimsical intrusions.

Topics of discussion range from matters of state to the rise of luxury, freedom of the press (not "Pressefreiheit" but "Pressefrechheit", 212), to man and the nature of human existence. Though it invariably falls to the vicar to proffer the moral anecdotes, Göchhausen cannot restrain himself from delivering blistering broadsides on contemporary life. Social institutions are the principal target of his rambling diatribes, and his discourse is liberally salted with admonitions to 'work and pray'; this, in his view, is the only guaranteed antidote to the aberrations of society. Novels, fashion journals, and the theatre are constant objects of his derision, and he equates the <u>Komödienhaus</u> with a <u>Tollhaus</u> because both audience and actors have a 'ridiculous' involvement in sentimentality and trite love plots. But most importantly, Göchhausen's moral view regards the activities of middle-class society as symptomatic of its inner bankruptcy. At one point he interrupts his 'reader' to extort a confession of spiritual inadequacy:

> Was macht Ihr Weib mit dem Modejournal? Wozu <u>Euch</u>, in Eurem Städtchen von tausend Häusern, Lesegesellschaften? "Um uns Aufzuklären!. . ." Musst feine Büchlein lesen oder feine Begriffe von Aufklärung haben, wenn Ihr noch nicht einmal so klug seyd, einzusehen, dass Ihr. . . grose [sic] alberne Kinder seyd! Und wozu Euch Clubbs und Cassino's? habt Ihr zu viel Langeweile? 'Wir sind uns selbst zur Last daheim--. . ." (23)

The root of all evil is quite clearly the Enlightenment itself: "Aber, Herr Pfarrer, die Aufklärung ist dran schuld, glaub ich" (73). Göchhausen always manages to turn his conversations with his 'good friend' the vicar to questions of Christian ethics, but whereas the clergy depicted in most other works of 1790 are successful agents of secularization, Göchhausen's vicar is not. On one occasion, for example, he faces the conclusion that up-dating the faith is of no avail whatsoever. Although he himself had done everything to make the old faith both meaningful and contemporary and had omitted from sermons "all den alten schweren Wust von Katechismusdogmatik" (72), yet out of a considerable congregation he has scarcely one hundred communicants, and only a few women on Sundays: "kaum zwanzig alte Weiber in den Stühlen" (73). In Göchhausen's view, the philosophical century is unaccommodating to religion.

The traditionally homiletic form of _Erbauung_ has an important function in this work; it allows the vicar to launch into sermons on Göchhausen's behalf, and thus to instruct the reader by direct confrontation. Moral views are not insinuated by means of an entertaining plot. On one occasion he bases his sermon on faith versus works, "der moralischste Text, den es je gab. . . . der dogmatischmoralischste" (91). It is the vicar's clear conviction that man is justified by works alone, but in the course of his argument the concept of 'works' evolves into an affirmation of the merit of 'labour.' Thus the combination of prayer and labour is proclaimed as the most essential ethic in middle-class life. As Christian Salzmann's _Sebastian Kluge_ (1790) will illustrate even more clearly, man is justified by success.[35] Surely, we must argue, justification by 'works' and justification by 'success' are two totally different things; but logical argument is not particularly important for such moralists. By interpreting 'works' as 'work,' they are saying that success publicly justifies the man who has laboured for it. The vicar drives his points home with unparalleled tedium, but, as Göchhausen notes, with complete success: "er lies [sic] seine Gemeinde wie angenagelt, in den Stühlen . . . . sitzen, und sich satt weinen" (96). The reader's sympathetic involvement in the narrative was doubtless meant to have a didactic function as well.

Göchhausen, we noted, is not always content to speak through his vicar, but often interrupts his fiction to deliver his own homily. Even in unequivocally clear pronouncements, he resorts to varying degrees of bold-faced italics to assert his view that only the faithful Christian can face life joyously. The technique literally scars the pages of his work:

> Die Hauptregel, aus welcher die andern fliesen [sic], ist immer die, die zugleich die grose [sic] Lebensregel eines weisen und guten Menschen ist. Ueberlass dich dem U N V E R M E I D L I C H E N ganz unbedingt. RUHIG sterben kan auch der, der von künftiger Fortdauer gar nichts weis [sic]. Aber F R E U D I G die Auflösung erwarten,

kan, MEINER Ueberzeugung nach, nur der redliche gläubige,
seiner Seligkeit gewisse C H R I S T. (195)

The closing lines of Göchhausen's Büchlein promise his 'attentive
readers' a continuation in the near future, a not uncommon promise for
the period. Commending himself into his reader's care, he commends them
in turn unto God: "Und hiemit Gott befolen [sic] bis das neu' Büchlein
fertig ist" (248). The promised book appeared the same year.

[E.A. Göchhausen:] Meines Vaters Hauschronika, ein launiger Beytrag zur
Lebensweisheit, Menschen- und Weltkunde. Mit Belegen, Anecdoten und
Characterzügen (1790).

Göchhausen's 'whimsical contribution to wisdom and human understanding' is intended to enlighten his readers ("aufklären, wie man's
itzt nennt"), in the 'good old-fashioned sense of solid down-to-earth
wisdom and not the enlightenment which one nowadays buys at the word-
monger's' (xiii). True enlightenment, to Göchhausen's mind, means knowledge of God; and an awareness of the value of time he has granted us in
this earthly household: "wir müssen die Tage aus der Hand des Hausherrn
annehmen, wie Er sie in seinen Ewigen Haushaltungs-Kalender eingetragen
hat" (2). He writes for the epitome of middle-class provincialism:

> ". . . jedem geraden, einfältige Natur liebenden, Prunk-
> hassenden, den Menschen gern im Hauskleide, an seinem
> Feuerherde. . . sehenden Leser; jedem, der Hertzlichkeit
> und Wahrheit liebt, und die Kunst versteht, aus den
> kleinsten Zügen die wichtigsten und sichersten Resultate
> für Menschenkunde zu ziehen;. . . (xxvii)

Having assumed the role of editor of his father's personal papers
("Hab' aber das feine Büchlein nicht selbst gestellet, sondern mein Vater
seeliger", iv f.), Göchhausen divests himself of responsibility for style
and content. His main editorial function is limited to 'excerpting'
those parts of his father's private papers which best reveal the inner
man and which he deems of moral value for the simple souls ("gute, stille, biedere, einfältige Seelen, Männlein und Weiblein", 333), for whom
the book is intended. The work is variously called a "Noth- und Hülfs-
büchlein" (4), "Hauschronika" (4), "Tagebüchel" (318), "Universal-Haus-
apotheke" (431), and a "Spiegel zur Selbstbeschau" (504); one cannot es-

cape the impression that these half-truths are imitations of Sterne's whimsical manner. The final descriptive term recalls the "Spiegel" of the devotional tradition, and it is significant that Göchhausen's 'father' describes his manuscript as a mirror of his own soul (Spiegel meiner Seele) for the 'general contemplation' (20) of his readers. He concludes the work in a similar manner:

> "Nimm also für diesmal vorlieb, Gesindlein. . . mit diesem Spiegel zur Selbstbeschau. Siehe für dich allein, wie du gestaltet bist; werde besser und klüger. . ." (504).

The Preface informs us of its entertaining and instructive contents:

> Ist übrigens allerley nützlicher Lahr und viel guter Ding drin, auch wohl hie und da ein Schwank, wie es unter sittigen Leuten und guten Kumpanen von Alten her Brauch war. Ist also ein Büchlein, ernsthafft mit unter, auch ein wenig lustig zu lesen; . . . (iv)

The work is a composite of third-person narrative, first-person recollection, letters, and lengthy quotations from Haller, Wieland, Zinzendorff, Weishaupt, and Mirabeau, and abounds in morally instructive anecdotes and playlets, prayers, and 'wise sayings.' The tone is set by the author's own self-righteous and self-satisfied pulpit-thumping and by his many harangues--such as against the French Revolution and the Enlightenment. His perspective is always clear: "Erst bin ich Mensch, dann Staatsbürger, und dann freyer Lutheraner" (169); in practice, however, his priorities are the reverse: first a Lutheran, then a citizen, and then a human being. Göchhausen is a churchman who feels his institution threatened. He is certainly correct in calling his book an "allerley," and he begs his reader to take it for what it is, neither seeking nor finding in it more than it actually contains. Having 'prepared' the work (with an eye perhaps to the opening pages of Tom Jones) to satisfy all tastes and digestive systems ("so mancherley Geschmack, so mancherley Dauungswerkzeuge," 400) he wants each reader to 'take what he can use and leave the rest for others.'

Göchhausen does not regard the Hauschronika as a novel, presumably because it does not contain tales of love and adventure. Yet like the contemporary novelist, he tries to use Sterne's techniques and Richardson's idiom to 'steal into the human heart' by means of entertaining narratives. To his mind at least, he has succeeded in imparting truths by revealing his father's heart to an emotionally involved readership:

> Verzeyht Ihr mirs, gute Seelen, dass ich es wagte, Euch
> das Heiligthum des Hertzens meines Vaters aufzudecken?
> Ach, Ihr schenket ja wohl eine Thräne des Mitgefühls dem
> Künstler, der sich in Euer Hertz und Einbildungskraft
> hinein stahl! Hier ist Wahrheit; nicht Roman. Dies konnte
> nicht geschehen; es geschah! (245)

The plot is very skimpy indeed, its sole function being to explain how the manuscript came into the 'editor's' hands, and how the old man had recorded his reflections. The bulk of the work is devoted to preachment. As the author himself admits, if he had 'torn out the whole litany of reason and self-control [which, to speak with Daniel Defoe, constitute "not only the greatest beauties of the work, but are calculated for the infinite advantage of the reader"[36]], there would be scarcely little else left' (318). Göchhausen maintains a patronizing and patriarchal attitude towards his readers, explaining that while there are bound to be many things in the book they will not understand, he will give as much explanation as possible. However, he adds, one need not understand the book which one is reading provided it is a good one! The Bible is his case in point.

Set against the background of developments in the Character Novel, a review in the Neuer Teutscher Merkur for 1791 (Vol 2, p. 230) provides a particularly revealing commentary on Göchhausen's Hauschronika. The reviewer regards it as disconnected and odd, but nonetheless remarkable because of its psychological insights and what he feels to be veiled autobiography:

> Es ist ein sehr merkwürdiges Buch, schon als psychologische
> Erscheinung. Denn Sie werden bald finden, dass es unter
> mancherley Umhüllung immer der Verfasser selbst ist, der
> sich schildert; und ohne seinen Nahmen zu wissen, kann man
> gewiss seyn, dass man einen wahren Menschen vor sich sieht,
> und obendrein keinen alltäglichen.

[Christian Gotthilf Salzmann:] Sebastian Kluge. Ein Volksbuch (1790)

Whereas Göchhausen imparts his moral precepts by addressing the reader directly, illustrating his views by means of exempla, and by attempting a psychological portrayal of his hero, Salzmann's work clothes a moral view in a fictional autobiography. Each stage of the protagonist's life intends to illustrate the efficaciousness of Salzmann's principles, while the vicar counsels the hero on his path toward success and acts as an agent of secularization. Leonard Meister's Spaziergänge proclaims the traditional view of the office of pastor as advisor, consoler and benefactor of humanity (48), a view shared by the vicar in Johann Christian Müller's Physiognomist who also claims that every pastor is his people's most important confidant and authority (184). Salzmann's pastor is all of these things, but uses his office in a uniquely different way. He does not stress Christian charity with its renunciation of worldly goods, but uses the idiom of Christian faith to transmit modes of behaviour designed to bring about better adjustment to the secular form of life. Education for moral action is here a corollary of the adaptation of the middle-class to economic conditions; success in business is proof of grace. In Salzmann's vocabulary, one's time on earth is the principal which, when invested by the virtuous application of the ethic of work, guarantees returns with compound interest: "Jedem Menschen ist ein grosses Kapital gegeben, das sich stetig verzinst; das ist die Zeit" (15).

The only available edition of Sebastian Kluge is a commemorative issue of 1898, which the editors admit to having 'expurgated.' All parts 'which are foreign to the taste of the times have been omitted and certain adjustments made to present-day taste and morality, without thereby harming the spirit of the work' (iii). While one might well regret the lack of historical accuracy caused by the loss of the first edition, the present text provides unexpected evidence of the continued appeal of Salzmann's works.

According to the editor, they continue to exert a far greater educative influence among the people ("eine weit grössere volkserzieherische Kraft, iii), than thousands of other books that are put into the hands of children and [!] adults. Of all Salzmann's novels, Sebastian

Kluge was selected for republication as it is 'not without a certain
poetic power' (v). Salzmann had set himself the 'grand task' of trans-
mitting important truths by means of a life story: "durch Mitteilung
einer Lebensgeschichte" (vi). The goal of the hero's personal development is of particular importance as it reflects those ultimate values
which are considered the principal concerns of human development: by
using 'good advice' and 'faithful application of time and energy,'
Kluge acquires 'independence of judgment, ownership of property and
goods, honour and public esteem' (vi). One could hardly expect a narrow-
er secular interest. It is important to note the readership which Salzmann had in mind. The editor claims to quote Salzmann when explaining
that Kluge's "Lebenslauf" is actually written for those who are neither
scholars nor have the opportunity to read many books. Yet Salzmann believes 'that even scholars will learn much by it.' (iv)

   A brief summary of Sebastian Kluge will best illustrate the relationship between plot and moral instruction. The novel is little more
than an extended parable: "Exempel von einem Menschen, der durch gute
Anwendung seiner Zeit ein glücklicher Mensch geworden ist" (39). Kluge's
father takes him out of school at the age of eleven and teaches him to
despise God, his mother, and work. He leaves home on his father's death
and would have become a vagrant 'if God had not had other plans for him.'
He chances upon a village squire, who becomes his guardian and apprentices him with a farmer so that he might learn 'the virtues of the proper
use of time.' The boy soon learns to delight in heavy labour and thrills
to the crops he has planted. The local vicar's sermon on Christ's use of
the sabbath for healing instead of rest moves the lad so deeply that he
devotes his Sundays to finishing his schooling. Having surpassed his
fellow farmers in reading skills, he comes upon a book on crop rotation
and tries his hand at this method of farming, though the squire warns
that hastily attempted innovations court danger. In one year of labour
and study Kluge succeeds in filling a fallow field with clover 'like a
forest.' (Not even the fields must rest!) In six years he almost doub-
les his master's crops and cattle. The vicar's sermon honouring one's
parents moves him to visit his destitute mother; he leaves her his sa-
vings, then returns to the farm to toil, learn and save money. He becomes a gambler and loses everything; by a lucky chance, he wins it all back

and gives up his 'wicked' ways.

On another occasion he meets a stranger who teaches him to adjust
his socks so that he can hike better. Kluge thus learns the virtues of
dialogue: One can either learn something new or else give advice--and
if neither be the case it is still better than playing cards (25). At
the age of twenty-four he seeks a wife and is advised that resources come
before love. The squire's wedding gift is a part of the profits derived
from Kluge's labour; his interest on invested time is thus paid. On
first arising from the marriage bed, he proclaims that if a bachelor can
achieve so much, how much greater scope for an industrious couple! They
labour in the fields, stay at home after work instead of seeking diver-
sions in town, and save more money. When Kluge's wife institutes a coffee hour to break their endless day, he calculates that it would squander
5760 man-hours over a twenty-year period. Kluge continues to meet the
challenges of life: he buys a sour field cheaply and makes it productive
by labouring in his spare time; he sees his neighbour ruined through
stock-market speculation instead of toiling for gain; 'escapes the boredom' of his child's christening party by planting trees from which he
gathers a full harvest in a single year. He amasses a dowry for his
child by not heating the bedroom in winter, putting aside the wood he
would have burned, which he then sells in order to buy sheep. The sheep
reproduce, he sheers them annually, sells the wool and saves the money.
At long last he reaches the pinnacle of his career on his appointment as
Church Inspector:

> Ich konnte gut schreiben und rechnen, führte eine gute
> Ehe, gute Haushaltung und lebte mit allen Nachbarn in
> guter Eintracht. Solche Männer müssten Kircheninspektoren
> werden. (91)

The final chapter reveals, however, that Salzmann is not as severe
an opponent of rest as the book might suggest:

> . . . die Stunden der Nacht, die man mit Schlafen zubringt,
> sind gut angewendet, denn sie stärken den Körper, dass er
> dann am Tage desto mehr arbeiten kann. (95)

Salzmann's Sebastian Kluge is further demonstration of Max Weber's
thesis[37] that protestantism canonized man's earthly profession as a divine calling and justified economic endeavours as a kind of Divine Ser-

vice in which one's capacity to earn a living was regarded as a form of asceticism.

Here secularization has gone much further than in Göchhausen's books, for Sebastian Kluge is at least a rudimentary novel that hints at character 'development.' The next novel takes us a step further by attempting to portray how two young girls actually develop into womanhood and assume a useful role in society.

[Christiane Naubert:] Merkwürdige Begebenheiten der gräflichen Familie von Wallis (1790)

Linked with the tradition of Richardson by the effective combination of didactic intent, English setting, epistolary form, and women as central characters, this work is unique among the German novels of 1790. Its purpose is to illustrate thoughts on feminine education--Gedanken über weibliche Erziehung (i, 9)--so that Naubert's readers might learn 'what they are to strive for and be forewarned of what they must flee' (I, 10). It consists of ninety-three 'entertaining and instructive letters' (I, 40) exchanged between eight correspondents. The epistolary technique is used to present different views on the 'events' in the Wallis family that bear out Naubert's ideas on education.

The book opens with a letter from the Majorin von Sandwich in which she asks her friend, Gräfin von Wallis, whether she should send her thirteen year-old daughter away to school or educate her at home. Gräfin von Wallis replies that the best way to express her views is 'to sketch the outline of the plan she followed with some success' and to offer 'a few examples of the effects which the different educational methods' had upon her twin daughters. We thus have two protagonists instead of the customary single figure; it is as though Naubert were conducting an experiment, so that the reader might judge which of the daughters had the most salutary experience. The twins are seven years old when Gräfin von Wallis initiates her plan of education:

> Gelehrig sollten sie werden, ohne ein sklavisches Wesen
> anzunehmen; geschmeidig, ohne sich zu fürchten; zartherzig,
> ohne schwach zu werden (I, 11).

To this end, the girls spend the next three years at home learning to read and write, do sums, sew, and tend to the household chores. From eleven years of age onwards, they follow different paths.

One of the twins, Minna Wallis, is educated at home in the country, far from the influences of city life. When domestic chores are done, she retires to her father's study to hear his 'lectures on natural science' and to undertake 'experiments which transform learning into sheer pleasure.' As a result of her father's deistic approach Minna can 'look up to the God of Nature through Nature itself' (I, 23). She embarks on the study of history, based on 'the historical parts of the Bible,' and learns French and Italian. Her father is delighted with her progress and the author explains that 'if this beautiful approach, this mutual confidence between parent and child were generally observed,' much 'misery' would be avoided. (The heroine's fate in Die unglückliche Fürstin aus Wien, we may recall, supports this view.) Indeed, 'if parents would only try to strengthen their daughters' soul and power of judgement, there would be fewer cases where false choice offends a young woman's honour and destroys her parents' hopes' (I, 39). The Majorin von Sandwich is delighted with the 'instructive and entertaining' observations of her 'kind teacher' who is advising her 'what to avoid and what to imitate' (I, 45).

The danger in sending one's daughter away to school, as the story of Amalie Wallis illustrates, is that 'absence weakens her love for her mother' (I, 52). Amalie is sent to a boarding school where she learns the social graces befitting a young woman. On graduating, she is 'the loveliest, finest, most perfect young lady in England' (I, 67). No longer can she tolerate the 'unrefined' simplicity of country-life. She regards Minna's studious way of life as boring, 'and besides, males hate an educated woman' (I, 83). Her perfections, as her mother laments, are the superficialities, vanities, and cultivated boredom of upper-class society. Amalie is, in consequence, a hollow person, while Minna is all soul.

After a brief visit, Amalie leaves home again to live with a frivolous aunt in high society and becomes a coquette. Coquettry, as her mother explains, 'is not only a definite characteristic of wickedness, but usually the mark of a flighty soul without principles and is the basis of almost every female vice as well' (I,109). Indeed Amalie would have been surprised to learn that men are not at all interested in witless belles. Baron Holderness, representing the male attitude toward women in this novel, prefers Minna:

> . . . ich bin mehr als jemals überzeugt, ein Frauenzimmer muss erst denken, ehe sie gefallen kann! woher käme sonst der Unterschied bey diesen Zwillingsschönheiten? Amalie könnte Pygmalions Bildsäule vorstellen; aber Minna ist die Seele, welche sie belebet. Nicht dass es der ersten an Lebhaftigkeit fehlet, das weiss der Himmel; aber alles ist mechanisch. . . wie bey allen feinen Frauenzimmern in England; aber bey Minna so, wie bey keiner einzigen" (I, 104)

Letters subsequently exchanged between these and other correspondents in the novel reveal how the eighteen year-old twins fare on their own in the adult world. An account of their adventures would be superfluous here, as they follow the traditional pattern of the love story. It suffices to remark that Amalie falls into difficult (but instructive) straits because of her false values, while Minna is deceived by a world in which her pure soul and intellectual achievements are alien. One of the letters--richly seeded in penny-philosophy like the others--anticipates the conclusion of the novel and is central to Naubert's didactic interests--despair should never overwhelm a noble soul:

> Verzweiflung sollte niemals eine edle Seele überwältigen; der Unglückliche sollte nie die Hoffnung aufgeben,wenn auch heute das Schicksal ihm feind ist; denn Morgen kann es wieder lächeln. (I, 168)

After more than a thousand pages, the final letter of Gräfin von Wallis joyously describes the betrothal of her 'twin cherubs'; both are happy, and both are worthy of being so. Her daughters' marriage and enjoyment of sound domesticity was 'the constant wish of her whole life.' She delights in the knowledge that the ultimate goal of her daughters' education--by adventure and misadventure--has finally been revealed; the girls are mature and worthwhile persons, ready to enter upon a life of social responsibility. Although Amalie's education had first made her unhappy in the adult world and Minna's upbringing was not immediately crowned with deserved good fortune, Gräfin von Wallis derives a moral: The mistaken views in Amalie's education 'ceded at first to woe and then to better example,' while 'the disappointed expectations' of Minna were 'the testing of a pure virtue which heaven visibly acclaims' (II, 545 ff.)

208

The question still remains as to whether the Sandwich girl should
be brought up at home or sent to school. Gräfin von Wallis suggests an
answer by explaining that education at home had provided Minna with all
the resources she needed 'to triumph over her tests.' Amalia, we are informed had to be 'rescued' from the shallowness of high society 'like
kindling from a fire,' while her frivolous aunt, who had lured her from
the wholesomeness of home, had come to ruin (II, 552).

Whereas Naubert's historical novels received highly favourable reviews, she was thoroughly trounced for being 'a boring biographer' when
the present novel was reviewed in the Allgemeine Deutsche Bibliothek for
1791 (vol 104, p. 418):

> Es gibt sehr langweilige gräfliche Familien; diese ist eine
> davon und ihr Geschichtsschreiber ein langweiliger Biograph.
> Diese soll in Richardsonscher Manier geschrieben seyn; aber
> die Begebenheiten, Raisonnements und die Art der Darstellung
> sind gleich gemein und uninteressant. Ist dies dicke Buch
> aus Geldnoth zusammengeschrieben; so ist der Verf. zu be-
> dauern. Es muss unerhörte Geduld dazu erfordert werden,
> so etwas auf das Papier zu bringen, und man sollte denken,
> Schwefelhölzer zu machen wäre eine bey Weitem unterhalten-
> dere und nützlichere Arbeit.

[Wilhelm Friedrich Heller:] Sokrates (1790)

The works we have just reviewed were designed as vehicles for the
author's homilies, and were entirely fictional. Yet some writers, as we
have seen, felt that their views would be more convincing if their
'truth' could be authenticated by the lives of historical figures. This
is the thought behind Wilhelm Heller's Sokrates and Ignaz Fessler's
Marc-Aurel. They placed their heroes in fictional situations and used
the teachings of Socrates and Marcus Aurelius as a foil for general observations. These works might equally well have served as examples of
the historical novel of 1790, but are included here as rudimentary
character novels as they shed light on the manner in which biography was
turned to didactic purposes.

Heller explains that Sokrates was the culmination of boyhood interest and an enthusiasm he tried to impart to his female pupils (I, v).
Regarding the historical Socrates as the epitome of reason, moderation
and virtue (I, 3, 32, et passim), he consequently considers his novel

a timely offering to contemporaries who are afflicted by the evil times
(I, 71). Socrates was in all respects 'a very useful man; nothing was
more agreeable or more instructive than his company' (I, 165). Heller
wants his story to be both engaging and instructive, as he hopes to en-
sure Socrates' continued influence; indeed the 'mere narration of his
life works miracles' (I, 305 f.). Following the principles of his historical model, who 'opposed the trends of his times' (I, 39), Heller op-
poses popular taste in the novel. Yet it will be obvious at first glance, he explains, that "der Meisner'sche Alcibiades" (I, v)[38] induced him
to write Sokrates. Though Meisner's hero 'as boy, youth, and man holds
greater attraction for the fashionable world' (I, v), he insists that his
own novel is of greater value. Indeed, 'Socrates' life showed more
beautifully and clearly than Agathon's, quid virtus et quid virtus et
quit sapientia possit' (viii). Frequent references to the author of
Agathon, whose works Heller presumes his female readers to have read
(100), clearly suggest that Heller regarded Wieland's Bildungsroman as a
model. His lengthy dialogues on beauty, virtue and wisdom--after the
pattern of Agathon--would seem to bear this out.

Heller's situation reflects the quandary of many novelists: he
knows his public wants to be entertained, while he himself wishes to
teach. 'A few conversations between Socrates and his mistress would be
more welcome than the more serious dialogues with his philosophical
friends'; but as that sort of thing can be found easily elsewhere, he
hopes that noble souls would care for once to lend an ear to a Greek sage:
"allein man hat solcher süsen [sic] Dinge schon so viel, dass ich von
ädlen Selen [sic] hoffen darf, sie werden auch einmal einen griechischen
Weisen gern hören" (I, vi f.). Philosophy, he assures us, as though
countering those of his colleagues who rail against the 'philosophical
century,' is not a dangerous thing. Socrates' philosophy by no means
prevented him from fulfilling his duties as a citizen, for he earned his
keep by working (I, 32).

Though only the first book of Heller's novel is extant, we may
assume it is representative of the whole. According to Heller himself
the parts but differ in one major feature: Part One could give no scope
for action, whereas Part Two was to contain the hero's most important
deeds (I, viii). In each part, however, Heller was faced with the

problem of authenticating his fictionalized portrayal of Socrates. His
Preface, for example, claims Plato and Xenophon as his authorities, and
explains that Moses Mendelssohn's "Charakter des Sokrates" served him as
a guideline (I, v). He seems particularly indebted to four of Plato's
socratic dialogues, though he never specifically mentions any one: the
Euthyphro, which portrays Socrates as a teacher seeking to shake the
Athenians' confidence in their untested opinions; the Apology, in which
Socrates explains to his judges that his mission is to arouse the Athenians from dogmatic slumbers and make them reflect upon the meaning and
purpose of their lives; the Crito, in which the imprisoned Socrates argues that the true end of existence is not life per se, but living well;
and finally the Phaedo, in which he discusses the immortality of the
soul. One suspects that the model for Heller's Aristipp (184 ff.) can
be found in Plato's Protagoras, but whereas Plato's Aristippus is noted
for his insistence on the intelligent control of pleasure as opposed to
either slavish adherence or abstinence, Heller's Aristipp does not deal
with that issue. The names of his characters seem authentically Greek,
although not all appear in Plato. Antiphon (I, 75 ff.) Kristobal (I,
89 ff., 226 f.), and Nikomachides (I, 261) can be found in Aristotle,
while Antisthenes (I, 86 ff.) figures in Aristophanes' comedy The Clouds.

Heller's documentation suggests scholarly precision in only one
instance. Claiming that 'Socrates' genius remains a dark and insoluble
puzzle for us,' he refers his reader to the studies of C. Meiners and
L.J.K. Justi, both apparently entitled "Über den Genius des Socrates"
(I, 117).[39] On informing his reader elsewhere that 'Socrates was, according to all that we know of him, the most incomparable, wisest and noblest
man,' he refers us in a footnote to Lavater's Physiognomische Fragmente,
'where many fine things are said about him' (I, 23).[40] It is curious
that he should claim Wieland's Musarion as his source for the Delphic
oracle's injunction, "Know thyself," (I, 285) instead of referring to
Plato's Apology. For the rest, he is content to allude to unnamed 'writers of antiquity' (I, 34), but is never consistent in his use of footnotes to substantiate sources or to qualify his observations. Relatively
insignificant points are sometimes annotated, whereas major arguments often are not. Heller's use of quotations seems to have been dictated by
convenience.

Heller is only partly concerned with demonstrating that he has studied the sources. Of greater significance is the excitement he feels in portraying, without the need of scholarly proof, an historical figure who is 'uncommonly famous' (I, 4). He knows of no other mortal, he writes, whose virtue, doctrine, and death earned the admiration of all people in all ages. Not even Jesus attained this stature (I, 10 f.). Whatever one thinks of Socrates, he adds, quoting Justin Martyr with forced logic, Christ is that Reason which the whole human race shares; all men who live according to Reason are Christians. Just such a man was Socrates (I, 140). For this reason Heller had wanted to write a "Parallelbiographie" of Christ and Socrates (I, 286 f.), a task that would have required a Plutarch to carry it off: "aber es gehört ein plutarchischer Geist dazu" (I, 269).

The content and form of Heller's book were suggested by two features of Socrates' life: his ideas and his technique of presenting them. As Heller writes, when explaining the socratic method to his readers: "Und so sprach er mit Jedermann, der ihm Stand hielt, über die wichtigsten Gegenstände des menschlichen Lebens" (I, 31). The novel mainly consists of a series of discussions between Socrates and various representatives of society on such topics as virtue, honesty, moderation, fashions, faith in God, and scorn of wealth. Whereas the title and Preface lead one to expect a 'life' of Socrates, the text offers selected 'samples' of the rich fare, which are supposed to whet our appetite for more:

> Die Probe von dem Umgang des Sokrates mit seiner Familie
> kann uns lüstern machen nach einigen Aeuserungen [sic] seines
> Herzens und Verstandes gegen Freunde. Wir werden einige
> Beweise aus Xenophon anführen (I, 51).

Each scene or discussion presents a single facet of Socrates' character and thought. They are linked together by third-person narratives and by author-commentaries that summarize the significance of each scene and occasionally offer a preview of what is to follow. The technique results in a plodding rhythm and an irksome tendency towards polemics. However, the approach is germane to Heller's didacticism, for his main purpose consists in offering a moral corrective: "In den Tagen der Schöngeisterei und Kraftgeniesucht ist es wohl der Mühe wert, zu erfahren, wie der Weltgenius in Griechenland gesprochen habe" (I, vi f.). We need only

cite a few examples to demonstrate how Heller adapts Socrates' life to
contemporary needs.

The book opens with a description of 'the world into which the
great man stepped.' Socrates was 'the teacher of his contemporaries and
a model of wisdom for all future centuries' at a time when 'the beautiful
days of Greece were on the verge of decline' (I, 3). Heller holds up the
person of Socrates as a sublime model for emulation while exploiting the
decline of Greek culture to forewarn his fellow-countrymen of Germany's
impending moral collapse. He asserts that luxury, disunity, and Persian
"Galanterie" undermined the 'beautiful structure of the Greek state' and
then directs a tirade against foreign customs and contemporary philosophies that are now hastening the ruin of the German state:

> . . . ach! so wirst du sinken, Teutonia, mein Vaterland,
> wenn brittische Whims, französische Moden, abenteuerliche
> Aufklärung, Schwärmerey, und Unduldsamkeit, und fremde
> Statskabalen [sic] deinen Geist irre führen, und deine
> Kräfte zermalmen! (I, 8)

In another scene we overhear Socrates questioning Pistias the Armourer
concerning the secrets of his craft. Socrates wishes to learn why
Pistias' armour is so expensive and how he manages to make a breastplate
for a 'disproportionate person' so that it is well-fitting and harmonizes
with the person's form. Pistias replies that the perfection of his art
depends upon imitating nature: "wenn er [der Harnisch] gut passt, so ist
er auch nach dem Modell der Natur proportionierlich" (I, 28). Leaving
the fictional Socrates to expound the importance of imitating nature,
Heller turns to the 'fair ladies of the fatherland' and chastises them
for their ridiculous 'corsets and narrow shoes': "Ihr Schönen meines
Vaterlandes, denkt an eure Schnurbrüste und engen Schue [sic], wenn
Sokrates von Harnischen spricht!" (I, 31). Somewhat later Socrates explains that whoever is ungrateful to his parents must expect ingratitude
from others. Using biblical language, Heller intrudes into the narrative
to explain, curiously enough, that one can find contemporary corrobora-
tion for Socrates' view in the works of Laurence Sterne:

> Wehe dem Menschen, vom Weibe geboren, der dieses liest, und
> die Heiligkeit der kindlichen Pflichten nicht in der Tiefe
> des Herzens empfindet! Der liebenswürdige Yorick dachte
> hierinn, wie Sokrates: die Dankbarkeit, sagt er, ist die

schönste Pflanze der Menschentugenden; denn sie wächst
auf der Staude der Woltätigkeit [sic] (I, 51).

After numerous episodes and dialogues in which we see Socrates 'as
sculptor and philosopher, moralist and man of the world, husband and
warrior,' Heller presents his hero as 'the speaker of the people, as de-
fender of suppressed innocence' (I, 238). Here too, his Socrates aims
'to instruct his fellow-citizens in virtue and wisdom' (I, 267). Heller
presents his static hero as the epitome of perfected man; he is the
authoritative preacher of reason and virtue who converts others to a new
way of life and helps the German reader to understand social problems
from Heller's viewpoint. The closing scene gives final authentication
when one of Socrates' pupils approaches the Delphic Oracle. As Socrates
had done in Plato's Apology (but with different intent and results), the
pupil asks who is the best and wisest man:

> Grose [sic] Gottheit! wer ist der Weiseste unter den
> Menschen? Die Antwort ward ihm unter Blizen [sic] und
> Donnern: Sokrates (I, 308)

[Ignaz Aurelius Fessler:] Marc-Aurel (1790)

Fessler's novel, which the Allgemeine Deutsche Bibliothek for
1790 (vol 94, pp. 445-46) regarded as "einer von der neuen Gattung historischer Romane, wo Geschichte zum Grunde liegt, die aber durch Hinzudichtung mancher Umstände erweitert wird und verschönert", and which
Marion Beaujean regards as a Bildungsroman,[41] aims at portraying the principles and actions (I, 1) of a 'sublime colossus' (III, ii) and paragon
of virtue (IV, 202). The author wishes to show some of his readers the
'greatness and bliss' to which man is raised by utilizing 'a reason sublime beyond prejudice and a virtue based on human nature' (I, i). Marcus
Aurelius, we are told, lived for virtue and for the happiness of man.
This, in brief, is 'the whole story of his life, which immortalizes him
in the hearts of all decent people' (I, iii). Fessler writes to pay
homage (III, i) to a man 'who deserves not merely our admiration, but our
imitation' (III, ii), and 'whose moderation would have made him worthy
of ruling the world' (III, iii).

Fessler describes his work as a "Darstellung" (II, ii), a "Schil-

214

derung" (III, i) and as an "Umriss" (III, i), which 'graphically portrays Rome's invincible hero' (III, ii). We are informed with facile modesty that it is not a professional 'essay' (II, ii), but a 'small and insignificant' work, the 'fruit of the author's solitary and quiet hours' (II,i) We may be reasonably certain that Fessler would not wish Marc-Aurel to be regarded as a novel, for his article "An die ästhetischen Kunstrichter der Deutschen", published in Archiv der Zeit [1796, Vol 1, p. 242], defends his historical novels against such terminology. They should be called "historische Gemälde", their aim being to fill in the gaps of history by psychological combination and by sketching the instructive characters of one's heroes. He also argues in the Preface of Abalard (1806) that his principal aim in writing books based on historical figures was to reveal the hero's states of mind by casting them in a fictional form: "Man forderte die Bedingungen des historischen Romans von mir, der ich nur Geisteszustände durch ein romantisches Kleid sichtbar machen wollte."[42] The Allgemeine Deutsche Bibliothek for 1790 seems to have appreciated this approach by remarking that Fessler presents his hero so that we observe even his earliest education ("Bildung"), and 'the character which emerged from it.'

Fessler has in fact adapted the general 'principles' of Marcus Aurelius' Contemplations, albeit often without specific reference to the original. He promotes those virtues which we find described in Aurelius' work as "goodness, self-respect, truthfulness, reasonableness, co-operativeness, and high mindedness," these being construed as "the elevation of [one's] thoughts above the stirrings of the flesh" (Contemplations, Bk. 10, par. 8). Some scenes are explicitly based upon the Contemplations, and are amply footnoted. In one scene, for example, the fictional hero reveals himself as a just man who loves those who offend him. He expresses the view that loving one's enemy is natural to those who regard all men as brothers and who understand that offenders act out of ignorance or against their own will. Insults harm no one, the hero explains, for the citadel of one's personality remains unassailed; calumny and scorn cannot work counter to virtue (II, 155). A lengthy footnote paraphrases the Contemplations (Bk. 7, para. 22) and notes the correct reference. When the Rusticus of the novel maligns Marc-Aurel by suspecting him of incontinence, Fessler adds a note explaining why he construed

Rusticus' character in this manner:

> Ein harter Mann muss Rusticus gewesen seyn, weil <u>Marc-Aurel</u>
> selbst bekennt (Betracht. Erst B. 17) dass er es der Vor-
> sicht verdanke, dass ihn der Zorn über den <u>Rusticus</u>, worein
> er oft gerathen ist, nie zu einer Handlung hingerissen hat,
> die er jetzt zu bereuen Ursache hatte. (II, 217)

Again the reference is correct, although the interpretation is open to
question. However, Fessler is frequently inclined to place entirely
alien concepts on the lips of Aurelius. A significant case in point is
the hero's definition of virtue as 'a perfect reason, or a correct and
firm knowledge of the rules according to which one must act, united with
a skill acquired through practice of acting according to these rules in
all cases' (I, 82). The concept of adhering to moral precepts reflects
Fessler's views, whereas Aurelius speaks of hearkening to "your directing
mind, the ruler of your soul" (Bk. 5, para. 26).

A typical form of authentication, however, is expressed in the
claim that his hero's words are characteristic of the historical man:
"<u>Marc-Aurels</u> Aeusserung ist charakteristisch" (IV, 67). A major theme
of the <u>Contemplations</u>, for example, is that of man's social responsibility: "An exile is he who flees from social principle. . ." (Bk. 4,
para. 9); "Just as you yourself complete a social system, so must your
every action complete a life directed to social ends" (Bk. 9, para. 23).
These views are important for Fessler's novel. Aurelius, Fessler informs
us, never considered it beneath his dignity to appear among all levels of
society as a teacher, 'because he knew that moving examples have a stron-
ger and more certain effect than cold laws and threatened punishments'
(III, 321). Thus Fessler uses "rührende Beispiele" in the form of dramatic dialogues to illustrate the bald statements and assertions of his
account. Contrived scenes based on the generalities derived from Aurelius' views form the main structural component of the work; these are
linked by descriptive narratives and by the author's prosaic commentaries,
which summarize the principles his characters have enacted or discussed,
and forecast future scenes. Fessler explains his approach in these
terms:

> Marc-Aurel wollte Gutes thun, und er fand Zeit, Gelegenheit,
> Mittel genug dazu. . . Mit welchem glücklichen Erfolge
> für das allgemeine Wohl dies öfters geschah, sollen

216

folgende Gespräche zeigen. (II, 273)

Fessler is never loath to change circumstances to fit his narrative aims, but whenever he takes a gross liberty, as we noted earlier, he adds his reasons in a footnote. Whenever his hero acts out of character, (as in the emotional episode with his mistress), and speaks in a manner foreign to the temperate man of reason whom Fessler claims him to be, a footnote justifies the portrayal 'before the court of literary taste':

> Die Absicht, auf Hypatias [Marc-Aurels Geliebte] schwärmerische Einbildungskraft zu wirken, rechtfertigt Marc-Aurels weitläuftige, in die Erzählung. . . eingewebte Beschreibung vor dem Richterstuhl des Geschmackes. (II, 84)

Historicity, however, remains subordinate to the demands of creating a pleasing and instructive fiction, and Fessler may well have been thinking of that part of the Contemplations where Aurelius wrote: "Speak, both in the Senate and to anyone you may address, with fitting grace, but without pedantic precision." (Bk. 8, para. 30).

Certainly, the reviewer in the Allgemeine Deutsche Bibliothek for 1790 (vol. 94, pp. 445-46) was pleased with the result. He noted that 'these fictions certainly have verisimilitude and charm, and the author writes with dignity and in a carefully worked style.' He did not at all object to Fessler's having supplemented the facts of history by embellishing his narrative. The reviewer of the second volume in the same journal for 1791 (Vol 104, p. 179) singles out Fessler's lack of talent for writing love scenes and suggests that if the author continues to 'spin out his digressions we can expect a fair number of volumes' yet to come.

Fessler's hero first appears among the suppressed population of Rome as a Messiah: "Die im Staube zertretene Menschheit rufte [sic] zu ihrem mächtigen Schutz-Genius"--and Marcus Aurelius came (9). Like young Jesus in the temple, Marc-Aurel absorbs the instruction of his masters, thus developing his character and revealing what he is to become as a man:

> Je eifriger der Knabe den Unterricht seiner Lehrer sich eigen machte, destomehr entwickelte sich auch sein Karakter, und zeigte dem scharfsichtigen Beobachter deutlich, was er als Mann in der Folge werden könnte,werden würde. (112)

Yet Providence had 'singled him out before the human race as an object for adoration and emulation,' and his teacher observed in these childhood years 'unmistakable seeds' of the man he would once be (13). But having thus prepared us for psychological insights into the gradual development of his hero's personality and secular mission, Fessler falls back upon the technique of the episodic narrative. The hero is not actually shown to develop at all. The eight-year old Marc-Aurel speaks with the same command of rhetoric (I, 51) and with the same 'perfect reason' (I, 82) as the mature man. The scenes are a series of incidents and situations strung out, as it were, across the supporting pillars of brief didactic commentaries that the author inserts into his fiction. It falls to these commentaries to indicate that the young hero is developing into the virtuous ruler of Rome. The novel as biography depends on these signposts. Thus Fessler asserts after many tedious dialogues that Marc-Aurel is "auf der reitzvollen [sic] Laufbahn der Weisheit und der Tugend" (I, 66) and that he is actively engaged in seeking truth (I, 128); later we are informed that he has become committed to virtue, friends, and fatherland: "Gewonnen war jetzt Marc-Aurel für Tugend, Freunde und Vaterland. Gewonnen für immer" (II, 258). As the novel draws to a close we are told that Aurelius is near the fulfillment of his mission: "nahe der Vollendung seines mühsamen Laufes" (IV, 202); when the hero dies on the final page, Fessler concludes that he had achieved his goal: "Marc-Aurel hatte vollendet" (IV, 316). Without the author's clear statements demarking critical stages of his hero's advance through life, the rudiments of the Bildungsroman would have passed unperceived.

[Georg Christoph Kellner:] Klingstein: Eine Geschichte, mit Szenen aus dem spanischen Successionskrieg (1790)

Kellner's Klingstein advances beyond the character novels of Naubert and Fessler by actually portraying the testing of a soul. The hero's impassioned imagination (glühende Einbildungskraft, 101) aroused and nourished from early childhood by his predilection for novels and stories of adventure, thrusts him out of conventional society until at the last he finds fulfillment in domestic bliss. Kellner calls his work a biography (7) and a character sketch (174) of a man whose life must be described under a fictitious name to protect a remaining member of the family. Once this last member has taken his place "in den Regionen wo Sokrates, Konfuz, Zoroaster, Rousseau and alle praktischen Weisen der Erde Lorbeern tragen, zu denen sie sich durch stechende Dornen hindurch wanden" (7), Klingstein's real identity will be revealed. The Preface decries the prevailing commercialism in choosing book-titles (die mer-kantilischen Spekulationen der Titelwahl bei Büchern, 5) and assures the reader that whatever one might think of the present title, the work is indeed true and based upon authentic sources. It is not, Kellner ex-plains, a history of the Wars of Spanish Succession. Now, its immediate impact is that of a fast-paced chronicle, ranging in style from melodra-matic sentimentality to cinematographic clarity and staccato rapidity in the battle scenes. It is in these life-like scenes that Kellner most amply demonstrates that the book bears the stamp of truth (das Gepräge der Wahrheit); yet the other 'truth' of the novel is its demonstration that too vigorous an imagination courts danger.

Highlighting the functions of soul, spirit and imagination in the development of its hero, Kellner's short novel comes closer than any we have seen so far to revealing inner biography as Blanckenburg had advo-cated. Although he achieves neither the symbolic technique of Moritz' Hartknopf nor the psychological approach of Anton Reiser, his technique of motivating the action in terms of the hero's temperament suggests that he was aware of the possibilities that lay in this direction. What Salz-mann, for instance, had portrayed as outward adjustment to moral pre-cepts, becomes in Kellner's hands the delineation of forces within the individual; the pronouncement of ethical codes has ceded to the forward thrust of crucial experiences:

> Hört Leser! wie, gleich einem reissenden Strom, der Bett
> und Ufer verlässt, die Felder überschwemmt, Felsen
> losspult, Häuser umwirft, Bäume aus den Wurzeln mit
> fortreisst; wie, gleich diesem Strome, und wozu dieser
> Vorfall unsern Heinrich Klingstein mit fortriss. (45)

Heinrich Klingstein, the son of a pious protestant blacksmith, grows up in a small town that is so imbued with 'bourgeois pride that its inhabitants preferred to be miserable townsmen ruined by luxury than happy country-folk' (10). His father would have 'no truck with such

219

tomfoolery" (10), kept to himself, and introduced his son to readings of battles and heroism in the <u>Kaiserchronik</u>. Heinrich's quick imagination is aroused and nourished, and a passing interest in literature soon becomes a monomania. He copies assiduously from chronicles and novels of knights and robbers and then tries his own hand at the writer's craft. His father grows uneasy at his son's preoccupation with the fantasy-world of war, urges him in vain to learn a trade, and eventually turns in despair to the village pastor, who assures him that the Deity (die Gottheit, 23) has other plans for young Heinrich. The Deity has destined Klingstein to lead a tumultuous life and finally to gain the secular prize of domestic quietude--a plan to which the pastor is party. The lad is destined to live 'by the fruits of his spirit' (23).

The pastor is impressed by Heinrich's aptitude for scholarship and makes arrangements for him to spend some years in a boarding school, where he excels. But Heinrich's secret purpose in studying so diligently is to prepare himself to become a 'hero' like his fictional models, and he devotes all his spare time to the study of chronicles, strategy, and applied mathematics. The school principal and the pastor, as the author observes, are duped into thinking that the aspirations of this young fantast are marks of 'scientific thirst' (29). In time young Klingstein stands 'like a majestic heaven-wards striving cedar of Lebanon' (36). But in his eagerness to realise his fantasy-world of cavalier skirmishes and bravado, he breaks away from the restrictions of city-life and the oppressive slavery of school (Stadtzwang und Schulsklaverei, 52) and 'escapes' to university. The 'freedom' of university enables him to live 'in a fantastic dream' (69 f.), where he quickly becomes an audacious wag with a flair for sabres. On hearing of his wild life, the pastor consults with Heinrich's father, and the two men send Klingstein to another university to study theology. The young man's mind is once again turned to philology and learned rubbish: "so ward denn seine Thätigkeit wieder Sprachstudium und gelehrter Wortkram" (100); but at every opportunity he turns his 'impassioned imagination" (101) to tales of war. Even in his sleep, 'indescribable ecstasy' and 'burning figaments of the imagination' makes him 'the happiest of enthusiasts.' (121) His unarmed attack on two armed officers who had insulted him brings him to the attention of the

Prince, who immediately appoints him adjutant. After bloody battles and daring escapades in the Wars of Spanish Succession, through which he blisters his way unscathed, Klingstein finally becomes a famous general.

As Klingstein grows older and as the novel draws to a close, he becomes markedly less robust. The 'fiery imagination' burns itself out, and the ardent youth becomes a serene old man. This, we are given to understand, is how Klingstein's character developed. 'All noble passions in their most sublime strength gradually found a place in Klingstein's great soul'; all that is, except love, 'this fair goddess of life' (175). We have come to expect love plots in novels of the period, but here we find only a slight concession to the convention. The woman whom Klingstein meets and marries near the end of his days is a "Mädchen voll zarter Weiblichkeit; voll zarten Gefühls von weiblicher Ehre!" (185) Klingstein's love is not the passion of a young firebrand, but the compassionate friendship between a man and a woman which finds its highest expression in marriage and a home. Kellner's description of the hero and the bride-to-be is one of the rare occasions when he intrudes into his narrative to instruct his reader:

> Liebe, die auf wonniges Anschaun geistiger Vorzüge [sic]
> und nicht allein auf physischen Trieb gründet, setzt
> alle menschlichen Kräfte und Triebe mit allen menschlichen
> Pflichten in das schönste Ebenmaas [sic] (186)

This moral is demonstrated in the closing scenes of the novel, when Klingstein enjoys a happy retirement with his wife and aging parents, who gather around him in warm admiration. Then all die, leaving him an old man with his books and memories of military exploits. Kellner invokes his readers to experience the bliss of the closing scenes and trusts that they too have felt that Klingstein was not only a hero but a human being as well:

> Wem schwillt hier nicht das Herz von seligster Wonne!
> Wer fühlt es hier nicht mit mir, dass Klingstein
> nicht nur Held, dass er auch Mensch war! (189)

The urge to set forth on adventures, as it is expressed in the Bildungsroman, is a sign of the inner need to break with one's spiritual past and conquer new areas of experience. But as Goethe's Werther observed,[43] distance is like the future: the most restless vagabond soon

longs for his homeland and finds in his home, and in the arms of his
wife, all the bliss which he sought in vain in the wild barren world:

> Oh, es ist mit der Ferne wie mit der Zukunft! . . .
> So sehnt sich der unruhigste Vagabund zuletzt wieder
> nach seinem Vaterland und findet in seiner Hütte, an
> der Brust seiner Gattin,. . . all die Wonne, die er
> in der weiten, öden Welt vergebens suchte.

The reviewer in the Allgemeine Deutsche Bibliothek for 1791
(vol 104, p. 417) had little patience with Kellner's novel and no sympathy with its implications. Instead of achieving success, the hero of
'this extremely boring book' should have gotten a licking when he was
young:

> Was der Sohn eines Schmidts aus Gerbenstein in Hessen in
> seinen Schuljahren treibt, in welchen er sehr fleissig,
> übrigens aber ein wilder Junge ist; was er mit seinem Papa
> und seinem Lehrern in seinem Geburtsorte und in Holzminden
> plaudert; wie er nachher auf Universitäten geht und dort
> auf pöbelhafte Weise böse Händel anfängt; wie er nachher
> einen Unteroffizier verwundet und dafür von dem Prinzen,
> welcher Chef des Regiments ist, nicht etwa zu einer
> wohlverdienten Strafe ad posteriora verurtheilt, sondern
> zum Adjutanten und Liebling ernannt wird; wie er nun
> Tapfer im Successions-Kriege ficht, General wird und
> endlich heyrathet - das erzählt uns Herr G. Chr. K. in
> diesem höchst langweiligen Buche, worin auch abscheuliche
> Verse vorkommen, und dem, zu unserm Schrecken, laut Vor-
> rede noch eine [Familiengeschichte der Rosenbusche] von
> eben der Art folgen soll.

The reviewer's impatience with Kellner's swashbuckling hero is
understandable; Klingstein first strikes one as the churlish instigator
of pointless schemes and escapades. There are suggestions, however, that
Kellner was using his hero as a means for exploring the relationship between freedom and discipline, imagination and reason. He contrasts the
free play of the young man's imagination in the opening pages of the novel with the practical middle-class demands of earning one's living and
becoming a useful member of society. Klingstein begins to develop when
we are told that 'the Deity' (23) intended him to experience the clash
of opposing interests. From this point onwards his mind is 'awakened'
and 'nourished' (29) until his parallel development in physical stature
and 'scientific knowledge' (35) make him, as we have seen, 'like a

majestically heavenwards-striving cedar of Lebanon' (36). In rare reflective moments Klingstein ponders the relationship between mind and body, licence and common sense. Thus his apostrophe to his 'brain' concedes that although the mind directs the body, the body itself actually
achieves one's goals. Because of his basically impulsive attempt at physical conquest of his world, Klingstein escapes the 'bondage' of urban
life and the 'oppressive' school system (53). Kellner wants to teach his
reader through his hero's experience that the imagination must follow
reason and not run on ahead of it:

> Die Fantasie muss dem Verstande folgen, und nicht vor ihm
> herlaufen. Man soll ja Student werden. Nur erst, wenn
> mehr Jugendhitze verrauscht ist. (52)

The remainder of the book tries to show how reason gains control of imagination, and how Klingstein himself begins to realize that his reality
is in fact a dream world (69 ff.). We are meant to view his military
experiences as enforcing, and later encouraging, the disciplined use of
imagination. He develops into a practical man, a successful tactician.
Sound judgement gradually dominates his life until, as we have seen,
'all noble passions gradually [find] a place in Klingstein's noble soul'
(175). The hero finds domestic bliss in marriage, the middle-class para-
dise so often extolled in novels of the period.

[Friedrich von Oertel:] Kilbur, ein Beitrag zur Geschichte des sitt-
lichen Gangs menschlicher Natur (1790-91)

Whereas Kellner's novel portrays the actions of an essentially
unreflective character who is thrust onward through life by sheer imagination, Oertel's Kilbur reveals a process of reflective maturation. The
plot is secondary to reflections on the nature of human development, and
Oertel explains that the customary descriptions of journeys and encounters cannot be given much scope in his novel (II, 285). The traditional
reader of novels will 'perhaps' be recompensed for his boredom (II, 5) by
gaining insight into the impulse for order--Trieb zur Ordnung (I, 145)--
which is the key to the progressions in the physical and spiritual worlds
--die Progressionen in Körper- und Geisterwelt (II, 60). This type of
pleasing and useful truth (Nützliche Wahrheit, die zu gefallen weiss,

II, 426) is the great demand which one can make of any writing; an author's acceptance and fulfillment of this challenge compensates his work for many shortcomings in style and learning (II, 426). Similar assertions are made elsewhere in the novel, but nowhere more clearly than when Oertel expresses the aim of his book through the words of his narrator:

> Ich werde aus der Geschichte meiner Knaben- und Jünglings-
> jahre. . . bis dahin, wie ich anfing, ein Wesen für mich zu
> seyn, nichts anführen, als was durchaus nötig ist, um mich
> so zu zeigen, wie ich bin; was die Entstehung und Entwick-
> lung meines Karakters schildert und also zum Zweck dieses
> Buches gehört. Wer einen gewöhnlichen Roman zu lesen ge-
> glaubt und gehofft hat, dem muss freilich vieles, was ich
> hier anführe, überflüssig, plauderhauft und langweilig
> scheinen, weil er dann nur Situationen, Begebenheiten,
> Schilderungen, Verwicklungen und Entwicklungen erwartet
> und nichts für entbehrlicher hält, als was nach Philosophie
> schmeckt. . . (I, 238 f.)

To be sure, Oertel wishes to entertain, but only in so far as such amusement is instructive and useful. The union of delight and instruction can only be achieved, he claims, by revealing: "die innere Wahrheit. . . welche man in sich selbst, im eignen Herzen findet, die man also gleichsam daraus hervorspinnen muss" (I, 239). Here as elsewhere, Oertel is in striking accord with Blanckenburg's Versuch über den Roman, which suggested that the novelist should concern himself with participation in the vital issues of humanity and thereby bring the human race closer to perfection (xiv f., 41, 389, et passim). Such participation is effected, both in Blanckenburg's theory and Oertel's practice, by unfolding inner biography and revealing the processes at work in human development. The novelist's principal concern is philosophic truth:

> In Kindheit und Jugend werden Herz und Geist gebildet, so
> wie sie in reifern Alter sich zeigen, und hier, wie überall,
> ist Ursach' und Würkung, Keim und Entwicklung. Es ist
> schön und lehrreich, zu zeigen, wie der Mensch ist, aber
> schöner und lehrreicher noch, zu zeigen, wie er wurde
> (II, 1). . . Es ist hier von philosophischer, nicht von
> historischer, Treue die Rede, also davon, ob unter so und
> so gegebenen Umständen das und diess erfolgen konnte und
> musste. (Oertel, II, 6)

Blanckenburg had insisted that the basic motif of a novel should be the protagonist's inner condition (17 f.) "Innere Geschichte" (392) was to be, indeed, the 'essential' and 'particular' concern of the whole genre. We should see "das Innere der Personen" (58) set in motion in the novel, and find ourselves moved as a consequence. Everything which flatters our 'impulse for perfection' (30) arouses within us the most pleasing of all emotions. The reader must be transposed into the 'mind' of the characters and into the world in which they interact, so as to be able to perceive the cause-and-effect relationships of human existence. Novelists, he had asserted, cannot plead ignorance of their characters' inner states and must graphically depict the relationship of inward and outward states (288). Characters in the fictional world, like those in the real world, are to suffer as a means to perfection: "Die Personen sollen, in des Dichters kleiner Welt, (eben so wie in der grossen, wirklichen) zu ihrer Besserung, zu ihrer Vervollkommnung leiden" (166).

Oertel speaks in a similar idiom and enunciates a concept of Bildung which is representative of the fully developed (i.e. secularized) Bildungsroman. Suffering and transformation are one, and their intergration into a Self is the essence of human existence and immortality:

> Leiden und sich verändern ist eins, und diese Veränderungen
> in ein Ich sammeln, mit dem Faden, den uns Schicksale und
> Bewusstseyn in die Hand geben, der Vollendung entgegen
> gehn, aus dem Mannichfaltigen in Eins--so war ich da, so
> dort. . . immer anders und immer ich--das ist der Kern
> des Menschenlebens, Daseyn, Realität und Unsterblichkeit.
> (II, 240 f.)

Oertel's novel is a portrait--Gemählde (II, 426)--in which everything is true to the inner being of his hero, "innerlich wahr" (I, 15), and in which he aims at showing how the inner state of man is bound to the outer man by numerous invisible bonds: "wie das Innere durch unzählige, unsichtbare Bande mit dem Aeussern zusammenhängt" (I, 150). We can never firmly grasp the principles of ethics, Oertel explains, until we learn how inward and outward states interact, for every action is the image of a thought. The secret history of an individual is more useful to society than any compendium of ethics:

> Wir können nie zu einem festen Satz in der Sittenlehre
> kommen, wenn wir nicht lernen, wie das Aeussere auf das
> Innere und diess dann wieder auf jenes würkt. Jede
> Handlung ist nur der Körper, das Bild eines Gedankens [sic];
> . . . Die geheime Geschichte eines Individuums ist

nützlicher als irgend ein Kompendium der Sittenlehre.
(I, 331).

Our life consists of 'moments,' our character of 'minutiae,' and only
when these are portrayed can we grasp the whole (II, 232). Human life
is all the more beautiful, the more it compares to the seasonal changes
in a year (I, 88).

Like Heller in Sokrates, Oertel exhorts the reader to 'know thyself,' but reveals 'a more profound significance than one usually ascribes to the motto of the temple at Delphi' (II, 176). The motto
'points toward that inner meaning whose intensity and energy [!] must be
felt if we are to be true and at one with ourselves: "diesen innern Sinn,
dessen Intensität, dessen Energie man bestimmt. . . fühlen soll, um dann
wahr, mit sich selbst eins zu seyn" (II, 176). The 'inner meaning' must
be the basis upon which a system of ethics is built (II, 176). Self-
knowledge is synonymous in Oertel's view with the attainment of the True,
the Good, and the Beautiful (II, 440), and it is central to his secularized view of Bildung that 'no single road' (I, 8) leads to the ultimate goal, which we experience as 'quietude and independent happiness'
(I, 8). While the paths to self-knowledge are many, the process is the
same for all conditions of men: each passing day holds 'a new condition'
for each individual, and it is our vocation (Bestimmung) to exercise all
our powers and capabilities unceasingly. Peace of mind is produced by
knowledge of outward things and inner capacities (äusserer Dinge und innern Vermögen) and such knowledge is brought about in the degree that
we expand our 'organs' for its apprehension (II, 60 f.). Thus Oertel's
fictional autobiographer proclaims that he himself had to pass through
despair and suffering in order to attain true knowledge; the novel thus
focuses on:

> . . . die Auftritte des Schmerzes, des Jammers, ja der
> Verzweiflung. . . durch die ich gehen mußte, eh' ich zu
> einer wahren Kenntniß der Dinge und von da zu der beruhi-
> genden Philosophie gelangte, die izt über das Vergangene
> mich tröstet, die Gegenwart mir verschönert, und die
> Zukunft in ihr anmutigsten Gestalt mir zeigt (I, 113)

It is of the greatest significance for the history of the character novel that Oertel has a completely secular concept of Bildung (in
terms of its moral, ethical, and spiritual implications), and that he

226

holds that individuality is a man's unique worth: "Nur der Mensch ist
schätzbar, der eignes Gepräg hat" (I, 24). Yet although the process of
Bildung is secular in intent, it is strikingly religious in tone. This
is illustrated most clearly in the many contemplative monologues, or what
we might call secularized prayers for self-assurance and faith in oneself,
which Oertel's characters address to a 'being' of greater magnitude than
man. It is perhaps significant that the protagonist turns to this numinous Being after first having entreated the muses and 'divine philosophy'
for grace:

> Nur euch, ihr Musen, nur dir, himmlische Philosophie, die
> vor allem Kenntniss sein selbst lehrt, weih' ich mich von
> nun an! Führt mich in euer innerstes Heiligthum ein!
> Lehrt mich fühlen und denken, einzig wahr leben. . .
> Vor allem aber schenkt mir Mut und Glauben an mich selbst,
> dass ich. . . in mir selbst Bewusstseyn eignen Werths
> erwerbe! (II, 211 f.).

> . . . und du, o allwaltendes, unbegreifliches Wesen,
> dessen Dasyn ich glaube und fühle, so wie das meinige. . .
> du, dessen Regierung allgemein weise und gut ist, dessen
> Rathschlüsse seelig machen alles was lebt, seeliger noch,
> was du zur Reihe vernünftiger Geschöpfe empor hobst,. . .
> O du, leite du mich zu dem, was mir gut ist! (II, 212)

Man can only reach the 'inner sanctum of wisdom' by passing through the
'labyrinth of sin,' and this "Labyrinth der Sünde" consists of nothing
other than contemporary social relationships: "die Verhältnisse unsrer
itzigen Welt" (I, 223). Freedom from 'sin' (I, 223), in Oertel's view,
means liberation from the bondage of social institutions and is synonymous with self-knowledge or independence of thought (II, 424). Only
where such freedom exists can there be 'true goodness' (I, 285).

Oertel's purpose in writing a fictional autobiography is to offer
guide-lines for life, and to demonstrate their effectiveness by revealing
the inner necessity which conditions his hero's development. He writes,
'for others,' to 'give them hints along the path they must tread,' and to
show that the path is practicable (II, 8). Like the reader of the devotional Speculum, Oertel's reader is to find himself reflected in the novel (II, 5). The 'reward' of one's pilgrimage through life 'lies in oneself, in the elevated feeling that virtue, religion and noble self-denial
bestow' (I, 213). This 'elevated feeling' of harmony constitutes his
ideal of personality. Because Oertel understands Bildung as a progression

of inner states, it follows for him that they should be portrayed in a
novel. He strives for revelation of character through introspection, but
he falls considerably short of his aim. He claims throughout the work
that the essence of human life is "cause and effect, seed and growth"--
Ursach' und Würkung, Keim und Entwicklung (II, 1)--and implies that this
should be reflected in one's narrative. In practice, however, his work
supports a different view: "Nur in einem Archiv, wo Schätze solcher Bemerkungen [über Tugend und Wahrheit] eingetragen worden, kann und mag
eine gute Gesetzgebung entworfen werden" (II, 4). Oertel shows an inclination toward the full implementation of Blanckenburg's theory, but
fails to portray his hero's development concretely.

The structure of the work is as follows: After having outlined
his theme and some of his basic assumptions, Oertel introduces his reader
to Kilbur, the fictional autobiographer, who recalls the broad outlines
of his life and encloses corroborating papers from various sources.
Each collection of papers has its own incapsulated narratives and letters.
The resultant assemblage of 'archives' makes the character of Kilbur
secondary to reflections on the nature of human delopment. Kilbur's
function in the presentation of his inner biography is to insert narratives between the sequences of incapsulated papers, and to enlarge upon
the documented experience of the earlier stages of his life by drawing
upon his experience of later life. Bewildering though this labyrinth of
documentation may be, Oertel is clearly implementing his principle that
'man's inner life is bound to his outer life by numerous invisible bonds'
(I, 150). Kilbur finally attains self-knowledge, the highest truth which
Oertel can envisage, and, as in many other novels of the period, this
ultimate truth is embodied in marriage: "nur die Ehe weist uns einen
festen Platz in der Haushaltung Gottes an, nur durch sie erhalten wir
einen Stand, werden wir nützlich, würken wir in's Ganze" (II, 395).

The principles of devotional literature (Spiegel) that urges introspection in terms of the path of Christian salvation reasserts itself
in Oertel's work. Kilbur is a secularized mirror of the inner man, and
is marked by a personal relationship between reader and author: "Sieh
doch alles. . . nur als eine Schilderung meiner selbst an: als Freund
. . . darf ich genau so schreiben." (II, 33 f.). Oertel himself claims
to have discovered this relationship in 'essays and novels,' particularly

in Montaigne, and much later in Rousseau's Confessions and Moritz' Anton
Reiser. Here was a 'rich treasure of self-confessions' in which one
gained insights into oneself (I, 371). But--as he himself says--he could
not quite attain this level himself, for he lacked 'the noble boldness
of a Rousseau or a Moritz' (I, 14).

Oertel's work was not reviewed until 1794, when a writer in the
Allgemeine Deutsche Bibliothek (vol 116, pp. 106-108) recognized the novel as something quite out of the ordinary:

> Dieses Buch hat sehr unverkennbare Vorzüge vor den ge-
> wöhnlichen Romanen, deren Zahl sich jetzt in Deutschland
> so unendlich vervielfältigt. Hier sind nicht Abentheuer
> auf Abentheuer gehäuft, um die Phantasie müssiger Menschen
> in beständiger Spannung zu erhalten, wenn man sich unfähig
> fühlt, durch Wahrheit und ächte Philosophie die Leser
> besserer Art zu interessiren; sondern die Geschichte ist
> nur der Faden, an welchem sehr nützliche Lehren für das
> praktische Leben, feine Beobachtungen, Züge, die von
> ächter Seelenkunde zeugen, lebhafte Schilderungen und
> manche nicht alltägliche Raisonments über wichtige
> Gegenstände angereiht sind.

He is reserved about Oertel's tendency to believe in premonitions and
visions, and claims that such dispositions are inappropriate for a
writer:

> Hie und da zeigt der V. einen kleinen Anstrich von
> Schwärmerey besonders einen Hang zu dem Glauben an Vor-
> bedeutungen und Visionen, welches man ihm zwar gönnen
> kann, aber wofür ein Schriftsteller doch nicht den Sinn
> noch mehr zu erwecken suchen sollte.

Similar viewpoints, were expressed with regard to Moritz' Hartknopf.

Oertel's Kilbur contains certain moral views and expresses attitudes toward the craft of fiction that are more fully developed in Moritz'
writings. Man's "Sinn für das Wahre" (I, 166) increases infinitely
through observation and knowledge of human nature, Oertel explains.
Truth is the 'sole deity' (I, 331), and alone is enduring, unified and
perfect: "Nur das Wahre hat Bestand, Einheit und Vollkommenheit" (I,
383). Sensitive souls experience "Vorgefühle, Ahnungen" (II, 23) of a
supreme force which one can only call Providence (II, 280). True goodness can only be found in freedom: "Nur wo Freiheit ist, da ist wahre
Güte" (I, 285); and in such freedom man may do everything that is not

against the eternal law of the Good and the True (II, 367 f.). The course of Kilbur's life 'taught that he was not so much created to find, as
to be found' (II, 72), a condition of life that is central to each individual person. Thus for Oertel it is not necessary to seek uplifting
insights in the lives of great men of history alone (as Heller and Fessler had done); the life of even the common man, no matter how socially
insignificant he may be, offers ample scope provided it bears the stamp
of inner truth:

> Darum muß der Beitrag auch des unbedeutendsten Menschen,
> wenn's einen solchen giebt, dem Forscher des Wahren schätz-
> bar und werth seyn, sobald er den Stempel der inneren Treue
> und Truglosigkeit darauf gedrückt sieht. . . . So hab' ich
> diese Papiere angesehen, als ich mich entschloß, sie der
> Leserwelt darzustellen. Wer möchte nicht gern, dacht'
> ich, sich selbst in einem andern wiederfinden? (II, 4)

Moreover, Oertel is expressing a secular view of existence, in which
philosophical terms have replaced the Christian idioms of God, faith,
grace, redemption.[44]

C O N C L U S I O N

As used in 1790, the term "novel" applied to a broad range of popular fiction, from Kratter's lubricious Das Schleifermädchen aus Schwaben to Oertel's innovative character novel Kilbur and Moritz' Anton Reiser. Though writers of the period had no critical definition of the genre, they continued a practice of 1780 by scorning the 'usual novel' with its trite love plots, lack of realism, false sentiments, and moral ambiguity. Yet they often accommodated a public which, to their mind, expected a novel to be a tissue of adventures and involved love affairs. Marketability was a prime consideration in the writing of novels, and Oertel's observation that the German book-trade was the axis around which literature and author revolved seems well founded. Published largely in fascicles and showing little literary concern for development of plot and character, or for coherent presentation of ideas and themes, most novels strike one as factory-products. Indeed as Becker observed of 1780, with literary mass-producers like J.F.E. Albrecht and Christiane Naubert, one can actually speak of an industry. Though many writers expressed the wish to write something different and to be free of the commercial constraints of pleasing both publishers and public, the German novels of 1790 reflect a monotonous tendency to cling to outworn techniques and motifs. Most novels preserve vestiges of the baroque romance, reveal a sentimentality reminiscent of Richardson, and seem to imitate the already conventionalized narrative techniques of Fielding and Sterne. It is perhaps remarkable that as far as the novel of 1790 is concerned, the Sturm und Drang movement need never have taken place.

Though we find no support for Becker's assertion that Ritter-Räuber und Schauerromane dominate the novels of this period, thread-bare traditional knights, and the occasional robber, appear in two historical novels with an occasional touch of thinly contrived gothic horror; robbers appear in three love stories. A supposedly haunted castle figures as a background for Shandean self-parody in Freiherr von Knigge's Das Zauberschloss oder Geschichte des Grafen Tunger, but of course the novel is not a serious attempt at writing a horror story. One wonders if

K. Tschink's unavailable <u>Geschichte eines Geistersehers; aus den Papieren</u> <u>des Mannes mit der eisernen Larve</u> (1790) might have been a genuine attempt in the genre. The <u>Reiseroman</u>, not found in 1780, would seem to form a coherent group in 1790--though only Geiger's satirical <u>Reise eines</u> <u>Erdbewohners in den Mars</u> is extant. With perhaps the exception of J.H. Campe's unavailable <u>Reise von Braunschweig nach Paris</u> (1790), the other three--Ch. F. Dreyssig's <u>Reisen des grünen Mannes durch Teutschland und</u> <u>Ungarn</u>, the anonymous <u>Meine Reisen am Pulte beim Scheine einer Argant-</u> <u>Lampe</u>, and <u>Wie geht's auf der Welt, oder Besuche in all vier Weltteile</u>-- are, to judge by their titles, more interested in satire than travel.

Important changes did nonetheless take place in 1790. Dialogue novels, which constitute one-sixth of the production in 1780, are no longer found, though Johann Kausch' unavailable <u>Kabale im Civildienst, ein</u> <u>dramatischer Roman</u> (1790) may have been one. 'Elevated' and epistolary novels, predominant in 1780, virtually disappeared as authors turned their attention to middle-class situations and heroes, and to mixed narratives with various combinations of letters, dialogues, and manuscripts. Novels can no longer be categorized along traditional lines as Becker had done for 1780. Most now shift narrative techniques at will, and, in sharp contrast to the previous decade, all now have at least a latent tendency toward social criticism. A prime example of diversification in the novel, and of its propensity for including what once would have been regarded as extraneous material, is the preponderance of non-narrative digressions. As distinct from sub-plots, such digressions disregard the reader's interest in the story and often open the narrative to quite lengthy discourses on the most divergent topics. These digressions find a legitimate place in 29 of the 35 extant novels of 1790 whenever the authors want to broach a new topic. Self-consciously intrusive authors figure in over half the novels of 1790, a slight increase over the previous decade.

If practically all novels of 1780 appeared anonymously, somewhat less, namely 63 % of the extant novels, were published without identifying the author in 1790. Significantly, the majority of these have strong affinities with the romance--the 'usual novel' so often maligned in novels and reviews of the period. The increasing self-confidence of authors might also have played a part in publishing fewer anonymous novels than in 1780. This view certainly seems to be borne out by the prefaces. While most novelists of 1780 wrote lengthy prefaces to justify their novels before public and reviewers, just over half the novels of 1790 have introductions: eleven of these are serious apologies, while the other seven are purposefully whimsical preambles.

While writers of 1790 assert with their predecessors that their aim is instruction and delight, it is significant that just half of their novels are genuinely didactic. Of the nine Novels of Love and Adventure, seven of which claim to promote sexual morality and middle-class values, only two really aim at serious instruction. For the rest, instruction is a mere pretext for publishing entertaining fiction. This feature is also found in the Historical Novel, only two of which are genuinely didactic. One of these focusses on a bourgeois heroine, a victim of the sexual exploitation of her aristocratic mentors, while the other preaches middle-class morality against an aristocratic background. Dealing with bourgeois concerns seems to lend a degree of moral credibility not to be found in the romance. Only five Satirical Novels, those exposing government institutions and the 'fraudulent' claims of religion, are genuinely didactic. The other five, by authors who do not take themselves very seriously, are designed more for entertainment. All ten Character Novels, on the other hand, are consistently committed to genuine didacticism. As with the other novels of the period, this feature is generally associated with the middle-class milieu.

Novels of Love and Adventure, which preach virtue by revealing the dangers of erotic love, constitute one-fifth of the extant fiction of 1790. Vitiated by crass distinctions between vice and virtue, a complete dependence upon stock-types and situations, and by a sentimentality verging on bathos, they represent a low ebb of the traditional romance. Contemporary reviewers were unimpressed with them. However, in two-thirds of these novels bourgeois heroes have assumed functions traditionally reserved for the upper classes.

The Historical Novel, absent in 1780, perpetuates the stereotyped aristocratic heroes and situations of the traditional romance under the often tenuous pretence of historical precision. Reflecting an interest in the contemporary revaluation of historiography, with its canons of chronological order, truthfulness, impartiality, and the 'pragmatic'

233

technique of motivating events, it added a new dimension to popular fiction. However, it generally retained the episodic narrative. In an attempt to show that the 'truth' of their moral views was borne out by the events of recorded history, novelists strove to make the events usually associated with traditional fiction more credible through a pretence of scholarly documentation. Four of the six extant historical novels of 1790 actually designate themselves "Histories" (Geschichten). Contemporary reviewers, who in 1790 were conversant with the term "historical novel", regarded the genre as a hybrid because of its mixture of fact and fancy. Indeed historians seem to have felt that the novelist might so misuse historical sources that all certainty would disappear. Such concerns were not unfounded. Sharing the Enlightenment view on the progressive perfection of culture, the historical novelist regarded the 18th century superior to other epochs and promoted the prejudice that the Middle Ages were a period of barbarism, superstition, and ignorance. All novels of this type purport to deal with events from the medieval period. Though the Historical Novel was not successful in all it tried to accomplish, it remains a significant experiment in a new direction.

Political satires, which constitute half the extant Satirical Novels of 1790, are equally dependent upon the traditional devices of love and intrigue as a scaffolding for their clichés. Consisting largely of tirades, harangues and polemics against governments and their ministers (and frequently satirizing secret societies), they never challenge the sovereign's right to rule. Even satires on the French Revolution expend all their ire on the licentiousness of the courts, political favouritism and priests, blaming them for the oppression of the lower classes. Aristocratic heroes predominate precisely because they are the object of attack. With the exception of these works and a single love story, the novel of 1790 is apolitical. A reviewer of the period correctly observed that this type of satire had already been overworked to such an extent that only an uncommonly high degree of wit and whimsy could give it some appeal and a semblance of novelty.

Wit and whimsy can only be found in the four satirical novels that parody the novel itself. Despite their tendency to highlight the obvious and to labour motifs, the prominence of attempts at self-parody could

suggest the beginnings of a new type of humorous novel. It is interesting that all four of these have bourgeois heroes, two of which are would-
be artists who find they lack talent. Fielding remains a prime model.
At the same time, however, satirical novelists of the period made no significant advances over Don Sylvio von Rosalva. Wieland had already
adeptly exploited all the devices that his imitators slavishly repro-
duced.

The Character Novel of 1790, the type that attempts to edify the
reader by offering insights into the hero's personality, introduces a
new element into popular fiction that holds promise for the future development of the genre. Experimentation with the psychological portrayal
of character--just beginning in 1780--now seems a major concern. Indeed
the theory of 'pragmatic' narratives advanced by historiographers is most
fully implemented in this type of novel. Significantly, Fessler objected
to having Marc-Aurel termed a historical novel on the grounds that he was
more interested in character than in events. He suggested the term
"historical portrait" as he aimed at complementing the facts of recorded
history with psychological insight. Even Göchhausen's Meines Vaters
Hauschronika, one of the weakest novels of this type, was regarded by a
contemporary reviewer as a remarkable book because of its uncommon psychological approach. As Blanckenburg had expressed it in 1774, the novelist should show possible people of the real world and reveal the inner
condition of man. In practical terms, writers of character novels seem
to feel with Oertel (Kilbur, II, 438 ff.) that novels can and should make
morality practical by extending our knowledge of man; this is to be
achieved through subtlety of characterization. This view is echoed in
other types of the period. Georg Kellner claimed in Die Familiengeschichte der Rosenbusche (IV, 225), for instance, that writers should
emulate Goethe's Werther and Rousseau's La Nouvelle Heloise because these
works present us with "true copies of real human characters." It is significant that this new directional thrust in the writing of novels should
be provided by a type which shows least dependence upon elements of the
romance, has the highest proportion of bourgeois heroes, and the greatest
real interest in promoting middle-class values; it is the only type in
which the protestant vicar plays a serious (though often secularized)
role. Whereas Catholicism was attacked in five of the thirty-five novels

of 1790 (and neglected in the rest), and vicars and priests were pilloried in three, we observe in the Character Novel a desire to modify
Christian insights along secular lines.

The most significant Character Novels, Oertel's Kilbur, and
Moritz' Hartknopf and Anton Reiser--recognized by contemporary critics
as unusual and new--reveal a conscientious application of Blanckenburg's
theory of the novel: the reader is educated by directly experiencing the
inner world of viable fictional characters in their journey through life,
and by then applying this insight to his own immediate milieu. Many for-
mulations in these novels reveal an almost literal agreement with Blanckenburg's essay. Apart from his analytical technique of revealing what
Lessing called "inner probability" and Schiller "philosophical truth",
Oertel's major contribution lies in his expression of a completely secular concept of Bildung and his view that a man's unique worth is his individuality.

Moritz' epoch-making character novels are the highlights of 1790--
not only because of their innovations in content and narrative technique,
as separate studies show, but because of their consistent development and
treatment of themes and ideas. Anton Reiser explores psychologically the
effects of a restrictive childhood that left little scope for individual
development, thus creating the fully developed prototype of the Bildungsroman; Andreas Hartknopf explores symbolically the protagonist's transition from Christian orthodoxy to the secular religion of aestheticism.

The most important single change in the German novel of 1790 lies
in its shift to bourgeois concerns. Economic stability, frugality, family honour and marital fidelity, respect for one's elders, the preserva-
tion of quiet domesticity, and responsibility toward one's social class
are advocated in varying degrees and combinations in the majority of novels. This holds true even when one suspects that instruction is a pretext for writing entertaining fiction, or when writers expose the frail-
ties of the upper classes. Even the aristocratic milieu of the Middle
Ages as portrayed in Historical Novels is a foil for promoting the
blessedness of marriage and for revealing the folly of social ambition.
All the young firebrands and fantasts, from the love story to the more
sophisticated Character Novel, are eventually brought to heel and are

incorporated into the security of the middle-class milieu. Because of
the dominant role played by bourgeois heroes and values, the traditional
romance with its epic heroes and incredible adventures has ceded pride
of place to the common man. Fully developed bourgeois heroes--completely
absent a decade earlier--figure in 60 % of the novels of 1790. The
bourgeois 'middle novel,' defined by Jean Paul in the light of such works
as Tom Jones, The Vicar of Wakefield, Tristram Shandy, and Wilhelm
Meisters Lehrjahre, and regarded by Becker as 'modern' in 1780, is clearly coming of age.

STATISTICAL TABLE

of Themes and Techniques

in 35 extant novels of 1790

According to types

	Love (9)	Historical (6)	Satirical (10)	Character (10)	Total (35)
Epistolary	1	0	0	1	2
Dialogue	0	0	0	0	0
Mixed narratives	5	5	8	7	25
First person	1	0	1	1	3
Third person	3	1	1	2	7
Episodic	9	4	8	4	25
Self-conscious author	6	3	5	4	18
Documented	3	5	3	4	15
Prefaces	1	2	7	8	18
Anonymous	7	6	7	2	22
Non-narrative digressions	7	5	8	9	29
Romance elements	8	5	6	2	21
Love Plots	9	6	8	6	29
Aristocratic heroes	3	5	4	2	14
Bourgeois heroes	6	1	6	8	21
Artist as hero	1	0	2	2	5
Genuinely didactic	2	2	5	10	19
Sexual Morality	6	3	2	5	16
Middle-class values	7	5	6	8	26
Ends in marriage	8	1	2	4	15
Vicar/Priest as Counsellor	1	0	2	5	8
Anti-church	1	0	4	0	5
Political Themes	1	0	4	0	5
Anti-French	1	0	4	0	5
Anti-"novel"	5	2	5	3	15
Secret Societies	1	1	6	2	10

NOTES TO INTRODUCTION

1. I allude, of course, to the reprint series published by J.B. Metzlersche Verlagsbuchhandlung, Stuttgart.

2. Allgemeine Litteraturzeitung for 12 May 1790 issued a statistical table of all books, either new or reprinted, which were promoted at the Frankfurt and Leipzig Easter Fair 1790. A supplementary table on the year's publications was issued on 13 November 1790. The tables contain: "alle deutsche, angeblich fertig gewordene, Bücher, so viel nach den freylich oft unsichern Schlüßen hat geschehen können, die man aus den Titeln auf den Inhalt der Bücher ziehen kann. . ." According to the total figures listed under the rubric "novels," 112 first editions seem to have appeared in 1790. I have documented 120 titles.

3. Such an approach is based on a number of assumptions, not least of which are that the fiction of a given era reflects the 'temper of the times', and that the Bildungsroman forms a coherent genre. Lothar Köhn (Entwicklungs- und Bildungsroman; Ein Forschungsbericht, Stuttgart, 1969), reveals that although the term is applied descriptively to works of fiction from the Middle Ages to the present day, there is no consensus as to its precise definition and applicability.

4. Cf. Walter Nutz, Der Trivialroman: Seine Formen und seine Hersteller. Ein Beitrag zur Literatursoziologie (Köln, 1962); Marion Beaujean, Der Trivialroman in der zweiten Hälfte des 18. Jahrhunderts (Bonn, 1964); Martin Greiner, Die Entstehung der modernen Unterhaltungsliteratur: Studien zum Trivialroman des 18. Jahrhunderts (Stuttgart, 1964); Kurt-Ingo Flessau, Der Moralische Roman: Studien zur gesellschaftskritischen Trivialliteratur der Goethezeit (Köln, 1968); Heinz Otto Burger, ed., Studien zur Trivialliteratur (Frankfurt am Main, 1968).

5. Cited in deBoor and Newald, Geschichte der deutschen Literatur, Vol VI, Pt. i (München, 1957), p. 384.

6. Hermann Bausinger, "Wege zur Erforschung der trivialen Literatur," in Burger, Studien, p. 18.

7. Dietrich Naumann, "Das Werk August Lafontaines und das Problem der Trivialität", in Burger, Studien (note 4 above), p. 85.

8. Eva D. Becker, Der deutsche Roman um 1780 (Stuttgart, 1964) (hereafter cited as Becker) notes (p. 1) that the distinction between Kunstroman and Trivialroman is untenable for the pre-romantic novel.

9. Becker, pp. 2 ff. See also J.M.S. Tompkins, The Popular Novel in England 1770-1800 (1932; Reprinted University of Nebraska Press, Lincoln, 1961), p. 172: "In the early 'eighties the novel begins to stir with new life. The yearly output increases, new themes, settings and characters appear, and the general level of relevance and coherence rises. The date must not be pressed.

10. Becker, pp. 2 ff.

11. Manfred W. Heiderich, dissertation in progress The German Novel in 1800: an analysis and critical bibliography (Queen's University, Kingston). My current project Bibliographie des Deutschen Romans 1750-1800: Verzeichnis vorhandener Originalromane will hopefully make this field even more accessible.

12. Ibid., pp. 43 ff.

13. Ibid., p. 54.

14. Jean Paul, "Vorschule der Aesthetik", Sämtliche Werke, Historisch-Kritische Ausgabe (Weimar, 1927-63), XI, 238.

15. Kurt-Ingo Flessau, Der Moralische Roman (note 4 above), p. 15.

16. Helmut Germer, The German Novel of Education 1792-1805: A Complete Bibliography and Analysis (Bern, 1968).

17. Georg Christoph Lichtenberg, Werke (Hamburg, 1967), p. 157.

NOTES TO CHAPTER I

1. J.J. Eschenburg, <u>Entwurf einer Theorie und Litteratur der schönen
    Wissenschaften. Zur Grundlage bei Vorlesungen</u>. Neue 2. umgearbeite-
    te Ausgabe (Berlin und Stettin, bey Friedrich Nicolai, 1789), p.336.

2. For the range of usage see <u>Kritische Friedrich Schlegel Ausgabe</u>,
    vol II, ed. Hans Eichner (München, 1967), lii-lci, and Dieter Kimpel,
    <u>Der Roman der Aufklärung</u> (Stuttgart, 1967), pp. 6 ff.

3. Joachim Heinrich Campe, <u>Vaeterlicher Rath für meine Tochter</u> (Braun-
    schweig, 1791), p. 59. Cited in George Jäger, <u>Empfindsamkeit und
    Roman</u> Stuttgart, 1969), p. 61.

4. The scene is taken from Fielding's <u>Jonathan Wild</u> (1745), in which the
    hero plunges into the sea from a boat. Within two minutes he is
    ". . . miraculously. . . replaced in his boat, and this without the
    assistance of a dolphin or sea-horse, or any other fish or animal,
    who are always ready at hand when a poet or historian pleases to call
    for them to carry a hero through the sea. . . The truth is, we do
    not choose to have any recourse to miracles, from the strict obser-
    vance we pay to that rule of Horace: Nec Deus interdit, nisi dignus
    vindice nodus-. . ." Cited from Fielding, <u>Jonathan Wild</u> (New York,
    1962), pp. 106 ff. Rambach does not acknowledge his debt to Fiel-
    ding, nor does he include Fielding's reference to Horace.

5. G.C. Kellner, <u>Familiengeschichte der Rosenbusche</u> (IV, 225): "Goethe's
    Werther und Pope's Heloise- - - warlich! mehr treue Kopien würklicher,
    wenn gleich seltner Menschenkaraktere, als mancher nicht untersuchen-
    de Verächter der Darstellungskunst glauben mag- - - Werther, Heloise
    vergassen Freundschaft, Religion, Gesundheit und Leben. Eine eigne
    heilige Empfindung war ihnen alles; und diese ware Liebe." Pope's
    poem "Eloisa to Abelard" was published in 1717. Kellner must be
    thinking of Rousseau's <u>Julie ou La Nouvelle Héloise</u> (1761).

6. Horace, "The Art of Poetry", in <u>The Complete Works of Horace</u> (ed.
    Caspar J. Kraemer, New York, 1936), p. 408.

7. Marianne Ehrmann, "Ueber die Lektür," <u>Amaliens Erholungsstunden</u>
    (Stuttgart, 1790), vol 1, p. 27. Cited in Georg Jäger, <u>Empfindsam-
    keit und Roman</u> (Stuttgart, 1969), p. 72.

8. See Erich Trunz' editorial remarks in Goethe's <u>Werke</u>, Hamburger Aus-
    gabe, Band 6, p. 530 f.

9. Cf. the following titles:
    Aramenes, <u>Die Durchlauchtigste Margaretha von Oesterreich</u>. . . 1716.
    August Bohse, <u>Die Liebenswürdige Europäerin Constantine</u>. . . 1698.
    Lycosthenes, <u>Der Durchlauchtigste Arbaces. . . Nebst seiner
    Durchlauchtigsten Damaspia</u>. . . 1726.
    Ormenius, <u>Die Liebes-Geschichte der Durchlauchtigsten Prinzessin
    Medea aus Cypern</u>. . . 1719.
    V.S., <u>Die Jüttische Kasia, Oder der Durchlauchtige Adamarez Und die
    Durchlauchtige Adamia</u>. . . 1732.

Elsewhere Müller's parody describes the "new world" of novels which
led his hero's imagination astray: "Jetzt lag eine neue Welt vor
ihm offen: [Zieglers] die asiatische Banise, [Prevosts] Cleveland,
der Mirakuloso Florisanti, die siebenmal unglücklich und siebenmal
glücklich ausgeschlagene Ehe, [Bohses] die liebenswürdige Europäer-
inn Konstantine, die schöne Georgianerinn Rethima, [Anton Ulrichs]
Aramena, [Richardsons] Pamela, manche Robinsonade. . . alles das
zeigte ihm Seiten und Kräfte des Herzens, an die er von selbst noch
lange nicht gedacht haben würde, Es begonnte ihm in der Gegend der
Herzgrube zu drängen und zu engen, es wirbelte ihm im Kopfe, alles
was Mädchen hiess wurde ihm interessant und er nahm sichs ernstlich
vor, sich ehester zu verlieben (II, 337 f.).

10. Kurt-Ingo Flessau, <u>Der Moralische Roman</u> (Köln, 1968), p. 33: "Aus
dem Spiel mit der Erotik wird, nicht zuletzt wohl auch aus kommer-
ziellen Erwägungen, das Angebot kaum verhüllter Sinnlichkeit."

11. Lohbauer's subscription list is included here for purposes of comparison even though it was not first published in 1790. It first
appeared in the periodical "Der Beobachter" in 1788. See Bibliography.

12. <u>Deutsche Literatur in Entwicklungsreihen</u> (ed. Fritz Brüggemann,
Darmstadt, 1966), vol.15, pp. 58 ff. See also pp. 258 ff.
"Der Buchhändler ging, nachdem er sowohl den Domine als den Sebaldus
bis vor die Tür seines Ladens begleitet hatte, bedächtig in seine
Schreibstube zurück, um zu überlegen, ob nicht eine Spekulatie zu
machen wäre.
Mynheer van der Kuit war ein Buchhändler, der das Handwerk verstand,
und trieb es auch als ein Handwerk. Ein Buch sahe er als ein Ding
an, das verkauft werden könnte. Weiter kümmerte ihn nichts dabei.
Aber hierzu wusste er auch alle Vorteile zu suchen und noch besser
sich dabei vor allem Nachteile zu hüten. Dabei bemühte er sich
nicht etwan um kleine gemeine Vorteile, z.B. für ein neues Buch
einen pfiffigen Titel zu ersinnen, über ein verlegenes Buch, nebst
einer neuen Jahrzahl, einen neumodischen Titel zu schlagen. . .
Nein! [Er] spekulierte ins Grosse."

13. It is interesting in this respect that Müller von Itzehoe's <u>Herr
Thomas</u> parodies Thilo's narrative technique as treating the basic
theme: "Mädchen, willst Du mich? Antw. Ja!- - Den Schulz [sic]
oder Thilo mögt ich sehen, der mir aus diesem kurzen Katechismus
einen Roman machen könnte! Laßt einen Epithalamienfabrikanten kommen, bezahlet den Pastor, füttert die Gäste. . . und packet das
junge Paar ins Bett;. . . ."

14. Harvey Waterman Thayer, <u>Laurence Sterne in Germany</u> [1905] (Reprinted
New York, 1966), p. 20.

15. Hans Ehrenzeller, <u>Studien zur Romanvorrede von Grimmelshausen bis
Jean Paul</u> (Bern, 1955).

16. Johann Gottfried Herder, "8. Humanitätsbrief," <u>Sämmtliche Werke</u>
(ed. B. Suphan, Berlin,1877-1913), vol 18, p. 121.

17. Nicolai's important Preface to the <u>Allgemeine Deutsche Bibliothek</u>

for 1768 (vol. 8) explains that the contributors will be fair to the
readers and not "cast dust in their eyes.": Die Verfasser des All-
gem. Deutschen Bibliothek suchen nie. . . den Lesern, die ein Buch
kaum zu Gesicht bekommen haben, Staub in die Augen zu streuen, sie
übereilen sich nicht, sondern überlegen ihr Urteil. Ehe sie es
niederschreiben, vergeht indess die Zeit, und haben die Leser unter-
dessen das Buch selbst gelesen, so ist dies dem Kunstrichter gar-
nicht unangenehm, der sich nicht scheuet, seine Rezension mit dem
Buch selbst vergleichen zu lassen."

His Preface to volume 12 (1770, p. iv) points out that reviews will
not be restricted to good books. All kinds will be reviewed in order to reveal "the true condition of literature": "Verschiedene Gelehrte sind der Meinung gewesen, dass es besser sei, wenn man nur
bloss wichtige und gute Bücher anzeigte und die mittelmässigen und
schlechten ganz wegliesse. Ohne Zweifel würde eine periodische
Schrift, die dieses täte, dem Leser eine viel angenehmere Aussicht
eröffnen, aber sie würde ihm nicht den wahren Zustand der Literatur
vor Augen legen." His own method will show the degree of insipidity
and ignorance that prevails:. . . [zeigt] in welchem Grade leider!
noch Seichtigkeit, Nachbeten, Pedanterie, Zänkerei, ja, Unwissen-
heit, Aberglauben und Barbarei herrschen. Man lernet diese Mängel
am besten aus den mittelmässigen und schlechten Büchern kennen,
mit denen Deutschland jährlich in ungeheurer Anzahl überschwemmt
wird."

18. Sander alludes of course to Nicolai's Allgemeine Deutsche Bibliothek.

NOTES ON CHAPTER II

1. Wolfgang Kayser, "Die Anfänge des modernen Romans im 18. Jahrhundert," DVLG, 28 (1954), 417-446.

2. Ibid., pp. 421 ff.

3. Ibid., p. 425. See, however, my article "Johann Beer's Approach to the Novel" (Seminar, vol VII, No. 1, March, 1971, 31-41) which shows Beer's practise of self-conscious literary techniques in the 1680's and thus regards him as a distinctive prototype of the eighteenth-century novelist prior to English influences. His innovations seem to have gone unnoticed, and it is really Wieland and his English models who bring about the change in fiction. See also Steven R. Miller, Die Figur des Erzählers in Wielands Romanen, Göppingen,1970.

4. Ibid., p. 427. See also Kayser, "Wer erzählt den Roman," Die Vortragsreise (Berne, 1958), p. 88.

5. Franz K. Stanzel, Typische Formen des Romans (3rd ed., Göttingen, 1967), p. 16.

6. Schiller, "Über die tragische Kunst", in Werke, Bd. II, Darmstadt, 1962, p. 497.

7. Stanzel, p. 23.

8. Peter Michelsen, Laurence Sterne und der deutsche Roman des achtzehnten Jahrhunderts (Göttingen, 1962). (Hereafter cited as Michelsen)

9. Michelsen, pp. 52 ff.

10. Ibid., p. 52, note 11. Further editions (published in Hamburg): 1776, 1777, 1778; pirated editions: Hanau/Höchst 1776/77, Berlin 1776, Frankfurt/Leipzig 1776/77. Thayer (Sterne in Germany, p. 29) discusses Friedrich Just Riedel's assessment of Sterne, which was published in his Sämmtliche Schriften (Wien, 1787, 4. Th. 4. Band, p. 133): Riedel "shows appreciation of Shandy complete and discriminating, previous to the Sentimental Journey. . . In a volume dated 1768 and entitled 'Über das Publikum: Briefe an einige Glieder desselben,' written evidently without knowledge of the Journey, Riedel indicates the position which Shandy had in these years won for itself among a select class. Riedel calls it a contribution to the 'Register' of the human heart and states that he knows people who claim to have learned more psychology from his novel than from many thick volumes in which the authors had first killed sentiment in order then to dissect it at leisure."

11. Michelsen, p. 62.

12. Michelsen (p. 65) documents this with but two of many possible examples: Thus Bode renders "reviewers of Great Britain" as "Journalisten der gelehrten Republik," and Sterne's references to the English works "Valentine and Orsan" and "The seven Champions of England" as

"Der gehörnte Siegfried" and the "Sieben Haimonskinder." According to Michelsen (p. 66), Johann Lorenz Benzler's justified criticism of Bode's translation in the Preface to his own rendition (Tristram Shandy's Leben und Meinungen, von neuem verdeutscht, [1]Leipzig, 1801, [2]Hannover, 1810) appeared at a time when Sterne's novel no longer held any acute significance for the literary life of Germany.

13. Michelsen, p. 69.

14. Harvey Waterman Thayer, Laurence Sterne in Germany. A Contribution to the Study of the Literary Relations of England and Germany in the Eighteenth Century (1905) (New York, 1966), p. 36.

15. Michelsen, p. 123. Cf. Sterne's famous comment in Tristram Shandy (Bk. I, ch. 22): "By this contrivance [the digression] the machinery of my work is of a species by itself; two contrary motions are introduced into it and reconciled, which were thought to be at variance with each other. In a word, my work is digressive, and it is progressive too,--and at the same time."

16. Michelsen, p. 130. Cf. Lessing (Hamburgische Dramaturgie, 93): "Wir übersetzen. . . jetzt fast durchgängig humour durch Laune." Michelsen points out (p. 30, note 21) that in Lessing's view the translation was incorrect.

17. C.E.F. Schulz, Litterarische Reise durch Deutschland (Leipzig, 1786), vol 2, pp. 85 ff.

18. Thayer, Sterne pp. 33 ff.: "The Sentimental Journey is the record of a sentimental experience, guided by the caprice of a whimsical will. Whimsicality is a flower that defies transplanting; when once rooted in other soil it shoots up into obscurity, masquerading as profundity, or pure silliness without reason or a smile. The whimsies of one language become amazing contortions in another. The humour of Shandy, though deep-dyed in Sterne's own eccentricity, is still essentially British and demands for its appreciation a more extensive knowledge of British life in its narrowest, most individual phases, a more intensive sympathy with British attitudes of mind than the German of the eighteenth century, save in rare instances, possessed."

19. Michelsen, p. 109.

20. Ibid., p. 115.

21. Michael Poser defines this non-narrative form in Der abschweifende Erzähler (Bad Homburg, 1969), p. 12: "Die Romanabschweifung ist ein Stück nicht-erzählerischer, direkt dargebotener Weltanschauung-- sei sie nun satirisch, witzig, meditativ, pastoral oder wie immer eingefärbt. . . dieses Stück Weltanschauung erscheint in einer rhetorischen Situation, die darin besteht, dass der Autor den Leser durch sekundäre Mittel, vor allem durch eine der vertretenen Meinung entsprechende Selbstdarstellung, zur Annahme der vorgeführten Weltanschauung anreizt."

22. Henry Fielding, Jonathan Wild (New York, 1962), p. 84. Rambach

plagiarized Fielding's novel and condensed it into a short-story which was published in 1790 in the collection Kniffgenies (see bibliography).

23. It is interesting to compare Daniel Defoe's views on digressions as expressed in the Preface to the Farther [sic] Adventures in the Life and Adventures of Robinson Crusoe of York, Mariner (1719) (London, 1966): ". . . all those reflections, as well religious as moral, which are not only the greatest beauties of the work, but are calculated for the infinite advantage of the reader." The influence of Robinson Crusoe on the German novel is well documented. See, for example, Dieter Kimpel, Der Roman der Aufklärung (Stuttgart, 1967), pp. 26 ff. Writers of 1790, however, were trying to imitate Sterne rather than Defoe.

24. The article, entitled "Ueber den Missbrauch des Freundschafts-Kusses und der Umarmungen--Eine Rede im Cirkel seiner Freunde gehalten, von T. Stille" reads in part (p. 295): "Kuss und Umarmung beym Abschied oder Wiederfinden des Zwillingsbruders unserer Seele, bey Entdeckung eines neuen schönen Zuges seines Geistes und Herzens, in den seligsten Augenblicken des Lebens wo das innigste Gefühl des Wohlwollens gegen den Freund die Sprache hemmt, gegeben und empfangen, entehrt auch den Mann so wenig,als die Thräne sanfterer Theilnehmung an den Schicksalen unsrer Lieben. Nur wird der Mann nicht siegwartisch empfinden, wo er denken, nicht weinen, wo er handeln soll. . ."

25. Fielding, An Apology for the Life of Mrs. Shamela Andrews (1741), ed., Sheriden W. Baker, (Berkeley and Los Angeles, 1953), p. 27: "Mrs. Jervis and I are just in Bed, and the Door unlocked; if my Master should come--Odsbobs! I hear him just coming in the Door. You see I write in the present Tense, as Parson Williams says. Well, he is in Bed between us, we both shamming a Sleep, he steals his Hand into my Bosom, which I, as if in my Sleep, press close to me with mine, and then pretend to awake. . . ."

26. Hermann Riefstahl, Dichter und Publikum in der ersten Hälfte des 18. Jahrhunderts, dargestellt an der Geschichte der Vorrede, Diss. Frankfurt, 1934. Hans Ehrenzeller, Studien zur Romanvorrede von Grimmelshausen bis Jean Paul (Bern, 1955).

27. Fielding, Jonathan Wild (New York, 1962), p. 59.

28. Eva D. Becker, Der deutsche Roman um 1780 (Stuttgart, 1964) p. 179. Becker explains that she is indebted to E.R. Curtius for the term.

29. Similarly Bahrdt passes over a scene of Ala Lama because not even Chodowiecki, the most famous book illustrator of the period, could have coped with it--"Kein Chodowiecki vermag die Scene zu zeichnen" (II, 110).

30. Blanckenburg, Versuch über den Roman, 1774, p. 527. Blanckenburg is here speaking of writers of travels who write in imitation of Sterne's A Sentimental Journey, but this does not affect the applicability of his remarks to the novel of 1790.

31. Tristram Shandy, Bk. VI, ch. 1.

NOTES TO CHAPTER III

1. Eva D. Becker, Der deutsche Roman um 1780 (Stuttgart, 1964), p. 43.

2. Becker, p. 104.

3. Marion Beaujean, Der Trivialroman in der zweiten Hälfte des 18. Jahrhunderts (Bonn, 1964), p. 85.

4. J.B. Basedow, Ausgewählte Schriften, hrsg. von Hugo Göring (Langensalza, 1880), p. 62, cited in Kurt-Ingo Flessau, Der Moralische Roman (Köln, 1968), pp. 27 ff.

5. Flessau, Der Moralische Roman, p. 36.

6. Horace, De Arte Poetica, 11. 39-40.

> Sumite materiam vestris qui scribitis aequam
> Viribus et versate diu quid ferre recusent,
> Quid valeant humeri.

> (Take up a subject equal to your strength, O writers,
> And mull over well what loads your shoulders will bear,
> And what they will not.)

7. The full life of this character is portrayed in Kellner's Klingstein. Eine Geschichte, mit Szenen aus dem spanischen Successionskriege, 1790, but the details have little or nothing in common with the account in Familiengeschichte. The novel is discussed in Chapter VI.

8. Kellner is referring to Jean-Baptiste Du Halde, S.J., Description geographique, chronologique, politique et physique de l'Empire de la Chine et de la Tartarie chinoise, 4 vol, (Paris, 1735), first translated by R. Brookes as The general history of China, containing a geographical and physical description of the Empire of China, Chinese Tartary, Corea and Tibet. . . (London, 1736) (Queen's University holds).

   Translated into German as: Johann Baptiste Du Halde Ausführliche Beschreibung des chinesischen Reichs und der grossen Tartarey. . . mit einer Vorrede von Herrn Abt Mosheims, darin die neuesten Chinesischen Kirchengeschichten erzählet werden. . . 4 Bde. (J.C. Koppe: Rostock, 1747-56).

   A Russian translation followed in St. Petersburg, 1774.

9. Cf. King Lear, I, 2:

> Why bastard? Wherefore base,
> When my dimensions are as well compact,
> My mind as generous, and my shape as true,
> As honest madam's issue? Why brand they us
> With base? With baseness? Bastardy? Base, base!
> Who in the lusty stealth of nature take
> More composition, and fierce quality / Than doth within
>   a dull, stale, tired bed / Go to th' creating a whole
>   tribe of fops / Got 'tween asleep and wake?

NOTES OF CHAPTER IV

1. Georg Lukács, <u>Der Historische Roman</u> (Berlin, 1955), p. 11: "Es fehlt dem sogenannten historischen Roman vor Walter Scott gerade das spezifisch Historische: die Ableitung der Besonderheit der handelnden Menschen aus der historischen Eigenart ihrer Zeit." Reinhold Grimm (<u>Deutsche Romantheorien: Beiträge zur einer historischen Poetik des Romans in Deutschland</u>, Frankfurt a.M., 1968, p. 15), was the first to point out that Lukács has not definitively resolved the problem of the historical novel.

2. Lukács, p. 45: "Historische Echtheit bedeutet für ihn [Scott] die zeitbedingte Eigenart des Seelenlebens, der Moral, des Heroismus, der Opferfähigkeit, der Standhaftigkeit usw. Dies ist an der historischen Echtheit Walter Scotts wichtig, unvergänglich und für die Geschichte der Literatur epochemachend. . . ."

3. Lukács, p. 56: "Diese historische Treue ist bei Scott gerade die Wahrheit der historischen Psychologie der Gestalten, des echten hic et nunc (hier und jetzt) ihrer seelischen Beweggründe und ihrer Handlungsart."

4. Lukács (pp. 11 ff.) is impressed by what he calls the realistic social novel of 18th-century England represented by Fielding, Smollett and Defoe, and its portrayal of contemporary morals and psychology. He sees in such novels as <u>Moll Flanders</u> and <u>Tom Jones</u> a broad realistic portrayal of contemporary history which is linked with the fortunes of their characters. See also Scott's Introductory Epistle to <u>The Fortunes of Nigel</u>.

5. See, for example: Donald Davie, <u>The Heyday of Sir Walter Scott</u> (London, 1961); Robert C. Gordon, <u>Under Which King? A Study of the Scottish Waverley Novels</u> (London, 1969); Robin Mayhead, <u>Walter Scott</u> (London, 1968).

6. See Lieselotte E. Kurth, "Historiographie und historischer Roman. Kritik und Theorie im 18. Jahrhundert," <u>Modern Language Notes</u> 79 (1964), 337-362. Kurth point out that the standard reference works such as <u>Reallexikon der deutschen Literatur</u> (hrsg. von Paul Merker und Wolfgang Stammler, 2. ed., Berlin, 1958) are incorrect in claiming that the historical novel is a creation of the late romantic and early realistic 19th century. Whereas Marion Beaujean (<u>Der deutsche Trivialroman</u>, Bonn, 1964, p. 97) claims that the historical novel seems to have appeared suddenly around 1785, Kurth's examples are some 20 years older.

7. See, for example, Nicolai's <u>Sebaldus Nothanker</u>, Bd. 1,2. (1773), (<u>Deutsche Literatur in Entwicklungsreihen</u>, Bd. 15, p. 53)

8. Cited in Sigmund von Lempicki, <u>Geschichte der deutschen Literaturwissenschaft bis zum Ende des 18. Jahrhunderts</u>, 2. vermehrte Auflage (Göttingen, 1968), p. 417.

9. Lempicki, p. 416.

10. Lempicki, p. 418.

11. Lempicki, p. 419.

12. Lempicki, p. 416.

13. D.H. Hegwisch, <u>Allgemeine Uebersicht der deutschen Kulturgeschichte</u> <u>bis zu Maximilian dem Ersten. Ein Anhang zur Geschichte des Kaisers</u> (Hamburg, bey Bohn, 1788.) [230 pp.] A precis of the work recognizing it as a memorable and instructive study appeared in the <u>Allgemeine Deutsche Bibliothek</u> for 1792 (vol 108, pp. 206-11).

14. Lempicki, p. 427.

15. For a concise survey of French theory and practice see Vivienne Mylne, "Fiction, History and Truth," <u>The Eighteenth-Century French</u> <u>Novel: Techniques of Illusion</u> (Manchester, 1965), pp. 20-31, on which the following is based.

16. Sigmund von Birken had expressed essentially the same view in his Preface to Anton Ulrich's <u>Aramena</u> (1669 ff.): "Dergleichen Geschicht‐ mähren [Romane] / sind zweifelsfrei weit nützlicher / als die wahrhafte Geschichtsschriften: dann sie haben die freiheit / unter der decke die Wahrheit zu reden / und alles mit-einzuführen / . . . womit man gern den Verstand üben und zur tugendliebe bereden wollte."

17. Faksimiledruck nach der ersten Fassung von 1774, hg. und mit einem Nachwort versehen von E. Th. Voss (Stuttgart, 1964).

18. Cited in Jörg Schönert (<u>Roman und Satire im 18. Jahrhundert</u>, 1969, pp. 84 ff.). Misconstruing Engel's term "der politische Geschichtsschreiber" as "novelist", Schönert argues that Engel was actually urging <u>novelists</u> to write "true practical history". See also Georg Jäger, "Die pragmatische Geschichtsschreibung" in <u>Empfindsamkeit</u> <u>und Roman</u> (Stuttgart, 1969), p. 115: "Die Romantheorie des 18. Jahrhunderts ist durch den Pragmatismus, die Form der aufklärerischen Geschichtsschreibung, wesentlich geprägt. Die Prinzipien des Pragmatismus (psychologische Entwicklung aus menschlichen Triebfedern, Kausalnexus und Finalität, Anschaulichkeit einer idealen Gegenwart, Ablehnung der Trennung von Erzählung und Reflexion) werden auf den Roman übertragen."

19. See, for example: Freiherr Franz von Bilderbeck, <u>Alexander, eine</u> <u>historisch-romantische Skizze</u> (Offenbach, 1800), and the anonymously published <u>Wilhelm Griskircher oder die Belagerung von Wien: ein</u> <u>historisch-romantisches Gemälde aus dem 17ten Jahrhundert</u> Wien, 1800). I am indebted for this information to Manfred W. Heiderich's dissertation (in progress), "The German Novel in 1800" (Queen's).

20. J.A. Bergk, <u>Die Kunst, Bücher zu lesen. Nebst Bemerkungen über</u> <u>Schriften und Schriftsteller</u> (Jena, 1799) [München, 1968], p. 249.

21. Bergk, p. 253.

22. See Schiller's letter of 10 Dezember 1788 to Caroline von Beulwitz: . . . Ich werde immer eine schlechte Quelle für einen künftigen Geschichtsforscher seyn, der das Unglück hat, sich an mich zu wenden. Aber ich werde vielleicht auf Unkosten der historischen

Wahrheit Leser und Hörer finden und hie und da mit jener ersten
philosophischen zusammentreffen. Die Geschichte ist überhaupt nur
ein Magazin für meine Phantasie, und die Gegenstände müssen sich
gefallen lassen, was sie unter meinen Händen werden."

23. "Die Nachrichten, welche diese alten Dokumente von Heinrichen und
von den in seine Geschichte verwickelten Personen enthalten, über-
geben wir Euch in heutiges Deutsch übertragen, und wünschen, dass
sie Euren Beifall finden mögen." (ii).

24. Heinrich Zedler, Grosses vollständiges Universal-Lexikon aller
Wissenschaften und Künste, 64 vols. (Halle, 1732-54). I have resorted to this work in this and following accounts in order to indicate the type and quality of historical information which would
have been readily available to historical novelists if they had
cared to consult it. I am not suggesting that Heinse used Zedler
as a source and invented other details, as Zedler himself must have
had sources which were also available to Heinse. Responses to my
written enquiries to German libraries indicate Zedler as the only
accessible source. Special assistance in this regard was kindly
rendered by Dr. Heinz Gittig, Direktor des Auskunftsbüros deutscher
Bibliotheken, Berlin (DDR).

25. Christine Touaillon, Der deutsche Frauenroman im 18. Jahrhundert
(Wien und Leipzig, 1919), pp. 345 and 402.

26. Touaillon, p. 346.

27. Generally, Friedrich II is supposed to have been the last Babenberg.
Friedrich Schlenkert, ("Graf Albert von Babenberg", Altdeutsche
Geschichten romantischen Inhalts, 1790, p. 347) regards Graf Albert
von Babenberg as the last of his line: "Der Henker schlug ihm
[Grafen Albert] den Kopf und mit ihm dem edlen Stamme der Babenber-
ger seinen letzten Ast ab."

28. It is interesting to note that the Luitgard in Schlenkert's short-
story "Werner, Graf von Walbek" (Altdeutsche Geschichten, 133) is
described in precisely the same terms as the heroine in Naubert's
Barbara Blomberg (54). The Luitgard of Naubert's Werner, Graf von
Bernburg does not resemble her at all. The articles on the Counts
of Bamberg (variously spelled Papenberg, Babenberg, and Bernburg)
and the Counts of Walbeck in Zedler's encyclopedia give us some indication as to how characters and events might have become confused
in the popular mind. We read, for example, that the city of Bernburg, which was ruled by Lothario, Graf zu Walbeck, was burned by
the Wends in 996. Lothario was poisoned for having hindered Eckhard
von Meissen [Luitgard's father) from becoming Emperor. Lothario
left an only son, "Werinharius" or "Wernizus" for whom the estate
of Bernburg was purchased. He abducted his promised bride, Luitgard, in 999 when her parents changed their minds about the marriage.

29. Naubert implies this throughout the novel. See, for example, p. 54:
"Meine Leser fragen, wie Barbara bey dem ungewöhnlichen Geiste, den
ihr die Geschichte zuschreibt, bey einiger Erfahrung in den Sitten
der Welt, und bey der Gabe, das zu sehen und zu beurtheilen, was sie

umgab, sich so leidentlich als ein todtes Werkzeug zu allem habe
brauchen lassen, was man wollte, und wir sehen uns genöthigt zu Aufklärung dieser Räthsel. . . zu sagen, dass ihr Herz so redlich und
truglos, als ihr Verstand hell und aufgeklärt war. . . ."

30. See Touaillon, p. 280: "Sein Anfang ist lebendig und witzig und es
fehlt nicht an realistischen Zügen; bald aber verlaufen diese Spuren eines erwachenden Talents in Sand und eine ungestaltete Masse
aus ganz verschiedenen, oft nur äusserlich zusammengehefteten Be-
standteilen, deren Inhalt, Ton, Sprache und Komposition beständig
wechselt, bleibt übrig. Die ursprünglichen Absichten der Verfasser-
in geraten in Vergessenheit, sie greift neue Gedanken auf und lässt
sie wieder fallen, Hauptpersonen verschwinden und tauchen erst nach
langer Zeit wieder auf, um ohne Liebe und Interesse schnell abgetan
zu werden, während neue Personen hervortreten, obwohl die Handlung
ihrer nicht bedarf. Blosse Gesprächsszenen ohne Bedeutung für das
Ganze werden breit ausgesponnen, wichtige Ereignisse und Entwicklungen in Eile erledigt. In allem zeigt sich grosse Nachlässigkeit,
durch die aber immer wieder Spuren von Begabung [!] durchblitzen."

NOTES TO CHAPTER V

1. Jörg Schönert, Roman und Satire im 18. Jahrhundert. Ein Beitrag zur Poetik (Stuttgart, 1969), p. 7. This is the most recent and most comprehensive study of this subject, but makes very ponderous reading. For a more concrete treatment see Maria Tronskaja, Die Deutsche Prosasatire der Aufklärung (Berlin, 1969), who observes (p. 86) the rise of the satirical novel at the beginning of the 1770's.

2. Schönert, p. 106.

3. Schönert, pp. 3.

4. Kurt-Ingo Flessau, Der moralische Roman. Studien zur gesellschaftskritischen Trivialliteratur der Goethezeit (Köln-Graz, 1968), p. 15. (Hereafter referred to as Flessau)

5. Schönert, p. 34.

6. Gilbert Highet, The Anatomy of Satire (Princeton, 1962), p. 18.

7. Schönert, pp. 163 ff. "Gerade am Beispiel des satirischen Romans kann deutlich werden, inwieweit der Roman der Forderung nach 'Autonomie' der Kunst folgt, wie sie um 1790 laut wird."

8. Ibid., p. 3.

9. Ronald Paulson, Satire and the Novel in 18th-Century England (New Haven and London, 1967), p. 20.

10. Highet, The Anatomy of Satire, p. 16 ff.

11. Schönert, Satire, p. 106.

12. Henry Fielding, The History of Tom Jones: A Foundling (New York, n.d.), p. i f.

13. Irvin Ehrenpreis, Fielding: Tom Jones (London, 1964), p. 35.

14. Flessau, Der moralische Roman, p. 12.

15. J. Chr. Adelung, Grammatisch-kritisches Wörterbuch. . . ., 3. Thl., Leipzig, 1798, Sp. 280: "In weiterer Bedeutung, gesellschaftlich, zu den gesellschaftlichen Verhältnissen gehörig." Cited in Flessau, p. 19.

16. Flessau, p. 38.

17. Ibid., p. 26.

18. Ibid., p. 20 ff.

19. Eva D. Becker, Der Roman um 1780 (Stuttgart, 1964), p. 43 ff.

20. Highet, The Anatomy of Satire, p. 18 f.

21. Flessau, p. 38 f. Further evidence in support of Flessau's views can be found among most writers of 1790 even when they are not intending to be satirical. Cf. Oertel's Kilbur (I, 12): "Itzt hab' ich wieder Ruh' und Frieden erlangt, und weiss sie besser zu

benutzen als damals. Um mich her hat Einsamkeit, nur von ihren Freuden begleitet, sich gelagert; ländliche Stille umsäuselt mich, ich
liege an der ewigen Quelle alles Guten Wahren und Schönen, an den
Brüsten unsrer Mutternatur. . ." The antithesis of such pastoral
tranquility is expressed in Knigge's Zauberschloss (5): "In dem
Städtchen, wo ich wohnte, hatte die goldne Aufklärung schon herr-
liche Fortschritte gemacht; Es gab da schöne Geister und Deisten und
Weltbürger, gelehrte Frauenzimmer, Clubbs, Lese-Gesellschaften, ein
Coffeehaus, ein Liebhaber-Concert, Mitglieder geheimer Gesellschaf-
ten. . . Die Prediger sprachen von Denkfreyheit, die Aerzte von Char-
latanerie, die Advocaten von Uneigennützigkeit. . ." Cf. also Marion
Beaujean, Der Trivialroman in der zweiten Hälfte des 18. Jahrhunderts
(Bonn, 1964), p. 79: "So finden die politischen Tagesereignisse wohl
einen Niederschlag in der Literatur, aber das Darstellungsvermögen
reicht so wenig zu einer wirklich grossen Satire, wie die geistige
Bewältigung neue Ansätze findet."

22. Marion Beaujean (Trivialroman, p. 78) describes J.F.E. Albrecht's
Die Regenten im Tierreich (Leipzig, [1]1790, [2]1793) as perhaps the
most political novel written in Germany at this time. Unfortunately
the work is not extant.

23. Flessau, Der moralische Roman, p. 10 f.

24. Siegfried von Lindenberg, Leipzig, 1784.(Faksimiledruck)Fkft/M. 1971.

25. Schönert, Roman und Satire, p. 56.

26. Ibid., p. 78.

27. Marion Beaujean, Trivialroman, p. 76.

28. Schönert, p. 56. See also Maria Tronskaja (note 1 above), pp.41-51.

29. Henry Fielding, The Life of Jonathan Wild the Great ([1]1743, [2]1754),
cited in William Irwin, The Making of Jonathan Wild (Hamden, 1966),
p. 38. Text in modern orthography published New York, 1962, p. 89.

30. Hilaire Belloc claims in The French Revolution that Louis XVI was
cured of his impotence by an operation in 1777. Paul B. Bernard
explains in Joseph II (New York, 1968, p. 68): "It did not take
[Joseph II] long to find out that apart from requiring a slight sur-
gical intervention, the King had been guilty of inexcusable laziness
and lack of ambition in the conjugal bed. The Emperor sternly lec-
tured the young couple and the result was that within the year Marie
Antoinette could write her mother that she was at last expecting an
heir."

31. Albert Goodman, The French Revolution, 4th rev. ed. (London, 1967)
pp. 78 ff.

32. See Jost Hermand's Nachwort to the reprint of Carl Ignaz Geiger,
Reise eines Erdbewohners in den Mars (Stuttgart, 1967).

33. For the following see Sten G. Flygt, The Notorious Dr. Bahrdt
(Nashville, Tennessee, 1963).

34. "Infinite power is infinite power, said the doctors

who maintained the <u>reality</u> of the nose. - It extends
only to all possible things, replied the Lutherans.

By God in heaven, cried the Popish doctors, he can make
a nose, if he thinks fit, as big as the steeple of
Strasburg." (<u>Tristram Shandy</u>, Bk. IV)

35. R.L. Kahn, <u>Kotzebue. His Social and Political Attitude: The Dilemma of a Popular Dramatist in Times of Social Change</u>, Diss. Toronto
1950, p. 187: "The German audience was accustomed to the portrayal
of types on the stage. In attempting to find social criticism in
Kotzebue, one must never forget that these traditional types are
always present in the plays; the words they speak are perhaps not
always Kotzebue's views--they are what everyone would expect to
hear; but Kotzebue's views are only too often little better than re-
petitions of the conventional and traditional criticisms directed
against society during the eighteenth century." This holds true for
the present novel as well.

36. <u>Aramena, eine syrische Geschichte für unsere Zeiten</u>, umgearbeitet
von S. [ophie] A. [lbrecht], 3 Thle., 8⁰, Berlin, ¹1782-86, ²1790.
The original title was: <u>Der durchlauchtigen Syrerin Aramena Liebes-
geschichte.</u>

37. <u>Erbauungen für Jedermann</u>, 2 Thle., Flensburg (Christiani, Schleswig), 1786, (Listed in Heinsius).

38. Highet, <u>The Anatomy of Satire</u>, pp. 77 ff.

39. Christian Gotthilf Salzmann, <u>Carl von Carlsberg oder über das
menschliche Elend</u>, Th. 1-6 (Schmieder, Carlsruhe, 1784). Beaujean explains in <u>Der Trivialroman</u> (p. 63) that this was a very popular
work whose fame gave rise to numerous imitations. Müller's comment
on Heinrich Stilling refers of course to Johann Heinrich Jung-Stilling's autobiographical novel <u>Heinrich Stillings Jugend</u> (1778),
<u>Jünglingsjahre</u> and <u>Wanderschaft</u> (2. and 3. part, 1778) and <u>Heinrich
Stillings häusliches Leben, eine wahrhafte Geschichte</u> (1789)

40. I was unable to trace this title.

41. I have adopted a contemporary translator's rendering of the original
title: <u>Essays on Physiognomy; for the Promotion of the Knowledge
and the Love of Mankind</u>. Written in the german [sic] Language by
I.C. Lavater, and translated into English by Thomas Holcroft, London, printed for Robinson. 1789.
<u>The Allgemeine Deutsche Bibliothek</u> for 1790 (vol 96, p. 272), passed
off this translation with the remark that it contained some pictures
that were neither in the German nor French editions.

42. J.C. Lavater, <u>Physiognomik. Zur Beförderung der Menschenkenntniss
und Menschenliebe</u>, Vervollständigte neue Auflage der verkürzt herausgegebenen physiognomischen Fragmente (Berlin, 1834), p. 14: "Die
Physiognomik kann eine Wissenschaft werden, so gut als die Physik;--
denn sie ist Physik! So gut als die Arzneikunst; denn sie ist ein
Theil der Arzneikunst! So gut, als die Theologie; denn sie ist
Theologie! So gut, als die schönen Wissenschaften; denn sie gehört

zu den schönen Wissenschaften. . . Sobald eine Wahrheit oder eine
Erkenntnis Zeichen, sobald ist sie Wissenschaft. . ."

43. As a consequence of the secularisation of literature, as we will see
in Chapter VI, writers were gradually incorporating esoteric philosophies into their novels and were portraying the spiritual growth of
heroes destined for a 'higher existence'. Müller could scarcely have chosen a better medium for lampooning Lavater's views than a satirical autobiography which exploits the techniques of the Bildungsroman.

44. Richard Newald, Geschichte der deutschen Literatur (München, 1957)
vol 6/1, p. 199.

45. See Helmut Germer, The German Novel of Education 1792-1805. A complete Bibliography and Analysis (Berne, 1968), p. 45.

46. Cf. Kellner. Familiengeschichte der Rosenbusche (I, 19 f.): Wahres
Glück für Lavatern, dass in der Zeit nicht Autorensucht[unseren
Helden] beseelte; hätt' er seine Beobachtungen aufgesetzt und mit
feinen Kupfern geschmückt, herausgegeben; wahrlich! schon im Anfang
dieses Jahrhunderts wär dann eine Physiognomik erschienen, dickbe-
leibt und possierlich genug, um allen folgenden Zeiten den Appetit
nach einer neuen Lavaterschen ganz zu verderben." Bahrdt's Yhakanpol (p. 254) notes: "Lavater ist ein Schwärmer, der sich in hoch-
tönende Worte einhüllt und selbst von dem allen keinen deutlichen
Begriff hat."
Hilfrich Peter Sturz' serious essay "Erklärung über die Physiognomik", in Schriften, Band 2 (Carlsruhe, 1784) p. 378 to which Lavater
himself added notes, observes, however: "Ich bin von der Wahrheit
der Physiognomik, von der Allbedeutsamkeit jedes Zuges unsrer Gestalt so lebhaft als Lavater überzeugt. Es ist wahr, dass sich der
Umriss der Seele in den Wölbungen ihres Schleyers bildet, und ihre
Bewegung in den Falten ihres Kleids."

47. Cf. Sturz, "Erklärung über die Physiognomik" (loc. cit. II, 381):
". . . und wir sind alle, weniger oder mehr, empyrische Physiognomi-
ker; wir finden im Blick, in der Miene, im Lächeln, im Mechanismus
der Stirne bald Schalkheit, bald Witz, bald forschenden Geist."

48. Lavater (Physiognomik, p. 5) explains this "infallible key" in the
following manner: "Die Physiognomik... ist die Seele aller menschlichen Urtheile, Bestrebungen, Handlungen, Erwartungen, Fürchten,
Hoffnungen... Von der Wiege an, bis zum Grabe, in allen Ständen und
Altern, bei allen Nationen, von Adam an, bis auf den letzten, der
sterben wird; vom Wurm an, den wir zertreten, bis auf den erhabensten
Weisen, ist die Physiognomik der Grund von Allem, was wir thun und
lassen."

49. Lavater (Physiognomik, p. 21) explains: "Alle Menschen in der Welt,
die Augen und Ohren haben, haben Anlagen zur Physiognomik. Aber
unter zehn Tausenden wird nicht Einer ein guter Physiognomist
werden."

NOTES TO CHAPTER VI

1. Marion Beaujean, Der Trivialroman in der zweiten Hälfte des 18. Jahrhunderts (Bonn, 1964), p. 182 f.

2. Hans Jürgen Haferkorn, "Der freie Schriftsteller," in Archiv für Geschichte des Buchwesens, hrsg. von der Historischen Kommission des Börsenvereins des Deutschen Buchhandels e.v., Buchhändler Vereinigung GmbH, Band V, 1964, pp. 523-712. Haferkorn (p. 528) establishes the rise of the professional writer from 1760 till 1800.

3. Ludwig W. Kahn, Literatur und Glaubenskrise (Stuttgart, 1964), p. 8, refers to Walter Gebhardt, Religionssoziologische Probleme im Roman der deutschen Aufklärung, Diss. Giessen, 1931.

4. Fritz Martini, "Der Bildungsroman: Zur Geschichte des Worts und der Theorie," DVLG 35 (1961), p. 47.

5. Karl von Morgenstern, "Über das Wesen des Bildungsromans", Inländisches Museum, 1819, Heft 3, p. 13. Cited in Martini (note 4 above) p. 57. Cf. Karl Philipp Moritz, Anton Reiser, ein psychologischer Roman (Leipzig, n.d.), p. 335: "Dieser Teil [Teil IV, 1790] enthält auch einige vielleicht nicht unnütze und nicht unbedeutende Winke für Lehrer und Erzieher sowohl als für junge Leute, die ernsthaft genug sind, um sich selbst zu prüfen. . ."

6. Cf. Ludwig Kahn, Literatur und Glaubenskrise, p. 15: "Wenn man daher von Säkularisation spricht, ist festzustellen, dass es sich nicht notwendigerweise um eine Abwendung vom Religiösen, um Entreligionisierung und Verweltlichung handelt, sondern zugleich um eine Ausbreitung des Religiösen auf Gebiete, die vorher nicht eigentlich und wesentlich religiös waren. Was wir finden, ist nicht Schwund des Religiösen, sondern eine Lösung des Glaubens von Kirche, Dogma und institutioneller Gebundenheit, ein Zerbrechen der zentralen religiösen Form, so dass das Religiöse jetzt aus der Mitte auf Randgebiete verströmt und neue Bereiche ergreift. . ."

7. See for the following Friedrich Wilhelm Wodtke, "Erbauungsliteratur, in Paul Merker und Wolfgang Stammler, eds., Reallexikon der deutschen Literaturgeschichte (Berlin, 1925-31), and Kahn, Literatur und Glaubenskrise, passim.

8. Martin Opitz, Buch von der Deutschen Poeterey [1624] (Tübingen, 1963), p. 7.

9. Johann Christoph Gottsched, "Von den poetischen Nachahmungen," in Versuch einer Critischen Dichtkunst, [reprint of the 4th edition, 1751] (Darmstadt, 1962), p. 161.

10. Eric A. Blackall, The Emergence of German as a Literary Language 1700-1775 (Cambridge, 1959), p. 92.

11. Marianne Spiegel, Der Roman und sein Publikum im frühen 18. Jahrhundert: 1700-1767 (Bonn, 1967), pp. 52 ff.

12. Helmut Germer, The German Novel of Education 1792-1805. A complete
    Bibliography and Analysis (Bern, 1968), p. 6, note 7. Cf. Wilhelm
    von Humboldt's comment in a letter to Goethe of 23 August 1804:
    "Man las in allen Schulen kapitelweise die Bibel. Da war Geschichte,
    Poesie, Roman, Religion, Moral, alles durcheinander. . . Aus dieser
    Quelle schöpfte bis jetzt der gemeine Mann alles, wodurch er mehr
    als blosses Lasttier war." Kurt-Ingo Flessau (Der Moralische Roman,
    Köln, 1968, p. 9) observes: "Die Bildungsbedürfnisse der Bürger in
    ansprechender Form zufriedenzustellen und zugleich die Gebildeten
    abwechslungsreich und angenehm zu unterhalten, beabsichtigen die
    Herausgeber der Wochenschriften. . .[die] eine Vorstufe der mora-
    lischen Romane [darstellen].

13. Sebaldus Nothanker, in Deutsche Literatur in Entwicklungsreihen,
    Bd. 15, ed., Fritz Bruggemann (Darmstadt, 1967), pp. 149 ff.

14. Southern Germany, under the aegis of the Roman Catholic Church,
    never contributed directly to literary secularisation. Beaujean
    points out (Der Trivialroman, p. 185, note 275) that Catholic devo-
    tional literature increased in comparison with protestant works.

15. Dieter Kimpel, Der Roman der Aufklärung (Stuttgart, 1967), pp. 68 ff.

16. H. Schöffler, Protestantismus und Literatur: Neue Wege zur engli-
    schen Literatur des 18. Jahrhunderts [1922], 2. Aufl. 1958, pp. 163
    ff., cited in Kimpel, op. cit., p. 68. See also Haferkorn, op. cit., p. 540.

17. Samuel Richardson, Clarissa, or the History of a Young Lady...,
    (London, 1748), vol VII, p. 350.

18. See the German Museum, or Monthly Repository of the Literature of
    Germany, the North and the Continent in general. Vol II, for the
    Year 1800. London. . . . . p. 639:

    "Albertine and Albertina; an imitation of Richardson's Clarissa. . .
    vol I, II. printed in 1788, the remaining volumes in 1789 and 1790,
    Berlin, Arnold Wever vol I, pp. 382 8vo., II, 379, 8vo."

    "A German translation of Richardson's Clarissa was published a short
    time after the original had appeared in England; but as at that time
    the German language just began to emerge from a state of infancy,
    this translation was no longer fit to be put into the hands of young
    people, and greatly stood in need of being carefully revised and
    dressed in modern and more elegant garb. But the author of Alberti-
    na has done more than this in order to improve it. The original
    being much too voluminous and expensive for the generality of rea-
    ders of this class of composition [!], the author has judiciously
    reduced it to one third of its bulk, without thereby mutilating the
    beautiful body of the original; and by translating the scene of ac-
    tion to Germany, has rendered it still more interesting for German
    readers."

    Another reviewer, in the Neuer Teutscher Merkur for 1790 (vol 2,
    pp. 435 ff.), also discusses this new translation. He notes that
    although the reading of Clarissa and Pamela has fallen out of style,
    Richardson's 'characters are drawn with such unparalleled felicity,

the interspersed psychological observations are so true, the consequences for taste and morals so important,' that the German public
ought to welcome a new edition.

Chr. H. Schmidt's sixteen-volume translation of <u>Clarissa</u> appeared
in Mannheim, 1790-91.

19. Cited in Schmidt, <u>Richardson, Rousseau und Goethe</u>, p. 35.
This account is also found in Maria Tronskaja, <u>Die deutsche Prosasatire der Aufklärung</u> (Berlin, 1969), p. 103.

20. Eva D. Becker, <u>Der deutsche Roman um 1780</u> (Stuttgart, 1964), p. 12.

21. Haferkorn, op. cit., pp. 525 ff.

22. Arnold Hirsch, <u>Bürgertum und Barock im Deutschen Roman: Zur Ent-
stehungsgeschichte des bürgerlichen Weltbildes</u> [1934], 2. Aufl.
(Köln, 1957), p. 128.

23. Fritz Stemme, "Die Säkularisation des Pietismus zur Erfahrungsseelenkunde", <u>ZfdPh</u>, 72 (1953), pp. 144-158.

24. Cited in Stemme, p. 147.

25. Kimpel, <u>Der Roman der Aufklärung</u>, p. 107.

26. Haferkorn, op. cit., p. 528.

27. Cf. Thomas Mann, <u>Gesammelte Werke</u> (Frankfurt am Main, 1960), vol XI,
p. 616: "Was ist denn der deutsche Bildungsroman anderes als die
Sublimierung und Vergeistigung des Abenteurromans."

28. Ch. F. Blanckenburg, <u>Versuch über den Roman</u>, Faksimiledruck der
Originalausgabe von 1774 (Stuttgart, 1965), pp. xiv f.

29. Jörg Schönert (<u>Roman und Satire im 18. Jahrhundert</u>, Stuttgart, 1969
p. 81) notes Blanckenburg's admission of having often written contrary to his own theories.

30. Wilhelm von Humboldt, "Theorie der Bildung des Menschen" (1793),
in <u>Gesammelte Schriften</u> (Berlin, 1903). Photomechanischer Nachdruck
(Berlin, 1968), Bd. 1, p. 283.

31. Walter Muschg, <u>Tragische Literaturgeschichte</u>, 3. Aufl. (Bern, 1957),
p. 297.

32. Schrimpf, ed., K. Ph. Moritz, <u>Andreas Hartknopf</u>, Nachwort, p. 32.

33. Robert Minder (<u>Die Religiöse Entwicklung</u>. . . p. 219) cited in
Schrimpf, op. cit., p. 28.

34. August Langen, "Karl Philipp Moritz' Weg zur symbolischen Dichtung",
<u>ZfdPh</u> 81 (1962), p. 174. For the most complete Moritz bibliography
see Thomas P. Saine, <u>Die Ästhetische Theodizee: Karl Philipp Moritz
und die Philosophie des 18. Jahrhunderts</u>, München, 1971.

35. Kahn, <u>Literatur und Glaubenskrise</u>, p. 52: "Die andere Seite ist die
Rechtfertigung--nicht durch den Glauben, sondern durch den Erfolg."
Max Weber, <u>Gesammelte Aufsätze zur Religionssoziologie</u> (Tübingen,
1922) I, 80; cites Richard Baxter: "It is for action that God main-

taineth us and our activities; work is the moral as well as the natural end of power. . . It is action that God is most served and
honoured by. . ." Cited in Kahn, p. 117.

36. Daniel Defoe, The Life and Surprising Adventures of Robinson Crusoe
of York, Mariner [1719] (London, 1966). See Preface to the Farther
[sic] Adventures.

37. Max Weber, "Die protestantische Ethik und der Geist des Kapitalis-
mus", Gesammelte Aufsätze zur Religionssoziologie, op. cit., cited
in Kahn, p. 7.

38. Heller refers to August Gottlieb Meissner's Alcibiades, 4 Tle.,
(Leipzig, [1]1781-88, [2]1785-88). Beaujean incorrectly explains (Der
Trivialroman, p. 104) that Meissner's work marks the beginning of
the historical novel in Germany and depends upon the traditional
Fürstenspiegel, which portrayed the life and ideals of rulers. Its
interest for Heller doubtless lay in the fact that Alcibiades recounts a young prince's journey with a pedagogue in order to develop
himself into a virtuous ruler. Virtue here is understood as restraint, humility, and kindliness.
Lieselotte Kurth's examples of the historical novel are some twenty
years older. [see bibliog.]

39. Heller's footnote reads: "C. Meiners über den Genius des Sokrates,
in den verm. philo. Schriften, 3 Th. Und L.J.K. Justi über den
Genius des Sokrates: Leipz. 1779. Auch deutsches Museum, Junius
1777." Meiner's article "Vom Genius des Sokrates, eine philosophische Untersuchung", is found in Deutsches Museum (Leipzig, in der
Weygandschen Buchhandlung, Junius, 1777), 481-510. Meiners examines
the historical accuracy of Socrates' witnesses and concludes in part
that Socrates was a model of human virtue even though he left no
writings to prove it: "Wenn jemals ein Mann als Muster menschlicher
Tugenden bekannt gewesen ist, so ist es Sokrates. Ohngeachtet wir
von ihm keine Zeile haben, so hat ihn bloss seine Rechtschaffenheit
und seine Klugheit zum dauerhaftesten und glänzendsten Ruhm empor
geschwungen" (488). The purpose of the essay is to show (500 ff.)
that the facticity of Christianity cannot be demonstrated with miracles because Socrates' life itself was a miracle prior to the
Christian faith.

40. Cf. J.C. Lavater, Physiognomik: Zur Beförderung der Menschenkenntniss und Menschenliebe, Vervollständigte neue Auflage der verkürzt
herausgegebenen physiognomischen Fragmente (Berlin, 1834), p. 39:
"Und doch war Socrates aus Allem, was wir von ihm wissen, der wei-
seste, beste, unvergleichlichste Mensch."

41. Marion Beaujean explains briefly that ". . . Fesslers Marc-Aurel
(1799) [sic], der noch einmal das Gelassenheitsideal in antikem
Gewande aufgreift und in einem Erziehungs- und Bildungsroman ent-
rollt," is, like Heller's Sokrates, an imitation of Meissner's
Alcibiades (Der Trivialroman, p. 105). See note 38 above.

42. See article "Fessler", Allgemeine Deutsche Biographie.

43. Goethe, <u>Die Leiden des jungen Werthers</u>, in <u>Werke</u>, Hamburger Ausgabe, Bd. 6, p. 29.

44. Cramer's <u>Erasmus Schleicher</u> [[1]1789, [2]1791] deserves a comment here even though its dates of publication leave it outside the scope of this study. The novel is a secularized story of spiritual quest, in which the hero, in Cramer's words, treads a path toward divine wisdom: "Unerschütterlich und mit festem Schritte geht er seinen Weg, den er sich selbst vorgesetzt hat: er mag ihn nun durch Dornen, oder unter duftenden Blüthenbäumen über Rosen hin führen. Nichts hält ihn auf! nichts führt ihn seitwärts! nichts schreckt ihn zurück!" [Faksimiledruck der Ausgabe von 1792 hrsg., H.F. Foltin, 1971] (IV, 126 f.) The final chapter, significantly entitled "Amen! ! !", proclaims a humanistic gospel. A reviewer in the <u>Allgemeine Deutsche Bibliothek</u> for 1790 (vol 96, pp. 141 ff.) recognized this as a new kind of novel: "Kein Roman von gemeinem Schlag aus einer Romanfabrik in Dachstuben, sondern die Arbeit eines sehr guten Kopfes, die sich durch Originalität und richtige Zeichnung der Charaktere. . . dem Leser vortheilhaft auszeichnet."

BIBLIOGRAPHY

It has been a concern of this study to examine those works of prose fiction which might properly be considered first editions of 1790, and to establish definitive details of their authorship and publication. The present critical bibliography of first editions published in 1790 represents my conclusions after comparison and integration of bibliographical information obtained from four types of source: the standard reference works (Goedeke, Heinsius, Kayser, Kosch, Meusel, Holzmann/Bohatta), the British Museum Catalogue, personal communications from and search in Central Catalogues and libraries in Germany and Austria, and examination of the actual primary sources either in the original, on microfilm or xerox.

I. PRIMARY SOURCES

Where I have been able to obtain a microfilm or xerox copy of the primary source or to consult the original (Section A below), the title and publication data provided in the Bibliography are based on the title page of the text. Where it has been impossible to locate a copy of the original (Section C and D below), the data provided are based on the bibliographical sources listed in Part II of the Bibliography. Square brackets indicate interpolations from these sources or evidence found in the texts themselves. Where possible, works are listed alphabetically according to the author. The majority (62 %) were published anonymously, many others under a pseudonym. In such cases attribution of authorship was made by consensus of bibliographical sources.

Titles marked with an asterisk (*) indicate xerox or microfilm copies held by The Douglas Library, Queen's University, Kingston, Canada.

Albrecht, Johann Friedrich Ernst (1752-1814)

*Dreyerlei Wirkungen. Eine Geschichte aus der Planetenwelt. tradirt und so erzählt. [Published anon.]

Band I   Germanien, bey Peter Sandhof, 1789 [265 pp.]
Band II   Germanien, bey Peter Sandhof, 1789 [254 pp.]
Band III   Germanien, bey Peter Sandhof, 1789 [192 pp.]
Band IV   Germanien, bey Peter Sandhof, 1789 [284 pp.]
Location: Staats- und Universitätsbibliothek Frankfurt a.M..
            Sign. Biblioth. G.Fr. 1070

Band V   [Germanien, bey Peter Sandhof, 1790]
Band VI   [Germanien, bey Peter Sandhof, 1791]
Source: Deutsche Staatsbibliothek, Berlin, (DDR)
            Sign. Yw 531 b [presumed lost]

*Band VII Germanien, bey Peter Sandhof, 1792 [260 pp.]
*Band VIII Germanien, bey Peter Sandhof, 1792 [116 pp.]
Location: Senckenberg-Bibliothek Frankfurt a.M., Sign. 8° 13989

Albrecht, Johann Friedrich Ernst

*Fackland,oder Schaden macht klug. Von Albrecht, Verfasser der neuen Biographien der Selbstmörder.

Erster Teil, Wien, bey Johann David Hörling, Buchhändler, 1790
                                                    [195 pp.]
Zweiter Teil, Wien, bey Georg Trummer [n.d.] [190 pp.]
Location: Osterreichische Nationalbibliothek Wien, Sign. 250. 135-
           A. Fid. (72-269)

Albrecht, J.F.E.

*Uranie. Königin von Sardanapalien im Planeten Sirius/ ein Werk Wessemi Saffras des genannten Weisen, aber eines Thoren unter seinen Brüdern/ verteutscht von einem niedersächsischen Land-prediger. Zu finden Ueberall im Jahr 1790.

[Erster Theil 254 pp.] [Zweyter Theil 238 pp.]
Location: Staats- und Universitätsbibliothek Hamburg, Sign. A/11766.

Bahrdt, Karl Friedrich (1741-1 92)

*Ala Lama oder der König unter den Schäfern, auch ein goldner Spiegel.

2 Bd. [published anon.] [Bd. I - 316 pp; Bd. II - 383 pp.]
Frankfurt und Leipzig, 1790.
Location: Universitätsbibliothek Wien, Sign. I I20.029
           Universitätsbibliothek Berlin, Sign. Yq 5582

Bahrdt, Karl Friedrich

> Geschichte des Prinzen Yhakanpol, lustig und zugleich orthodox-
> erbaulich geschrieben von dem Magister Wromschewsky. Mit einer
> Vorrede vom Doctor Hofstede, Grossinquisitor. Adrianopel [Halle],
> 1790.
> Source: Staatsbibliothek Marburg, Sign. Yw 2569 [presumed lost]
>   Universitätsbibliothek Berlin, Sign. Yq 55825 [pres. lost]
>
> Copy consulted: Geschichte des Prinzen Yhakanpol, lustig und zugleich
>   erbaulich geschrieben, von D. Carl Friedrich Bahrdt.
>   Görliz, bei Hermsdorf und Anton, 1795. [460 pp.]
>   [Personal copy of Dr. Sten G. Flygt, Department of German,
>   Vanderbilt University, Nashville, Tennessee.]

Fessler, Ignaz Aurelius (1756-1839)

> *Marc-Aurel. [published anon.]
>
> Erster Theil. Breslau, bei Wilhelm Gottlieb Korn, 1790 [260 pp.]
> Zweiter Theil. Breslau, bei Wilhelm Gottlieb Korn, 1790 [436 pp.]
> Dritter Theil. Breslau, bei Wilhelm Gottlieb Korn, 1792 [488 pp.]
> Vierter Theil. Breslau, bei Wilhelm Gottlieb Korn, 1792 [216 pp.]
> [Heinsius: 1799; Marion Beaujean lists 1799 as first edition]
> Location: Universitätsbibliothek Berlin, Sign. Yr 68058

Geiger, Carl Ignaz (1756-1791)

> Reise eines Erdbewohners in den Mars. [published anon.]
>
> Philadelphia [Frankfurt a.M., bei Johann Gottlob Pech] 1790.
>   [86 pp.]
> [Edition used: Faksimiledruck der Ausgabe von 1790 mit einem
> Nachwort von Jost Hermand, J.B. Metzlersche Verlagsbuchhandlung,
> Stuttgart, 1967.]

Göchhausen, Ernst August (1740-1824) [pseud. Martin Sachs]

> *Ein Büchlein zur Beförderung einfältiger Lebensweisheit unter
> verständigen und ehrlichen Bürgern und Landleuten. Von einem
> Oberdeutschen Landmann. Nebst einem Conterfey in Fine,
> [published anon.]
> Erfurt, bey Georg Adam Keyser, 1790 [248 pp.]
> Location: Staatsbibliothek Marburg, Sign. NP 14336

Göchhausen, Ernst August

> *Meines Vaters Hauschronika, ein launiger Beytrag zur Lebensweis-
> heit Menschen- und Weltkunde. Mit Belegen, Anecdoten und Charac-
> terzügen.
>
> Herausgegeben von Martin Sachs.
> Erfurt, bey Georg Adam Keyser, 1790. [516 pp.]
> Location: Universitätsbibliothek Berlin, Sign. Yq 53235

Hegrad, Friedrich (1757-18??)

*Felix mit der Liebesgeige von Fr. Hegrad. [2.Aufl.] [1.Aufl.1790]

Erster Theil, Prag und Leipzig, in der Schönfeld-Meissnerischen
Buchhandlung, 1791 [204 pp.]
Zweiter Theil,Prag und Leipzig, in der Schönfeld-Meissnerischen
Buchhandlung, 1791 [167 pp.]
Location: Ernst-Moritz-Arndt-Univerität Greifswald, Sign.Kl.Nstr. 826

Heinse, Gottlob Heinrich (1766-1812)

*Heinrich der Eiserne, Graf von Hollstein. Eine Geschichte aus dem
vierzehnten Jahrhundert. In Zwey Theilen. [Tl.I, 202 pp; Tl.II,
288 pp.]
[published anon.] 1790.
Location: Bayrische Staatsbibliothek München, Sign. P.o. germ. 593^{s}

Heller, Wilhelm Friedrich (1757-179?)

*Sokrates von Wilhelm Heller.

Erster Theil, Frankfurt am Main, bei Friedrich Esslinger, 1790
(308 pp.] [Part II unavailable.]
Location: Universitätsbibliothek Wien, Sign. I 95.867
Universitätsbibliothek Berlin, Sign. Vs 6259

Kellner, Georg Christopf (? -1809)

*Familiengeschichte der Rosenbusche. Aus authentischen Quellen.

4 Theile. [1035 pp.] [published anon.]
Leipzig, bei Carl Friedrich Schneidern, 1789-90.
[Tl. I, 1789, 256 pp.; Tl II, 1790, 175 pp.; Tl. III, 314 pp.;
Tl. IV, 1790, 390 pp.] [published as Vols. 33-36 in the series
Neue Original-Romane der Deutschen, 1790]
Location: Staatsbibliothek Marburg, Sign. Yw 3748/30

Kellner, Georg Christoph

*Klingstein. Eine Geschichte, mit Szenen aus dem spanischen
Successionskriege, von G.Chr. K.

Breslau, bey Ernst Gottlieb Meyer, 1790. [189 pp.]
Location: Universitätsbibliothek München, Sign. 8° Maassen 2701

Kellner, Georg Christoph

*Molly und Uranie. Novelle. Mit einem Dialog: Ueber die Schöpf-
ung aller Welten und aller Geister, die sie bewohnen und ihre
Schönheiten geniessen. Von G.C. Kellner.

Mannheim, bey Schwan und Götz, 1790 [270 pp.]
Location: Staatsbibliothek Mainz, Sign. 55/84

Knigge, Adolf Franz Friedrich, Freiherr von (1752-1796)

*Das Zauberschloss oder Geschichte des Grafen Tunger.

Herausgegeben von Adolph Freyherrn Knigge.
Hannover, bei Christian Ritscher, 1791 [2. Aufl.] [308 pp.]
Location: Universitätsbibliothek Greifswald, Sign. Nstr. 871
Landesbibliothek Gotha, Sign. Po 2590

Kotzebue, August von (1761-18190

*Die gefährliche Wette. Ein kleiner Roman in zwölf Kapiteln.

Von August v. Kozebue [sic] Berlin, [I. Aufl. 1790] 1800. [96 pp.]
Location: Niedersächsische Staats- und Universitätsbibliothek,
Göttingen, Sign. 8. Fab. Rom. VI. 4520

Kratter, Franz (1758-1830)

*Das Schleifermädchen aus Schwaben. [published anon.]

[Bd. I, 311 pp., Bd. II, 348 pp.[Frankfurt am Mayn, bey
Friedrich Esslinger, 1796. [2. Aufl.] [1. Aufl. 1790]
Location: Universitätsbibliothek Wien, Sign. I 90.995
Queen's University Microfilm PT 26A and 26B
Deutsche Staatsbibliothek Berlin, Sign. Yr. 76812

Moritz, Karl Philipp (1757-1793)

Anton Reiser. Ein psychologischer Roman. [Berlin, 4 vols,1785-90]

Neue Ausgabe, Leipzig-Insel-Verlag, 1959
[Meusel lists: Anton Reiser; ein philosophischer Roman].

Moritz, Karl Philipp

*Andreas Hartknopf. Eine Allegorie.

Berlin, bei Johann Friedrich Unger, 1786. [published anon.]
[160 pp.]
Location: Universitätsbibliothek Wien, Sign. I 396.845 Adl.
Deutsche Staatsbibliothek, Berlin, Sign. Yw 2271 a
Universitätsbibliothek Göttingen, Sign. 8 Fab. Rom.VI, 2773

Moritz, Karl Philipp

*Andreas Hartknopfs Predigerjahre. [published anon.]

Berlin, bei Johann Friedrich Unger, 1790. [140 pp.]
Location: Universitätsbibliothek Wien, Sign. I 396.845 Adl.
Deutsche Staatsbibliothek, Berlin, Sign. Yw 2271 a
Universitätsbibliothek Göttingen, Sign. 8 Fab. Rom. VI,2773

Müller, Johann Christian Wilhelm

*Fragmente aus dem Leben und Wandel eines Physiognomisten. Ein
Pendant zu Musäus physiognomischen Reisen. [published anon.]

Halle,bey Francke und Bispink, 1790 [460 pp.]
Location: Universitätsbibliothek Berlin, Sign. Yr. 41808

Müller, Johann Gottwerth (genannt von Itzehoe) (1743-1828)

*Herr Thomas, eine komische Geschichte vom Verfasser des Siegfried von Lindenberg.

Tl I/II   Göttingen, bey Johann Christian Dieterich, 1790.[456 pp.]
Tl I/III Göttingen, bey Johann Christian Dieterich, 1791.[463 pp.]
Location: Niedersächsische Staats- und Universitätsbibliothek,
          Göttingen, Sign. 8° Fab. VI, 5037
          Deutsche Staatsbibliothek, Berlin, Sign. Yq 62802

Müller, Johann Gottwerth

Komische Romane aus den Papieren des braunen Mannes und des Verfassers des Siegfried von Lindenberg. Siebenter Band welcher
den ersten und zweyten Theil des Herrn Thomas enthält.

Göttingen, bey Johann Christian Dieterich, 1790

*Komische Romane aus den Papieren des braunen Mannes und des Ver-
fassers des Siegfried von Lindenberg. Achter Band welcher den
dritten und vierten Theil des Herrn Thomas enthält.

Göttingen, bey Johann Christian Dieterich, 1791.
[Goedeke notes correctly that the two titles, "Herr Thomas" and
"Komische Romane aus den Papieren. . ." actually refer to two
simultaneous editions of the same novel.]
Location: Landesbibliothek Kiel, Sign. Lm 34
          Deutsche Staatsbibliothek, Berlin, Sign. Yq 62802

Naubert, Christiane Benedicte (1756-1819)

*Alf von Dülmen. Oder Geschichte Kaiser Philipps und seiner
Tochter. Aus den ersten Zeiten der heimlichen Gerichte. [publ.
                                                          anon.]
Leipzig, in der Weygandschen Buchhandlung, 1791.[2.Aufl.] [544 pp.]
Location: British Museum, Catalogue 12548. b. 6.
          Universitätsbibliothek Greifswald, Sign. Bn 242$\underline{b}$

Naubert, Christiane Benedicte

*Barbara Blomberg, Vorgebliche Maitresse Kaiser Karls des Fünften.
Eine Originalgeschichte in zwei Theilen. [published anon.]

Erster Theil, Leipzig, in der Weygandschen Buchhandlung,1790.
                                                        [396 pp.]
Zweiter Theil, Leipzig, in der Weygandschen Buchhandlung,1790.
                                                        [440 pp.]
Location: British Museum, Catalogue 12548. d. 13
          Landesbibliothek Weimar, Sign. Dd, 4:288 a.b.
          Universitätsbibliothek, Jena, Sign. G.B.o. 754

Naubert, Christiane Benedicte

Merkwürdige Begebenheiten der gräflichen Familie von Wallis.
2 Theile, Leipzig, 1791 [2.Aufl.] [Published anon.]
Location: Landesbibliothek Hannover, Sign. IV 9 B 8°

Naubert, Christiane Benedicte

    *Brunilde. Eine Anekdote aus dem bürgerlichen Leben des dreizehn-
ten Jahrhunderts. [published anon.]

    Leipzig, in der Weygandschen Buchhandlung, 1790 [84 pp.]
    Location: Niedersächsische Staats- und Universitätsbibliothek,
          Göttingen, Sign. 8° Fab. VI, 4410

Naubert, Christiane Benedicte

    *Werner, Graf von Bernburg. [published anon.]

    Erster Theil, Leipzig, in der Weigandschen Buchhandlung, 1790
                                              [388 pp.]
    Zweiter Theil,Leipzig, in der Weigandschen Buchhandlung, 1790
                                              [374 pp.]
    [Continuous pagination through both parts for 762 pp.]
    Location: British Museum, Catalogue 12548. b. 21.

Oertel, Friedrich von (1764-1807)

    *Kilbur, ein Beitrag zur Geschichte des sittlichen Gangs mensch-
licher Natur von Friedrich von Oertel.

    Erster Theil, Leipzig, in der Weidmannschen Buchhandlung, 1790
                                              [411 pp.]
    Zweiter Theil, Leipzig, in der Weidmannschen Buchhandlung, 1791
                                            [465 pp.]
    Location: Wissenschaftliche Bibliothek der Stadt Erfurt, Sign.Lg.6860
          Staatsbibliothek Marburg, Sign. Yw 3291

Rehkopf, Heinrich Wolfrath (1767-1814)

    *Franz Wall, oder der Philosoph auf dem Schafot [published anon.]

    In zwey Theilen.
    Halberstadt, bey Johann Heinrich Gros. seel. Wittwe., 1791[2.Aufl.]
                                              [264 pp.]
    Location: Universitätsbibliothek München, Sign. 8° Maassen 3298

Salzmann, Christian Gotthilf (1744-1811)

    *Sebastian Kluge. Ein Volksbuch von C. G.Salzmann (Geb. 1744,
gest. 1811)
Für die Gegenwart bearbeitet von Eugen Isolani. Mit einem Geleit-
wort von Lic. Dr. Karl Leimbach, Kg. Provinzialschulrat zu Breslau.

    Glogau, Carl Flemming, Verlag, Buch- und Kunstdruckerei, A.G.
    [Preface is dated: "Dresden, im Aprill 1898" and claims that the
present text is an abbreviated version of Salzmann's original
which "erschien im Jahre 1790 bei Siegfried Lebrecht Crusius in
Leipzig".]
    [Unable to locate original edition.]
    Location: Universitätsbibliothek Wien, Sign. I 228.182
          Universitätsbibliothek Berlin, Sign. Ling 14479 [pres.lost]

Tresenreuter, Sophie (geb. von Thomson) (1755-?)

    *Geist der Memoiren der Herzogin Mathilde von Burgund. In den Begebenheiten verschiedener Personen aus dem zwölften und dreizehnten Jahrhundert. 3 Thle. [published anon.]

    Erster Theil, Schleswig, bei Kaven und Compagnie, 1789 [215 pp.]
    Zweiter Theil, Leipzig und Altona, bey Johann Heinrich Kaven, 1790
[164 pp.]
    Dritter Theil, Leipzig und Altona, bey Johann Heinrich Kaven, 1790
[184 pp.]
Location: Universitätsbibliothek München, Sign. 8° Hist. 5560

Werder, Heinrich

    *Eduard Rosenhain oder Schwachheiten unsers Jahrzehends.
[published anon.]

    Leipzig, bey Friedrich Gotthold Jacobäer, 1790. [294 pp.]
Location: Landesbibliothek Gotha, Sign. Poes. 8° 2949

Anon.

    *Die unglückliche Fürstin aus Wien.

    Hamburg, bei Benjamin Gottlob Hoffmann. 1790 [288 pp.]
Location: Osterreichische Nationalbibliothek, Sign. 117.416-A
              Universitätsbibliothek Greifswald, Sign. Kl. Nstr. 153

Anon.

    *Heinrich und Henriette oder Die traurigen Folgen eines raschen Entschlusses. Eine Robinsonade.

    Gera, bei Heinrich Gottlob Rothe, 1799 [2.Aufl.] [243 pp.]
Location: Landesbibliothek Gotha, Sign. Poes. 8° 3040

Anon.

    *Kabale und Liebe, eine Hofbegebenheit von einem Ungenannten.

    Frankfurt am Main, bei Gebhard und Körber, 1790 [220 pp.]
Location: Deutsche Staatsbibliothek Berlin, Sign. Yw 3295 a

B. OTHER WORKS FIRST PUBLISHED IN 1790 AND DISCUSSED IN THIS BOOK

Bahrdt, Karl Friedrich

   *Dr. Karl Friedrich Bahrdts Geschichte seines Lebens, seiner Mein-
   ungen und Schicksale. Von ihm selbst geschrieben.

   Erster Theil, Berlin, bei Friedrich Vieweg, dem älteren, 1790
                                                          [390 pp.]
   [final pages ends: Halle, gedrukt bei F.D. Francke]
   Zweiter Theil, Berlin, bei Friedrich Vieweg, dem älteren,[368 pp.]
   [Part II has two title pages, one marked "Berlin, 1790", and the
   other "Berlin, 1791"]
   Dritter Theil, Berlin, 1791, [406 pp.]
   Vierter und letzter Theil, Berlin, 1791, [287 pp.]
   [Page 287 of vol IV ends: Geschrieben und vollendet d. Isten Mai,
   1790]
   [Pages 288-297 list 126 of Bahrdts works appearing from 1758-1791]
   Location: Universitätsbibliothek Wien, Sign. I 98.384
              Deutsche Staatsbibliothek Berlin, Sign. At 8781 a

Haken, Johann Christian Ludwig (1767-1835)

   *Die graue Mappe, aus Ewald Rinks Verlassenschaft. [4 Bde.]
   [published anon.]

   [Kayser lists: 1.Aufl. 1790-94; 2.Aufl., with author's name, 1818.]
   Dritter Band, Berlin, bei Johann Friedrich Unger, 1791, [302 pp.]
   Vierter und letzter Band, bei Johann Friedrich Unger, 1791,
                                                          [302 pp.]
   Location: Staats- und Universitätsbibliothek Göttingen. [No catalg.Nr]
              Landesbibliothek Gotha, Sign. Poes. 8° 2478

Kaffka, Johann Christoph [actual name: Engelmann] [1754-1815]

   *Ruinen der Vorzeit, 2 Bde. [published anon.]

   Breslau und Leipzig, bey Wilhelm Gottlieb Korn, 1793.
   [Bd. I 298 pp; Bd. II, 215 pp.]
   [Kayser and Kosch list only 1790. Heinsius 1793.]
   [Contents of vol I: I) Eduard der Kühne, oder die Flucht des
   englischen Prätendenten 2) Sonderbare Begebenheit aus den un-
   glücklichen Tagen Carls des Zweyten, Königs von England 3) Die
   Herzoginn Cerifalco 4) Die Grafen P. in Venedig 5) Des Grafen
   Julius von F. Rettung aus den Händen der Inquisition in Madrid.
   Eine historische Begebenheit aus dem Jahre 1745./ Contents of
   Vol II: I) Wildgraf Hugo, Comthur des Tempelherren-Ordens.
   Geschichte aus den Zeiten seiner Aufhebung. 2) Die unglückliche
   Gräfinn Chateaubriant aus den Zeiten Franz des Ersten. 3) Die
   Krystallseherinn. Eine Zaubergeschichte. 4) Die Einsiedlerinn.]
   Location: Universitätsbibliothek Berlin, Sign. Yr 59114

Meister, Leonard (1741-1811)

   *Leonard Meisters neue schweizerische Spaziergänge.

   St. Gallen, bey Huber und Comp. 1790 [288 pp.]
   Location: Universitätsbibliothek Wien, Sign. I 145. 986
               Universitätsbibliothek Berlin, Sign. Gesch. 15449

Rambach, Friedrich Eberhard (1767-1826)

   *Thaten und Feinheiten renommierter Kraft- und Kniffgenies.
   2 Bd. [published anon.]

   [Kayser lists: "mit Hagemeister und Ludw. Tieck, 2 Thle., Berlin,
   n.d."] (Goedeke notes that Rambach had his pupils complete the
   story of Klostermayer, Bd. II, 141 ff.] Bd. I, Berlin, bei
   Christian Friedrich Himburg, 1790 [408 pp.] Contents of Vol I:
   I) Geschichte Jonathan Wilds des Grossen [a plagiarized and edited
   version of Fielding's novel Jonathan Wild]; 2) Leben Nikel Lists
   bekannten Räubers der güldenen Tafel in Lüneburg.]
   Bd. II Berlin, bei Christian Friedrich Himburg, .791 [334 pp.]
   [Contents of Vol II: I) Geschichte Carls Prices: 2) Mathias
   Klostermayer; oder der Bayersche Hiesel.]
   Location: Universitätsbibliothek Wien, Sign. I 395.403

Sander, Christian [also Levin] (1756-1819)

   *Salz, Laune und Mannichfaltigkeit, in comischen Erzählungen.
   [published anon.]

   Hamburg, bei Benjamin Gottlob Hoffman, 1790 [382 pp.]
   Location: Landesbibliothek Kiel, Sign. 8ᵃ Ls. 593
               Deutsche Staatsbibliothek Berlin, Sign. Zk 11051

Schlenkert, Friedrich Christian (1757-1826)

   *Altdeutsche Geschichten romantischen Inhalts. Bearbeitet von
   Schlenkert.

   Erstes Bändchen, Zürich, bei Ziegler und Söhne, 1790, [347 pp.]
   [Contents of this volume: 1) Erkanger und Berthold, Kammerboten
   von Schwaben (108 pp.); Graf Werner von Walbek (190 pp.)
   3) Graf Albert von Babenberg (46 pp.)
   Location: Landesbibliothek Gotha, Sign. POES. 2829

Stutz, Johann Ernst August (1767-18-2)

   *Erzählungen von E.A. Stutz. In Zwei Theilen. Wohlfeilere Ausgabe.

   [Thl. I: 206 pp., Thl. II: 212 pp.] Berlin und Stettin,in der
   Nicolaischen Buchhandlung, 1817, [I. Aufl. 1790]
   [Contents of vol I: 1) Kranow 2) Adimor und Elise, eine grie-
   chische Erzählung, wo nicht wörtlich, doch meist wahr 3) Die Rache
   4) Eginhard und Emma 5) von Melldorf 6) Kabale 7) Undank- Eine
   wahre Geschichte 8) Dankbarkeit- Eine wahre Geschichte 9) Die
   beiden Freundinnen; //Contents of vol II: 1)Ines de Cordova und
   Marquis de Lerma - Eine spanische Geschichte 2) Geschichte eines

Reisenden - Aus Briefen gezogen 3) Der Zauberer.
Location: Niedersächsische Staats- und Universitätsbibliothek,
         Göttingen, Sign. 8° Fab. VI, 3413
         Landesbibliothek Dessau, catalogue number unknown.

Thilo, Friedrich Theophilus (1749-1825)

   Lebensscenen aus der wirklichen Welt.

   [Volumes 1-8 only.]   [1784-89]
Source: Landesbibliothek Coburg, Sign. D III 9/40-51

   *Lebensscenen aus der wirklichen Welt. Vom Verfasser der
   Emilie Sommer.

   12 Bändchen. [Heinsius, Kayser, Kosch: 1784-90; Goedeke:
   178?-90.]
   Neuntes Bändchen, Leipzig, bey Paul Gotthelf Kummer, 1789,[284 pp.]
   Zehntes Bändchen, Leipzig, bey Paul Gotthelf Kummer, 1789,[284 pp.]
   Elftes Bändchen, Leipzig, bey Paul Gotthelf Kummer, 1790,[283 pp.]
   Zwölftes Bändchen,Leipzig, bey Paul Gotthelf Kummer, 1790,[306 pp.]
Location: Niedersächsische Staats- und Universitätsbibliothek,
         Göttingen, Sign. 8° Fab. Rom. VI, 4830^C

C. NO LONGER EXTANT FIRST EDITIONS OF 1790 WITH TRACEABLE AUTHORS

Albrecht, Johann Friedrich Ernst

   Der Ehebruch: eine wahre Geschichte dramatisch bearbeitet.

   Leipzig, 1790 [published anon.]
Source: Staats- und Stadtbibliothek Augsburg, Sign. Yr. 6846
          [presumed lost]
          Wissenschaftliche Bibliothek der Stadt Erfurt,
          Sign. Lg. 431 [presumed lost]

Albrecht, Johann Friedrich Ernst

   Die Regenten des Tierreichs. Eine Fabel. 3 Bde. Zürich, 1790-92
Source: Universitätsbibliothek Berlin, Sign. Yy 7681 [presumed lost]

Albrecht, Johann Friedrich Ernst

   Eigenmächtige Reisen in eine andere Welt. Vom Verfasser der
   Lauretta Pisana. Prag, 1790. [Also under the title: Neue Biographien der Selbstmörder]

   [Staats- und Universtitätsbibliothek Göttingen reports that its
   copy: Frankfurt und Leipzig, 1794; Sign. Fy 22 158 has been sold]
Source: Staats- und Stadtbibliothek Augsburg. No catalogue number.
          [presumed lost]

Armbruster, Johann Michael (1761-1814)

Romantische Erzählungen und Skizzen; Wahrheit und Dichtung, 2 Bde.
St. Gallen, 1790-93.

Source: Universitätsbibliothek Berlin, Sign. Yq 55814 [pres. lost]

Baczko, Ludwig Adolf von (1756-1823)

Leben und Leiden meines Vaters Jonathan Eiche, von Benjamin Eiche,
Kaufmann und Malzenbrauer zu Tilse in Preussen. Königsberg, 1790

Bahrdt, Karl Friedrich (1741-1792)

Alvaro und Ximenes, ein spanischer Roman.

Halle, bei Francke und Bispink, 1790 [published anon.]
Source: Staatsbibliothek Marburg, Sign. Yw 2565 [presumed lost]
Universitätsbibliothek Berlin, Sign. Yq 55814 [pres. lost]

Bahrdt, Karl Friedrich

Leben und Thaten des weiland hochwürdigen Pastor Rindvigius.
Ans Licht gestellt von Kasimir Renatus Denarré, Oberpaster in
Ochsenhausen, auf Kosten der Familie. [Libau, 1790]

Source: Staatsbibliothek Marburg, Sign. Yw 2568 [presumed lost]

Bakel, ...

Origines, eine komische Geschichte. 2 Thle. Weissenfels, 1790.

Source: Landesbibliothek Coburg. No catalogue number. [pres. lost]

Baur, Samuel (1768-1823)

Liebe, was sie ist, und seyn sollte; Beobachtungen, Lehrungen
und Warnungen. Gotha, 1790.

Becker, Gotthelf Wilhelm Rupert (?-1823)

Geschichte der Regierung Ferdinands des Katholischen,Königs von
Spanien, 2 Bde. Prag und Leipzig, 1790-91. [History or novel?]

Benkowitz, Karl Friedrich (1764-1807)

Lebensscenen aus der Vor- und Nachwelt. Halle, J.C. Hendel, 1790.

Source: Landesbibliothek Coburg, Sign. D. II. 11/13 [presumed lost]

Bornschein, Johann Ernst Daniel (1774-1838)

Der französische Abentheurer, oder Denkwürdigkeiten Greg. Merveils
4 Bde., Gera, 1790-91.

Büschel, Johann Gabriel Bernhard (1758-1813)

Julies und Rhea, oder. . . Rom, Kazzofermo und Monastrelta. 1790.

Campe, Joachim Heinrich (1746-1818)

Reise von Braunschweig nach Paris. . . Braunschweig, 1790.

Dreyssig, Christoph Friedrich

Reisen des grünen Mannes durch Teutschland und Ungarn.
2 Thle. Halle, 1788-90.

Durach, Johann Baptist (1766-1832)

Skizzen von Heroismus und Biedersinn, Wien, 1790.

Source: Bayrische Staatsbibliothek München, Sign. P.o.germ. 284 f.
[presumed lost]

Fischer, Heinrich Ludwig

Das Buch vom Aberglauben. . . und falschen Wahn. 1790.

Geiger, Franz Xaver

Schöne Lebensgeschichte des guten und vernünftigen Bauersmanns
Wendelinus. Augsburg, 1790.

Gorgy, Jean-Claude [pseud. Jacobine Lykurge]

Blansey, ein Roman. . . 2 Bde., Neuwied, 1790.

Hamaliar, Martin

Der Sieg über die Versuchungen zur Sünde. Schemitz, 1790.

Hänisch, G.

Gottfried Wacker, eine lehrreiche Geschichte für Professionisten
und Bürger. Freiberg, 1790.

Heuberger, Johann Wilhelm (1767-?)

Der französische Gilblas, oder Abenteuer Heinrich Lansons.

3 Thle., Neuwied, 1790-91. [Kayser lists "Lansons": Kosch,
Lamsons".]

Jenisch, Daniel

Bemerkungen auf einer Reise durch die Stadt und Landschaft
Narrenburg gesammelt. Von Demokritus dem jungen. Mit ihrem
Landkärtchen. Abdera [Augsburg] auf kosten des gesammten
Magistrats. 1790.

Kausch, Johann Joseph (1751-1825)

Kabale im Civildienst, ein dramatischer Roman, Grottkau, 1790.

Source: Staatsbibliothek Marburg, Sign. 4 in: Yp 5057/+/
[presumed lost]

Kayser, A. Ephraim

Charlottens Ankunft in der besseren Welt. Regensburg, 1790.

Lenz, Karl Gotthold (1763-1809)

Geschichte der Weiber im heroischen Zeitalter. Hannover, 1790.

Mösle, ...

Lottchen, oder Roman vieler Romane. Eine wahre Geschichte aus dem menschlichen Leben. 2 Thle. Wien, 1790.

Müller, Johann Ernst Friedrich Wilhelm (1764-1826) [pseud. Filidor]

Romantische Gemälde der Vorwelt.

2 Bde., Leipzig, 1789-90. [Kayser lists 1789-90; Heinsius, 1789]

Pradatsch, Babette

Der Sieg der Natur, in dem Jahrhunderte, in dem wir leben. . .
Prag und Leipzig, 1790.

Presser, S.G.

Oko von Okowsky, oder über das menschliche Elend in einer andern Gegend als der Salzmannschen.

Breslau, bey Johann Friedrich Korn, 1790.

Rassmann, Christian Friedrich (1772-1831) [pseud. Hortensio]

Eine Blume auf dem Grab des. . . Karl Hundertmark.
Halberstadt, 1790.

Reichenbach, Johann Friedrich Jacob (1759-1839)

Kunigunde von Rabenswalde, eine Scene aus dem 12. Jahrhundert.
Leipzig, 1790.

Reichlin von Meldegg, Fr. August Freiherr von

Karl von Lindenhain; eine Geschichte in Briefen.
2 Thle. Stuttgart, 1790.

Riedel, Johann Christoph Ludwig

Die Aufklärung nach der Mode, oder eine komisch-tragische Geschichte, wie sie die Welt aufstellt, zur Berherzigung meiner Brüder.
Neustadt an der Eich, 1790.

Source: Staatsbibliothek Marburg, Sign. Yw 3296 /+/ [pres. lost]

Schirlitz, Karl Eph.

Karl Rosenheim und Sophie Wagenthal, oder Beitrag zur Erkenntnis
des menschlichen Herzens, in Briefen. Meißen, 1790.

Schlenkert, Friedrich Christian

Adelheid von Burgund. o.O. 1790.

Schulz, Joachim Christian Friedrich (1762-1789)

Concino-Concini, oder Empörung eines Königs gegen seine Diener.
Deutsche Monatsschrift, Julius, 1790.

Schulz, Joachim Christian Friedrich

Martinuzzi, oder Leben eines geistlichen Parvenüs in Beziehung
auf neuere Erscheinungen. Weimar, 1790.

Schulz, Joachim Christian Friedrich

Geschichte der grossen Revolution in Frankreich, Berlin,
Vieweg, 1790. [History or novel?]

Seidel, Karl August Gottlieb (1754-1822)

Kleine skizzierte Geschichten und Romane, von verschiedenen
Verfassern.
[published anon.] Weissenfels, 4 Bde.,[1]1788-90;[2]Leipzig, 1811.

Seidel, Karl August Gottlieb

Adolph Wollmann, nach seinem geführten Tagebuch.
2 Bde. Dresden und Leipzig, 1790.

Stellheim, ...

Karl und Clementine von Rosensee; eine Geschichte deutscher
Zärtlichkeit. Wien 1790.

Textor, Friedrich Ludwig

Wallfahrten des Candidaten Kilian Hieronymus zu seinen Glaubens-
brüdern. Frankfurt, 1790.
[Also under the title: Silhouetten aus dem schwarzen Orden; ein
Beitrag zur Charakteristik der Weisen und Narren dieses Ordens.
Frankfurt, 1794]

Tschink, Kajatan

Geschichte eines Geistersehers; aus den Papieren des Mannes mit
der eisernen Larve.
Herausgegeben von Kaj. Tschink. 3 Thle. Wien, 1790.

Vulpius, Christian August (1762-1827) [pseud. Tirso di Milano]

Zauberromane. 2 Thle. Hamburg 1790/91.
[Kayser, 1790/91. Heinsiue, 1790.]
Source: Österreichische Nationalbibliothek Wien, Sign. 722.210-A
[presumed lost]

Walther, K.S.

Edmund, oder die Gefahren der allzugrossen Weesheit; nach dem
Französischen. Dresden, 1790.

D. UNAVAILABLE FIRST EDITIONS OF 1790 WITH UNTRACEABLE AUTHORS

Anon.

Anselms und seines Freundes poetische Reisen nach Kaklogallinien
im Jahre 1789. Leipzig, 1790.

- Begebenheiten Augusts von Schmaragden und seiner Geschwister.
  Leipzig, [1790].

- Begebenheiten und Scenen des menschlichen Lebens.
  Leipzig, 1790.

- Thessaline Bertring, oder die Reize der allmähligen Näherung.
  Ein Roman in Briefen.
  Heidelberg, 1790.

- Blandine, oder wahre Geschichte einer schönen Berlinerin in
  Briefen an ihre Freundin Laura.
  Berlin, 1790.

- Briefe zwischen Heinrich und Franziska.
  Berlin, 1790

- Caroline [Karoline] oder der Wechsel des Glücks, eine englische
  Geschichte.
  Liegnitz, 1790.

- Courtnay, ein Beitrag zur geheimen Geschichte der Königin Elisabeth.
  Leipzig, 1790.

- Dolbreuso, oder der Mann nach der Welt; eine wahre Geschichte.
  2 Thle. Gera, 1790.

- Ehrmann und Tonnette, eine wahre Geschichte zweier Liebenden in
  Briefen.
  Wien, 1790.

- Es war eben noch Zeit, oder Geschichte des Herrn von Warneck.
  Eisenbach, 1790.

- Euseb, oder die Früchte der Tugend in diesem Jahrhundert.
  Wien, 1790.

- Der böse Findling, oder der Schauerturm.
  Wien und Prag, 1790.

Anon.

>Franz, oder die Tugend belohnt sich selbst.
>2 Thle. Pressburg, 1790.
>Source: Staats- und Universitätsbibliothek Göttingen, Sing. 8°
>Fab. Rom. VI, 2028 g [presumed lost]

Anon.

>Die Gefahren zur See, eine Folge rührender Gemälde.
>Leipzig, 1790.

- Das heimliche Gericht. Eine dramatisirte Geschichte.
  Leipzig, 1790.

- Gespräch zwischen einer ungarischen und deutschen Hose.
  Hamburg, 1790.

- Gianetta, oder das Verderben des Mannes.
  O.o. 1790

- Gildeb und Komin, oder ein wahrer Freund kennt keine Komplimente.
  Wien, 1790.

- Elika Gräfin von Gleichen. Eine wahre Geschichte a.d. Zeiten
  der Kreuzzüge.
  2 Bde. Wien, 1790.

- Heinrich, König von Frankreich, Liebesgeschichten.
  Leipzig, 1790.

- Heinrich von Waldorf und Emilie von Weissenheim.
  2 Thle. Heidelberg, 1790.

- Herrmann [sic] und Julie, mehr als Roman.
  Leipzig, 1790.

- Karrikatur und Menschheit.
  Grätz, 1790.

- Kiashuta der Wilde, vom Stamme der Mohaws [sic]. Eine Geschichte
  aus dem letzten amerikanischen Kriege.
  Leipzig, 1790.

- Kleine Romane aus der wirklichen Welt.
  Leipzig, 1790.

- Konrad Knapp, oder der Kreuzfahrer. Ein romantisches Gemälde
  aus der Vorwelt.
  Frankfurt und Leipzig [Wien?], 1790.

- Koralg und Zamor, oder der berühmte Amerikaner.
  2 Thle. Freiberg, 1790.

Anon.

Das Landmädchen bei Dresden, oder die Gefahren der Residenz.
Gera, 1790.

- Leichtsinn und Reue, oder Louise von Willing [Willnitz].
Hirschberg, 1790.

- Liebesbegebenheiten des Herzogs [der Herzogin] von Ahrenberg.
Leipzig, 1790.

- Marano und Omra, oder die Kette des Schicksals, eine amerikanische
Geschichte.
Leipzig und Wien, 1790.

- Meine Lebensgeschichte, lauter reine Wahrheit; oder: Beweis ohne
Syllogismen daß es in Europa auch Cannibalen giebt.
Zürich, 1790.

- Meine Reisen am Pulte beim Scheine einer Argant-Lampe.
3 Thle. Coburg, 1790.

- Reizvolle Aussicht ins Ehebette, nicht nach dem Laufe der Welt,
eine Geschichte.
2 Thle. Glogau, 1790-91.

- Schilderungen, glückliche Liebschaften aus dem wirklichen Leben.
Leipzig, in der Weygandschen Buchhandlung, 1790.

- Sieg der ehelichen Liebe.
Breslau, 1790.

- Tägliche Unterhaltungen für alle vier Jahreszeiten, oder Auswahl
interessanter Erzählungen und Romane.
6 Bdchen., Wien 1790-91.

- Traurige Wahrheit für Jünglinge jeden Standes. Wahrheiten im
Romangewande, ein Pendant zu dem Buche: für Töchter edler Herkunft.
Altenburg, 1790.

- Wie geht's auf der Welt, oder Besuche in all vier Welttheile.
2 Thle., Leipzig, 1790.

II. SECONDARY SOURCES

A. BIBLIOGRAPHICAL WORKS

Allgemeine Deutsche Biographie. Hrsg. durch die Historische Kommission
bei der Bayerischen Akademie der Wissenschaften.
Bd. I-56. Leipzig: Duncker und Humblot. 1875-1912.

Brümmer, Franz. Lexikon der deutschen Dichter bis Ende des 18. Jahrhunderts. Leipzig, 1884.

Das Gelehrte Teutschland, oder Lexicon der jetzt lebenden teutschen
Schriftsteller, angefangen von Georg Christoph Hamberger, fortgeführt
von Johann Georg Meusel. 5. Aufl. 1796-1806. Reprint Georg Olms
Verlagsbuchhandlung, Hildesheim, 1966.

Eppelsheimer, Hans W., ed., Bibliographie der deutschen Literaturwissenschaft, Frankfurt am Main, 1957 ff.

Frey, John R. "Bibliographie zur Theorie und Technik des Deutschen Romans
(1910-1938)," MLN, 14 (1939), 557-67.

- - - "Bibliographie zur Theorie und Technik des Deutschen Romans
(1939-1953)," MLN, 69 (1954), 77-88.

Goedeke, Karl. Grundriss zur Geschichte der deutschen Dichtung:
Aus den Quellen.
> Dresden; vol 4,I (^{1}1891) ff 224, 225, 227, 228, 230, 232.
> vol 5   (^{2}1893) ff 274, 276-281.
> vol 6   (^{2}1898) ff 295.

Hayn, Hugo and Gotendorf, Alfred N. Bibliotheca Germanorum Erotica et
Curiosa: Verzeichnis der ges. deutschen erotischen Literatur mit Ein-
schluss der Übersetzungen, nebst Beifügung der Originale. Vols 1-8,
München, ^{3}1912-14.

Heinsius, Wilhelm. Allgemeines Bücher-Lexikon oder vollständiges Alpha-
betisches Verzeichnis der von 1700 bis zu Ende 1810 erschienenen Bücher,
welche in Deutschland und in den durch Sprache und Literatur damit verwandten Ländern gedruckt worden sind.
4 vols Johann Friedrich Gleditsch: Leipzig, 1812.

Holzmann, Michael and Bohatta, Hans. Deutsches Anonymen-Lexikon:
1501-1850. Vols 1-7. Weimar, 1902-28.

Kayser, Christian, ed. Index Locupletissimus. . . Vollständiges Bücher-
lexikon enthaltend alle von 1750 bis zu Ende des Jahres 1832 in Deutschland und in den angrenzenden Ländern gedruckten Bücher.
Bd.VI, Anhang Romane. Leipzig, 1836.

Körner, Josef. Bibliographisches Handbuch des Deutschen Schrifttums.
Dritte völlig umgearbeitete und wesentlich vermehrte Auflage. Bern,1949.

Kosch, Wilhelm. Deutsches Literatur-Lexikon:
Biographisches und Bibliographisches Handbuch. Zweite, vollständig neu
bearbeitete und stark erweiterte Auflage. 4 vols Bern, 1949-58.

Meusel, Johann Georg. Lexikon der vom Jahre 1750 bis 1800 verstorbenen teutschen Schriftsteller. 13 vols Leipzig, 1802-1813 (1816). Reprint Georg Olms Verlagsbuchhandlung, Hildesheim, 1967-68.

Neue Deutsche Biographie. Hrsg. von der Historischen Kommission bei der bayerischen Akademie der Wissenschaften. Duncker und Humblot: Berlin, 1961.

B. CRITICAL WORKS

Allott, Miriam. Novelists on the Novel. London, 1959.

Alter, Robert. Rogue's Progress: Studies in the Picaresque Novel. Cambridge, Massachusetts, 1965.

Appel, J.W. Die Ritter-, Räuber- und Schauerromantik: Zur Geschichte der deutschen Unterhaltungs-Literatur. Leipzig, 1859.

Appel, J.W. Werther und seine Zeit. Oldenburg, 1896.

Arndt, J. Die seelische Welt im Roman des achtzehnten Jahrhunderts. Diss. Giessen, 1940.

Ayrenschmalz, Armin. Zum Begriff des Abenteuerromans: Eine gattungstheoretische Untersuchung. Diss. Tübingen, 1962.

Bach, Anneliese. "Das epische Bild im Bildungsroman von Goethe bis Thomas Mann." GRM, 43 (1962), 371-86.

Bauer, Rudolf. Der historische Trivialroman in Deutschland im ausgehenden 18. Jahrhundert. Diss. München, 1930.

Bausinger, Hermann. "Zur Struktur der Reihenromane." Wirkendes Wort, 6 (1955-56), 296-301.

Beaujean, Marion. Der Trivialroman in der zweiten Hälfte des 18. Jahrhunderts: Die Ursprünge des modernen Unterhaltungsromans. Bonn, 1964.

Beck, H. Die Erbauungsliteratur der evangelischen Kirche Deutschlands. Erlangen, 1883.

Beck, W. Die Anfänge des deutschen Schelmenromans. Zürich, 1957.

Becker, Eva D. Der deutsche Roman um 1780. Stuttgart, 1964.

Belloc, Hilaire. The French Revolution. London, 1966.

Bergk, J[ohann] A[dam]. Die Kunst, Bücher zu lesen: Nebst Bemerkungen über Schriften und Schriftsteller. Jena, 1799. Photomechanical Reprint München, 1968.

Bernard, Paul P. Joseph II. New York, 1968.

Black, J.B. The Art of History: A Study of Four Great Historians of the Eighteenth Century. London, 1926.

Blackall, Eric A. The Emergence of German as a Literary Language 1700-1775. Cambridge, 1959.

Blanckenburg, Friedrich von. Versuch über den Roman. Leipzig und Liegnitz: bey David Siegers Wittwe, 1774. Faksimile-druck der Originalausgabe, ed. Eberhard Lämmert. Stuttgart, 1965.

Bobertag, Felix. Geschichte des Romans und der ihm verwandten Dichtungs-gattungen. Erste Abteilung: Bis zum Anfange des 18. Jahrhunderts. Breslau, 1876.

Boeschenstein, Hermann. Deutsche Gefühlskultur: Studien zu ihrer dichterischen Gestaltung. Grundlagen 1770-1830. Bern, 1954.

Bössenecker, H. Pietismus und Aufklärung. Diss. Würzburg, 1958.

Borcherdt, Hans Heinrich. Der Roman der Goethezeit. Urach and Stuttgart, 1949.

Biessenden, R.F. Samuel Richardson. London, 1958.

Bruford, W.H. Die gesellschaftlichen Grundlagen der Goethezeit. Weimar, 1936.

Burger, Heinz Otto, ed. Studien zur Trivialliteratur. Frankfurt a.M., 1968.

Carlsson, Anni. Die deutsche Buchkritik: Von den Anfängen bis 1850. Stuttgart, 1963.

Catholy, Eckehard. Karl Philipp Moritz und die Ursprünge der Deutschen Theaterleidenschaft. Tübingen, 1962.

Chladenius, Johann Martin. Allgemeine Geschichtswissenschaft, worinnen der Grund zu einer neuen Einsicht in alle Arten der Gelahrtheit geleget wird. Leipzig, 1752.

Danziger, Marlies K. "Heroic villains in 18th-century criticism." Comparative Literature, II (1959), 35-46.

Davie, Donald. The Heyday of Sir Walter Scott. London, 1961.

Dibelius, Wilhelm. Englische Romankunst: Die Technik des englischen Romans im achtzehnten und zu Anfang des neunzehnten Jahrhunderts. Palaestra, XCII: Berlin, 1910.

Eckhardt, M. Der Einfluss der Madame Guyon auf die norddeutsche Laienwelt im 18. Jahrhundert. Diss. Köln, 1928.

Ehrenpreis, Irvin. Fielding: Tom Jones. London, 1964.

Ehrenzeller, Hans. Studien zur Romanvorrede von Grimmelshausen bis Jean Paul. Bern, 1955.

Eichner, Hans. "Zur Deutung von 'Wilhelm Meisters Lehrjahren.'" Jahrbuch des Freien Deutschen Hochstifts. Tübingen, 1966, 165-196.

Engel, J[ohann] J]acob]. Über Handlung, Gespräch und Erzählung. Faksimiledruck der ersten Fassung von 1774, ed. E.Th. Voss. Stuttgart, 1964.

Engelsing, Rolf.   "Der Bürger als Leser: Die Bildung der protestanti-
                    schen Bevölkerung Deutschlands im 17. und 18. Jahr-
                    hundert am Beispiel Bremen." <u>Archiv für Geschichte
                    des Buchwesens</u>, ed. Historische Kommission des Börsen-
                    vereins des Deutschen Buchhandels, Frankfurt, a.M.,
                    1960/61, vol 3   205-368.

Eschenburg, Johann J.   <u>Entwurf einer Theorie der schönen Wissenschaften</u>:
                    <u>Zur Grundlage bei Vorlesungen</u>. Neue 2. umgearbeitete
                    Ausgabe. Bey Friedrich Nicolai: Berlin und Stettin,
                    1789.

Flessau, Kurt-Ingo.   <u>Der moralische Roman: Studien zur gesellschafts-
                    kritischen Trivialliteratur der Goethezeit</u>.
                    Köln/Graz, 1968.

Flygt, Sten Gunnar.   <u>The Notorious Dr. Bahrdt</u>. Vanderbilt University
                    Press: Nashville, 1963.

Floersheim, A.   "Der 'Versuch über den Roman' des Freiherrn Chr. v.
                    Blankenburg: Ein Beitrag zur Geschichte der Roman-
                    theorie." Diss. München, 1925. [Michelsen (<u>Laurence
                    Sterne</u>, p, 167 note 30) explains that this work is no
                    longer extant.]

Foltin, Hans Friedrich.   "Die minderwertige Prosaliteratur: Einteilung
                    und Bezeichnungen." <u>DVLG</u>, 39 (1965), 277-283.

Forster, Eduard Morgan.   <u>Aspects of the Novel</u>. London, 1927. [German
                    edition, <u>Ansichten des Romans</u>. Suhrkamp Verlag:
                    Frankfurt, 1962.]

Forstreuter, K.   <u>Die deutsche Icherzählung: Eine Studie zu ihrer
                    Geschichte und Technik</u>. Berlin, 1924.

Francke, Hans.   "Zum Problem des Unterhaltungsroman." <u>Bücherkunde</u>,
                    II, (1944), vol 3/4, 44-50.

Frey, J.R.   "Author Intrusion in the Narrative: German Theory and
                    Some Modern Examples." <u>GR</u>, 23 (1948), 274-89.

Garte, Hansjörg.   <u>Kunstform Schauerroman</u>. Eine morphologische Begriffs-
                    bestimmung des Sensationsromans im 18. Jahrhundert
                    von Walpoles "Castle of Otranto" bis Jean Pauls
                    "Titan". Diss. Leipzig, 1935.

Gebhardt, Walter.   <u>Religionssoziologische Probleme im Roman der deutschen
                    Aufklärung</u>. Diss. Giessen, 1931.

Genin, L.E.   "Die volkstümliche deutsche Räuberdichtung im 18.
                    Jahrhundert als Protest gegen den Feudalismus."
                    <u>Zeitschrift für deutsche Literaturgeschichte</u>.
                    6 (1960), 727-46.

Gerhard, Melitta   <u>Der deutsche Entwicklungsroman bis zu Goethes Wilhelm
                    Meister</u>. Halle, 1926. [Zweite, unveränderte Auflage,
                    Bern, 1968.]

Germer, Helmut. The German Novel of Education 1792-1805: A Complete
Bibliography and Analysis. Diss. Vanderbilt Universi-
ty, 1966 . Bern: Herbert Lang, 1968.

Géruzez, Eugène. Histoire de la Littérature Francaise Pendant la
Revolution (1789-1800). Paris, 1884.

Gooch, George P. Germany and the French Revolution. New York, 1966.

Goodwin, Albert. The French Revolution. 4th rev. ed. London, 1967.

Gordon, Robert C. Under Which King? A Study of the Scottish Waverley
Novels. London, 1969.

Greiner, Martin. Die Entstehung der modernen Unterhaltungsliteratur:
Studien zum Trivialroman des 18. Jahrhunderts.
Hrsg. und bearb. von Therese Poser. München, 1964

Greiner, Walter. Studien zur Entstehung der englischen Romantheorie an
der Wende zum 18. Jahrhundert. Tübingen, 1968.

Günther, H.R.G. "Die Psychologie des Pietismus." DVLG, 4 (1926),
169 ff.

Hackermann, R. Die Anfänge des Romans in der Zeitung. Diss. Berlin,
1938.

Haferkorn, Hans Jürgen. Der freie Schriftsteller: Eine Literatur-
soziologische Studie über seine Entstehung in Deutschland zwischen 1750-1800. Diss. Göttingen, 1960.
Archiv für Geschichte des Buchwesens. Hrsg. von der
historischen Kommission des Börsenvereins des
Deutschen Buchhandels, Frankfurt/M., 1964.
Band 5, 523-712.

Harris, Kathleen. Beiträge zur Wirkung Fieldings in Deutschland
(1742-92). Diss. Göttingen, 1960.

Heine, Carl. Der Roman in Deutschland von 1774 bis 1778.
Halle a.S., 1892.

Hettner, Hermann. Geschichte der deutschen Literatur im 18. Jahrhundert.
3rd. ed., Braunschweig, 1923.

Highet, Gilbert. The Anatomy of Satire. Princeton, New Jersey, 1962.

Hirsch, Arnold. Bürgertum und Barock im deutschen Roman: Zur Ent-
stehungsgeschichte des bürgerlichen Weltbildes.
2. Aufl. Köln, 1957.

Hirsch, Arnold. "Barockroman und Aufklärungsroman." Études Germani-
ques, 9 (1954), 97 ff.

Hornaday, Clifford Lee. Nature in the German Novel of the Late
Eighteenth Century: 1770-1800. New York, 1966.

Huet, Pierre Daniel. Traité de l'origine des romans. Faksimiledruck
nach der Erstausgabe von 1670 und der Happelschen
Übersetzung von 1682. Mit einem Nachwort von Hans
Hinterhäuser. Stuttgart, 1966.

Irwin, William Robert.   The Making of Jonathan Wild: A Study in the
                          Literary Method of Henry Fielding.
                          Hamden, Connecticut, 1966.

Jack, Ian.   Sir Walter Scott. London, 1958.

Jäger, Georg.   Empfindsamkeit und Roman: Wortgeschichte, Theorie und
                         Kritik im 18. und frühen 19. Jahrhundert.
                         Stuttgart, 1969.

Jäger, Hans-Wolf.   Politische Kategorien in Poetik und Rhetorik der zwei-
                         ten Hälfte des 18. Jahrhundert. Stuttgart, 1970.

Jenisch, E.   "Vom Abenteurer- zum Bildungsroman." GRM, 14 (1926),
                         339-351.

Jentsch, Irene.   Zur Geschichte des Zeitungslesens in Deutschland am
                         Ende des 18. Jahrhunderts. Diss. Leipzig, 1936.

Jentsch, Rudolf.   Der deutsch-lateinische Büchermarkt nach den Leipzi-
                         ger Ostermess-Katalogen von 1740, 1770 und 1800 in
                         seiner Gliederung und Wandlung. Leipzig, 1912.

Joachimi, Marie.   Die Weltanschauung der deutschen Romantik. Jena und
                         Leipzig, 1905.

Kahn, Ludwig W.   Social Ideals in German Literature: 1700-1830.
                         New York, 1938.

Kahn, Ludwig W.   Literatur und Glaubenskrise. Stuttgart, 1964.

Kahn, Robert L.   Kotzebue. His Social and Political Attitudes: The
                         Dilemma of a Popular Dramatist in Times of Social
                         Change. Diss. Toronto, 1950.

Kahn, Robert L.   "Personality Factors in Kotzebue's work." Philologi-
                         cal Quarterly, 30 (1951), 69-85.

Kahn, Robert L.   "Kotzebue's treatment of social problems."
                         Studies in Philology, 49 (1952), 631-42.

Kahn, Robert L.   "Kotzebue's Weltanschauung." Modern Language Forum,
                         38 (1953), 41-55.

Kapp/Goldfriedrich.   Geschichte des deutschen Buchhandels: Vom Beginn
                         der klassischen Literaturperiode bis zum Beginn der
                         Fremdherrschaft (1740-1804). Bd. III. Leipzig, 1909.

Kayser, Wolfgang.   "Die Anfänge des modernen Romans im 18. Jahrhundert
                         und seine heutige Krise." DVLG, 28 (1954), 417-446.

Kayser, Wolfgang.   Entstehung und Krise des modernen Romans.
                         5th rev. ed. Stuttgart, 1968.

Kayser, Wolfgang.   Die Vortragsreise: Studien zur Literatur. Bern, 1958.

Killy, Walter.   Deutscher Kitsch: Ein Versuch mit Beispielen.
                         Göttingen, 1961.

Kimpel, Dieter.   Der Roman der Aufklärung. Stuttgart, 1967.

Klaiber, Th.   Die deutsche Selbstbiographie. Stuttgart, 1921.

Klein, Albert.   <u>Die Krise des Unterhaltungsromans im 19. Jahrhundert.</u>
                 Bonn, 1969.

Kluckhohn, Paul.   <u>Die Auffassung der Liebe in der Literatur des 18. Jahr-</u>
                 <u>hunderts und in der deutschen Romantik.</u>
                 2. Aufl. Halle, 1931.

Köhn, Lothar.   "Entwicklungs- und Bildungsroman: Ein Forschungs-
                 bericht (Erster Teil)" <u>DVLG</u>, 42 (1968), 427-73.

Köhn, Lothar,   <u>Entwicklungs- und Bildungsroman: Ein Forschungsbe-</u>
                 <u>richt.</u> Stuttgart, 1969.

Korff, H.A.   <u>Die Dichtung von Sturm und Drang: Im Zusammenhang</u>
                 <u>der Geistesgeschichte.</u>
                 Leipzig, 1928.

Kost, E.   <u>Die Technik des deutschen Romans von Musäus bis Goethe,</u>
                 <u>besonders in ihren Beziehungen zu den Romanen Fiel-</u>
                 <u>dings und Smollets.</u> Diss. Tübingen, 1922.

Kreuzer, Helmut.   "Trivialliteratur als Forschungsproblem." <u>DVLG</u>,
                 41 (May 1970) 173-191.

Kunze, Horst.   <u>Lieblingsbücher von dazumal.</u> Eine Blütenlese aus den
                 <u>erfolgreichsten Büchern von 1750-1860: Zugleich ein</u>
                 <u>erster Versuch zu einer Geschichte des Lesergeschmacks.</u>
                 München, 1938. Republished as: <u>Gelesen und geliebt.</u>
                 <u>Aus erfolgreichen Büchern 1750-1850</u>.
                 Berlin, 1959

Kurth, Lieselotte E.   "Historiographie und historischer Roman: Kritik
                 und Theorie im 18. Jahrhundert." <u>MLN</u>, 79 (1964),
                 337-62.

Langen, A.   <u>Der Wortschatz des deutschen Pietismus.</u>
                 Tübingen, 1954.

Langenbucher, Wolfgang.   <u>Der Aktuelle Unterhaltungsroman: Beiträge</u>
                 <u>zur Geschichte und Theorie der massenhaft verbreiteten</u>
                 <u>Literatur.</u> Bonn, 1964.

Lefebvre, Georges.   <u>The Coming of the French Revolution: 1789.</u>
                 Trans. R.R. Palmer, 4th ed.
                 Princeton, 1967.

Lempicki, Sigmund von.   <u>Geschichte der deutschen Literaturwissenschaft</u>
                 <u>bis zum Ende des 18. Jahrhunderts.</u>
                 2nd ed. Göttingen, 1968.

Lenglet du Fresnoy, Nicolas.   <u>De l'Usage des romans, où l'on fait voir</u>
                 <u>leur utilité et leurs differens [sic] caractères:</u>
                 <u>avec une bibliothèque des romans.</u> Amsterdam, 1734.

Lockmann, Wolfgang. Die Entstehung des Erzählproblems: Untersuchungen
zur deutschen Dichtungstheorie im 17. und 18. Jahrhundert. Meisenheim am Glau. 1963.

Lukaćs, Georg. "Die klassische Form des historischen Romans."
Sinn und Form, 6 (1954), 329-47, 554-93.

Lakaćs, Georg. Der historische Roman.
Berlin, 1955. English edition: Boston, 1963.

Lukaćs, Georg. Die Theorie des Romans: Ein geschichtsphilosophischer
Versuch über die Formen der grossen Epik.
3rd. ed. Neuwied und Berlin, 1965.

Magon, Leopold. "Friedrichs II. 'De la littérature allemande' und
dessen Gegenschriften: Zur Geschichte des literari-
schen Publikums im Deutschland des 18. Jahrhunderts."
Acta litteraria Academiae Scientarum Hungaricae.
2 (1959), 317-46.

Mahrholz, W. Deutsche Selbstbekenntnisse: Ein Beytrag zur Geschichte der Selbstbiographie von der Mystik bis zum
Pietismus. Berlin, 1919.

Mandelkern, Karl Robert. "Der deutsche Briefroman: Zum Problem der
Polyperspektive im Epischen." Neophilologus,
44 (1960), 200-208.

Martens, Wolfgang. Die Botschaft der Tugend: Die Aufklärung im Spiegel
der deutschen moralischen Wochenschriften.
Stuttgart, 1971.

Martini, Fritz. "Der Bildungsroman: Zur Geschichte des Wortes und
der Theorie." DVLG, 35 (1961), 44-63.

Mayer, Hans. Von Lessing bis Thomas Mann: Wandlungen der bürger-
lichen Literatur in Deutschland.
Pfullingen, 1959.

Mayhead, Robin. Walter Scott. London, 1968.

Merkel, Rudolf. "Buchdruck und Buchhandel in Ansbach: Von den Anfängen bis zum Ende des 18. Jahrhunderts." Archiv für
Geschichte des Buchwesens. Hrsg. von der Historischen
Kommission des Börsenvereins des Deutschen Buchhandels,
e.V. Band V., 957-1187.

Meyer, H. Entwurf einer Kunstgeschichte des 18. Jahrhunderts.
Stuttgart, 1805.

Michel, Karl Markus. "Das Härlein an der Feder: Romananfänge aus der deutschen Trivialliteratur." <u>Romananfänge: Versuch zu einer Poetik des Romans</u>. Ed. Norbert Miller, Berlin, 1965, 205-72.

Michelsen, Peter. <u>Laurence Sterne und der deutsche Roman des 18. Jahrhunderts</u>. Göttingen, 1962.

Mielke, Hellmuth. <u>Der deutsche Roman</u>. Dresden, 1912.

Mildebrath, B. <u>Die deutschen "Aventuriers" des 18. Jahrhunderts</u>. Diss. Würzburg, 1907.

Miller, Norbert. "Die Rollen des Erzählers: Zum Problem des Romananfangs im 18. Jahrhundert." <u>Romananfänge</u>. Ed. Norbert Miller, Berlin, 1965, 37-91.

Miller, Steven R. <u>Die Figur des Erzählers in Wielands Romanen</u>. Göppingen, 1970.

Minder, Robert. <u>Die religiöse Entwicklung von Moritz auf Grund seiner autobiographischen Schriften: Studien zum 'Reiser' und 'Hartknopf'</u>. Berlin, 1936.

Minners, K. <u>Die Theorie des Romans in der deutschen Aufklärung mit besonderer Berücksichtigung von Blanckenburgs Versuch über den Roman</u>. Diss. Hamburg, 1922.

Minor, Jakob, ed. <u>Fabeldichter, Satiriker und Popularphilosophen des 18. Jahrhunderts</u>. Berlin und Stattgart, 1884.

Mittner, Ladislao. "Freundschaft und Liebe in der deutschen Literatur des 18. Jahrhunderts." <u>Stoffe, Formen, Strukturen: Studien zur deutschen Literatur</u>. Hrsg. von Albert Fuchs und Helmut Motekat. München, 1962.

Müller, Jan-Dirk. <u>Wielands späte Romane. Untersuchungen zur Erzählweise und zur erzählten Wirklichkeit</u>. München, 1971.

Müller, Johann Gottwerth. <u>Über den Verlagsraub, oder Bemerkungen über des Herrn D. Reimarus Vertheidigung des Nachdrucks im April des deutschen Magazins 1791</u>. Leipzig, bey Friedrich Schneidern, 1792.

Müller-Fraureuth, Carl. <u>Die Ritter- und Räuberromane: Ein Beitrag zur Bildungsgeschichte des deutschen Volkes</u>. Halle a.d.S., 1894.

Mylne, Vivienne. <u>The Eighteenth-Century French Novel: Techniques of Illusion</u>. Manchester, 1965.

Neumann, Hilde.   Der Bücherbesitz der Tübinger Bürger von 1750-1850.
                   Ein Beitrag zur Bildungsgeschichte des Kleinbürger-
                   tums. Diss. Tübingen, 1955.

Nutz, Walter.   Der Trivialroman, seine Formen und Hersteller: Ein
                   Beitrag zur Literatursoziologie.
                   Köln, 1962.

Ohrenstein, I.   Die Theorie des Romans seit dem "Wilhelm Meister".
                   Diss. Wien, 1922.

Otto, K.   Wielands Romantechnik. Diss. Kiel, 1922.

Paulson, Ronald.   Satire and the Novel in Eighteenth-Century England.
                   New Haven and London, 1967.

Poser, Michael von. Der Abschweifende Erzähler: Rhetorische Tradition
                   und deutscher Roman im achtzehnten Jahrhundert.
                   Bad Homburg, 1969

Price, Lawrence M. "The English domestic novel in Germany 1740-1799."
                   Libris et Litteris: Festschrift für Hermann Tiemann
                   zum 60. Geburtstag. Hamburg, 1959, 213-20.

Proskauer, Paul Frank.   The Phenomenon of Alienation in the Work of
                   Karl Philipp Moritz, Wilhelm Heinrich Wackenroder,
                   and in "Nachtwachen' of Bonaventura.
                   Diss. Columbia University, 1966.

Rau, F.   "Der ästhetische Aspekt der Erbauungsliteratur."
                   Neuphilologische Mitteilung, 55 (1954), 305-10.

Reichert, K.   "Utopie und Staatsroman: Ein Forschungsbericht."
                   DVLG, 39 (1965), 259-87.

Reisner, J.   Über den Begriff Kitsch. Diss. Göttingen, 1955.

Rieder, H.   "Die triviale Literatur." Die Pforte. Monatsschrift
                   für Kultur.
                   [Esslingen] 8 (1957/8), 467-77.

Riefstahl, Hermann. Dichter und Publikum in der ersten Hälfte des
                   18. Jahrhunderts, dargestellt an der Geschichte der
                   Vorrede. Diss. Frankfurt, 1934.

Robson-Scott, W.D. German Travellers in England 1400-1800.
                   Oxford, 1953.

Rumpf, W.   Das literarische Publikum und sein Geschmack in den
                   Jahren 1760-1770. Diss. Frankfurt, 1924.

Saine, Thomas P.   Die Ästhetische Theodizee: Karl Philipp Moritz und die
                   Philosophie des 18. Jahrhunderts. München, 1971.

Schenda, Rudolf.   Volk ohne Buch: Studien zur Sozialgeschichte der
                   populären Lesestoffe 1770-1910.
                   Frankfurt am Main, 1970.

Schlözer, August Ludwig.   Vorstellung seiner Universal-Historie.
                   2 Tle. Göttingen und Gotha, 1772/73.

Schmidt, Erich.   Richardson, Rousseau und Goethe: Ein Beitrag zur
                   Geschichte des Romans im 18. Jahrhundert.
                   Jena, 1875.

Schneider, F.J.   Die Freimaurerei und ihr Einfluss auf die geistige
                   Kultur in Deutschland am Ende des 18. Jahrhunderts.
                   Prag, 1909.

Schönert, Jörg.   Roman und Satire im 18. Jahrhundert: Ein Beitrag
                   zur Poetik. Stuttgart, 1969.

Schücking, L.L.   "Literaturgeschichte und Geschmackgeschichte."
                   GRM, 5 (1913), 561-77.

Schulte-Sasse, Jochen.   Die Kritik an der Trivialliteratur seit der
                   Aufklärung: Studien zur Geschichte des modernen
                   Kitschbegriffs. München, 1971.

Schultze, Ernst.   Die Schundliteratur: Forderungen, Folgen, Bekämpfung.
                   Halle, a.d.S., 1909.

Sengle, Friedrich. Wieland. Stuttgart, 1949.

Sengle, Friedrich. "Bemerkungen zur Technik und Geist der populären
                   Biographie: Am Beispiel von O. Heuscheles. 'Herzogin
                   Anne Amalie'."
                   Euphorion, 46 (1952), 100-106.

Sichelschmidt, Gustav.   Liebe, Mord und Abenteuer: Eine Geschichte der
                   deutschen Unterhaltungsliteratur.
                   Berlin, 1969.

Singer, Herbett.   Der Galante Roman. 2. durchgesehene Auflage.
                   Stuttgart, 1966.

Singer, Herbert.   Der deutsche Roman zwischen Barock und Rokoko.
                   Köln/Graz, 1963.

Sommerfeld, Martin.   "Romantheorie und Romantypus der deutschen
                   Aufklärung."   DVLG, 4 (1926), 459-90.

Spiegel, Marianne. Der Roman und sein Publikum im frühen 18. Jahrhundert:
                   1700-1767. Bonn, 1967

Stange, F.   "Die Bedeutung des subjectivistischen Individualismus für die europäische Kunst von 1750-1850." DVLG, 9 (1931), 94 ff.

Stanzel, Franz K.   Typische Formen des Romans. Göttingen, 1964.

Stefansky, G.   "Die Krisis des religiösen Glaubens im deutschen Geistesleben des 18. Jahrhunderts." Euphorion, 30 (1929), 137-153.

Stemme, Fritz.   "Die Säkularisation des Pietismus zur Erfahrungsseelenkunde." Zeitschrift für deutsche Philologie, 72 (1953),144-158.

Stephan, H.   Der Pietismus als Träger des Fortschrittes in Kirche, Theologie und allgemeiner Geistesbildung. Tübingen, 1908.

Stern, Guy.   Fielding, Wieland and Goethe: A Study in the development of the novel. Diss. Columbia, 1954.

Stöckle, F.K.E.   Jean Pauls Romantechnik. Diss. München, 1924.

Thalmann, Marianne.   Der Trivialroman des 18. Jahrhunderts und der romantische Roman: Ein Beitrag zur Entwicklungsgeschichte der Geheimbundmystik. Berlin, 1923.

Thayer, Harvey Watermann.   Laurence Sterne in Germany: A Contribution to the Study of the Literary Relations of England and Germany in the Eighteenth Century. (1905). Reprinted New York, 1966.

Thombury, Ethel Margaret.   Henry Fielding's Theory of the Comic Prose Epic. New York, 1966.

Tompkins, J.M.S.   The Popular Novel in England 1700-1800. Lincoln, Nebraska, 1961.

Touaillon, Christine.   Der deutsche Frauenroman des 18. Jahrhunderts. Wien und Leipzig, 1919.

Trainer, James.   Ludwig Tieck: From Goethe to Romantik. The Hague, 1964.

Tronskaja, Maria.   Die Deutsche Prosasatire der Aufklärung. Berlin, 1969.

Voss, Ernst Theodor.   Erzählprobleme des Briefromans, dargestellt an vier Beispielen des 18. Jahrhunderts. Diss. Bonn, 1960.

Wangermann, Ernst. From Joseph II to the Jacobin Trials: Government
Policy and Public Opinion in the Habsburg Dominions
in the Period of the French Revolution.
London, 1959.

Weber, H. von   "Geschäft und Technik des Unterhaltungsromans."
Zwiebelfisch, 4 (1913), 161-170.

Wessenberg, I. von   Elementarbildung des Volks im 18. Jahrhundert.
Zürich, 1814.

Wessenberg, J.H.   Über den sittlichen Einfluss der Romane: Ein Versuch.
Constanz, 1826.

Winterscheidt, Friedrich. Deutsche Unterhaltungsliteratur der Jahre
1850-1860. Bonn, 1970.